Contents

NIMBLE BOOKS LLC

Blood On Our Hands

The American Invasion and
Destruction of Iraq

Nicolas J.S. Davies

NIMBLE BOOKS LLC

Nimble Books LLC

1521 Martha Avenue

Ann Arbor, MI, USA 48103

http://www.NimbleBooks.com

wfz@nimblebooks.com

+1.734-330-2593

Version 1.0; last saved 2010-05-20.

Printed in the United States of America

ISBN-13: 978-1-934840-98-6

ISBN-10: 1-934840-98-X

∞ The paper used in this publication meets the minimum requirements of the American National Standard for Information Sciences—Permanence of Paper for Printed Library Materials, ANSI Z39.48-1992. The paper is acid-free and lignin-free.

Dedicated to Ben Ferencz

Thank you for your encouragement and support, and for a lifetime of commitment to peace and justice.

From Buchenwald to Nuremberg to The Hague, you have laid the foundation of a bridge from the Hell of war to a just and peaceful world.

It will be up to my generation and my children's generation to finish building the bridge and to walk across it.

Because of your life's work, human beings will one day live in a world at peace, and the horrors of war will be only a dark chapter in our collective memory.

Law Not War!

PREFACE

We seem to have lost our sense of direction as a nation. The United States of America has, until recently, been an inspiration throughout the world. Its Declaration of Independence challenged the power of hereditary monarchs. Sovereignty belonged to the people. It spoke of inalienable rights to life and liberty in a democratic society. In two devastating world wars, courageous young Americans were in the forefront of brutal battles against tyranny and oppression. Presidents Woodrow Wilson and Franklin Delano Roosevelt sponsored new legal institutions to maintain global peace. The United Nations Charter prohibited the use of armed force unless authorized by the Security Council under strict conditions of self-defense. Dwight D. Eisenhower, Supreme Commander of all Allied military forces, after being elected U.S. President, warned in 1958 that "the world no longer has a choice between force and law. If civilization is to survive, it must choose the rule of law." U.S. President George Bush (the elder) in his State of the Union Address in 1991, appealed for a world order "where the rule of law, not the law of the jungle governs the conduct of nations." What happened to the dream?

The United States was the principal architect for the International Military Tribunal, formed in Nuremberg at the end of World War Two, to bring to justice, in an indisputably fair trial, some of the worst perpetrators of incredible Nazi crimes. One of America's most able jurists, Supreme Court Justice Robert N. Jackson, was designated by the American President to be Chief Prosecutor for the United States. Aggression, War Crimes and Crimes against Humanity were clearly criminal offenses punishable under international law. Jackson's proudest accomplishment was the confirmation by the Tribunal that illegal war-making was "the supreme international crime", since it encompassed all the other crimes. It was made absolutely clear by the U.S. at Nuremberg that international law must apply equally to all nations. "To pass these defendants a poisoned chalice," said Jackson, "is to put it to our own lips as well." General Telford Taylor, a very distinguished lawyer and Chief of Counsel for twelve, less-publicized subsequent trials conducted by the U.S. at Nuremberg, put it best: "There is no moral or legal basis for immunizing victorious nations from scrutiny. The laws of war are not a one-way street." Have we forgotten the lessons we tried to teach the rest of the world?

Nicolas J.S. Davies paints a "monumentally tragic picture" as he describes the tension between "realists" who favor the use of force and "idealists" who depend upon the rule of law. He notes the futility of weapons of mass destruction and the changes on military policy that became known as American "unilateralism". He documents the deceptions by various administrations using the CIA and other clandestine forces to bring about "regime change" when deemed necessary to protect certain U.S. "vital interests". His eighteen chapters spell out many of the details of the violations of international law that may have frightened some of our enemies but certainly alienated many law-abiding friends. The reader of this book should ask: "Whose blood, on whose hands?"

Following the attacks on the World Trade Center in New York by Muslim extremists, the American public was understandably in a state of shock, if not panic. President George W. Bush declared war on terrorism. Of course, an idea cannot be killed by a gun but only countered by a better idea; but that fact was forgotten as "Realists" seized the reins of power and asserted presidential powers not readily apparent in the U.S. Constitution. Understandably, no one wanted to appear unpatriotic by challenging the Supreme Commander. Nicolas Davies, as well as others, had the courage to begin challenging the legality of many of the actions being undertaken by the Bush Administration. Meanwhile brave young people went off to kill and be killed and large numbers of innocent civilians died in vain.

The author's documented criticism of the administration of George W. Bush and his cabinet in connection with the illegal invasion of Iraq is particularly devastating. Ever since the "Downing Street Papers" were published by reliable British newspapers in 2004, it has become abundantly clear that, if true, a prima facie case has been made that leaders of the Bush Administration deliberately conspired to deceive the American public about the existence of weapons of mass destruction in order to gain support and legitimacy for the unauthorized and hence illegal overthrow of the regime of Saddam Hussein. To be sure, everyone is presumed innocent until found guilty after a fair trial. Newspaper stories are not very credible evidence, but, in cases of such great public importance, suspicions give rise to an obligation of the accused to come forth with the complete truth. Unfortunately, that has not yet happened.

The world remains torn by brutal wars, yet not since Nuremberg and Tokyo has anyone ever been tried for the crime of aggression. The International Criminal Court, that was created in The Hague and is now operational, provides in its Statute that aggression is a crime, but the court cannot deal with it until certain new high hurdles are overcome. It was the United States, under the influence of conservative Senator Jesse Helms, Chairman of the Senate Foreign Relations Committee, and his protégé John Bolton, that the U.S. did everything in its power to kill the Court or cripple it in its cradle. It is anticipated that the new administration of Barack Obama will see things differently and will try to uphold the noble principles of the Nuremberg trials and the wisdom of Justice Robert Jackson.

It is to be hoped that allowing aggression to be tried by an independent international criminal tribunal will help deter such crimes in the future. ICC jurisdiction is not retroactive. The deeds of the George W. Bush Administration will be judged in the Court of public opinion and the Davies book is a good starting point. With a new administration in Washington, led by a respected lawyer recognizing the need for change, there is renewed hope that America's reputation may yet be restored to its former glory.

I served as a combat soldier in World War Two and witnessed the horrors as we landed on the beaches of Normandy and liberated many Nazi concentration camps. We must stop the glorification of war and rely on compromise, compassion, tolerance, understanding and the rule of law. I have spent almost all of my life trying to prevent illegal war-making. Much progress has been made in the evolution of international criminal law and respect for human lives everywhere. But the shame of Rwanda and current unresolved conflicts still rests with us and much more still remains to be done. There never has been and never can be a war without atrocities since war-making is the biggest atrocity of all. All disputes must be settled only by peaceful means, as required by the U.N. Charter that binds all nations. If the U.S. is to regain its image as a moral leader in the world, we must return to the rule of law that applies equally to all. As noted by Davies, change in policy is possible if the futility of past policies is recognized. The details will be found in the pages that follow.

BENJAMIN B. FERENCZ
J.D. Harvard Law School, 1943
Chief Prosecutor, Einsatzgruppen Trial, Nuremberg, 1947
For biography and citations please see www.benferencz.org

INTRODUCTION. AUTHORITY AND MILITARY POWER

The word *guerilla* originated in Spain during the Peninsular War (1808-1814). At the height of Napoleon's power, his *Armee D'Espagne* marched into Spain, quickly defeated the Spanish army, and installed the Emperor's brother Joseph Bonaparte on the throne of Spain. However, the Spanish people would not accept defeat. The army melted into the civilian population, took up arms again, and fought the French in a debilitating campaign of small engagements to deny Napoleon the fruits of his conquest. The resistance of the *guerillas* was fueled by the brutality with which the French suppressed the initial popular uprising in Madrid in May 1808, in particular the summary execution of 5,000 prisoners immortalized in a well-known painting by Francisco Goya.

The *guerillas* played an essential part in Napoleon's downfall. Their resistance prompted the British to send a small force to Portugal, and then forced Napoleon to leave half (270,000) of his French-born troops in Spain when he ordered his *Grande Armee* into Russia in 1812, a huge factor in his defeat. General Arthur Wellesley (later the Duke of Wellington) took command of British forces on the Peninsula in 1809. Informed by Britain's experience during the American Revolution, he believed by 1811 that Spanish popular resistance was the key to victory, in spite of the formidable military imbalance in favor of Napoleon's all-conquering army. Wellesley wrote in a dispatch that, although there were 353,000 French troops in Spain, "they have no authority beyond the spot where they stand."[1]

Napoleon's armies had marched across Europe on the tide of the French Revolution, overthrowing *anciens regimes* and liberating their

---

1. Paul Kennedy, *The Rise and Fall of the Great Powers* (New York: Random House, 1987), 134-6.

downtrodden people. Their authority was rooted in the revolutionary ideas of Voltaire, Immanuel Kant and Thomas Paine. But by the time they invaded Spain in 1808, the ideals of Liberty, Equality and Fraternity had lost their meaning to the populations they had liberated. Paper money, the world's first central bank and other innovative financial devices could not alter the essential fact that France, with a population of 28 million and many economic disadvantages, was not able to support an army of a million men spread all over Europe. The underlying imbalance was even greater once France's access to its colonies on other continents was cut off by the Haitian Revolution and the British naval victory at Trafalgar. So the French empire of the Revolution became an empire of conscription, plunder, and brutality. War was paid for by more war, and domestic stability in France was purchased by exploiting the labors of the rest of Europe. The revolution lost its authority, and its soldiers in Spain confronted the consequences.

Wellesley's report that the French forces in Spain had "no authority beyond the spot where they stand" seems intensely relevant to the American experience in Iraq. Israeli journalist Nir Rosen described the U.S. army in Iraq in similar terms, as "lost in Iraq ... unable to wield any power, except on the immediate street corner where it's located."[2] A man with a gun always has a certain kind of authority "on the spot where he stands" or "on the immediate street corner where [he]'s located," but how does that translate into authority that extends beyond one spot, the kind of authority required to actually govern a country? Evidently, both Napoleon in Spain and the American policy-makers in Iraq failed to solve this problem, despite past military successes and abundant confidence at the outset in both cases.

---

2. "Anatomy of a Civil War: Writer Nir Rosen on Iraq's Descent Into Chaos," *Democracy Now*, November 27th 2006. http://www.democracynow.org/2006/11/27/anatomy_of_a_civil_war_writer

As in the Peninsular War, the lack of authority or legitimacy doomed the American enterprise in Iraq from the outset. Mismanagement, corruption and brutal military tactics compounded the problem, but I do not believe that these were the decisive factors. In fact, ordinary people all over the world saw the more fundamental illegitimacy of the American venture in Iraq as the underlying problem all along, even as their concerns were dismissed out of hand by policy-makers and media pundits in Washington.

American policy-makers and professional experts in 2002, like Napoleon and his advisers 200 years earlier, looked at the military equation in Iraq and saw only huge imbalances in their own favor. Many years and a million deaths later, some of them must wonder how they could have got it all so wrong, but few will ever acknowledge that the mass of the world's people had it right. The experts' vested interest in their own jobs and credentials does not permit such a self-effacing assessment.

This is not a new phenomenon. Irrationality in high places can be contrasted with common sense among ordinary people throughout the wars of the twentieth century. In *Century of War*, published in 1994, Gabriel Kolko referred to the "inherent, even unavoidable institutional myopia" by which "options and decisions that are intrinsically dangerous and irrational become not merely plausible but the only form of reasoning about war and diplomacy that is possible in official circles."[3] His examples from Flanders to Vietnam made it clear that he was describing the rule rather than the exception. The moral of his tale was that the greatest dangers we face as modern human beings come more often from our own irresponsible leaders and their cadres of experts than from the dangers they claim to protect us from.

---

3. Gabriel Kolko, *Century of War* (New York: The New Press, 1994), 456.

One of the few Washington insiders who saw the weakness of the American position in Iraq from the outset was former U.S. National Security Adviser Zbigniew Brzezinski. In *Out of Control: Global Turmoil on the Eve of the 21st Century*, he had examined some of the dilemmas facing the United States in the post-Cold War world. He observed that, while the United Nations had growing authority but lacked power, the United States had unprecedented military power but lacked authority.[4] He imagined a constructive relationship between the two that might combine global power with global authority to restore stability. However, he did not foresee that self-serving American efforts to subordinate the authority of the U.N. to American interests would undermine both the fragile authority of the United Nations and the power of the United States, leading to even greater instability.

Like Wellesley, Brzezinski understood that the exercise of military power can be constructive or destructive of social and political order, and that authority and legitimacy are essential to accomplishing anything constructive or lasting on these fronts. Brzezinski was born in Poland and educated in Canada, which may give him a greater capacity for objectivity than his colleagues in the American foreign policy bureaucracy.

Incredibly, American foreign policy experts treated the hopeless brutality of the U.S. occupation of Iraq as a completely separate issue from the illegality of the invasion. When I raised the issue of the illegitimacy of the U.S. position in Iraq with a Democratic Senate staffer in May 2007, she told me: "That's in the past. The question is what to do now." The rather obvious principle that a restoration of legitimacy was always the necessary first step toward resolving the crisis in Iraq was taboo throughout years of political debate in the United States as the catastrophe unfolded.

---

4. Zbigniew Brzezinski, *Out of Control: Global Turmoil on the Eve of the 21st Century* (New York: Scribner, 1993), 150-52.

The underlying assumption of recent American thinking on foreign policy is that authority stems automatically from other kinds of power, such as military and economic power, rather than existing, or not, as a distinct form of power with its own characteristics and prerequisites. In fact, authority is the first thing that must be established before any form of state power can be effective and constructive. The evolution of such a dangerously unrealistic view in the United States can be traced to its history as a rising power over the past two centuries, in which its expanding role in the world, combined with its revolutionary background and the relative decline of the European powers, did indeed lead to real authority in world affairs. In hindsight, this process may appear to have been inevitable, or may even be credited to magical formulae such as "manifest destiny."

But a serious reading of history makes it clear that American statesmen, politicians and international lawyers worked very hard to construct the mechanisms by which American power actually came to acquire authority and legitimacy in the eyes of the world, and that these efforts were essential to the emergence of the United States as the leading power of the "American century". At the end of the 19th century, American diplomats and international lawyers led the legalist movement to construct a new legal framework for international politics. They negotiated mechanisms to peacefully resolve disputes; to establish international courts; to codify customary international law into explicit, enforceable international treaties; and to regulate the conduct of war so as to limit its most brutal consequences.

They achieved limited but real progress, leading to the Hague peace conferences (1899 & 1907), the League of Nations, the Permanent Court of International Justice (1922), the Kellogg Briand Pact (1928) to "renounce war as an instrument of national policy," and eventually the United Nations Charter (1945), which brought together many of the elements of those earlier treaties and institutions in a comprehensive system dedicated to peace as the predominant value and goal in international affairs.

International law professor Francis Boyle has written extensively about the legalist movement in American foreign policy. He has highlighted the fact that it is often wrongly confused or conflated with moralist approaches to international affairs. In *The Foundations of World Order*, he made it clear that the American legalists were more pragmatic than this would suggest.[5]

Throughout history, questions of international law had been reduced to conflicting, often self-serving, moral arguments, but this had clearly failed to prevent war, with all its human, political and economic costs. The effort to codify customary international law through multilateral treaties was a response to this failure, not an extension of it. For most of the past century, the legal regulation of international behavior to provide a peaceful framework for life, politics and commerce has been correctly recognized as a pragmatic mutual interest of all civilized nations.

By 1945, their failure to prevent two world wars convinced the world's governments that this framework needed to be significantly strengthened, not abandoned. Hence the United Nations Charter was granted the universal status that the League of Nations had never achieved. President Roosevelt told the U.S. Congress that the new framework

> ought to spell the end of the system of unilateral action, the exclusive alliances, the spheres of influence, the balances of power, and all the other expedients that have been tried for centuries—and have always failed. We propose to substitute for all these a universal organization in which all peace-loving nations will finally have a chance to join. I am confident that

---

5. Francis Anthony Boyle, *Foundations of World Order: The Legalist Approach to International Relations, 1898-1922*, (Raleigh: Duke University Press, 1999).

the Congress and the American people will accept the results
of this conference as the beginnings of a permanent structure
of peace.

The United States Senate had learned the bitter lesson of its failure to
ratify the League of Nations treaty after 1919, and it voted to ratify the
United Nations Charter without reservation by 89 votes to 2.

The American view that the United States can use these mechanisms and institutions or ignore them as it sees fit to advance its own
interests is an outgrowth of the dominant position that the U.S. has
occupied in the world since 1945. The disappointment of Hans Morgenthau and others at the failure of international law to prevent the First
and Second World Wars led to a "realist" school in U.S. foreign policy,
from which Brzezinski, Henry Kissinger and the neoconservatives all
derive much of their intellectual credibility. Morgenthau's observation
that states will very often act in their own interest in disregard of international law has been used opportunistically in policy circles as a rationale for the United States to join the outlaws.[6]

This opportunism exploits the fundamental dichotomy in the role of
the United States in the world. Is the United States simply a country
like any other, acting in its own national interest? Or does it play a special role in the universal interest of stability, peace and prosperity that
is shared by all peoples? These two may coincide in some cases, but
they also conflict in many others. In practice, the role the United States
plays in the world is justified alternately on each of these bases, but the
basis on which it chooses one over the other has become transparently
opportunistic.

When it suits the United States government to claim that it is simply exercising the rights of a sovereign country, as in its aggressive response to the September 11th attacks, it does so. On the other hand,

---

6. Hans L. Morgenthau, *Politics Among Nations, 7th Edition*, (New York: McGraw
Hill, 2005).

when its own goals can be advanced more effectively by claiming that it is acting as a supranational defender of universal interests, then it does this instead, as in its policy toward Iraq and Iran. And of course it often combines elements of both, but once again the combination is on a purely opportunistic basis. Its commitments under international law, the only legitimate or credible framework on which such a fundamental conflict of interest could be reconciled, are rejected as a yardstick, or in many cases even treated as an obstacle to be out-maneuvered.

This blatantly illegitimate posture has undermined the United States' position of authority and brought it increasingly into conflict with other countries, and with the very institutions and treaties that its own diplomats worked so hard to construct. It led in 1986 to a ruling against the United States by the International Court of Justice (ICJ) over its illegal use of military force against Nicaragua, and to overwhelming votes of condemnation in the U.N. General Assembly over its attack on Grenada (108 votes to 9) in 1983 and over what the U.N. resolution called its "flagrant violation of international law" against Panama (75 votes to 20) in 1989.

The U.S. foreign policy establishment's response to this crisis of legitimacy has been to withdraw from the compulsory jurisdiction of the ICJ; to oppose both the formation and the functioning of the new International Criminal Court; to withdraw from other multilateral treaties; and to hire new experts and lawyers to devise far-fetched rationales for exempting U.S. behavior from international legal constraints on a case by case but increasingly systematic basis. When British Foreign Secretary Robin Cook told U.S. Secretary of State Madeleine Albright that the British government was having difficulty "with its lawyers" over the NATO plan to attack Yugoslavia in 1999, she suggested that the British government should follow the U.S. example and "get new lawyers."[7]

Unfortunately, the demise of the Soviet Union came at a critical moment in this process and only emboldened the theorists of the new "sole superpower" to expand America's imaginary freedom of action beyond anything they would have dared to imagine in earlier times. The centerpiece of this dangerous experiment, which was not by any means limited to the "neocons," was the more aggressive use of military force to achieve foreign policy objectives.

The role of the U.S. Department of Defense was quietly redefined and expanded in a succession of strategy documents and reviews. Under the heading of "Defense Strategy" in one of its *Quadrennial Defense Reviews (QDR)*, the U.S. Department of Defense redefined its mission in ways that conflicted directly with the post-World War II foundations of international law and order.[8]

Ignoring what is arguably the United States' most solemn international commitment under the U.N. Charter to use military force only in self-defense or at the request of the U.N. Security Council, the new logic of American exceptionalism led to the following statement: "When the interests at stake are vital ... we should do whatever it takes to defend them, including, when necessary, the unilateral use of military power. U.S. vital national interests include, but are not limited to ... preventing the emergence of a hostile regional coalition ... .(and) ensuring uninhibited access to key markets, energy supplies and strategic resources.".

By framing this policy as "defending" vital interests, the document presented what international law defines as aggression against other

---

7. James Rubin, "Countdown to a Very Personal War," *Financial Times*, 30 September 2000, 9.

8. Available at Federation of American Scientists' web site: http://www.fas.org/man/docs/qdr/sec3.html

sovereign countries as a form of "defense.". The *Quadrennial Defense Review* in question was not published by Donald Rumsfeld's Defense Department but in May 1997 by the Clinton administration.

Arguments based on "vital interests" are dangerous precisely because they are persuasive to the citizens of any country. But countries' "vital interests" frequently come into conflict with each other, so that justifying military action based on these grounds simply resurrects the central historical problem of international relations. This is the very problem that the legalist approach to international relations was designed to resolve. The U.N. Charter provides an overarching framework for peacefully resolving conflicting national interests in the modern world precisely by prohibiting this sort of unilateral military action. The British government publicly cited "vital interests" as the justification for its invasion of Egypt in 1956, but it had neglected to consult its legal advisers. When he was finally consulted after the crisis, Sir Gerald Fitzmaurice, the senior legal adviser at the Foreign Office, had to explain that, "The plea of vital interest, which has been one of the main justifications for wars in the past, is indeed the very one which the U.N. Charter was intended to exclude."[9]

Any country that decides to renege on its most solemn treaty commitments faces predictable problems in its international relations. For the United States, there is also a constitutional problem. Article VI (2) of the United States Constitution declares: "This Constitution, and the Laws of the United States which shall be made in Pursuance thereof; and all Treaties made, under the Authority of the United States, shall be the supreme Law of the Land; and the Judges in every State shall be bound thereby, any Thing in the Constitution or Laws of any State to the Contrary notwithstanding."

---

9. Anthony Howard, "War against Iraq - the Legal Dilemma," *The Times*, March 11 2003. http://www.timesonline.co.uk/tol/comment/article1118185.ece

The designation of international treaties as part of the "supreme Law of the Land" should be a significant barrier to the formation of a foreign policy that violates the foundations of international law and order. But in the United States, politicians, "think tanks," and corporate media have succeeded in marginalizing their own Constitution along with the U.N. Charter and the foundations of international law. The government's new lawyers have concocted legalistic, semantic justifications for U.S. actions and rejected the jurisdiction of any international body that could objectively evaluate their legality. And the American public across the political spectrum has been brainwashed to believe that none of this really matters. It was only with the invasion of Iraq that the U.S. government's illegitimate foreign and defense policy ran head-long into the light of day, and that the terrible consequences of its delusions began to become clear to the public.

It is vital to understand that, notwithstanding the NATO attack against Yugoslavia in 1999 and the endless American war in Afghanistan, since 2001, this new strategy had actually conquered nothing but the fertile imaginations of American policy-makers prior to the invasion of Iraq. The United States had not successfully invaded and occupied another country on the scale of Iraq anywhere in the world since the aftermath of the Second World War. The American experience in Korea, Vietnam and elsewhere should have given grounds for extreme caution. And yet it was precisely those who urged caution who were dismissed as irresponsible, idealistic, or soft, while the wishful thinkers who cooked up this murderous scheme were treated as bold innovators worthy of unquestioning public confidence. The behavior of American officials and opinion-makers was entirely consistent with Gabriel Kolko's critique of the "inherent, even unavoidable institutional myopia" by which "options and decisions that are intrinsically dangerous and irrational become not merely plausible but the only form of reasoning about war and diplomacy that is possible in official circles."

An essential component of this monumentally tragic picture is the role of American business leaders in fostering and supporting the dangerous "institutional myopia" that Kolko recognized. But the promotion of policies of aggression by American commercial interests is far from a new development. On February 12th 1946, even as the former wartime allies, the U.S. and the U.S.S.R., were trying to gauge each other's intentions in the post-war world and hoping to preserve a fragile peace, Dr. Virgil Jordan, President of the National Industrial Conference Board, laid out a diabolical plan to an audience of business leaders at the Union League Club in Philadelphia:

> Let us first offer the utmost capacity of our economic power for reconstruction to every people who will undertake to abolish all national military expenditure, and disarm down to the level of the local constabulary. Let us, secondly, demand the unlimited right of continuous inspection and control of every industrial operation and process, of every public policy which may have the most remote relationship to armament and warfare. And, finally, let us make, keep and improve our atomic bombs for this imperative purpose; let us suspend them in principle over every place in the world where we have any reason to suspect evasion or conspiracy against this purpose; and let us drop them in fact, promptly and without compunction wherever it is defied.[10]

By 1949, influential American opinion-makers were calling for a massive nuclear attack on the Soviet Union to exploit the opportunity provided by the American monopoly on nuclear weapons and to prevent the Soviets from building their own nuclear deterrent. George Fielding Eliot, the respected former war correspondent of the *New York Herald Tribune*, wrote: "We cannot allow the present Soviet government to come into possession of the atomic bomb plus the means to

---

10. D. F. Fleming, *The Cold War and its Origins*, (Garden City: Doubleday, 1961), 392-4.

deliver atomic bombs in North America. ... we must use our military superiority to support an ultimatum."[11]

As with calls for U.S. aggression against Iran today, Eliot insisted it would not be sufficient to target nuclear facilities, because the Soviets could respond by invading Western Europe: " ... the only way to prevent, or mitigate, such massacre would be to strike quick and hard at the centers of Soviet power, and so shatter the will and smash the strength of the Soviet monster that his reactions against helpless people will be no more than dying convulsions ... Every man, every pound of metal, every effort that is not imperatively needed for the maintenance of security should go into the creation and delivery of offensive air-atomic blows against the source of our danger - the Soviet Union itself."

The American media have consistently played the role of cheerleaders for aggression and militarism, demonizing potential enemies and echoing the "institutional myopia" of policy-makers. *Colliers* magazine, with a circulation of millions, devoted its entire October 1951 issue to a fictional history of World War III, to which highly respected Americans contributed articles. Edward R. Murrow imagined the view from the B-36 that dropped the first atomic bomb on Moscow. Lowell Thomas wrote, "I saw them 'chute into the Urals". Arthur Koestler described the "glorious vision" of the American re-education plan for the Soviet people. And Pulitzer-prize-winning cartoonist Bill Mauldin provided cartoons of Russia under American occupation. The premise of the story was that the United States had responded to a Soviet attack on Yugoslavia with "saturation A-bombing of the U.S.S.R."[12]

---

11. George Fielding Eliot, *If Russia Strikes*, (Indianapolis: Bobbs-Merrill, 1949), 206-52.

12. *Colliers*, October 27th 1951; cited in Richard Barnet, *Roots of War*, (New York, Atheneum, 1972), 299-300.

But wiser heads still prevailed among American leaders. In 1949, General Eisenhower responded sternly to advocates of American aggression in a speech in St. Louis that our present-day supremacy theorists would do well to read. He said, "I decry loose and sometimes gloating talk about the high degree of security implicit in a weapon that might destroy millions overnight ... *Those who measure security solely in terms of offensive capacity distort its meaning and mislead those who pay them heed.* No modern nation has ever equaled the crushing offensive power attained by the German war machine in 1939. No modern nation was broken and smashed as was Germany six years later" (my emphasis).

U.S. Army Chief of Staff General Omar Bradley warned against "too heavy trust in air power, against reckoning our safety on fantasy rather than facts." Bradley was staggered by the immorality of what other influential Americans were suggesting: "Ours is a world of nuclear giants and ethical infants. We know more about war than we know about peace, more about killing than living."[13]

The views advanced by Paul Wolfowitz and others since 1989 are eerily similar to those of Virgil Jordan and his colleagues in the late 1940s. American military, political and business leaders continue to seek the Holy Grail of a U.S. monopoly on military power and the ability to destroy enemies without American casualties by using proxies, covert action by special forces, air power, long-range missiles, nuclear annihilation, weapons in space or some magical combination of all of these. Unmanned drones are only the latest in this long string of American weapons whose false promise has been even more dangerous than the lethal effects of the weapons themselves. William Appleman Williams analyzed this recurrent fantasy of American omnipotence forty-five years ago. He concluded that it had taken root during America's brief

---

13. Max Werner, *The Daily Compass*, July 1st 1949; cited in Fleming.

post-World War Two monopoly on nuclear weapons.[14] Every great power that has developed new, more powerful weapons than its adversaries has expanded its military strategy to exploit the competitive advantage they confer. But the virtually unlimited destructive power of nuclear weapons has been a double-edged sword for the United States, bringing it the tantalizing chimera of ultimate power, but no practical way to achieve it.

But U.S. political leaders supported by powerful business and institutional interests keep resurrecting this nightmare of offensive power, to drain the resources of each new generation of Americans and to threaten and kill new generations of human beings all over the world. These interests have succeeded in repeatedly undermining peace and progress for more than sixty years. One way or another, they cannot do so indefinitely, but the critical question is whether they can be stopped by civil society, before their irresponsible policies lead to national bankruptcy or, even worse, global catastrophe.

Throughout this story, the reader will find powerful commercial and bureaucratic interests driving U.S. policy to capitalize on the new military imbalance in favor of the United States since the end of the Cold War: to recover control over Middle Eastern oil just as the historical demand-supply curve enters its most critical and lucrative phase; to intimidate or destroy any government that challenges U.S. interests; to increase U.S. military spending beyond even Cold War levels; and, in contrast to the Cold War, to develop actual war-fighting in the permanent "War on Terror" or "Long War" as a profit center for weapons manufacturers, military suppliers and other contractors.

Corporate-funded think-tanks have played a critical role since the 1970s in developing the ideological and theoretical groundwork for

---

14. William Appleman Williams, *The Tragedy of American Diplomacy*, (New York: Dell, 1962).

these policies, promoting militarism in American society and manufacturing public consent for policies that would otherwise just seem unnecessary, irrational and dangerous. The present form of the myopia that Kolko identified is not just an accidental feature of bureaucratic institutions. It is driven by commercial interests that define success in terms of near-term corporate profits. But an essential component of their ideology is to rationalize and market policies that kill and inflict misery on millions of people. From any longer-term perspective, Kolko is right that this is a destructive, dangerous, immoral and ultimately suicidal way to organize America's political economy.

In the following chapters, I have described how the development of these dangerous and illegitimate policies climaxed in the American invasion and destruction of Iraq. I have drawn as much as possible on first-hand and objective sources: human rights reports by the U.N. Assistance Mission for Iraq; declassified and leaked official documents; first-hand accounts by independent journalists, Iraqi bloggers and American soldiers; the work of academic, medical and military researchers; and the rare instances when Western media reporters escaped the confines of the Centcom briefing room in the Green Zone or embedding with U.S. forces and their editors elected to publish what they discovered.

Western reporting on the war was corrupted from the start by the Pentagon's "embedding" program, and quickly degenerated to a mainly stenographic exercise orchestrated by the Centcom Press Office. The echo chamber of the U.S. corporate media fleshed out this artificial narrative to create an imaginary, virtual Iraq in the mind of the American public, feeding a political debate that bore no relation to the real war that its government and armed forces were waging, the country they were destroying or the lives of its inhabitants. I have done my best to dispel the myths created by this 21st century propaganda machine and to uncover the reality that it was built to obscure.

Throughout the book, you will find that the underlying questions of authority, legitimacy and responsibility keep coming to the surface, like a pool of blood seeping through the carpet. The inescapable conclusion is that the strategic and commercial interests that launched the United States into this crisis by a complete disdain for the laws of international behavior then clung relentlessly to their original goals, compounding the crime of aggression with the further crime of genocide against the people of Iraq. The United States' ultimate goal was a severely limited state of sovereignty for the Iraqis, one defined and circumscribed by U.S. interests and therefore an inherently illegitimate basis for the invasion and occupation of their country.

I hope that this cautionary tale will give the reader a new way of looking at the fundamental foreign policy problems facing the United States at the beginning of the twenty-first century, and the danger that the illegitimate basis of current U.S. policy poses both to Americans and to the people of the world. In 1945, American leaders faced the imperative of bringing the cycle of world wars between the great powers to an end before they completely destroyed civilization. The United States found itself in a position of unprecedented power in a ruined world, with 40% of the world's remaining wealth and economic activity. America's leaders might have assumed that they could lead the world solely on the basis of their economic and military power, but they had the wisdom and the humility to recognize the need for authority and legitimacy that would endure beyond that moment of American supremacy. Through the United Nations Charter and the continuing development of international law, they sought to legitimize America's newfound power within a nominally democratic and humanistic international system, with the world's common interest in peace as its unifying principle and overarching value.

It is a tragedy of global and historic proportions that America's leaders have progressively reneged on these critical commitments. Just as the United States faces a decline in its relative economic position vis-àvis China, Europe, and other powers, its leaders have abandoned the framework that their predecessors so carefully crafted to ensure continued peace and prosperity in what is, in the long run, an inevitably multi-polar world. Just when the United States needed urgently to redirect its resources to develop new energy technologies and to cooperate with other countries to address problems that impact the whole world, from global warming to poverty and disease to the unsustainable depletion of important natural resources, our leaders chose a diametrically different path, the path of unrestrained militarism.

The economic consequences of this tragic choice were not hard to predict. Already, during the Cold War, the United States steered its best brains and technology into its military industrial complex and quickly ceded its leadership in the manufacture of consumer products to Germany and Japan, the very countries it had militarily defeated. As the U.S. military budget was downsized in the 1990s, the United States recovered some of its commercial leadership and produced the next generation of consumer technology, based on the personal computer and the Internet. But between 2000 and 2008, its military budget more than doubled from $300 billion to more than $700 billion per year, and it ceded its leadership in more civilian industries to China, Japan, Europe and even India and South Korea.

But the path America chose was in fact a well-worn road that many have travelled before us. In *The Rise and Fall of the Great Powers*, Paul Kennedy described a very similar trajectory in the history of every country that has risen to prominence in the world since the sixteenth century. He found that rising powers enjoy enormous competitive advantages over older ones, so that every preeminent nation must eventually adjust to the economic tides of history and find a new place in a world it can no longer dominate. Relative economic strength is the most powerful determinant of a country's position in the world, while military forces and weapons technology are only a secondary form of power that wealthy nations develop to protect and support their expanding economic interests. An economically dominant country can very quickly convert some of its resources into military power when the need arises, as the United States did in the 1940s. But this does not work in reverse, as Great Britain discovered in the 1950s. Using its military power to try to hold onto its empire proved counter-productive, and peaceful transitions to independence formed a much stronger basis for future relationships with former colonies. The drawdown of its global military commitments was an essential part of its difficult but ultimately successful transition to a post-colonial future.[15]

But the transition from hegemony to coexistence is a delicate one in every case, and it is always made more dangerous by the temptation to use military force to try and preserve and extend a country's dominance. By their very nature, great powers do develop powerful military forces and weapons. It is very difficult for the leaders of a great power to understand that the gradual decline of their relative position cannot be averted by the right military strategy. Within military bureaucracies, careers rest upon the ability to develop such strategies, whether they can ultimately succeed or not. Officials who tell their superiors that their weapons and armies cannot solve their problems do not win promotion to senior positions, so that alternative voices and strategies are systematically excluded from consideration at the highest levels of government.

It usually takes a crisis, like Suez in 1956 for Britain, or Iraq and Afghanistan for the United States, to bring reality to the fore. The history of great powers using military force to try and stave off the tides of economic history has proved to be counter-productive and often calamitous. The ultimate success of these transitions hinges on the capacity of powerful bureaucratic institutions to come to terms with the limits

---

15. Kennedy, *ibid.*

of their own power and to develop radically different policies, an inherently problematic and counter-intuitive process.

But the United States faces such a transition at a particularly inopportune moment in history for strategists seeking military means to prolong its dominance. Not only has the world experienced two world wars in the past century, but much of the world has only recently liberated itself from European colonialism, making it acutely resistant to American efforts to solve any of its problems by military intervention and occupation. As Richard Barnet observed in 1972, as America finally began to extricate itself from Vietnam, "at the very moment the number one nation has perfected the science of killing, it has become an impractical instrument of political domination."[16]

So, unless Americans want the twenty-first century to be dominated by a desperate struggle for power that will bankrupt the United States, unleash global chaos, and conceivably destroy our civilization, we have to find a suitable framework for this inevitable transition. Since Britain, France, and other European colonial powers have entered their post-colonial period, they have become leaders in the development of international law. This is not by coincidence. Even as the United States has come to see compliance with international law as an impediment to its ambitions, the post-colonial European powers have found that it provides them with precisely the framework for peaceful coexistence and commercial competition in a multi-polar world that its architects intended.

As the United States begins its inevitable transition to a post-imperial role in the world, it will find such a framework equally necessary. Only two other alternatives seem realistic. One would be a struggle for raw destructive power that would destroy the United States as surely as its enemies. The other would be a futile effort to establish a

16. Barnet, *ibid.*, 21.

completely new system of global order even as the United States' ability to shape it diminishes. Eisenhower's warnings against delusions of offensive military power and the dangers of the military-industrial complex and Roosevelt's vision of the United Nations seem prescient, or at least as relevant to our time as to their own. The United Nations Charter and the continuing development of international law remain a necessity, albeit an imperfect one, for the future of the United States and the world. To fill the largest gap in the existing framework, enforcement and judicial systems must have the authority to hold even the most powerful countries accountable under international law, and the United States must accept their jurisdiction in the common interest of its own people and the world at large.

It is important to keep the dangers we face in proper perspective. The problems facing the United States are by no means intractable if they are correctly understood and addressed. As Paul Kennedy examined the position of the United States in 1987, he concluded: "In all of the discussions about the erosion of American leadership, it needs to be repeated again and again that the decline referred to is relative not absolute, and is therefore perfectly natural; and that the only serious threat to the real interests of the United States can come from a failure to adjust sensibly to the newer world order."

Since Paul Kennedy wrote that in 1987, we have unfortunately witnessed precisely such a failure. Instead of seizing the opportunities for peace and disarmament presented by the end of the Cold War, American leaders followed the path that Kennedy warned against, seeking to capitalize on America's military superiority to resuscitate its waning position of economic dominance. Although the necessary adjustments now require even more profound changes in American society than they would have twenty years ago, they nonetheless follow a well understood pattern of transition from militarization to peacetime production that many countries have followed successfully, not least America's former enemies, Germany and Japan.

Because the United States has now travelled farther along the path of militarism, the necessary changes now seem more radical than any that Americans in positions of power appear willing to consider or discuss. Tragically, the prospect of abandoning their illusions of permanent dominance is so distasteful to America's leaders that they have been prepared to inflict misery, pain and death on millions of people in a desperate effort to avoid the necessary adjustments. As American policies generate wider conflict in more parts of the world, the imperative for transformation is only becoming more urgent.

Chapter 1. A Brief History of Regime Change

The United States had not attempted a full-scale invasion of an Iraq-sized country since 1945, in part because it had found easier and more effective ways to eliminate foreign governments that challenged its interests. As John Bolton complained bitterly to a panel at the 2007 Conservative Party Conference in England, "The U.S. once had the capability to engineer the clandestine overthrow of governments. I wish we could get it back."[17]

In reality, "regime change" had never been a simple task, and many of Bolton's predecessors had felt the same impotence that he felt confronting Iran and other independent actors on the world stage in 2007. But "regime change" had achieved enough short-term successes to encourage the belief in American elite circles that the "capability to engineer the clandestine overthrow of governments" was an effective, even essential, component of U.S. foreign policy. The actions of the CIA and other covert agencies have certainly been counter-productive to U.S. interests on many occasions, but their activities have enjoyed consistent support in Washington, based on an unwavering commitment to the expansion of American global political and economic power that is shared by a consensus of the American ruling class whether in or out of government.

Noam Chomsky has observed that America's enemy throughout this period has been neither communism nor terrorism but "independent nationalism".[18] The U.S. government has consistently embraced governments that have accommodated American commercial and geostrategic interests regardless of their system of government, while it has worked actively to topple those that have asserted their own national interests over those of the U.S. government or of American corpora-

---

17. Ros Taylor, "Bolton calls for bombing of Iran," *The Guardian*, September 30 2007.
18. Noam Chomsky, *Failed States*, (New York: Metropolitan, 2006), 110.

tions and investors. Ideology has not been the determining factor, let alone whether a government employs terrorism, as indeed the U.S. government has frequently done itself. As Gabriel Kolko wrote in *Confronting the Third World* in 1988, "The irony of U.S. policy in the Third World is that while it has always justified its larger objectives and efforts in the name of anticommunism, its own goals have made it unable to tolerate change from *any* quarter [his italics] that impinged significantly on its interests."[19]

The official transition from "communism" to "terrorism" as the justification for U.S. policies has made the distinction between fear-based rhetoric and the interests that drive actual policy more transparent than ever to most of the world. The obvious fact that America's chosen enemies are not all terrorists has led to the introduction of more nebulous terms like "moderate" for subservient governments and "extremist" for independent ones. Thus countries with elected or popular governments as diverse as Venezuela, Cuba, Iran and Russia are "extremist," or "undemocratic" while U.S. allies such as Saudi Arabia, Egypt, Morocco, Colombia and Ethiopia are termed "moderate" in spite of being absolute monarchies, military dictatorships or corrupt oligarchies who retain power through systematic violence against their own people. The critical factor in the way these countries are characterized in American political discourse is their position in relation to U.S. interests, not their internal political organization.

Following the Second World War, the Americans and British succeeded in preventing the emergence of independent nationalist governments in the countries they liberated from German occupation or in the European colonies they recaptured from Japan. The Western allies brutally suppressed the very resistance groups that had fought with them against the Germans in Greece and against the Japanese in the

---

19. Gabriel Kolko, *Confronting the Third World*, (New York: Pantheon, 1988), 292.

Philippines, Korea, Indonesia and Indochina. In Korea, local resistance forces had already formed a provisional government, the Korean Peoples Republic (KPR), by the time U.S. forces reached Seoul. But when the KPR's officials came to present themselves to the U.S. general in command, he refused to recognize them and the southern half of Korea was instead placed under U.S. military occupation. The British rearmed Japanese troops to fight local resistance forces in Indonesia and Indochina, as well as redeploying the Security Battalions that the Germans had recruited and trained to fight resistance forces in Greece. In each of these countries, the allies' anti-democratic actions in the immediate post-war period led to long-term conflicts whose effects still linger sixty years later.[20]

American officials went to extraordinary lengths to influence elections in liberated European countries. Under an arrangement between the CIA and the American Federation of Labor's (AFL) Free Trade Union Committee, the AFL's Irving Brown delivered cash to non-Communist union leaders in France and Italy to buy elections and break strikes.[21] Socialists and Communists won a plurality of the votes in the Italian election in 1946, and then joined forces to form the Popular Democratic Front for the next election in 1948.[22] With assistance from the Roman Catholic church, U.S. officials directed an unprecedented and well-financed propaganda campaign to influence that election, employing prominent Italian-American spokesmen like Frank Sinatra, anti-Soviet propaganda films and radio messages, and 10 million pre-printed letters from Italian-Americans to their friends and rela-

---

20. D. F. Fleming, *The Cold War and its Origins 1917 - 1960*, (Garden City: Doubleday, 1961), 174 - 187; also Howard K. Smith, *The State of Europe*, (New York: Knopf, 1949), 225 - 32.

21. Ronald Radosch, *American Labor and United States Foreign Policy*, (New York: Random House, 1969).

22. William Blum, *Killing Hope*, (Monroe, Maine: Common Courage, 2004), 27 - 34.

tives. On a more concrete level, President Truman announced a complete cut-off of U.S. aid if the FDP should win.

The FDP was reduced from a combined 40% of the votes in 1946 to 31% in the 1948 election, and the Christian Democrats won with 48.5%, a plurality they would never exceed as they led increasingly corrupt right-wing governing coalitions for the next 46 years. Italy was saved from an imaginary communist dictatorship, but more importantly from an independent democratic socialist program that was committed to workers' rights and to protecting small to medium-sized Italian businesses against competition from American multinationals. The Soviet Union took a hands-off approach to the Italian election and to British-backed repression in Greece, and the Western allies did likewise in Eastern Europe.

The United States employed a similar strategy for elections in Japan in 1951 and 1954 to ensure the success of the Liberal Democratic Party. These campaigns in Italy and Japan created a model that was employed by the CIA and other U.S. agencies like the National Endowment for Democracy all over the world for the next 60 years: propaganda to raise the specter of communist dictatorship; alliances with local ruling classes; huge sums of money funneled to the election campaigns of favorable candidates; and clandestine infiltration of news media by the CIA.

Inevitably though, independent nationalist governments began to emerge. Mohammed Mossadegh was an elected prime minister in Iran who had enough popular support to survive a two year long British naval blockade and a boycott by Western oil companies after he nationalized his country's oil industry, breaking off a long-term contract with British Petroleum (BP). In August 1953, the CIA joined Britain's MI6 in backing a successful military coup to replace Mossadegh, and thus developed a second model for "regime change," one that dispensed with the problem of elections altogether.[23]

The following year, the CIA went to even greater lengths to overthrow the elected, independent government of Jacobo Arbenz in Guatemala.[24] President Truman had aborted a planned CIA coup against Arbenz in 1952, but the United Fruit Company continued to pressure the U.S. government to take action. Its specific grievance against Arbenz was that Guatemala had paid the company only $525,000 for some unused land as part of a modest land reform program. The company claimed the land was worth $16 million, and protested that it had only valued the land at the lower figure to avoid paying higher taxes. United Fruit was not used to Guatemalan governments challenging its interests and was determined to reestablish its powerful position in Guatemala before it could deteriorate any further. The U.S. government saw Guatemala's actions in the same light, as an example that could lead other governments in the region to challenge dominant U.S. business interests.

Nevertheless the first coup attempt in March 1953 failed because the Guatemalan Army would not turn against the government. The CIA raised the stakes for its next effort, with arms depots and airstrips in Nicaragua, Honduras, and the Panama Canal Zone. It offered bribes to senior military officers; placed propaganda branding Arbenz as a communist, which he was not, in newspapers all over Latin America; planted caches of Soviet weapons in Guatemala and Nicaragua to back up its propaganda; and trained a small army of mercenaries under Guatemalan exile Castillo Armas to invade the country, supported by 30 planes flown by American pilots. CIA planes with Guatemalan markings launched a false flag attack on Honduras, while another CIA plane sank a British ship waiting in port to load Guatemalan coffee and cot-

---

23. *Ibid.*, 64 - 72.
24. *Ibid.*, 72 - 83.

ton. The whole plot was obvious and clumsy, and documents exposing it soon fell into Arbenz's hands. But the CIA pressed ahead regardless.

When Guatemala brought its evidence to the U.N. Security Council, the U.S. was able to persuade all but four members to either abstain or vote against the Guatemalan resolution, but both Britain and France spoke in favor of the resolution before abstaining, and Secretary General Dag Hammarskjold wrote later that he considered resigning over the United States' manipulation of the Security Council.

Foreign Minister Toriello offered to reopen negotiations with United Fruit, but the U.S. had gone too far to turn back. After a group of Guatemalan military officers persuaded Arbenz to step down, U.S. Ambassador Peurifoy summoned the Guatemalan Chief of Staff, handed him a list of Guatemalans who were to be executed within 24 hours and demanded that the CIA's mercenary leader Castillo Armas be installed as President. The reign of terror which followed set the stage for the next 40 bloody years of Guatemalan history: thousands were arrested; many were tortured and killed; seven United Fruit labor organizers were found murdered; 72,000 people were officially branded as communists and banned from holding public office, or even from owning a radio; all land reform was reversed; 75% of the population was disenfranchised by a new Spanish literacy requirement; and all political parties, trade unions and peasant organizations were banned. A young Argentinian doctor who was working in Guatemala at the time was radicalized by the repression that he witnessed—he was Dr. Ernesto "Che" Guevara. He eventually fled Guatemala for Mexico, where he met a young Cuban exile named Fidel Castro and joined his revolution.

Following its successes in Italy, Iran and Guatemala, the U.S. government was persuaded that the CIA's methods could be more cost-effective than "sending in the Marines," as it had done throughout Central America and the Caribbean earlier in the 20th century. This was particularly appealing to the Eisenhower administration as it struggled to disengage from the Korean War and sought ways to avoid future military debacles. An added advantage of CIA "covert" operations was that, by their very nature, the American press could be silenced with a quiet word to editors to prevent them from betraying "national security" secrets. The media could then report only the official cover story, turning them into powerful coconspirators in the propaganda component of these operations.

The success of these early operations was at first hard to replicate. Two coups failed against President Figueres in Costa Rica, permitting that country to progress socially, economically and politically beyond what the U.S. government tolerated elsewhere in Central America. Between July 1957 and October 1958, the CIA was involved in as many as eight unsuccessful plots against Egypt and Syria to undermine their brief union as the United Arab Republic. There was nearly a replay of *Murder in the Cathedral* after Eisenhower told Secretary Dulles that he hoped "the Nasser problem could be eliminated". Dulles took this literally, and he and his brother, the director of the CIA, returned with a fully formed plan to assassinate President Nasser, which Eisenhower insisted was not what he had intended.[25]

In 1957 and 1958, the CIA supported an unsuccessful rebellion against the Sukarno government in Indonesia, during which an American pilot, Allen Pope, was shot down and captured in Ambon and imprisoned for four years. Three successive coups in Laos between 1958 and 1960 only turned the country into a CIA playground for the next decade, and hardly constituted an alternative to military action. As in neighboring Cambodia and Vietnam, the United States eventually dropped a greater tonnage of bombs on Laos than the allies had dropped on Germany and Japan combined throughout the Second World War.

---

25. Wilbur Crane Eveland, *Ropes of Sand: America's Failure in the Middle East*, (New York: Norton, 1980), 292.

Its mixed but significant results in the 1950s established a prominent role in U.S. policy for the CIA Clandestine Service. Despite the secret nature of its operations, declassified documents, disaffected agents and congressional investigations have exposed much of this history. William Blum's book *Killing Hope* details other failed coups against Haiti (1961 & January 1991), the French government in Algeria (1960), the Dominican Republic (1958 & 1960), Chile (1970), Costa Rica again (1971), the Seychelles (1979 & 1981), Suriname (December 1982 and July 1983), and Angola (1992-3). There were no less than five failed C.I.A. coups in Panama before the U.S. invasion in 1989, another in Venezuela in 2002, and an apparent CIA role in a coup attempt in Equatorial Guinea in 2005.

Then there is the almost endless history of CIA support for attacks, terrorism, attempted assassination, sabotage and propaganda against Cuba. The most serious attacks included bombing raids in 1960 (3 Americans killed & 2 captured), the apparent bombing of a French ship unloading Belgian munitions in Havana (at least 75 killed), the Bay of Pigs invasion (at least 100 Cubans and 4 Americans killed), an absurd but dangerous collision at sea with an East German ship loaded with British buses bound for Cuba in 1964, a biological attack with swine fever that killed 500,000 pigs, the terrorist bombing of a Cuban airliner (73 dead, with the probable perpetrators, Michael Townley, Luis Posada Carrilles, and Orlando Bosch still free in the U.S.), and several assassination attempts against President Fidel Castro.[26]

On the "success" side of the ledger, that is to say that the immediate objective of overthrowing a government was accomplished, there were the Congo in 1960; back-to-back coups in Ecuador (1961 & 1963), Brazil (1961 & 1964), the Dominican Republic (1961 & 1963), Greece (1965 & 1967), and Bolivia (1964 & 1971); El Salvador (1961); Guyana (1964); In-

---

26. Blum, 184 – 93.

donesia (1965); Ghana(1966); Chile (1973); Nicaragua (1990); and Haiti (September 1991 and 2004). In most of these countries, the U.S.-backed coups were followed by severe repression, disappearances, extra-judicial executions, torture, corruption and prolonged setbacks for the democratic aspirations of their people.[27]

Merely to read the long list of these countries is sufficient to illu-strate one of the most predictable consequences of the CIA's opera-tions: the unmasking of the predatory aspects of U.S. foreign policy to populations all over the world. In the long-run, this stimulated a healthy skepticism towards U.S. policy and strengthened aspirations for real self-determination. Many of these countries have eventually formed governments that are among the most firmly committed to po-litical and economic independence from the United States.

The history of multiple coups, successive failed coups and endless machinations in so many of these countries makes it clear that the CIA Clandestine Service gradually deteriorated into a weapon with which to harass, destabilize and threaten other governments as much as a tool for installing friendly ones, which was in fact only a short-term result anyway in most cases. The intrinsic illegitimacy of externally driven regime change meant that any success at all depended on either the strength of the forces the CIA was backing within the country, the prior extent of U.S. influence or some combination of both. As we shall see, there was little reason to believe that any of the preconditions for suc-cessful regime change existed in Iraq in the 1990s, when the job was assigned to the CIA, or for that matter in 2003 when the task was reas-signed to the armed forces of the United States and the United King-dom.

---

27. See Blum, *ibid.*

CHAPTER 2. THE DESIRE FOR REGIME CHANGE IN IRAQ

The acknowledged history of CIA operations in Iraq began in 1958 with the revolution that overthrew the British-backed monarchy and brought General Abdul Qasim to power. The Pentagon immediately drew up plans for a U.S.-Turkish invasion, but it was called off, apparently under threat of a military response from Moscow. General Qasim soon began soliciting other Arab countries with a plan to dissolve the Western monopoly on Middle Eastern oil by founding what would eventually become OPEC, the Organization of Petroleum Exporting Countries. A declassified memo from the Near East Division of the CIA Clandestine Service revealed that the CIA quickly initiated efforts to "incapacitate" him. The memo elaborated, "We do not consciously seek subject's permanent removal. We also do not object should this complication develop."[28]

One of the CIA's agents in Iraq was an assistant military attaché at the Egyptian Embassy in Baghdad. He hired a 22 year old Iraqi named Saddam Hussein to assassinate Qasim on October 7th 1959. Hussein and his companions botched the job, and Hussein fled the country, wounded in the leg by one of his coconspirators. The CIA rented him an apartment in Beirut until he had recovered from his injury, and then moved him to Cairo. He became a frequent visitor at the U.S. Embassy, while still officially working for and being paid by the Egyptian intelligence service.[29]

Qasim proceeded to nationalize most of Iraq's oil industry in 1961. He was overthrown and killed by the Baath Party in 1963, and there are

---

28. Douglas Little, "Mission Impossible: The CIA and the cult of covert action in the Middle East," *Diplomatic History* 28:5 (November 2004) 663-70.

29. Richard Sale, "Saddam key in early CIA plot," United Press International, April 10 2003.

conflicting versions of the CIA's role in the coup. A few weeks later, King Hussein of Jordan told an Egyptian newspaper editor in Paris that the Baathists had held "numerous meetings" with the CIA as they planned the coup, mostly in Kuwait, and that, as in Guatemala, they supplied the new government with a list of suspected communists to be executed. Different reports have put the number killed following the coup at between four and ten thousand.[30]

By 1972, the Baath Party was in full control of Iraq, and had completed the nationalization of its oil industry. In April, Prime Minister Ahmed al-Bakr signed a friendship agreement and an arms deal with the Soviet Union. The Shah of Iran supported Kurdish rebels in northern Iraq who were fighting for "autonomy," and ultimately for a Kurdish state. They were led by Mustafa al-Barzani, a former ally of the Iraqi Communist Party who had spent twelve years in the Soviet Union. The rapprochement between the Iraqi government and the Soviets left Barzani isolated, but he did not want to become a puppet of Iran. So he sent a message to President Nixon via the Shah that he wanted American backing. The U.S. House Intelligence Committee staff later investigated CIA activities in Iraq and found repeated statements by Barzani that Iraqi Kurdistan was "ready to become the 51st state."[31]

The Intelligence Committee staff's findings were leaked and then published as the *Pike Report*, first in excerpts in the *Village Voice* in 1976, and then as a book by the Bertrand Russell Peace Foundation in Britain in 1977. They included a CIA memo from March 22nd 1974 that made the nature of U.S. support for Kurdish aspirations quite clear:

---

30. Roger Morris, "A tyrant forty years in the making," *New York Times*, March 14 2003; and Muhammad Hasanein Haikal, *Al-Ahram*, September 27 1963, cited in Hanna Batatu, The *Old Social Classes and the Revolutionary Movements of Iraq*, (Princeton: Princeton University Press, 1978), 985-6.

31. Staff Report of the House Select Committee on Intelligence, CIA - *The Pike Report*, (Nottingham: Spokesman Books, 1977), 56, 195-8, 211-7, cited in Blum, *Killing Hope*.

"We would think that Iran would not look with favor on the establishment of a formalized autonomous government. Iran, like ourselves, has seen benefit in a stalemate situation ... in which Iraq is intrinsically weakened by the Kurds' refusal to relinquish semi-autonomy. Neither Iran nor ourselves wish to see the matter resolved one way or the other." The Kurdish population of Iraq would pay a heavy price for many years to come for their role as pawns of this cynical policy.

The rise of oil prices after 1973 and the new-found power of OPEC brought Iraq and Iran closer, and border disputes and other issues between them were more easily resolved in this new environment. Very soon, none of Iraq's neighbors had any interest in supporting the Iraqi Kurdish rebels, and the traditional interest in quashing Kurdish aspirations for autonomy once again took precedence in Iran, Turkey and Syria. U.S. supplies to the Kurds in Iraq had been routed via Iran, and they were cut off by Iran in March 1975. The Iraqi government seized the opportunity to launch a major offensive against the Kurdish rebels. The Kurds cabled the CIA, "Complete destruction hanging over our head. We appeal you and USG (U.S. government) intervene according to your promises..." And to Secretary Kissinger: "Our movement and people are being destroyed in an unbelievable way with silence from everyone. We feel your Excellency that the United States has a moral and political responsibility towards our people who have committed themselves to your country's policy."

The *Pike Report* found that 200,000 Kurdish refugees who fled to Iran received inadequate assistance from Iran or the United States and that Iran forcibly returned 40,000 of them to Iraq. When the House Intelligence Committee staff confronted Kissinger with his abandonment of the Kurds, he famously retorted that "Covert action should not be confused with missionary work."

In 1979, the CIA's former asset, Saddam Hussein, became President of Iraq after rising through the ranks of the Baath Party. As President, he modeled himself on Joseph Stalin. There is chilling video footage of his first meeting with government officials. Hussein slowly read out the names of officials he claimed were plotting against him, and the officials in question were led away one by one, mostly to their deaths. It is possible that Hussein had remained an agent of Egyptian intelligence or the CIA during the twenty years between 1959 and 1979. He had certainly maintained friendly contacts with Western officials as a senior member of the Baathist government, even as he personally supervised purges, torture, and executions of his political opponents.

The beginning of Hussein's reign as President coincided with the Iranian Revolution, and he took full advantage of Western fears of Islamist Iran to obtain weapons and financial support. The United States gave Iraq export credits and sold it helicopters; the French provided Mirage fighters; the British other military equipment. The Americans, British, and Germans each provided components of Iraq's chemical weapons program, including a British-built chlorine factory in Fallujah.

In early 1980, there was small-scale fighting across the southern border between Iran and Iraq, with artillery exchanges and naval incidents. Then, on September 22nd, Iraq launched a full-scale invasion of Iran along a 400-mile front. This was Saddam Hussein's "Whirlwind War" to annex Iran's oil-fields, which are located primarily in Khuzestan in the south-west corner of Iran closest to Iraq.[32]

Six months later, at the cost of massive casualties on both sides, the Iraqis had made meager advances into Iran, capturing what was left of Khorramshahr, but not the main prize of Abadan, while the Iranians bombed Basra and held their own on many parts of the front. Then, on March 22nd 1981, 120,000 Iranian troops counterattacked at Dezful under cover of a sand-storm. They quickly recovered 1,500 square miles of territory, killed 4,000 Iraqis, took 15,000 prisoners and captured 300

---

32. Robert Fisk, *The Great War for Civilization*, (New York: Knopf, 2005), 179 - 217.

tanks. This was the first of Iran's "human wave" attacks. They left the Shah's British tanks behind and sent 14-year-olds on motor-bikes and "martyrs" with anti-tank missiles and small arms to confront Iraqi tanks, and they simply overran them.

As the tide of the war turned against Iraq and the Iranian Army advanced into the marshes south of Amara, the desperate Iraqis turned to unconventional warfare. They dammed the marshes, flooded them with thousands of gallons of gasoline from tanker trucks, then fired incendiary shells to ignite the fuel and turn the land into an inferno.

Iraq first used poison gas against Iranian troops in January 1981. As the war started going badly for Iraq, its gas attacks increased. Iran's human waves were to be exterminated like swarms of insects. There were 31 gas attacks in 1983, according to official Iraqi records, and Western journalists were already examining gas victims at hospitals in Tehran. Western governments dismissed their reports as Iranian propaganda, but the CIA must have known better. Its extensive contacts in Iraqi Kurdistan must have confirmed reports of gas attacks on three Kurdish villages in October 1983. And yet, only two months later, on December 20th 1983, former and future Defense Secretary Donald Rumsfeld was photographed shaking Saddam Hussein's hand as he requested permission to reopen the U.S. Embassy in Baghdad.

In 1994, the House Banking Committee published a report on "United States chemical and biological warfare-related dual-use exports to Iraq". The committee was primarily concerned with the residual impact of these dangerous substances on U.S. troops in 1991, but it also detailed how "the United States provided the government of Iraq with ... chemical warfare agent production facility plant and technical drawings, (and) chemical warhead filling equipment" among other items.[33]

---

33. Senate Banking Committee, The Riegle Report, "United States Dual-Use Exports to Iraq and Their Impact on the Health of the Persian Gulf War Veterans," May 25 1994.

But gas alone was not enough to defeat Iran's human waves. The Iraqi strategy depended on something else: satellite intelligence to detect when and where the human waves were forming. The U.S. Defense Intelligence Agency assigned sixty officers to provide this intelligence to the Iraqis. Some of the American officers also conducted on-site battle damage assessments and saw for themselves the horrific effects of the combination of satellite intelligence and chemical weapons that the U.S. and its allies were providing. From the Fao Peninsula on April 19th 1988, Lieutenant Colonel Rick Francona confirmed news reports that the Iraqis had used chemical weapons to recapture the peninsula, but his commanding officer, Colonel Walter Lang, told the *New York Times* that "the use of gas on the battlefield by the Iraqis was not a matter of deep strategic concern".[34]

Iraq's invasion of Kuwait in 1990 and the subsequent U.S. attack on Iraq have been the subject of much speculation. Did the U.S. give Saddam Hussein a "green light", or at least fail to hold up a red one? The reasoning behind Iraq's and the United States' actions seems to have included elements of miscalculation on both sides. Much has been made of U.S. Ambassador Glaspie's statement to Saddam Hussein on July 25th 1990 that the United States had "no opinion on the Arab-Arab conflicts, like your border disagreement with Kuwait". However, her later statement that no one expected Hussein to "take all of Kuwait" may be even more revealing of American planning.[35]

Iraq challenged Kuwait's independence as soon as it was granted by Britain in 1961, but was deterred from immediately annexing Kuwait by an airlift of British troops. The existence of Kuwait as a separate nation deprived Iraq of any good port on the Persian Gulf. Iraq continued to assert sovereignty over two strategic islands and to dispute the location

---

34. Patrick E. Tyler, "Officers say U.S. aided Iraq in war despite use of gas", *New York Times*, August 18 2002.
35. Flora Lewis, "Between-lines disaster", *New York Times*, September 19 1990.

of its border with Kuwait. During the Iran-Iraq War, Iraq claimed that Kuwait further violated its border and stole Iraqi oil from the Rumaila oil-field to the tune of $2.4 billion, and also that it was driving down the price of oil by exceeding its OPEC production quota. As Kuwait refused to negotiate on any of these issues, Iraq started massing forces on the Kuwaiti border in July 1990.[36]

Meanwhile, the United States was facing the prospect of a "peace dividend" at the end of the long Cold War. Debate was under way in Congress over what promised to be a much reduced defense budget, to the delight and relief of most Americans. But of course their joy was mirrored by trepidation within the Pentagon and the armaments industry, who desperately needed some sort of crisis to change the mood of the country and save their powerful positions and investments. In particular, the new B-2 stealth bomber, which would eventually cost $2.2 billion apiece, was facing the axe now that its original Cold War mission had become obsolete.

Whatever the U.S. communicated to Iraq, either by design or by mistake, the other actor in this drama, Kuwait, certainly received assurances of protection from Washington that encouraged it to reject negotiations with Iraq. King Hussein of Jordan told an interviewer in February 1991 that the orders given to the Kuwaiti Army, in the event of an invasion by Iraq, were to hold off the Iraqi forces for 24 hours, and then "American and foreign forces would land in Kuwait and expel them." The Kuwaiti Oil and Finance Minister said later, "We knew that the United States would not let us be overrun". Indeed, since 1980, the Carter Doctrine had designated the Persian Gulf as an area of vital interest that the U.S. was theoretically prepared to fight over. The Carter Doctrine applied to "an attempt by any *outside* force to gain control of the Persian Gulf region," and was aimed at the the Soviet Union, but

---

36. Blum, *Killing Hope*, 320 - 38.

President Reagan had already expanded it to apply to any threat at all against Saudi Arabia.

In 1990, the implosion of the Soviet Union colored the American response to the crisis from the outset. Michael Mandelbaum, the director of East-West studies at the Council on Foreign Relations, told the *New York Times*: "For the first time in 40 years we can conduct military operations in the Middle East without worrying about triggering World War III."[37] So a limited border incursion by Iraq or a seizure of the disputed islands would have been just the small war made to order for the U.S. military-industrial complex as it fought for its commercial and political life-blood in Washington. But Saddam Hussein and his advisors apparently understood this, and he characteristically upped the ante and, as Ambassador Glaspie noted, took all of Kuwait.

American aircraft carriers were converging on the Persian Gulf within 24 hours, as the Kuwaitis expected. And within the same 24 hours, Congress saved the B-2 bomber, and the promised peace dividend began to slip away into an imaginary America run by quite different people and interests. The *Los Angeles Times* reported on October 2nd 1990 that, "The defense budget compromise ... would spare much of the funding that has been spent each year to prepare for a major Soviet onslaught on Western Europe". In the interest-driven world of U.S. defense policy, the United States would continue to build and deploy weapons to fight a country that no longer existed, and it would find other enemies to indirectly justify the expense.

The next six months saw the United States reject every effort to resolve the crisis in Kuwait peacefully. Iraq immediately offered to withdraw on terms that would address some of its complaints and made repeated efforts to negotiate a withdrawal. As the U.S. war-deadline of

---

37. Clifford Krauss, "U.S. officials satisfied with Soviets' Gulf role," *New York Times*, September 20 1990.

January 15th 1991 approached, Arab diplomats reported that the Iraqis were ready to withdraw on the sole condition that the U.S. would not attack them, but this was not good enough.

At every level, institutional forces and vested interests were driving toward war, and George H. W. Bush was not the man to stand in their way. Former Assistant Secretary of Defense Lawrence Korb wrote in the *Washington Post* that inter-service rivalries were ensuring that each branch of the armed services was lobbying for a major role in the war-plan to demonstrate its value in the post-Cold War world. He wrote: "Even the reserves are scheduled to be sent ... The reserve lobby recognized that their future funding may be jeopardized if their units do not get involved."[38]

Beginning on January 15th, each of the U.S. armed services was granted an almost unlimited opportunity to demonstrate just how much devastation it could inflict on military and civilian targets in Iraq. The road from Kuwait to Basra became the "highway of death"—a "target-rich environment" for U.S. Navy and Air Force pilots. U.S. Army tanks fitted with ploughs buried Iraqi conscripts in their trenches. Inferior Iraqi tanks were death-traps, incinerated before their guns were within range. The road from Baghdad to the Jordanian border was a second highway of death, with little military traffic but plenty of buses, taxis and other passenger vehicles packed with people fleeing the capital. Baghdad and other cities were devastated—American and allied planes dropped 90,000 tons of bombs.

Anatole Turecki was in a better position than most Americans to correlate the bomb tonnage figures with the public relations campaign the Pentagon conducted around its new "precision" weapons. He was a Polish fighter pilot who was captured by the Soviets in 1939, flew a Spit-

---

38. Lawrence Korb, "The 'War' inside the Pentagon," *Washington Post*, November 25 1990.

fire in the Battle of Britain and then became a navigator on RAF Wellington bombers over Germany. By 1991, he was a professor of computer science in Florida and a world-class yachtsman. He told me at the time that Iraq was being ruthlessly carpet-bombed by waves of B-52s and that the American public was being sold a sophisticated dog and pony show of pseudo-military briefings and bomb-sight video footage. Subsequent official reports validated Turecki's analysis. Only 7% of the deluge of bombs and missiles raining down on Iraq were in fact "precision" weapons and, in any case, many of these experimental weapons failed to perform as advertised

This cynically deceptive demonstration of American weapons technology ended just in time for the Paris Air Show, and aircrews were ordered to fly to Paris without even cleaning their planes so that potential customers could see them in all the grime and glory of their victory. Sales went through the roof. The next two years were record ones for U.S. arms exports, and the U.S. would maintain a 40% to 50% share of the global arms market for the next 15 years. U.S. defense budgets fell modestly during the 1990s to about $300 billion per year, but Congress heeded President Bush's warning not to "naively cut the muscle out of our defense posture." The Cold War military infrastructure had been saved. As a shareholder in the Carlyle Group, a huge private equity firm heavily invested in the arms trade, the former President was rewarded with exploding profits during what most Americans had hoped would be a new era of peace and disarmament.

For Iraq, the agony only continued. A U.N. survey recorded the "near apocalyptic impact" of the bombardment, which had transformed what "had been until January a rather highly urbanized and mechanized society" into "a pre-industrial age nation". International sanctions slowed the rebuilding of the infrastructure after the war, as U.N. weapons inspectors began the futile and thankless task of searching for the mythical weapons that justified the continued collective punishment of the Iraqi people.[39]

Although the United States had targeted the Iraqi leadership during the war, Saddam Hussein and other senior leaders survived. The U.S. government was not prepared to order its forces to march on Baghdad and occupy the country in violation of its U.N. mandate in 1991, nor to give more than verbal support to the rebellions that followed the war, but that does not mean that it did not desire "regime change" in Iraq. In fact, it consistently pursued that goal throughout the twelve years that followed. Its three principal weapons were: the U.N. sanctions regime; persistent low-grade aerial bombardment, with opportunistic spikes of heavier bombardment; and CIA covert action. The eventual resort to war was a testament to the brutal futility of all three. According to the best estimates, the human cost of the sanctions included between 400,000 and 500,000 preventable deaths of children under the age of five.[40]

It is vital to understand that the entire basis of the U.N. sanctions regime and the "no fly zones" was a fiction. Legally and diplomatically, all of this was justified by unanswered questions surrounding Iraq's development of chemical and biological weapons and nuclear research during the 1980s and by the Iraqi government's use of air power to put down the rebellions that followed the war. But it was well understood in diplomatic circles that the United States and Britain had an ulterior motive that was independent of these questions. As former U.N. Assistant Secretary General Dennis Halliday put it in 2002, "The whole weapons inspection issue is really just a ruse. The real agenda of the Bush administration is a regime change." Halliday resigned from a 34-year

---

39. Paul Lewis, "After the war; U.N. survey calls Iraq's war damage near-apocalyptic," *New York Times*, March 22 1991.

40. M. M. Ali, J. C. Blacker, "Excess Mortality in Iraq," *Center for Population Studies*, University of London, 2003. http://www.lshtm.ac.uk/cps/public/index.html

career with the U.N. in protest over the U.N.'s role in this lethal cha-
rade, and was nominated for the Nobel Peace Prize. Hans Von Sponeck,
who replaced Halliday as the senior official supervising U.N. operations
in Iraq, followed his example and also resigned in protest.[41]

But the ability of American and British diplomats to maintain international support for the sanctions regime was not unlimited. It gradually eroded, leading eventually to outright opposition from other members of the Security Council. This disagreement climaxed in the Bush
administration's defiance of the Security Council and the U.S. and British invasion of Iraq. In hindsight, it is clear that this threat had always
existed, and the role played by other Security Council members in
maintaining the sanctions regime can be viewed as an effort to contain
the United States by offering it an alternative to war, as much as a
strategy to contain Iraq.

The failure of this effort bears out the lesson of the 1930s that support for a potential aggressor sends it the wrong message, forestalling
immediate aggression at the expense of encouraging it to expand its
aggressive ambitions in the long run. In the case of the United States,
appeasement fueled the belief among American policy-makers in the
1990s that the threat of aggression could be an effective tool by which
to impose its will on the world. Even as the resulting cataclysm swept
over Iraq, the United States escalated its ongoing war in Afghanistan
and launched a new campaign of familiar threats against Iran, demonstrating that its leaders had not by any means learned their lesson. As
history has repeatedly shown, aggression is an intoxicating and addic-
tive drug that clouds judgment, encourages brinksmanship and norma-
lizes terrible violence.

---

41. Hadani Ditmars, "Dennis Halliday," *Salon.com*, March 20 2002.
http://dir.salon.com/story/people/feature/2002/03/20/halliday/index.html?source=sear
ch&aim=/people/feature

1996 was a critical year for U.S. policy and for U.N. sanctions. The UNSCOM inspectors in Iraq were by now convinced that Iraq had destroyed all its nuclear, chemical, and biological programs and stockpiles in 1991. Their inability to prove this beyond any doubt was the only leverage the U.S. and British governments had left with which to justify continued inspections and sanctions. By the end of 1995, the worldwide outcry over sanctions had led to the development of the U.N. Oil for Food Program, which would soon go into effect and mitigate at least some of the dreadful effects of sanctions on the population. In the eyes of American policy-makers, this would reduce the punitive effect of the sanctions, and thus the pressure on the Iraqis to overthrow Saddam Hussein.[42]

The sharp end of the U.S. regime change strategy was the CIA's planning for a coup in Iraq, and the erosion of the sanctions regime now brought this to a head. The CIA had used the UNSCOM inspections as a cover to gain intelligence and make contacts in Iraq, but its principal allies were Iraqi exiles outside the country, led by Ayad Allawi and his Iraqi National Accord (INA). Allawi had been a medical student in London in the late 1970s who also worked for the Iraqi Mukhabarat secret police, informing on Iraqi students in Britain. In 1978 he approached Britain's MI6 intelligence service with an offer to act as a double agent. The Mukhabarat found him out, but after it failed in an attempt to assassinate him, he became a fully-fledged British agent. With MI6 backing, he founded the INA as a front for the Saudi intelligence service during the first Gulf War, to broadcast anti-government propaganda into Iraq.

In 1994 Allawi told his MI6 handlers that he had contacts in Iraq who could remove Saddam Hussein from power given the right outside support. MI6 introduced him to Steve Richter, the head of the CIA's

---

42. Scott Ritter, *Iraq Confidential*, (New York: Nation Books, 2005), 161-9.

Near East Division, and to Mohammed al-Shahwani, an Iraqi exile with a brother in the Special Republican Guard, who was already working with the CIA's Iraq Operations Group. The two exiles were installed in Amman, Jordan, and the coup was set for June 1996. It was to coincide with renewed UNSCOM inspections of Special Republican Guard facilities, which, unbeknown to senior weapons inspector Scott Ritter and his team, were to be used as a pretext for a U.S. attack on those facilities and as a trigger for the coup.

The CIA provided all the coup participants in Iraq with satellite radios to coordinate their actions. However, many of the exiles involved in the plot were in fact Iraqi double agents who were reporting the plotters' every move to the Mukhabarat. In January 1996 the Mukhabarat obtained one of the secure radios and was able to listen in on every detail of the plot for the next five months. On the eve of the coup, every one of the radios inside Iraq suddenly went silent. All the plotters had been arrested, and many would soon be dead.

This was more than a setback for the CIA. All its contacts in Iraq were now dead or in prison, and the exile groups it had been working with were riddled with double agents. The CIA's Clandestine Service, the United States' weapon of choice for overthrowing independent nationalist governments since 1945, was impotent against Iraq, fatally outspooked by its former allies in the Mukhabarat. This left U.S. policy adrift, desiring regime change, but without any of its traditional means of attaining it—no electoral process to manipulate, no forces within the country that could overthrow the government, and no exile forces with which to destabilize it.

With U.S. policy on Iraq at an impasse, a group of former Bush administration officials and neoconservative ideologues began a campaign for even stronger measures. They came together in June 1997 to form the "Project for the New American Century" (PNAC), essentially a campaign to capitalize on the vision of a more aggressive military policy laid out in the 1997 Quadrennial Defense Review. The 25 signatories to the original PNAC Statement of Principles included Richard Cheney, Donald Rumsfeld, Paul Wolfowitz, Lewis Libby, Eliott Abrams, and Jeb Bush.[43]

The initial PNAC publications did not have any clearer direction than Clinton's policies. They were simply calls for higher defense spending based on the thesis that Ronald Reagan won the Cold War by militarily outspending the Soviets and that larger military budgets were therefore the key to the future greatness of the United States. Their self-serving logic was easily dismissed by critics, but served as a rallying-point for military-industrial interests. In the first six months of its existence, the PNAC published a paper on NATO expansion and one on "U.S.-China Nuclear Coopertation" (sic), and not much else.

But the PNAC did not take long to find a focus for its assertiveness. In January 1998, as President Clinton prepared to give his annual State of the Union speech, nine of the better known PNAC members signed on with John Bolton, Richard Perle, and other foreign policy hawks to a very public letter to the President on the subject of Iraq. It stated correctly that "current American policy toward Iraq is not succeeding," and concluded, without supporting evidence, "that we may soon face a threat in the Middle East more serious than any we have known since the end of the Cold War."

The letter called for an explicit policy for "the removal of Saddam Hussein's regime from power" to replace the failed covert strategy. The bureaucrats magnanimously proposed: "We stand ready to offer our full support in this difficult but necessary endeavor," but the policy would inevitably depend on the blood and sacrifice of a completely different class of Americans. The letter also specified that "American policy cannot continue to be crippled by a misguided insistence on unanimity in

---

43. http://www.newamericancentury.org/

the UN Security Council," an explicit call for the United States government to violate the United Nations Charter and thus Article VI(2) of the United States Constitution (which stipulates that "...all Treaties made, under the Authority of the United States, shall be the supreme Law of the Land").

The lobbying of the PNAC and its allies achieved a significant short-term goal in October 1998 with the passage of the "Iraq Liberation Act of 1998." The central clause of this bill declared, "It should be the policy of the United States to support efforts to remove the regime headed by Saddam Hussein from power in Iraq." It went on to provide up to $97 million for weapons, military training, and propaganda operations, and called on Clinton to designate "Iraqi Democratic Opposition Organizations" who would be eligible to receive these funds and the weapons and military training they would pay for.[44]

The bill passed the House by 360 votes to 38, with even Dennis Kucinich and Lynn Woolsey among the Ayes. In view of all that has ensued since, the Nays deserve honorable mention: Neil Abercrombie, Donald Payne, William Lacy Clay, John Conyers, Danny Davis, Alcee Hastings, Lloyd Doggett, Ron Paul, John Lewis, Maxine Waters, George Miller, Jesse Jackson, Barbara Lee, Jose Serrano, Bobby Rush, Pete Stark, Edolphus Towns, and Ike Skelton, among those still in Congress in 2010. These wiser heads found no like minds whatsoever in the Senate, where the bill passed by unanimous consent.

Following the passage of the Iraq Liberation Act, President Clinton launched a four-day bombing campaign against Iraq on December 16th 1998. The apparent purpose of this attack seems to have been to test public and diplomatic reactions to the more overt use of force and the rhetoric that was later used to justify the invasion, by claiming to target sites that housed Iraq's alleged WMD programs. On the domestic front,

---

44. http://news.findlaw.com/hdocs/docs/iraq/libact103198.pdf

there was little public criticism of the attack itself, although many people regarded it as an effort to divert attention from Mr. Clinton's sex-scandal. On the diplomatic front however, it left the U.S. and Britain more isolated than ever. Russia briefly withdrew its ambassadors from Washington and London and—along with China and France—increased the pressure for the lifting of sanctions on Iraq. The Russian Duma voted overwhelmingly to withdraw unilaterally from the U.N. sanctions regime, but President Yeltsin did not act on the resolution.

Within a few months, U.S. forces were engaged in an eleven week bombing campaign against Yugoslavia, this time placing military action under the auspices of NATO and receiving greater international support. As in 1991 against Iraq, the drive to war was unstoppable once U.S. war interests were engaged. This campaign gave the United States a new foothold and an expanded military presence in an important part of Eastern Europe, while further eroding the authority of the U.N. Charter to prevent American aggression.

The NATO bombing was justified as an effort to protect Albanians in Kosovo from "ethnic cleansing" by the Yugoslavian authorities. But it was actually Serbs and Montenegrins that had been fleeing Kosovo since the 1980s because of discrimination and violence by the Albanian majority. In the 1990s, Albanian secessionists formed the U.S.-backed Kosovo Liberation Army, which escalated the campaign of terrorism and ethnic cleansing against Serbs and other minorities in Kosovo. Yugoslavian national police responded with acts of violent repression, which provided the pretext for NATO's bombing campaign and annexation of Kosovo.

Conditions in Kosovo only deteriorated under Western administration. Diana Johnstone, the author of *Fool's Crusade: Yugoslavia, NATO and Western Delusions*, described Kosovo in 2007 as "a poverty-stricken cauldron of discontent characterized by violent ethnic hatred, a political system manipulated by armed clans, a corrupt judicial system, and terrified minorities (notably Serbs and Roma) deprived of the most basic freedoms, such as being able to venture out of their besieged homes in order to shop, go to school or work their fields. Not to mention broken down public services, an economy totally dependent on foreign aid and criminal trafficking (drugs and sex slaves), and massive unemployment affecting a youthful population easily aroused to violence."[45]

But the annexation of Kosovo did succeed in creating a small militarized buffer state between Yugoslavia and the projected route of the AMBO oil pipeline through Bulgaria, Macedonia, and Albania. This pipeline is being built, with U.S. government support, to provide the United States and Western Europe with access to oil from the Caspian Sea, bypassing Russia, Turkey, Greece and Yugoslavia (now Serbia). Energy Secretary Bill Richardson explained the underlying strategy in November 1998. "This is about America's energy security," he explained. "It's also about preventing strategic inroads by those who don't share our values. We're trying to move these newly independent countries toward the west. We would like to see them reliant on western commercial and political interests rather than going another way. We've made a substantial political investment in the Caspian, and it's very important to us that both the pipeline map and the politics come out right."[46]

The AMBO pipeline is planned to be operational by 2011. Kosovo and Macedonia remain unstable, but AMBO Executive Vice President Gligor Tashkovich is confident that the United States will do whatever is necessary to protect the pipeline. Asked in 2005 who or what will vouch for the stability of Macedonia, he noted that "America will care what happens to Macedonia if an oil pipeline carrying oil supplying America

---

45 Diana Johnstone, "How to make a bad situation impossible – great power meddling in Kosovo", *Counterpunch*, June 2/3, 2007

46 George Monbiot,,"A discreet deal in the pipeline," *The Guardian*, August 15th 2001; http://www.freerepublic.com/focus/f-news/1976946/posts

runs through it."[47] If the United States eventually launches a military intervention in Macedonia to protect the AMBO pipeline, how many Americans will understand that this commitment in yet another faraway country has been implicit in U.S. policy since 1998?

On the far greater potential prize in Iraq, the Clinton administration had played the part expected of it in U.S. foreign policy circles by continuing the collective punishment of Iraq and preserving the public myth of Iraqi WMDs, while significantly eroding constraints on the use of U.S. military force in the post-Cold War world. Despite the derision of the neoconservatives, Clinton had served their interests well, even as he bequeathed the challenge of actual regime change in Iraq to his successor.

---

47 http://balkanalysis.blogspot.com/2005/01/ambo-pipeline-moves-forward-interview_09.html

CHAPTER 3. PLANNING AGGRESSION

Following one of the strangest electoral results in American history, George Bush held his first (and equally strange) National Security Council meeting on January 30th 2001.[48] The topic was "Mideast Policy," and some of the cabinet secretaries present had prepared for the meeting by ordering up briefings from their staff on the long-running Israeli-Palestinian crisis. But this understandable misreading of the agenda was swiftly corrected. After a cursory chat about Israel and Palestine, Bush turned to National Security Adviser Condoleezza Rice and asked her what was on the agenda. "How Iraq is destabilizing the region, Mr. President" was her scripted response.

Rice asked CIA Director George Tenet to deliver a prepared briefing which centered on an aerial photograph of a factory in Iraq, allegedly evidence that Iraq was once again producing chemical or biological weapons. After all present had pored over it for a while, Treasury Secretary Paul O'Neill asked, "I've seen a lot of factories around the world that look a lot like this one. What makes us suspect that this one is producing chemical or biological agents for weapons?" Tenet admitted that he had "no confirming intelligence."

Secretary of State Colin Powell made a case for "smart sanctions" that could win international approval by targeting Iraq's government instead of its people. Others speculated about how to improve U.S. intelligence on Iraq and advocated stepping up the ongoing bombing campaign. At the end of the meeting, it was decided that the State Department would work on a new sanctions regime, the Pentagon would explore military options, the CIA would try to improve its intelligence, and Treasury would put more financial pressure on the Iraqi government. The ultimate goal—regime change in Iraq—was already official U.S. government policy and was taken for granted.

---

48. Ron Suskind, *The Price of Loyalty*, (New York: Simon & Schuster, 2004), 70 - 86.

The planning continued over the next few months. At the Pentagon, the Defense Intelligence Agency (DIA) circulated documents with titles like "Foreign Suitors for Iraqi Oilfield Contracts." DIA analysts were already working on the post-regime-change distribution of the spoils, also taken for granted, rather than on a concerted effort to find out what was really going on in Iraq. At another NSC meeting, George Tenet pointed out that it was still only speculation whether Iraq had weapons of mass destruction or was restarting any weapons-building programs, but he was quickly quieted by Donald Rumsfeld. Indicating the junior aides present, Rumsfeld warned him, "I'm not sure everyone here has clearance to hear this."[49]

The planning for military action against Iraq was already well under way when Saudi terrorists crashed four airliners into New York, Washington and Pennsylvania on September 11th 2001. At 2:40 p.m. that day, Secretary Rumsfeld held a meeting at the Pentagon to discuss the U.S. response to the terrorist attacks. *CBS News* obtained a copy of Undersecretary Cambone's notes from the meeting under the Freedom of Information Act. They quoted Rumsfeld saying he wanted "best info fast. Judge whether good enough hit S.H. at same time—not only UBL. ... Go massive. Sweep it all up. Things related and not."[50]

The stated goal of the terrorist attacks was to goad the United States into actions that would gradually undermine its own military and economic power and turn it into what Osama bin Laden called a "suicide state". Al Qaeda was counting on a repressive and violent response from the U.S. government that would expose the hypocrisy of its much-vaunted commitment to human rights and civil liberties and unleash the destructive power of the U.S. armed forces on Muslim nations. This would lay bare the hard, iron fist of American militarism within the

---

49. *Ibid.*, 160-1.
50. *CBS News*, "Plans for Iraq attack began on 9/11," September 4 2002. Original document image at http://www.flickr.com/photos/66726692@N00/100545349/

velvet glove of American "soft power" and lead to widespread resistance. Al Qaeda astutely manipulated the warlike ambitions and "institutional myopia" of U.S. officials, who took the bait, hook, line and sinker. They responded by launching an unwinnable and self-destructive "war on terrorism", even as they rather meekly complied with Al Qaeda's most concrete demand by withdrawing U.S. forces from bases in Saudi Arabia in 2003. [51]

At a meeting at Camp David four days after the attacks, Deputy Secretary of Defense Paul Wolfowitz argued forcefully for an immediate attack on Iraq.[52] He had for some time been touting a plan to invade southern Iraq, annex Iraq's southern oil-fields, and install a puppet regime in the U.S.-occupied portion of the country. During the lunch break, Bush ordered this discussion shelved for the time being, but privately assured Defense Policy Board chairman Richard Perle that Iraq would be the next target of U.S. military action after Afghanistan.[53]

A few days later, Perle called a two-day-long Defense Policy Board meeting, attended by Rumsfeld, Henry Kissinger, James Woolsey, and Ahmad Chalabi among others. Former CIA Director Woolsey flew to London to try and dig up evidence to link Iraq to September 11th. Several of the Board's members signed a PNAC letter to Bush, declaring, "But even if evidence does not link Iraq directly to the attack, any strategy aiming at the eradication of terrorism and its sponsors must include a determined effort to remove Saddam Hussein from power in Iraq." The letter also proposed action against Hezbollah in Lebanon and a tougher line against the Palestinians.[54]

---

51. Mark Perry and Alistair Crooke, "How to Lose the War on Terror, Part 5: The Politics of Indignation", *Asia Times*, June 8 2006.

52. National Commission on Terrorist Attacks, *The 9/11 Commission Report*, (New York: Norton, 2004), 335.

53. Bryan Burrough, Evgenia Peretz, David Rose, David Wise, "The Rush to War," *Vanity Fair*, May 2004.

54. http://www.newamericancentury.org/Bushletter.htm

The obvious connection between America's dependence on Middle Eastern oil and the attacks by Saudi terrorists might have led U.S. officials to consider a change in energy policy to develop alternatives to vast imports of oil from the Persian Gulf. But any reflection on the roots of the crisis in U.S. policy was off limits. Addressing B-2 bomber crews of the 509th Bomber Wing at Whiteman AFB in Missouri on October 19th 2001, as they prepared to burn thousands of gallons of fuel en route to targets on the other side of the world in Afghanistan, Secretary Rumsfeld told them, "We have two choices. Either we change the way we live, or we must change the way they live. We choose the latter. And you are the ones who will help achieve that goal."

Within days, the debate regarding the U.S. response to the terrorist attacks had devolved into a choice between just attacking Afghanistan or using September 11th as a pretext for a much wider war, precisely the more aggressive and illegitimate use of U.S. military force that the PNAC and the neoconservatives had been advocating for several years. Now placed in important positions of power, the neocons would win this argument, with a short delay to accommodate what they saw as a diversion in Afghanistan.

The obvious third option, to respond to the terrorist attacks as a terrible crime that should be seriously investigated and prosecuted with the full force of national and international legal systems, is not mentioned in any reports of options seriously considered by U.S. officials. It seems that no one in official U.S. circles appreciated the benefit of responding to this crisis by strengthening the international rule of law, placing the United States firmly on the side of civilized society and treating those who planned the attacks as criminals. But notable experts outside government did speak out for just such a response. They included Benjamin Ferencz, the former Nuremberg Chief Prosecutor and architect of the International Criminal Court, and Sir Michael Howard, Professor of Modern History at Oxford University, who called the decision to declare a "war on terrorism" by U.S. authorities "a very natural but a terrible and irrevocable error."[55]

Michael Howard, a widely respected military historian, spoke to National Public Radio in the United States a few days after the attacks. A few weeks later, he gave a speech to the Royal United Services Institute in London, in which he expressed the hope that the U.S. government might somehow revoke its "irrevocable error."[56] Eight years later, his initial assessment that this would prove impossible seems prescient. He described how the British had responded to terrorism over the past 60 years in Palestine, Ireland, Cyprus and Malaysia:

> ... we never called them "wars": we called them "emergencies." [Sir Michael was being a bit of a revisionist here— the British actually coined the phrase "war on terrorism" during their campaign against Jewish terrorists in Palestine in the 1940s, but this failed policy may in fact have taught them the lesson he was trying to pass on.] This meant that the police and intelligence services were provided with exceptional powers, and were reinforced where necessary by the armed forces, but all continued to operate within a peacetime framework of civil authority. If force had to be used, it was at a minimal level and so far as possible did not interrupt the normal tenor of civil life. The object was to isolate the terrorists from the rest of the community, and to cut them off from external sources of supply. They were not dignified with the status of belligerents: they were criminals, to be regarded as such by the general public and treated as such by the authorities.

Howard went on to succinctly describe what made the American definition of a "war on terrorism" so dangerous:

> But to use, or rather to misuse the term 'war' is not simply a matter of legality, or pedantic semantics. It has deeper and

---

55 "Crimes against humanity," *National Public Radio*, September 19, 2001. http://www.benferencz.org/arts/61.html

56 Sir Michael Howard, "Mistake to declare this a war," *Evening Standard*, October 31, 2001. Full text at http://english.pravda.ru/main/2001/11/01/19888.html

more dangerous consequences. To declare that one is 'at war' is immediately to create a war psychosis that may be totally counter-productive for the objective that we seek. It will arouse an immediate expectation, and demand, for spectacular military action against some easily identifiable adversary, preferably a hostile state; action leading to decisive results.

"The use of force is no longer seen as a last resort, to be avoided if humanly possible, but as the first, and the sooner it is used the better .... Any suggestion that the best strategy is not to use military force at all, but more subtle if less heroic means of destroying the adversary are dismissed as 'appeasement' by ministers whose knowledge of history is about on a par with their skill at political management."

And he ridiculed the neoconservative vision of Iraq as the central front in this new "war."

"Figures on the Right, seeing themselves cheated of ... a short, jolly war in Afghanistan, demand one against a more satisfying adversary, Iraq; which is rather like the drunk who lost his watch in a dark alley but looked for it under a lamp post because there was more light there."

Of course, Michael Howard was taking the public statements of American officials at face value, as if this really was all about terrorism. We can understand from his reasoning that, if it really was about terrorism, this would be a self-defeating, counter-productive way to respond to it. On the other hand, if this was really about starting an endless war that could not be contained by national boundaries or the rule of law, in order to capitalize on America's new position as the world's single military "superpower," then a different reasoning might apply.

Whether the so-called "global war on terror" could possibly succeed on these terms is harder to analyze because, by its very nature, its goals are ill-defined and opportunistic, and the consequences of such widespread violence, destruction and chaos are inherently unpredictable. To the extent that this would be a sort of global counter-insurgency campaign against all sorts of political movements, much of Howard's analysis would still apply. In particular "the peacetime framework of civil authority" that could bestow a veneer of legitimacy on American actions would be undermined by a "war psychosis" and spiraling escalations of violence and militarism on all sides.

From the outset, few Americans understood that the so-called war on terror did not legally constitute a real war. The U.S. government opportunistically exploited this terminology to violate the U.S. Constitution and international human rights laws, but State Department Legal Adviser John Bellinger stated unequivocally, "We do not believe that we are in a legal state of war with every terrorist group everywhere in the world. Rather, the United States uses the term 'global war on terrorism' to mean that all countries must strongly oppose, and must fight against, terrorism in all its forms, everywhere around the globe."[57]

Bellinger repeated this precise formulation in press conferences, speeches and articles published all over the world. His campaign of public diplomacy to clarify the official position of the U.S. government and place it in a proper legal context contrasted dramatically with American political rhetoric that deliberately left its domestic audience at the mercy of the "war psychosis" that Michael Howard identified as the hidden danger of this policy.

And Elizabeth Wilmshurst, the former Deputy Legal Adviser at the British Foreign Office has pointed out that this sort of rhetoric did not provide any legal basis to circumvent international law: "This rather extraordinary war against terror, which is a phrase that all lawyers hate ... is not really a war, a conflict against terror, any more than the war against obesity means that you can detain people."[58]

---

57. John B. Bellinger III, "Legal issues in the war on terrorism," *London School of Economics*, October 31 2006.
http://www.lse.ac.uk/collections/LSEPublicLecturesAndEvents/pdf/20061031_JohnBellinger.pdf
58. Marie Woolf, "Legality of Iraq occupation flawed," *The Independent*, July 5, 2004.

In 2009, an Eminent Jurists Panel convened by the International Commission of Jurists and headed by former President of Ireland Mary Robinson reviewed the international response to terrorism since 2001. Echoing Michael Howard's warning about a "war psychosis", the jurists' report explained that the U.S. government had confused the public by framing its counterterrorism activities within a "war paradigm". It added that,

"The U.S.' war paradigm has created fundamental problems. Among the most serious is that the U.S. has applied war rules to persons not involved in situations of armed conflict, and, in genuine situations of warfare, it has distorted, selectively applied and ignored otherwise binding rules, including fundamental guarantees of human rights laws."

The ICJ panel concluded that, contrary to the claims of the U.S. government, the established principles of international law "were intended to withstand crises, and they provide a robust and effective framework from within which to tackle terrorism,"[59]

Perhaps the only thing that was really certain from the start was that the so-called war on terror would destroy millions of innocent people's lives. It was precisely the intrinsic and universal danger to human life and society posed by this type of international behavior that led the world powers to completely renounce "war as an instrument of national policy" in the Kellogg Briand pact (1928), to reiterate their commitment to peace even more forcefully in the United Nations Charter (1945) and instead to develop the "robust and effective framework" of international law. As the ICJ panel made clear, this framework was developed to provide a viable and preferable alternative to war, and to ad hoc responses to international problems driven by confusion and militarism.

---

59 Eminent Jurists Panel on Terrorism, Counter-Terrorism and Human Rights, *Assessing Damage, Urging Action*, (Geneva: International Commission of Jurists, 2009). http://icj.org/IMG/EJP-report.pdf

The short-term American success in assisting the Northern Alliance to overthrow the Taliban government in Afghanistan only encouraged American policy-makers to believe that their military power could indeed serve the purposes for which they intended to use it. The longer term problems created by American actions in Afghanistan were still far from evident to the general public, and this gave the U.S. government a political window of opportunity to move ahead with its plans against Iraq.

The next phase of this planning was exposed by a series of leaked British documents known as the "Downing Street Memos". These were official British government documents leaked to British journalist Michael Smith of the conservative *Daily Telegraph* by a government official whose identity has remained secret.[60]

The earliest of these documents was an Options Paper and an accompanying Legal Background Paper drawn up for Prime Minister Blair by the Defense and Overseas Secretariat in response to an initiative on Iraq from Washington. It was dated March 8th 2002. The Options Paper spelled out two choices: toughening the containment policy, or regime change. It called the latter "a new departure which would require the construction of a coalition and a legal justification." It went on to say: "A full opinion should be sought from the Law Officers if the above options are developed further ... Of itself, Regime Change has no basis in international law."

The Legal Background Paper rejected any notion that military action against Iraq could be justified by self defense in the absence of an Iraqi attack on another country, or as some form of humanitarian intervention. This left only the enforcement of U.N. resolutions as a possible justification, but this too was highly problematic.

---

60. Michael Smith, "Failure is not an option, but that doesn't mean they will avoid it," *The Daily Telegraph*, September 18, 2004. Full text of Downing Street Memos at http://www.afterdowningstreet.org/?q=node/840

The paper explained that the U.S. government interpreted Security Council resolutions in ways that were neither supported by the language of the resolutions themselves nor shared by other Council members, including the U.K. The no-fly zones over northern and southern Iraq were established in 1991 and 1992 to protect the civilian population from aerial attack by the Iraqi government. They were justified at the time as a limited, proportional and arguably humanitarian measure following soon after the end of hostilities and were approved by UN Legal Counsel Carl-August Fleischauer. The United States now claimed that the no-fly zones could be used for a quite different purpose, to enforce the disarmament provisions of resolutions 687 and 688, a view rejected by Britain and other Security Council members and not supported by any Security Council resolution.

The United States was also arguing that an individual state, such as itself, could make an independent determination that Iraq was in breach of its obligations under Security Council resolutions instead of deferring to the Security Council to make such a judgment. The Legal Background Paper categorically rejected this argument, adding: "We are not aware of any other State that supports this view."

The paper noted that the U.S. and British justification for Operation Desert Fox in 1998, based on S.C. resolution 1205, "was controversial anyway; many of our partners did not think the legal basis was sufficient as the authority to use force was not explicit. Reliance on it now would be unlikely to receive any support." This was putting it mildly—it did not add that the Russian Parliament had gone so far as to vote for the end of sanctions on Iraq following those attacks, nor that "many of our partners" had strongly condemned them.

The Legal Background Paper did not directly address the American or British view on regime change nor expand on the Options Paper's statement that it had "no basis in international law." None of the Security Council resolutions in question had threatened Iraq with regime change. On the contrary, many of them had explicitly reiterated "the commitment of all Member States to the sovereignty, territorial integrity and political independence of Kuwait and Iraq" to quote the wording used in resolution 1205. So military action intended to result in regime change would simply be an act of aggression, a violation of the resolutions it claimed to be enforcing and a serious violation of the U.N. Charter.

In spite of this substantial body of legal advice that military action to bring about regime change would constitute a serious international crime, the next document in the Downing Street Memos made it clear that Prime Minister Blair in fact committed the U.K. to precisely this policy within a matter of days, and that the United States was already committed to it. This document was a memo from British Foreign Policy Advisor Sir David Manning to Prime Minister Blair dated March 14th 2002 and marked "Secret - Strictly Personal." The memo described a dinner meeting between Manning and U.S. National Security Advisor Condoleezza Rice, at which Manning told Rice that Blair "would not budge in (his) support for regime change" and insisted only that it be "very carefully done:"

> I had dinner with Condi on Tuesday; and lunch with her and an NSC team on Wednesday (to which Christopher Meyer also came). These were good exchanges, and particularly frank when we were one-on-one at dinner. We spent a long time at dinner on Iraq. It is clear that Bush is grateful for your support and has registered that you are getting flak. I said that you would not budge in your support for regime change but you had to manage a press, a Parliament and a public opinion that was very different than anything in the States. And you would not budge in your insistence that, if we pursued regime change, it must be very carefully done and produce the right result. Failure was not an option. Condi's enthusiasm for regime change is undimmed. But there were some signs, since we last spoke, of greater awareness of the practical difficulties and political risks ... I think there is a

real risk that the Administration underestimates the difficulties. They may agree that failure is not an option, but this does not mean they will avoid it.

The next document was a memo to Manning from British Ambassador to Washington Sir Christopher Meyer, dated March 18th 2002, in which he described giving the same assurance to U.S. Deputy Secretary of Defense Paul Wolfowitz: "We backed regime change, but the plan had to be clever and failure was not an option ... I then went through the need to wrongfoot Saddam on the inspectors and the UN SCRs and the critical importance of MEPP (Middle East Peace Process) as an integral part of the anti-Saddam strategy."

The other two items in this first batch of leaked British documents were a letter to Foreign Secretary Jack Straw from Political Director Peter Ricketts and a memo from Straw to Blair from March 25th, 2002. These included efforts by the Foreign Office to assert the primacy of international law and fit British policy into some sort of legitimate context. Straw told Blair, "I believe that a demand for the unfettered readmission of weapons inspectors is essential, in terms of public explanation, and in terms of legal sanction for any military action." He warned Blair of what he called two "potential elephant traps." These were the illegality of regime change and the question of an additional mandate from the Security Council. "The U.S. is likely to oppose any idea of a fresh mandate. On the other side, the weight of legal advice here is that a fresh mandate may well be required."

Two weeks later, Blair visited Bush at his ranch in Texas, and stood with Bush as he spoke at a joint news conference on April 6th 2002: "I explained to the Prime Minister that the policy of my government is the removal of Saddam, and that all options are on the table ... The world would be better off without him and so will the future." Blair was less straightforward in his statement, "How we now proceed in this situation, how we make sure that this threat that is posed by weapons of mass destruction is dealt with, that is a matter that is open. And when the time comes for taking those decisions we will tell people about those decisions."[61]

Blair could not go public with his private and diplomatic commitment to regime change without generating serious opposition in Britain, so he played "good cop" to Bush's "bad cop." Bush was quite explicit about his intentions, and yet millions of people in Britain and the United States were reassured by Blair, Powell and others, that the unthinkable would not come to pass. They could not have been more completely or successfully deceived. The decision to use American and British military force to overthrow the government of Iraq had already been taken.

In May 2002, the United States and Britain began a campaign of much heavier bombing of Iraq. Britain's Ministry of Defense later published figures for allied missions flown and tonnages of bombs dropped between 2000 and 2002. They revealed that the rate of bombing during the next six months more than doubled compared with the previous year. The campaign climaxed in early September in a massive air raid by a combined fleet of 100 planes.[62] A year later, on July 17th 2003, U.S. Air Force General Michael Moseley, who commanded the campaign, bragged to a joint briefing at Nellis Air Force Base in Las Vegas that it "laid the foundations" for the invasion.[63] Centcom commander General Tommy Franks backed up Moseley's claim in his memoir *American Soldier*. He described a meeting at the White House in which Ms. Rice argued for a pause in the bombing when Bush was due to speak to the United Nations. Franks persuaded Bush to continue the bombing on

61. http://www.whitehouse.gov/news/releases/2002/04/20020406-3.html

62. Michael Smith, "RAF bombing raids tried to goad Saddam into war," *The Sunday Times*, May 29, 2005.

63. Michael Smith, "General admits to secret air war," *The Sunday Times*, June 26th, 2005.

the basis that the destruction of Iraq's defensive weapons was an essential part of the groundwork for the invasion.[64]

Tony Blair summoned a "Prime Minister's Meeting" on Iraq for July 23rd 2002. The most widely publicized of the Downing Street Memos was actually the minutes of this meeting, and Michael Smith was also given an incomplete copy of the "Cabinet Office Paper" that was distributed to the participants in preparation for the meeting.

The opening summary of the Cabinet Office Paper invited ministers to "agree that the objective of any military action should be a stable and law-abiding Iraq," but paragraphs 11 through 14 on "Justification" described the even more elusive quest for a law-abiding United Kingdom and United States. The fundamental illegitimacy of the plans being made was still the central problem: "U.S. views of international law vary from that of the U.K. and the international community. Regime change, per se, is not a proper basis for military action under international law." And yet, "U.S. military planning unambiguously takes as its objective the removal of Saddam Hussein's regime."

Since the meetings in March, the British had settled on a strategy of imposing a new inspection regime on Iraq as the only way to create a pretext for war that could be convincing to the U.N. Security Council. Iraqi obstruction would be an essential part of the pretext for war under this plan, but this would be unlikely to materialize in the early stages of the inspection process. The paper concluded: "We would be most unlikely to achieve a legal base for military action by January 2003." This implied that the U.S. government had established January 2003 as a target date for the invasion.

John Scarlett, the Chairman of the Joint Intelligence Committee, stated at the outset of the meeting that only "massive military action" would be likely to actually accomplish regime change. Sir Richard

---

64. General Tommy Franks, *American Soldier*, (New York: Regan Books, 2004).

Dearlove, the head of MI6, then told the meeting that there had been "a perceptible shift in attitude" in Washington and that "military action was now seen as inevitable. Bush wanted to remove Saddam, through military action, justified by the conjunction of terrorism and WMD. But the intelligence and facts were being fixed around the policy."

This statement was identified as a "smoking gun" by American critics of the war, but it was far from the earliest one, as we have seen. In fact, Bush had been quite explicit about his objective. It was only the sheer enormity of his plan that led most people to believe that his declared intentions could be dismissed as "cowboy" rhetoric and that wiser heads would prevail. In fact the United States and United Kingdom were already implementing a detailed war plan, and their actions on the political and diplomatic fronts were integral parts of that plan, not alternatives to it.

Defense Secretary Geoff Hoon alluded to the stepped-up bombing campaign, which was by now well under way, as "spikes of activity ... to put pressure on the regime." The Western press had been dutifully reporting the official story, that allied planes were only responding to threats to their safety from Iraqi missile batteries and radar sites, but Iraqi and other Arab media were providing more accurate accounts of the expanded bombing campaign, with pictures of casualties and bomb-damage.

Foreign Secretary Jack Straw said he understood that Bush was committed to war, but thought the timing was not yet decided: "But the case was thin. Saddam was not threatening his neighbors, and his WMD capability was less than that of Libya, North Korea or Iran. We should work up a plan for an ultimatum to Saddam to allow back in the U.N. weapons inspectors. This would also help with the legal justification for the use of force."

Then it was Attorney General Lord Peter Goldsmith's turn. He reiterated his previous advice, "that the desire for regime change was not a legal basis for military action. There were three possible legal bases: self-defense, humanitarian intervention, or UNSC authorization. The first and second could not be the base in this case."

Then, "the Prime Minister said that it would make a big difference politically and legally if Saddam refused to allow in the U.N. inspectors. Regime change and WMD were linked in the sense that it was the regime that was producing the WMD. ... If the political context were right, people would support regime change. The two key issues were whether the military plan worked and whether we had the political strategy to give the military plan the space to work." This is a revealing glimpse into Mr. Blair's view of the legal, political, and military aspects of the situation. Blair, like Bush, was ever the politician. As long as his military advisers could assure him that the military plan was viable, he had confidence in his own sense of what would work politically. The veneer of legitimacy that UN inspections could create was an essential part of his political strategy, but, as Elizabeth Wilmshurst later told the Chilcot inquiry, the legal questions were "simply an impediment that had to be got over before the policy could be implemented".[65]

---

65 Philippe Naughton and David Brown, "Lawyer's memo contradicts Jack Straw's evidence to Chilcot inquiry", *The Times*, January 26 2010.

CHAPTER 4. IMAGINING WEAPONS OF MASS DESTRUCTION

And so, the effort to convince the American and British public of the existence of non-existent Iraqi weapons became the central front in the "War on Terror." The phrase "War on Terrorism" had been transcribed into "War on Terror" soon after September 11th 2001, further blurring the nebulous objectives of the campaign and deepening the war psychosis that had alarmed Michael Howard in October 2001. Now these political conditions would be opportunistically exploited to launch the invasion of Iraq and its attempted destruction as an independent power in the Middle East. The awkward fact that Iraq had neither "weapons of mass destruction" nor any substantial links to terrorism would not deter Bush or Blair from pursuing its destruction "justified by the conjunction of terrorism and WMD" as the Downing Street Memos described it.

The commercially-dominated media in the United States played a key role in bolstering the false evidence of Iraqi "weapons of mass destruction" and links to terrorism. Throughout the 1990s, the CIA and Britain's MI6 had used time-tested methods to spread stories in the world's press about Iraq's imaginary weapons. U.N. weapons inspector Scott Ritter told a parliamentary inquiry in Britain that he was recruited in 1997 to take part in MI6's "Operation Mass Appeal." This operation planted stories, including unsubstantiated reports from UNSCOM's files provided by Ritter, in newspapers in Poland, India, and South Africa. These stories were designed to filter back into the echo chamber of the Western corporate media, where they would appear to corroborate and validate each other.[66]

---

66. "Scott Ritter: How the British Spy Agency MI6 Secretly Misled A Nation Into War With Iraq," *Democracy Now*, December 30, 2003.

But the major instrument of this propaganda campaign was the Iraqi National Congress (INC), an Iraqi exile group founded in 1992 by the Rendon Group, a Washington public relations firm under contract with the CIA. The INC was active in Iraqi exile politics throughout the 1990s, and received at least $52 million from the CIA and DIA (Defense Intelligence Agency) by the time its funding was finally cut off in 2004. It was managed by Ahmad Chalabi, an Iraqi banker convicted of embezzlement in Jordan. Chalabi eventually became a senior official in occupied Iraq in spite of his widely known, self-serving and duplicitous role in plotting the invasion and destruction of his own country.

On June 26th 2002, the INC sent a letter to the U.S. Senate Appropriations Committee to justify its U.S. funding. It identified its "Information Collection Program" as the primary source for 108 newspaper and magazine articles about Iraq's weapons programs and links to terrorism since October 2001. The articles in question appeared in publications all over the world, including the *New York Times*, the *Washington Post*, the *Wall Street Journal*, *Time*, *Newsweek*, *Vanity Fair*, the *Atlantic Monthly*, the *New Yorker*, the Associated Press, and other newspapers and TV outlets in the U.S.; the *Times*, the *Guardian*, the *Observer*, the *Daily Telegraph* and the *Economist* in the U.K.; Agence France Presse; and newspapers in Australia, Canada, Russia, the Czech Republic, Kuwait, Thailand, and Singapore.[67]

The false claims in these articles included detailed descriptions of fictitious chemical, biological and nuclear weapons programs, terrorist training facilities, and collaboration between Saddam Hussein and Osama bin-Laden. The INC presented Iraqi defectors and exiles directly to journalists and sympathetic U.S. officials to substantiate its claims. This wide dissemination of misinformation created the impression that

---

67. "List of articles cited by the Information Collection Program (ICP)," *Knight Ridder Newspapers*, May 15, 2004.
http://www.mcclatchydc.com/reports/intelligence/story/16633.html

multiple sources were corroborating each other, giving credibility to what was really complete fiction from a single source. This media campaign supported misleading statements by government officials to create a blizzard of mutually reinforcing propaganda. It drowned out the absence of any real evidence noted by the most knowledgeable experts, such as Scott Ritter and Senator Bob Graham, the Chairman of the Senate Intelligence Committee.

In fact, as Scott Ritter told CNN in July 2002, "No one has substantiated the allegations that Iraq possesses weapons of mass destruction or is attempting to acquire weapons of mass destruction." He elaborated "...chemical weapons have a shelf-life of five years. Biological weapons have a shelf-life of three years." So any weapons unaccounted for since 1991 were not even a potential threat in 2002. The only weapon Iraq had possessed that had a longer shelf-life was mustard gas, but it is a battlefield weapon rather than a strategic one, and could pose no threat to the United States or Great Britain. It is inconceivable that U.S. intelligence agencies lacked the elementary technical expertise to understand these basic facts.[68]

In his book *Iraq Confidential*, subtitled *The untold story of the intelligence conspiracy to undermine the U.N. and overthrow Saddam Hussein*, Ritter made it clear that, by 1995, he and his colleagues at UNSCOM were satisfied that Iraq had destroyed its entire arsenal of chemical and biological weapons, along with its nuclear weapons program, in 1991. The inspections process thereafter became a political tool of the American and British governments as they tried to justify the indefinite continuation of sanctions and their plots for regime change. As they launched their final public relations offensive in 2002, U.N. inspections once again became part of this strategy, not as a mechanism for disar-

---

68. "Scott Ritter: Facts needed before Iraq attack," *CNN*, July 17 2002.

mament, but as a component of the public relations campaign for war.[69]

This campaign followed a classic pattern. Bush or another official would make a very public statement, usually in front of the television cameras, that few Americans had the background knowledge to question. Then, as the falsity of the statement became more widely known, they would modify it, downplay it or move on to a fresh allegation that made the previous one seem less important. Much of the public would be left believing the original claim, even when it had been widely and publicly debunked. This pattern was so consistent that it would be naive to interpret it as anything but a cynical effort to mislead the public. It is also fair to say that the media were much more easily led than the public at large, who took to the streets by the hundreds of thousands to oppose the war even as the media loyally echoed the ever-changing official story.

The decisive public relations offensive was launched by Mr. Cheney in August 2002, with unequivocal statements that Iraq was reconstituting its nuclear weapons program. In conjunction with the diplomatic offensive that secured the British commitment to war, Cheney had claimed on March 24th that Iraq was "actively pursuing nuclear weapons at this time."[70] Now he very publicly elaborated on this, and argued forcefully for unilateral U.S. military action.

Cheney spoke to a Veterans of Foreign Wars convention in Nashville on August 26th. "There is no doubt that Saddam Hussein now has weapons of mass destruction," Mr. Cheney said. "There is no doubt that he is amassing them to use against our friends, against our allies and against us." Cheney claimed that his certainty was based on the testimony of Hussein Kamel, Iraq's Minister of Military Industries and Sad-

69. Scott Ritter, *Iraq Confidential*, (New York: Nation Books, 2005), 109-13 & 289-92.
70. http://transcripts.cnn.com/TRANSCRIPTS/0203/24/le.00.html

dam Hussein's son-in-law, who had revealed details of Iraq's weapons programs during his brief defection to Jordan in 1995, before he returned to Iraq and was killed. But Kamel's revelations all referred to the period before 1991, and the transcript of Kamel's UNSCOM debriefing includes the categorical statement that, following the Gulf War in 1991, "I ordered destruction of all chemical weapons. All weapons— biological, chemical, missile, nuclear—were destroyed." The other source on whom Cheney appears to have based his claims was Adnan al-Haideri, an Iraqi defector promoted by the INC and Judith Miller of the New York Times, but dismissed as a fraud by both the Pentagon and the CIA.[71]

On the terrorism front, Cheney claimed that one of the September 11th hijackers, Mohamed Atta, had met with the Iraqi consul in Prague in April 2001. This was the only tenuous link between Iraq and al-Qaeda that Woolsey had unearthed in Europe immediately after the attacks. Both the FBI and the Czech intelligence service had investigated it and concluded it to be false, not least because Atta was in Florida at the time. In March 2006, Cheney finally admitted that, "the degree of confidence in it, and so forth, has been pretty well knocked down now at this stage, that that meeting ever took place."[72]

While renewed U.N. inspections became a vital part of the public relations program for war, this went hand-in-hand with an effort to discredit them as an actual mechanism for disarmament. A frequent rhetorical flourish from U.S. officials was that "Saddam has had twelve years to disarm, and he hasn't done so". In fact, the model of intrusive inspections developed in the 1990s was not only effective in Iraq, but it created a good working model for resolving future weapons proliferation problems without recourse to war.

---

71. http://www.whitehouse.gov/news/releases/2002/08/20020826.html
72. http://www.whitehouse.gov/news/releases/2006/03/20060329-2.html

On both counts, it became vital for proponents of unilateral U.S. military power to portray this process as a failure. Even as the absence of WMDs in Iraq has completely validated UNSCOM's methods and findings, nobody in official American circles has acknowledged its success, let alone the obvious relative merits of inspections as opposed to war. Chief weapons inspector Scott Ritter is treated as some sort of counter-cultural figure in spite of being proved right in every respect, while the officials and pundits who got it all wrong are still trotted out as experts by congressional committees and so-called news programs on American television.

U.S. policy-makers did split into two factions over whether to revive U.N. inspections as part of the pretext for war, but this did not signify an actual effort to avoid war. On the one hand, the British and the U.S. State Department saw inspections as a politically essential concession to legitimacy, although the British were repeatedly advised that they would not in themselves provide a legal justification for regime change. On the other hand, hawks like Cheney and Rumsfeld were prepared to dispense with even the appearance of international legitimacy and to rely entirely on fear, flag-waving and lies to generate public support for the invasion.

The so-called moderates publicly presented their position as an effort to avoid war, but this was misleading. The only real difference between the position put forth by the "crazies," as Colin Powell called them, and his own and Blair's position was the extent to which their faction felt the need to create an illusion of legitimacy for the invasion by pretending that they were trying to avoid it and to comply with international law. Each faction played a vital political role in the overall policy, one by bringing along members of the public who had reservations about committing aggression, and the other by keeping up the drumbeat for war. In reality the crucial decisions had already been made, and the military plans were proceeding with the full support of both factions.

In September 2002, the effort to promote false intelligence on Iraqi weapons production and links to al-Qaeda was institutionalized in a new department at the Pentagon: the Office of Special Plans (OSP), under the authority of Douglas Feith, the Undersecretary of Defense for Policy. Its mission was to provide an alternative and hawkish interpretation of U.S. intelligence data to support the march to war. The OSP reported to Rumsfeld and Wolfowitz, and sometimes directly to Cheney and Rice, bypassing all the normal procedures by which U.S. intelligence agencies are supposed to compare notes and present policymakers with qualified and vetted intelligence.

The OSP also circumvented normal channels between the CIA and the Mossad in Israel, dealing directly with a similar Israeli operation run from Prime Minister Sharon's office. OSP employees illegally passed American secrets to Israel and to Ahmad Chalabi, who in turn passed them on to Iran. An OSP employee, Lawrence Franklin, was convicted of passing U.S. secrets to Israel and sentenced to 13 years in prison, but his sentence was later commuted to ten months of house arrest. Undersecretary Feith was also a subject of this investigation.[73]

In 2007, four and a half years too late, the Inspector General of the Department of Defense issued a scathing report on the OSP. He called its manipulation of intelligence data "inappropriate," but stopped short of recommending an additional criminal investigation. In June 2006 it was revealed that the Pentagon was operating a new office similar to the OSP, the Iranian Directorate, to provide policy-makers with alternative intelligence analysis on Iran.

Mr. Bush addressed the U.N. General Assembly on September 12th 2002, dedicating most of his speech to a sort of ultimatum on Iraq. In what was now a common pattern in the American case for war, he

---

73. Julian Borger, "The spies who pushed for war," *The Guardian*, July 17 2003; Robin Wright and Thomas E. Ricks, "Wider FBI probe of Pentagon leaks includes Chalabi," *Washington Post*, September 3 2004, A01.

made no distinction between the failure to fully account for weapons destroyed in 1991 on the one hand, and the possibility of more recent Iraqi weapons development on the other. He unconvincingly provided examples of the former as evidence of the latter and went on to make completely unfounded accusations: "We know that Saddam Hussein pursued weapons of mass murder even when inspectors were in his country. Are we to assume that he stopped when they left? The history, the logic, and the facts lead to one conclusion: Saddam Hussein's regime is a grave and gathering danger," and "Saddam Hussein has defied all these efforts and continues to develop weapons of mass destruction."[74]

To those listening who were more concerned by real threats from the United States than by imagined ones from Iraq, the overall import of Bush's speech was ominous. Just as Bush leapt from old accounting failures to imaginary new weapons, he likewise leapt from the need for compliance with Security Council resolutions to implied threats of aggression and regime change, leaving the world as worried as ever about America's real intentions: "The purposes of the United States should not be doubted. The Security Council resolutions will be enforced—the just demands of peace and security will be met—or action will be unavoidable. And a regime that has lost its legitimacy will also lose its power."

A fascinating thread in Bush's rhetoric throughout the "War on Terror" was his tendency to refer to his enemies in terms that could equally be used to describe his own policies. In this case, he referred to "regimes that accept no law of morality and have no limit to their violent ambitions...the threat hides within many nations, including my own...In one place—in one regime—we find all these dangers, in their most lethal and aggressive forms, exactly the kind of aggressive threat

74. Full text at http://news.bbc.co.uk/1/hi/world/middle_east/2254712.stm

the United Nations was born to confront." In similar looking-glass fashion, he provided a succinct analysis of the challenge that he was presenting to the United Nations itself: "All the world now faces a test, and the United Nations a difficult and defining moment. Are Security Council resolutions to be honored and enforced, or cast aside without consequence? Will the United Nations serve the purpose of its founding, or will it be irrelevant?"

Five days later, the U.S. government took another step in its effort to render the U.N. irrelevant when it published a new National Security Strategy (NSS) document that dismissed one of the cornerstones of customary international law, the *Caroline* principle regarding preemptive military action. The new so-called "doctrine of preemption" was in *Section Five - Prevent our enemies from threatening us, our allies, and our friends with weapons of mass destruction.* Consistent with the spurious arguments over Iraq's imaginary weapons and support for terrorism, it was presented as a response to "the overlap between states that sponsor terror and those that pursue WMD." The NSS document acknowledged the long-standing principle of international law established after the *Caroline* incident in 1837, which restricts preemptive or anticipatory self defense to a proportional response to an imminent attack, but it claimed a virtually unlimited expansion of this right, because "we must adapt the concept of imminent threat to the capabilities and objectives of today's adversaries ... (who) rely on acts of terror and, potentially, the use of weapons of mass destruction—weapons that can be easily concealed, delivered covertly, and used without warning."[75]

If preemption is applicable to weapons that can be "used without warning," the concept of imminence is rendered meaningless, as was presumably intended, and the mere possession of a single ballistic mis-

---

75. http://www.state.gov/r/pa/ei/wh/15425.htm

sile could constitute grounds for preemptive action. In the case of Iraq, the U.S. really went even further, essentially claiming that the mere existence of a hostile government that might one day develop such weapons could justify massive preemptive action to remove it from power. This was of course consistent with the 1997 Quadrennial Defense Review's threat of unilateral military action to prevent hostile alliances or to secure U.S. access to resources.

From the standpoint of international law, however, were this position ever to gain legitimacy, it would in effect remove all legal constraints on military action between modern states with modern weapons, since by this definition they all pose a constant and imminent threat to each other. Under existing international law however, any country that adopts such a position is simply violating Article 2 (4) of the United Nations Charter, which states, "All Members shall refrain in their international relations from the threat or use of force against the territorial integrity or political independence of any state, or in any manner inconsistent with the Purposes of the United Nations." The United States has arguably been in violation of Article 2(4) of the United Nations Charter since the publication of its 1997 Quadrennial Defense Review.

The irony of the American effort to unilaterally rewrite the *Caroline* principle because of terrorism was that this fundamental principle of international law was originally formulated as a result of American popular support for terrorism in Canada. By failing to prevent it's citizens from supporting, sheltering, and arming Canadian insurgents in 1837, the United States government placed itself in the same position as Afghanistan, Pakistan, Syria and other states that are accused of harboring terrorists in today's world. The argument that present-day terrorism and asymmetric warfare somehow render the *Caroline* principle obsolete is therefore absurd, since it was terrorism and asymmetric warfare that gave rise to it in the first place.

It is worth briefly reviewing the *Caroline* case in order to understand how this principle came to be established. In 1837, an insurgency was raging, not in Iraq or Afghanistan, but in Canada. A small, U.S.-owned steamer named the *Caroline* was being used to smuggle anti-British insurgents and shipments of arms across the Niagara River to their base on Navy Island in British territory. The British eventually responded by sending a boarding party in small boats to attack the *Caroline* at its mooring on the American side of the river in the middle of the night. One or maybe two Americans were killed and others wounded in the ensuing fight. The British captured the ship, towed it into the current, set it on fire, and left it to drift toward Niagara Falls. A contemporary newspaper picture showed the fiery wreck plunging over the falls.[76]

The incident understandably raised warlike passions on both sides of the border. Americans regarded the British raid as an act of aggression in American territory, while the British saw it as an act of preemptive or anticipatory self-defense. This raised the same general question as the "war on terror" about where the line should be drawn between legitimate preemptive self defense and aggression. The incident threatened to ignite a new war between Britain and the United States, and it delayed the resolution of other issues between the two countries, such as the location of the international border between Maine and New Brunswick and the disposition of Oregon. Commerce was affected, and business interests in both countries, notably British bankers and American land developers, were frustrated by this thorny obstacle to potentially profitable relations.

Finally, in 1842, the British government sent Lord Ashburton, a senior partner in Barings Bank, as a special ambassador to Washington, and the matter was peacefully resolved in an exchange of letters with the newly appointed U.S. Secretary of State Daniel Webster. The lan-

---

76. Martin A. Rogoff and Edward Collins, "The Caroline Incident and the Development of International Law," *Brooklyn Journal of International Law* 16, 1990, 493-8.

guage that resolved the crisis was written by Webster and agreed to by Ashburton, and it has served as the customary principle of international law regarding preemptive military action since that time. The critical wording in Webster's letter was as follows: "Respect for the inviolable character of the territory of independent nations is the most essential foundation of civilization," which may only be violated under "a necessity of self-defense, instant, overwhelming, leaving no choice of means, and no moment for deliberation." And "the act...must be limited by that necessity, and kept clearly within it." These principles are now known as the principles of necessity and proportionality, and they establish a very clear and indeed a high standard that must be met by any country that claims the right to violate the sovereignty of another in preemptive or anticipatory self-defense.

The *Caroline* principle was cited as definitive in the Nuremberg Judgment and is universally accepted in international legal and diplomatic circles. The notion that the government of one country can unilaterally modify or extend this principle has no more validity today than it did when the German defendants at Nuremberg made the same argument with respect to their "preemptive" invasion of Norway in 1940, a claim that the judges rejected on principle.

Following Bush's performance at the U.N. and the publication of the National Security Strategy, the debate moved to the U.S. Congress, where Bush was asking for a sweeping authorization for the use of military force against Iraq. Americans were promised that their government would finally present to Congress its evidence that Iraq was developing chemical, nuclear, and biological weapons so that an informed debate could take place. In fact, despite huge technological advances since 1962 and a decade of the most extensive and intrusive surveillance in history, the U.S. government lacked anything resembling Adlai Stevenson's evidence of Soviet missile sites in Cuba or any other documentary, photographic, or audio intercept intelligence that would have given credibility to its claims.

George Tenet, the Director of Central Intelligence, had shocked the Senate Intelligence Committee on September 5th by admitting that he had not even ordered a National Intelligence Estimate (NIE) on Iraq. The committee chairman, Senator Bob Graham, insisted that he produce one. The CIA eventually published this 90 page document on October 2nd and made it available to any Members of Congress who requested it. As Graham suspected, the intelligence assessment contained no confirmation that Iraq had developed any illegal weapons since the passage of Security Council resolution 687 in 1991.[77]

Then, on October 4th, the CIA gave Members of Congress a 25-page summary of U.S. intelligence on Iraq that repeated all the now familiar canards and painted a very different picture from the NIE. It claimed that U.S. agents knew the location of 550 specific sites in Iraq where chemical and biological weapons were stored, a claim that was completely absent from the NIE and utterly false. The so-called "summary" had nothing to do with the NIE it claimed to summarize. It was a blatantly political document that had been prepared several months earlier with the express purpose of making a case for war. Paul Pillar, a senior CIA analyst who worked on it, later told Public Broadcasting's *Frontline*, "The purpose was to strengthen the case for going to war with the American public. Is it proper for the intelligence community to publish papers for that purpose? I don't think so, and I regret having had a role in it."[78]

Senator Graham was outraged, and made an impassioned speech on the Senate floor, begging his colleagues to read the classified report as well as the declassified pro-war document. "Friends, I encourage you to read the classified intelligence reports which are much sharper than what is available in declassified form," he warned. "We are going to be

---

77. Bob Graham and Jeff Nussbaum, *Intelligence Matters*, (New York: Random House, 2004), 179-98.
78. http://www.pbs.org/wgbh/pages/frontline/darkside/view/

increasing the threat level against the people of the United States." Because the NIE was classified, he could not be more specific in open session, but the usually reserved and conservative Senator surprised his colleagues with an uncharacteristically graphic accusation: "Blood is going to be on your hands."

As the title of this book suggests, I believe that responsibility for aggression, genocide and other war crimes in Iraq extends well beyond the United States Senate. However, I agree with Lincoln Chafee, the only Republican Senator who voted against the Iraq war resolution, that for Senators of any political party, "Helping a rogue President start an unnecessary war should be a career-ending lapse of judgment."

On October 7th, Bush made his final and most deceptive pitch for the Congressional war resolution in a speech in Cincinnati. The transcript was published on the White House web site under the heading— "Iraq - Denial and Deception." It included at least 18 unsupported assertions that Iraq possessed nuclear, chemical, and biological weapons, and once again cited Hussein Kamel's UNSCOM testimony as supporting evidence. The climax of Bush's fear-mongering speech was that "we cannot wait for the final proof—the smoking gun—that could come in the form of a mushroom cloud."

Four days later, Bush's warnings were heeded and Graham's were ignored. The Senate, under a Democratic majority, passed a bill "To authorize the use of United States armed forces against Iraq" by 77 votes to 23. The House, under Republican rule, passed the war resolution by a smaller relative margin of 296-133. Graham's Democratic Senate colleague from Florida, Bill Nelson, reported on his web site that 90% of his correspondence from constituents was urging him to vote against the resolution, but he voted for it anyway.[79]

---

79. Lincoln Chafee, *Against the tide: how a compliant Congress empowered a reckless President*, (New York: Thomas Dunne, 2008), 93.

With the backing of Congress secured, the U.S. government turned its attention back to the United Nations and, with British support, set out to negotiate a new Security Council resolution on Iraq. This was SC resolution 1441, passed on November 8th 2002, which required a full disarmament report from Iraq within 30 days and "immediate, unimpeded, unconditional, and unrestricted access" to all sites in Iraq for UNMOVIC and IAEA inspectors. The negotiations were intense, as the Americans and British were desperate to include language that could later be interpreted as an authorization for military action. They failed, and their subsequent claims that SCR 1441 provided a legal basis for the invasion were universally challenged, even by the British government's own legal advisers.

UNMOVIC was established under SCR 1284 in December 1999, and was designed to remedy many of the problems encountered by its predecessor, UNSCOM, which had carried out on-site inspections in Iraq since 1991. The most fundamental innovation was that all UNMOVIC staff were to be U.N. employees instead of personnel on loan from member countries. UNMOVIC's mandate was finally terminated in June 2007, and the final Compendium of its work has been published. This exhaustive report concluded, ".... in hindsight, it has now become clear that the UN inspection system in Iraq was indeed successful to a large degree, in fulfilling its disarmament and monitoring obligations."[80]

The UNMOVIC Compendium included five "Key Lessons" learned from the 16-year history of UNSCOM and UNMOVIC. Two of these were particularly relevant to the whole question of American interference with the inspections process in Iraq:

- Complete independence is a prerequisite for a UN inspection agency. The inspection agency must be

---

80. http://www.un.org/Depts/unmovic/new/pages/compendium.asp

independent as well as be seen to be totally independent. This is required to allay fears of misusing the inspection process either to support other agendas or to keep the inspected party in a permanent state of weakness.

- Proving the negative is a recipe for enduring difficulties and unending inspections.

On November 27th 2002, its later conclusions notwithstanding, UN-MOVIC set out on the first of a new round of inspections to try and "prove the negative" under the leadership of former IAEA chairman Hans Blix. Meanwhile, on December 7th, within the allotted time frame, Iraq submitted a 12,000 page document in which it confirmed that it had destroyed all its chemical and biological weapons and abandoned its nuclear weapons programs in 1991.

This report also named 150 foreign firms, including 24 American ones, that had provided components of its chemical, biological, and nuclear weapons programs. For example, on September 29th, 1988, American Type Culture Collection of Virginia shipped eleven different biological warfare agents to Iraq, including four types of anthrax, under a license from the U.S. Department of Commerce.

U.S. officials immediately dismissed Iraq's full disclosure as a fraud. As with previous Iraqi efforts to account for weapons it had destroyed, the Americans were only interested in gaps in the report that they could exploit to suggest that Iraq had retained some of its weapons, rather than the actual details of the report.[81] In this fashion, U.S. officials exploited gaps in the Iraqi report to provide plenty of material for President Bush's State of the Union speech on January 28th, 2003. Bush accused Iraq of retaining 25,000 liters of anthrax, 38,000 liters of botulinum toxin, 500 tons of sarin, mustard and VX nerve agent, and 30,000 chemical weapons shells. He shamelessly went on to declare before the

81. Tom Drury, "How Iraq built its weapons programs," *St. Petersburg Times*, March 16, 2003.

whole world that Iraq had purchased aluminum tubes to make centrifuges to enrich uranium, even though the International Atomic Energy Agency had already inspected the tubes in question and identified them as 81-mm rocket casings, noting that the composition of their inner surface was not suitable for use in centrifuges.[82]

The same speech included a reference to Iraqi uranium purchases in Africa, based on a document that the IAEA was able to identify as a forgery within hours of seeing it. The origin of this forged document has not been definitively established, but former U.S. intelligence officers identified the Office of Special Plans as the most likely culprit. They believed that OSP used Michael Ledeen of the American Enterprise Institute as a conduit to the Italian intelligence service, who then fabricated the document in Italy. This led to Joseph Wilson's mission to Niger, and ultimately to the deliberate exposure by senior U.S. officials of his wife's position as a career officer in the Clandestine Service of the CIA.[83]

The day before Bush gave his grand performance to Congress and a worldwide media audience, UNMOVIC chief Hans Blix had delivered an interim report on the progress of the inspections to the Security Council. His characterization of the unanswered questions UNMOVIC was trying to answer struck a marked contrast with Bush's presentation: "These reports do not contend that weapons of mass destruction remain in Iraq, but nor do they exclude that possibility. They point to lack of evidence and inconsistencies, which raise question marks, which must be straightened out, if weapons dossiers are to be closed and confidence is to arise."[84]

---

82. Michael R. Gordon, "Agency challenges evidence against Iraq cited by Bush," *New York Times*, January 10, 2003.

83. Philip Giraldi, "Forging the Case for War", *The American Conservative,* November 21 2005.

84. http://www.un.org/Depts/unmovic/Bx27.htm

Meanwhile, in London, the Foreign Office Legal Adviser Sir Michael Wood had obtained a copy of a statement made by British Foreign Secretary Jack Straw to Vice President Cheney that the British government would "prefer" an explicit Security Council resolution authorizing the invasion of Iraq, but that it would be "O.K." if they tried and failed to get one, "a la Kosovo" as Straw put it. Michael Wood drafted a stern memo to his boss on January 24th, reiterating the advice he had given consistently since 2001. He told Straw that his statement to Cheney was "completely wrong from a legal point of view".

Wood's memo, which was declassified during the Chilcot inquiry in 2010, made no bones about the gravity of the matter. "I hope there is no doubt in anyone's mind that, without a further decision of the Council, and absent extraordinary circumstances of which at present there is no sign, the U.K. cannot lawfully use force against Iraq to ensure compliance with its Security Council WMD resolution. *To use force without Security Council authority would amount to the crime of aggression.*" [author's italics][85]

In another note to Straw, Sir Michael told him, "To advocate the use of force without a proper legal basis is to advocate the commission of the crime of aggression, one of the most serious offenses under international law." And in yet another memo, the legal advisers warned Prime Minister Blair that invading Iraq would be seen as the most serious breach of international law by the U.K. since the Suez crisis. The only response of the Prime Minister's office to this memo was to ask, "Why has this been put in writing?" Wood also told the Chilcot inquiry that the Iraq crisis was " probably the first and only occasion" in his 30-year career that government ministers had rejected his legal advice.

---

85. Philippe Naughton and David Brown, "Lawyer's Memo Contradicts Jack Straw's Evidence to Chilcot Inquiry", *The Times*, January 26 2010; Michael Savage, "Invade and Be Damned: Foreign Office Lawyers Say Advice on Legality of War Was Ignored", *The Independent*, January 27 2010.

On January 31ˢᵗ, 2003, Bush and Blair held a private two-hour meeting at the White House, at which they discussed their final plans for the invasion. Bush was accompanied by Condoleezza Rice, Dan Fried, and Andrew Card; Blair by Sir David Manning, Jonathan Powell, and Matthew Rycroft. A five-page summary of the meeting written by Manning was leaked to international law professor Philippe Sands of University College, London, and then to Britain's Channel Four television news in February 2006. Most of the meeting revolved around the military plans for the invasion, but they also discussed their last-ditch diplomatic and political efforts to justify the war.

Manning wrote that their "diplomatic strategy had to be arranged around the military planning ... The start date for the military campaign was now penciled in for March 10th. This was when the bombing would begin." Bush and Blair both acknowledged during the meeting that the "weapons of mass destruction" had not been found, and were unlikely to be found before the invasion. Bush presented three alternative strategies to trigger the war, none of which were eventually adopted: painting an American U-2 spy plane in U.N. colors, and provoking the Iraqis into firing at it; bringing a defector out of Iraq to "give a public presentation about Saddam's WMDs;" and the assassination of Hussein.

The two leaders agreed to keep pursuing the diplomatic track at the United Nations. Manning paraphrased Bush as saying, "The U.S. would put its full weight behind efforts to get another resolution, and would twist arms and even threaten ... But he had to say that if we ultimately failed, military action would follow anyway." At that point, "we should warn Saddam that he had a week to leave. We should notify the media too. We would then have a clear field if Saddam refused to go." No one present raised any objection to either government's commitment to invade Iraq in March regardless of any developments on the diplomatic front. The critical decision had been made many months earlier, and the goal of the diplomatic efforts was to provide justification, not to provide an alternative to war.[86]

Five days later, Secretary of State Colin Powell made his infamous speech to the United Nations Security Council, which he later referred to as a "blot" on his reputation. Most commentators have portrayed Colin Powell as a "good soldier," a man who brought military values of discipline and loyalty to his political appointments after a long and distinguished military career. By contrast, Richard Betts, who directs the Institute for War and Peace Studies at Columbia University, has made a study of Chairmen of the Joint Chiefs of Staff and divides them into three categories: "routine-professional," "professional-political," and "exceptional-political." He places Powell in the third category: "exceptional-political."[87]

Colin Powell's first political appointment was on a White House Fellowship in the Office of Management and Budget under Frank Carlucci and Caspar Weinberger. Lieutenant Colonel Powell was 35 years old, and Richard Nixon was president. In the Carter administration, he served as assistant to Deputy Secretary of Defense Charles Duncan, with primary responsibility for the financial management of the Pentagon.[88]

Powell joined the Reagan administration in 1983, as assistant to his former mentor, then Secretary of Defense Caspar Weinberger, four months before the invasion of Grenada. He was deeply implicated in the Iran-Contra affair. He met frequently with Saudi Ambassador Prince Bandar as the Saudis funded the Contras in Nicaragua to the tune of $12 - 25 million per year. Then he arranged shipments of mis-

---

86. Don Van Natta, "Bush was set on path to war, British memo says," *New York Times*, March 27 2006.

87. Richard K. Betts, *Soldiers, Statesmen and Cold War Crises*, (New York: Columbia University Press, 1991), 235.

88. http://www.consortiumnews..com/archive/powell.html

siles to Iran and used the authority of his rank to thwart questions about the shipments from the U.S. military personnel carrying out his orders. After a brief stint out of the spotlight in Germany, he was appointed Deputy National Security Advisor in January 1987 and promoted to National Security Advisor 10 months later. Between each of his political appointments, he held military positions commensurate with his rise through the ranks to four-star general.

George Bush Sr. brought Powell back to the White House three months before the invasion of Panama, this time as Chairman of the Joint Chiefs of Staff. What was it about Colin Powell that made him indispensable to three U.S. presidents just as they were about to invade foreign countries? This could have been a coincidence, but maybe it was precisely Powell's consummate ability as a politician in uniform that made him so useful at these times.

When U.S. presidents want to go to war, someone like Colin Powell can perform an invaluable function. He can present a face to the public and to his colleagues in the military of a reluctant warrior who shares their concerns with the gravity of these decisions, conveying the sense that all other options have truly been exhausted and that the country faces a grave threat that it would be irresponsible to ignore. This was exactly the role that Powell played on February 5th 2003, and it is hard to imagine who else in the Bush administration could have been as persuasive to the American public and mass media.

Unlike Hans Blix, Powell began and ended his presentation with the assumption that Iraq did in fact possess chemical and biological weapons and a nuclear weapons program, but no skeptical listener heard anything in his speech that confirmed that assumption. His presentation mainly combined intercepted conversations between Iraqi officials and satellite imagery with reports by Iraqi exiles that served to explain their significance and to confirm what Powell and his colleagues wanted the public to believe.[89]

The first part of his presentation focused on evidence that the Iraqis must have been hiding something, based on the flurry of activity that often preceded UNMOVIC inspections. Some of these efforts may have constituted technical violations of resolution 1441's requirement for full cooperation, but none of them provided actual evidence of weapons development. He then presented his case on biological, chemical and nuclear weapons in that order.

The lengthy section on biological weapons focused on some mobile facilities to produce gas for weather balloons that were sold to Iraq by the British firm Marconi in 1987. Powell's assertions that they were really mobile "biological weapons factories" were based on the supposed testimony of four Iraqi exiles. The principal informant, Rafid Ahmed Alwan, code-named Curveball by the CIA, was presented by Powell as an "Iraqi chemical engineer who supervised one of these facilities ... [who] was present during biological agent production runs". Powell claimed that Alwan had witnessed an accident in 1998 in which "twelve technicians died from exposure to biological agents", but MI6 had already discovered that Alwan had only worked at that site until 1995.

Three days after Powell's speech, UNMOVIC inspectors visited the site in question and found that there were no doors on the end of the building where Alwan claimed that the mobile laboratories were taken in and out of the facility. After the invasion, the weather-balloon trailers were found and secured by U.S. forces, and both Bush and Blair made repeated public claims that they had found the "WMDs." These claims were so strident and persistent and their later retractions so

---

89. http://www.state.gov/secretary/former/powell/remarks/2003/17300.htm

muted that, in a poll taken three months after the invasion, 20% of Americans believed that the mythical WMDs had really been found.

On chemical weapons, the evidence was even weaker, which was probably why the mobile "biological weapons factories" took pride of place in the presentation. Powell simply repeated the familiar gaps in Iraq's accounting. He explained the lack of evidence of more recent production as evidence of Iraqi duplicity, based on brilliant adaptation of dual-use facilities: "Call it ingenious or evil genius, but the Iraqis deliberately designed their chemical weapons programs to be inspected."

On the nuclear side, for lack of anything better, he trotted out the old canard about the aluminum tubes, elaborating it with more details. He even cited the anodized coating that the IAEA had said would have to be milled off to make the tubes usable as centrifuges as evidence of technical advances in the imaginary Iraqi nuclear program. He went on to talk about the al-Samoud II rockets that UNMOVIC was already destroying, a technical violation of U.N. sanctions and a vindication of the inspection regime, but hardly a cause for war.

On this scant evidence, Powell hung at least a dozen categorical but false statements about Iraqi weapons:

"Saddam Hussein and his regime have made no effort—no effort—to disarm as required by the international community."

"We know from sources that a missile brigade outside Baghdad was disbursing rocket launchers and warheads containing biological warfare agents to various locations ... "

"The two arrows indicate the presence of sure signs that the bunkers are storing chemical munitions."

"Ladies and gentlemen, these are sophisticated facilities. For example, they can produce anthrax and botulinum toxin. In fact, they can produce enough dry biological agent in a single month to kill thousands of people."

"There can be no doubt that Saddam Hussein has biological weapons and the capability to rapidly produce more, many more."

"I'm going to show you a small part of a chemical complex called al-Moussaid, a site that Iraq has used for at least three years to transship chemical weapons from production facilities out to the field."

"With this track record, Iraqi denials of supporting terrorism take the place alongside the other Iraqi denials of weapons of mass destruction. It is all a web of lies."

And last but not least: "We have no indication that Saddam Hussein has ever abandoned his nuclear weapons program," once again ignoring Hussain Kamel's disclosures to UNSCOM in 1995.

Bush's and Powell's assertions fit neatly into their overall political strategy to win public support for the war. Keeping alive the illusion of a technical debate over the aluminum tubes is a good example. Faced with a choice between believing the impartial analysis of the IAEA and the questionable claims of the CIA, almost the entire world would unhesitatingly accept the IAEA's judgment. The only exception was the domestic political audience in the United States, where the media give extraordinary deference to the statements of U.S. government officials instead of evaluating competing claims on their merits. Thus a claim easily dismissed by the rest of the world was nevertheless a valuable tool in the domestic political debate over the coming war.

Powell's performance failed to win a new Security Council resolution, or to convince the diplomats or the people of the world that Iraq posed a greater threat to peace than the country actually threatening war, the United States. But Powell received rave reviews from his intended audience in the U.S. political and media establishment. His speech was thus a critical political step in the march to war.

CHAPTER 5. FULL LEGAL ADVICE

If Secretary Powell had any doubt that he had failed to sell the invasion of Iraq to the people of the world, the unprecedented worldwide demonstrations on February 15th, 2003 must have made the situation quite clear to him. Anti-war groups in Europe had been planning demonstrations for that day since November 2002, but they cannot have anticipated the confluence of events that made this date so historic.

The U.N. Security Council received another report from UNMOVIC and the IAEA on February 14th. The inspectors had visited many of the "WMD" sites identified by U.S. and British intelligence and found nothing more incriminating than a handful of empty warheads containing old chemical residue. As for Bush's mythical mushroom cloud, IAEA chief Mohammed ElBaradei told the Council, "As I have reported on numerous occasions, the IAEA concluded, by December 1998, that it had neutralized Iraq's past nuclear programme and that, therefore, there were no unresolved disarmament issues left at that time. Hence, our focus since the resumption of our inspections in Iraq, two and a half months ago, has been verifying whether Iraq revived its nuclear programme in the intervening years. We have to date found no evidence of ongoing prohibited nuclear or nuclear related activities in Iraq."[90]

Under a deluge of propaganda, the number of Americans who supported an invasion that was not approved by the Security Council had reached its highest level yet, but it was still only at 32-38% (depending how the question was posed), and half the population still opposed the war even with U.N. approval. A Gallup poll taken in 41 countries in Jan-

---

90. http://www.iaea.org/NewsCenter/Statements/2003/ebsp2003n005.shtml

uary clocked worldwide support for unauthorized military action at less than 10%.[91]

So this was the background as an estimated 30 million people took to the streets on February 15th in at least 60 countries. The world had never before seen global public opinion so mobilized on a single issue. The numbers were greatest in the countries whose governments supported attacking Iraq. The Guinness Book of World Records lists the 3 million people who took to the streets of Rome as the largest anti-war demonstration in history. Organizers in London and Madrid estimated their respective rallies at 2 million each. There were demonstrations all over the United States, with 400,000 demonstrators in New York and 200,000 in San Francisco. There were events on every continent, even in Antarctica, where a group of American scientists held an anti-war rally at McMurdo research station.

While many of these events were certainly well organized, the over-whelming numbers represented a spontaneous popular reaction to the prospect that the most powerful, technologically advanced war machine in history might be unleashed on the long-suffering people of Iraq. The mass demonstrations failed to stop the war, but they were a powerful sign of almost universal public outrage. The Spanish and Italian conservative governments that supported the war soon paid the inevitable political price, while others, as in Canada, were clearly warned against taking any part in the war.

And yet, in the United States, the corporate-controlled propaganda juggernaut rolled on. *Fairness and Accuracy in Reporting* examined the biased coverage of the march to war on the nightly T.V. news shows (CBS, ABC, NBC and PBS) in a report on February 12th. It found that only three out of 393 sources consulted on the war plan by American

---

91. http://www.pipa.org/OnlineReports/Iraq/IraqUNInsp2_Feb03/
IraqUNInsp2%20Feb03%20rpt.pdf; http://www.gallup-
international.com/download/GIA%20press%20release%20Iraq%20Survey%202003.pdf

television networks in the previous two weeks were people identified with anti-war views. 76% of sources were present or former government officials and only 6% of these were critical of the U.S. government's rationale for war. Even among non-official sources, only 26% of Americans interviewed on the air were skeptical of the rush to war, despite CBS's own polling which found that 61% of the public felt the U.S. should "wait and give the United Nations and weapons inspectors more time."[92]

As the next report due from the inspectors on March 7th drew nearer, it became clear that the U.S. and Britain had little hope of a new Security Council resolution that would authorize war against Iraq. On March 2nd, the *Observer* in London published a memo leaked by Katharine Gun, a whistle-blower at Britain's GCHQ intelligence headquarters, revealing that the U.S. National Security Agency (NSA) was conducting an "aggressive surveillance operation, which involves interception of the home and office telephones and the e-mails of U.N. delegates in New York." The memo was from Frank Koza in the Regional Targets division of the NSA, and the surveillance was aimed at the U.N. delegations of Angola, Cameroon, Chile, Mexico, Guinea, and Pakistan, who were considered to be the key swing votes for or against a war resolution.[93]

The leaked document said the operation was aimed at gleaning information not only on how Security Council members would vote on any second resolution on Iraq, but also "policies," "negotiating positions," "alliances," and "dependencies"—"the whole gamut of information that could give US policymakers an edge in obtaining results favorable to US goals or to head off surprises." The American media loyally ignored the story. The *New York Times'* deputy foreign editor,

---

92. http://www.fair.org/index.php?page=1628
93. Martin Bright, Ed Vulliamy and Peter Beaumont, "Revealed: US dirty tricks to win UN vote on Iraq war," *The Observer*, March 2 2003.

Alison Smale, told Norman Solomon, "Well, it's not that we haven't been interested, [but] we could get no confirmation or comment" on the memo from U.S. officials.[94] The *Washington Post* published one article on March 4th, but belittled the U.S. violation of diplomatic treaties as a minor incident, even as outrage over the "dirty tricks" campaign spread throughout diplomatic circles and the media in other countries. While the U.S. and British diplomats' quest for U.N. authorization for the war may have already been hopeless by this point, these revelations can only have deepened their alienation from their Security Council colleagues.

On March 5th, Russia, France, and Germany issued a joint statement that closed the door on any new resolution authorizing the use of force against Iraq. They made it clear that both Russia and France were prepared to use their veto power in the Security Council to uphold this position. They said:

> Our common objective remains the full and effective disarmament of Iraq, in compliance with Resolution 1441. We consider that this objective can be achieved by the peaceful means of the inspections.
>
> In these circumstances, we will not let a proposed resolution pass that would authorise the use of force. Russia and France, as permanent members of the Security Council, will assume all their responsibilities on this point.[95]

On March 7th, the Security Council heard from Blix and ElBaradei again. Dr. Blix reported that UNMOVIC was making progress in Iraq and that "it would not take years, nor weeks, but months" to complete its work and to transition to a regime of long-term monitoring to ensure that Iraq remained in compliance with Security Council resolu-

---

94. Norman Solomon, "Stop dodging the awkward truth," *The Observer*, March 9, 2003.

95. http://www.un.int/france/documents_anglais/
030305_mae_france_irak.htm

tions.[96] Dr. ElBaradei finally laid the Niger uranium story to rest, stating explicitly that it was based on a forgery: "Based on thorough analysis, the IAEA has concluded, with the concurrence of outside experts, that these documents—which formed the basis for the reports of recent uranium transactions between Iraq and Niger—are in fact not authentic." He went on to effectively dismiss all the allegations of nuclear activity in Iraq: "After three months of intrusive inspections, we have to date found no evidence or plausible indication of the revival of a nuclear weapons program in Iraq."[97]

Faced with an inspections program that was actually working and in fact working to undermine the case for war, and a veto threat from two Permanent Members, the U.S., the U.K., and Spain drafted a "compromise" resolution. It would not explicitly authorize military action but it would give the Council's assent to the idea that Iraq had failed to meet its obligations, and it would set an early deadline for a determination that Iraq had missed its "final opportunity" to avoid "serious consequences."[98]

The draft resolution was debated and discussed, but the majority of the council were no longer prepared to support a resolution that could give the U.S. and Britain any pretext for war. On March 10th, Secretary General Kofi Annan held a press conference at the opening of the new International Criminal Court in the Hague, a highly symbolic venue under the circumstances. He said, "The members of the Security Council now face a great choice. If they fail to agree on a common position, and action is taken without the authority of the Security Council, the legitimacy and support for any such action will be seriously impaired."[99]

---

96. http://www.un.org/Depts/unmovic/SC7asdelivered.htm
97. http://www.iaea.org/NewsCenter/Statements/2003/ebsp2003n006.shtml
98. http://www.un.org/News/dh/iraq/res-iraq-07mar03-en-rev.pdf
99 http://www.un.org/apps/sg/offthecuff.asp?nid=394

A reporter followed up on his statement:

> Q: Mr. Secretary-General, you said that an attack on Iraq without a second Council resolution would not be legitimate.. Would you consider it as a breach of the U.N. Charter?
>
> SG: I think that under today's world order, the Charter is very clear on circumstances under which force can be used. I think the discussion going on in the Council is to ensure that the Security Council, which is master of its own deliberations, is able to pronounce itself on what happens. If the U.S. and others were to go outside the Council and take military action it would not be in conformity with the Charter.

On March 7th, as the Security Council was meeting, Prime Minister Blair was given a 13-page document by his Attorney General, Lord Peter Goldsmith, that addressed the same question at greater length. The full text of this document was eventually leaked to the press in Britain and was made public in April 2005, two years into the war. The role of Attorney General in Britain is different to that in the U.S., and is more analogous to that of White House Counsel, to advise the Prime Minister on legal matters. Peter Goldsmith was not an international lawyer by training or experience, but the Chilcot inquiry revealed that an earlier draft of his advice written in January 2003 was consistent with all the other legal advice given to the British government that only a new Security Council resolution could authorize the use of force against Iraq.[100]

In the March 7th document, Goldsmith discussed legal arguments advanced by his U.S. counterparts at meetings he attended in Washington on February 10th and 11th 2003, and attempted to reconcile them with the British Law Officers' position up to that point that regime change in Iraq would constitute a clear violation of international law. The document therefore provided an opportunity to examine the

---

100. http://image.guardian.co.uk/sys-files/Guardian/documents/2005/04/28/legal.pdf

American arguments for the legality of the war as they presented them to their British allies, and to review them through the eyes of someone who knew that his country was committed to war and therefore had every interest in making the best possible case for it, but who also had a professional responsibility to warn Blair of the legal dangers he might face.

With little hope of a new resolution containing even an implicit pretext for the use of force against Iraq, much of his discussion revolved around the wording of SC resolution 1441. The central problem was that the resolution did not contain an authorization for the use of force. U.S. Ambassador to the U.N. John Negroponte had declared on the day that the resolution was passed, "As we have said on numerous occasions to Council members, this resolution contains no 'hidden triggers' and no 'automaticity' with respect to the use of force. If there is a further Iraqi breach, reported to the Council by UNMOVIC, the IAEA or a Member State, the matter will return to the Council for discussions as required in paragraph 12."

Goldsmith presented both sides of the argument and did his best to make the case for the American position, which appeared to have changed since Negroponte made that statement, but one cannot follow his arguments without seeing clearly the weight of the law on one side, and indeed his conclusions included warnings to the Prime Minister regarding his vulnerability to prosecution should he proceed with the invasion.

Goldsmith began by reviewing the three "possible bases for the use of force" under international law, namely self-defense; to avert overwhelming humanitarian catastrophe; and authorization by the Security Council acting under Chapter VII of the UN Charter. He dismissed the first two in this case, along with Bush's expanded doctrine of preemption:

I am aware that the U.S.A. has been arguing for recognition of a broad doctrine of a right to use force to pre-empt danger in the future. If this means more than a right to respond proportionately to an imminent attack (and I understand that the doctrine is intended to carry that connotation) this is not a doctrine which, in my opinion, exists or is recognized in international law.

Since this left only Security Council authorization as a possible justification, "the key question is whether resolution 1441 has the effect of providing such authorization." This "depends on the revival of the express authorization to use force given in 1990 by Security Council resolution 678." He broke this question into two parts: "Is the so-called 'revival argument' a sound legal basis in principle?" And "Is resolution 1441 sufficient to revive the authorization in resolution 678?"

Resolution 678 authorized Kuwait and its allies to use "all necessary means" to force Iraq out of Kuwait and "to restore international peace and security." Goldsmith claimed that resolution 687 (1991) "suspended, but did not terminate, the authority to use force in resolution 678." While the earlier resolution 686 noted only the "suspension of offensive combat operations," the wording of resolution 687 actually declared a "formal cease-fire" with no provision for "revival" of the authorization of military force. However, according to Goldsmith, "It has been the U.K.'s view that a violation of Iraq's obligations under resolution 687 which is sufficiently serious to undermine the basis of the cease-fire can revive the authorization to use force in resolution 678."

International legal experts disagree. Michael Byers of the University of British Columbia wrote in his book, *War Law*, that "the 1991 ceasefire resolution is clearly worded to terminate—not suspend—the previous year's authorization of military force." This would invalidate the entire revival argument, which was the only serious legal argument advanced for the legality of the invasion.[101]

Goldsmith acknowledged that, "The revival argument is controversial." He explained that it was approved by U.N. Legal Counsel Carl-August Fleischauer in August 1992 as a basis for establishing the southern "no-fly zone" over Iraq, but that Fleischauer and the British legal advisers concurred that "it is for the Security Council to assess whether any such breach of these obligations has occurred" before revival could come into effect. Only the United States took the position that an individual member state could make such a determination independently of the Council.

This question went to the heart of the whole issue of "revival." As long as the Security Council retained the position granted it under the U.N. Charter as the sole authority for the use of force, then the concept of revival was not a radical one. With or without revival, the Council remained the only body that could authorize military force, whether by revival of a prior resolution or by approval of a new one. On the other hand, a concept of revival that permitted individual countries to assume that role themselves would have undermined the exclusive authority over the use of force that is reserved to the Security Council by the U.N. Charter. This was not what the Fleischauer opinion authorized and indeed, when the U.S. and U.K. cited revival as justification for their attack on Iraq in 1999, this was strongly rejected by Russia and other Council members, as we saw in Chapter 2.

Goldsmith went on to say that "the arguments in support of the revival argument are stronger following the adoption of resolution 1441," because the resolution recalled "the authorization to use force in resolution 678 and that resolution 687 imposed obligations on Iraq as a necessary condition of the cease-fire." Once again Goldsmith linked the

---

101. Michael Byers, *War Law*, (New York: Grove Press, 2005), 44.

cease-fire to Iraq's continuing obligations in a way that was neither spelled out in SCR 687 nor accepted by other governments. He also cited the fact that paragraph 13 of resolution 1441 recalled previous warnings that "serious consequences will result from continued violations of its obligations."

Then he really went out on a limb, linking all these things together in a grand scheme based on misrepresentations of past Security Council practice and other countries' positions: "The previous practice of the Council and statements made by Council members during the negotiation of resolution 1441 demonstrate that the phrase 'material breach' signifies a finding by the Council of a sufficiently serious breach of the cease-fire conditions to revive the authorization in resolution 678 and that 'serious consequences' is accepted as indicating the use of force."

In reality, Goldsmith's interpretation of both these phrases, "material breach" and "serious consequences" was unique to Britain and the U.S. He himself mentioned statements by France, Russia, China, Mexico, Ireland and Syria that rejected any implicit authorization of force stemming from this language without a further decision by the Security Council. And past Security Council resolutions, including 678, had used the term "all necessary means" to authorize the use of force. Other Council members had insisted on using the weaker term "serious consequences" in resolution 1441 precisely to make it clear that they were not creating an automatic trigger for the use of force.

Goldsmith concluded his discussion of the principle of revival: "I disagree, therefore, with those commentators and lawyers who assert that nothing less than an *explicit* authorization to use force in a Security Council resolution will be sufficient." It was later revealed that "those commentators and lawyers" had included Goldsmith himself prior to March 7th 2003 (see Chapter 6). The only real evidence he cited in support of revival was the creation of the southern no-fly zone in 1992, an arguably proportionate response to a humanitarian crisis in the immediate aftermath of the Gulf War. That was a very different situation than the one the world was confronting in March 2003, when it was Iraq itself that faced the threat of invasion and "regime change" from the United States and the United Kingdom, something that had never been authorized by any Security Council resolution and which posed precisely the kind of "threat to the peace" that Chapter VII of the U.N. Charter was designed to prevent.

The structural inability of the Security Council to confront such a threat from any of its veto-wielding Permanent Members has been a recognized flaw in the U.N.'s collective security system from its inception. In 2004, 59% of Americans surveyed told the Chicago Council on Foreign Relations that "this should be changed so that if a decision was supported by all the other members, no member, not even the United States, could veto the decision." In fact the veto provision drew widespread condemnation as soon as the proposed composition and structure of the Security Council was made public in 1945. Albert Camus, then the editor of *Combat*, the former French Resistance newspaper, wrote most eloquently in an editorial on February 16th 1945:

> If this report is accurate, it is of considerable importance, for it would effectively put an end to any idea of international democracy. The world would in effect be ruled by a directorate of five powers. The decisions they take will be applicable to all other nations, but any one of the five could nullify a decision against its own interests by exercising its veto. The Five would thus retain forever the freedom of maneuver that would be forever denied the others.[102]

The inability of the Security Council to adequately confront the threat and then the act of aggression against Iraq has shaped this crisis exactly as Camus predicted. From the build-up to war through years of war and occupation, no action by the Security Council has effectively

---

102. Albert Camus, *Camus at Combat*, (Princeton: Princeton University Press, 2006), 172.

restricted "the freedom of maneuver" of the U.S. and U.K. governments. Consequently the Security Council has failed to uphold the protections guaranteed to all people by the U.N. Charter and international human rights laws, leaving the people of Iraq with only the same excruciating choices available to victims of aggression throughout history: collaboration, resistance, or flight and exile.

As to Goldsmith's second question, the "sufficiency of resolution 1441" as a trigger for revival, he posed the following question: "On the true interpretation of resolution 1441, what has the Security Council decided will be the consequences of Iraq's failure to comply with the enhanced regime?" (of inspections). He correctly read from paragraph 12 of the resolution that "the Council will convene immediately ... to consider the situation and the need for compliance with all of the relevant Council resolutions." Then he claimed that "there are two competing arguments" about what should happen next, if anything, based on the differing legal positions of the United States and other members:

> (i) that provided there is a Council discussion, if it does not reach a conclusion, there remains an authorization to use force;

> (ii) that nothing short of a further Council decision will be a legitimate basis for the use of force.

The American interpretation (i) was that the wording in SC resolution 1441 that Iraq was already in "material breach" had not only implicitly revived the authorization of force, but created a sort of open season on Iraq in which any of the countries formerly allied with Kuwait could attack Iraq independently and for their own purposes, even though no other members accepted this interpretation. In this view, the "final opportunity" granted Iraq in SC resolution 1441 was a magnanimous gesture to hold off the wolves, but the authorization of force had already been revived by the "material breach" acknowledged in the resolution.

Interestingly, the Americans seem to have undercut their own argument that the authorization for the use of force already existed by insisting in paragraph 4 of SCR 1441 that "failure by Iraq at any time to comply with, and cooperate fully in the implementation of, this resolution" would be "a further material breach." If the finding of a "material breach" in resolution 1441 was sufficient to trigger revival of the war authorization, then what was the importance of "a further material breach?" And if it wasn't sufficient to revive the authorization, then why would a further one make any difference?

And yet, the Americans were relying on "a further material breach" as a sort of last straw to tip the balance in favor of revival, clearly a political argument rather than a legal one, with the effect of progressively undermining the Council's authority as the sole arbiter of the use of force. This was consistent with Bush's threat to render the U.N. irrelevant, but, as Annan said, it was "not in conformity with the Charter."

The more general interpretation (ii) was that, in the event of Iraqi non-compliance, the Council would meet, as stated in paragraph 12 of SCR 1441, to "consider the situation and the need for full compliance with all of the relevant Council resolutions in order to secure international peace and security." As Goldsmith put it, "the issue should return to the Council for a further decision on what action should be taken at that stage," with the Council unequivocally fulfilling the role assigned to it by the U.N. Charter "to secure international peace and security."

Goldsmith debated these issues at length, but, towards the end of this section, he revealed his own discomfort with "the view that no further resolution is required." As he said, "The Council would be required to meet, and all members of the Council would be under an obligation to participate in the discussion in good faith, but even if an overwhelming majority of the Council were opposed to the use of force, military action could proceed regardless," reducing the Council discussion, as he put it, "to a procedural formality." Goldsmith could not bring himself to assert that that was the intention of the majority of the Council in voting for SCR 1441.

After a lengthy summary of all these arguments, Goldsmith stated his own view that, "In these circumstances, I remain of the opinion that the safest legal course would be to secure the adoption of a further resolution to authorize the use of force." He suggested that the authorization need not be explicit and that the draft resolution currently on the table would be sufficient, but he concluded, "If we fail to achieve the adoption of a second resolution, we should need to consider urgently at that stage the strength of our legal case in the light of circumstances at that time." The U.S. and U.K. governments did indeed "fail to achieve the adoption of a second resolution," but there is no evidence that they urgently reconsidered the strength of their legal case before launching their long-planned attack on Iraq.

The penultimate section of Goldsmith's brief was titled "Possible consequences of acting without a second resolution." He began, "In assessing the risks of acting on the basis of a reasonably arguable case, you will wish to take account of the ways in which the matter might be brought before a court. There are a number of possibilities." He then listed the ways in which a case for aggression or murder could be brought against the British government or against Blair himself, adding, "We cannot be certain that they would not succeed":

1.   The International Court of Justice in the Hague. The case could be referred to the Court either by a simple majority vote of the U.N. General Assembly or by another government that opposed the war. In the former case, the Court could only give an advisory opinion on the legality of the invasion. In the latter case, however, the U.K. would be bound by the Court's ruling, which might require a halt to military action. This would not be binding on the U.S. however, because it withdrew from the compulsory jurisdiction of the ICJ following its 1986 ruling on U.S. aggression against Nicaragua.

2.   The new International Criminal Court. This court did not yet have jurisdiction over the crime of aggression. However it could hear charges that the U.K. was violating international human rights law in its conduct of the war. The Campaign for Nuclear Disarmament (CND) had already put the British government on notice that it would report any violations of the Geneva Conventions to the ICC Prosecutor, but the ICC would not have jurisdiction unless British military and civilian courts failed to prosecute the crimes themselves.

3.   British courts. CND had already tried and failed in November 2002 to get a court ruling to stop military action against Iraq. However Goldsmith warned Blair of two other possibilities, "an attempted prosecution for murder on the grounds that the military action is unlawful and an attempted prosecution for the crime of aggression." He added that "Aggression is a crime under customary international law which automatically forms part of domestic law," so that "international aggression is a crime recognized by the common law which can be prosecuted in the U.K. courts."

Finally, and perhaps most significantly, Goldsmith ended his full legal advice with a paragraph headed "Proportionality." This is worth reading in full:

> I must stress that the lawfulness of military action depends not only on the existence of a legal basis, but also on the question of proportionality. Any force used pursuant to the authorization in resolution 678:
>
> -   must have as its objective the enforcement of the terms of the cease-fire contained in resolution 687 (1990) and subsequent relevant resolutions;
>
> -   be limited to what is necessary to achieve that objective;
>
> -   must be a proportionate response to that objective, i.e. securing compliance with Iraq's disarmament obligations.

> That is not to say that action may not be taken to remove Saddam Hussein from power if it can be demonstrated that such action is a necessary and proportionate measure to secure the disarmament of Iraq. But regime change cannot be the objective of military action. This should be borne in mind in considering the list of military targets and in making public statements about any campaign.
>
> Lord Goldsmith
> Attorney General
> 7 March 2003

So, if there was one thing that Blair was repeatedly and consistently told, it was that "regime change cannot be the objective of military action." And yet, as noted in the opening summary of the Downing Street Memo, "U.S. military planning unambiguously takes as its objective the removal of Saddam Hussein's regime." This had always been the central problem for the British Law Officers, and none of Goldsmith's convoluted reasoning about the wording of SCR 1441 had any bearing on it.

No other country accepted the U.S. government's interpretation of resolution 1441, including the British government's Law Officers until March 7th 2003. But even if one accepted the U.S. government's unique interpretations of every word of every resolution, as well as the controversial "revival" argument, they would only have authorized the use of military force to complete the destruction of Iraq's illegal weapons as per resolution 687. This was the task that Hans Blix and Mohammed ElBaradei were concluding had already been accomplished, and whose confirmation "would not take years, nor weeks, but months" by the peaceful, legitimate, and more reliable process of internationally-supervised inspections.

One can only conclude that the American desire for regime change in Iraq was unrelated to any of these arguments. Any shred of legitimacy that the United States government sought to gain by invoking the authority of the United Nations for the invasion was part of a purely political process rather than a legitimate exercise in collective security.

The British government was consistently and explicitly warned that the invasion of Iraq would constitute an act of aggression and a serious and criminal violation of international law.

CHAPTER 6. "THE CRIME OF AGGRESSION"

On September 26th, 2007, the Spanish newspaper *El Pais* published a leaked transcript of President Bush's meeting with Spanish Prime Minister Jose Maria Aznar that took place in Crawford, Texas, on February 22nd, 2003. This document provided final confirmation that, even as Powell was addressing the U.N. Security Council, the United States was 100% committed to the invasion of Iraq with or without U.N. authorization. This was therefore the real "threat to peace" that should have consumed the Security Council's most urgent attention instead of the United States' false claims against Iraq.[103]

After discussing the proposed terms of their joint draft resolution, Bush told Aznar, "If anyone vetoes, we'll go. Saddam Hussein isn't disarming. We have to catch him right now. Until now we've shown an incredible amount of patience. There are two weeks left. In two weeks we'll be militarily ready ... We'll be in Baghdad by the end of March."

This meeting took place barely a week after 2 million people marched against the war in Madrid. Aznar expressed concern over and over again that he and other European leaders needed a second resolution, however weak, to provide political cover for the invasion. "In fact," he acknowledged, "having a majority is more important than anyone casting a veto." Aznar urged patience, but Bush couldn't stand waiting any longer, as we see in this exchange:

> GWB: This is like Chinese water torture. We have to put an end to it.
>
> JMA: I agree, but it would be good to be able to count on as many people as possible. Have a little patience.
>
> GWB: My patience has run out. I won't go beyond mid-March.

---

103. Mark Danner, "The moment has come to get rid of Saddam," *New York Review of Books*, November 8 2007, 59 - 61.

As in many reports of Bush's private conversations, his tone throughout is reminiscent of a mafia boss discussing a move against a rival. He told Aznar of an Egyptian plan to grant exile to Saddam Hussein and then possibly assassinate him. But an agreement by Hussein to go into exile would not stop the United States from occupying the country—the invasion would proceed regardless. Clutching at straws, Aznar followed up on the exile question a bit later:

> JMA: Is it true that there's a possibility of Saddam Hussein going into exile?
>
> GWB: Yes. That possibility exists. Even that he gets assassinated.
>
> JMA: An exile with some guarantee?
>
> GWB: No guarantee. He's a thief, a terrorist, a war criminal ... People around him ... know his future is in exile or in a coffin.

And as for other Security Council members, Bush told Aznar, "Countries like Mexico, Chile, Angola and Cameroon have to know that what's at stake is the United States' security and acting with a sense of friendship toward us. Lagos has to know that the Free Trade Agreement with Chile is pending Senate confirmation ... Angola is receiving funds from the Millennium account that could also be compromised if they don't show a positive attitude. And Putin must know that his attitude is jeopardizing the relations of Russia and the United States."

As the days passed without a new resolution and the mid-March deadline approached, the illegality of the plan even threw Britain's role in the invasion into doubt. This was not because Blair finally heeded his government's legal advisers, but because the Chief of the Defence Staff, Admiral Sir Michael Boyce, refused to order British forces to make final preparations for the invasion without an assurance that it would be legal. Clearly his own legal advisers had reached the same conclusion as their civilian counterparts, and were perhaps influenced by Annan's statement on March 10th.

At that point, Boyce told the Prime Minister that he could not order his troops to invade Iraq without a written statement that it would be legal. For five critical days, from March 10th to the 15th, Britain's participation in the invasion was in legal limbo. A year later, on March 7th 2004, after retiring from the Royal Navy, Boyce explained his position to Antony Barnett of the *Observer*, "I asked for unequivocal advice that what we were proposing to do was lawful. Keeping it as simple as that did not allow equivocations, and what I eventually got was what I required ... something in writing that was very short indeed. Two or three lines saying our proposed actions were lawful under national and international law."[104]

Following the publication of Goldsmith's full legal advice in 2005, Boyce asked to speak to Barnett again. He explained that he was not shown Goldsmith's full legal advice in 2003 but that he wanted to make sure that Blair and Goldsmith would be held accountable for their decisions, and that he and his troops would not become their scapegoats:

> MB: My concern was always that the troops should feel absolutely confident that what they were doing was absolutely black-and-white legal ... So that's why I wanted to make sure we had this anchor which has been signed by the government Law Officer to show that at least we were operating under ... it may not stop us from being charged, but by God it would make sure we brought other people in the frame as well.
>
> AB: So if you were called to account it would also be Lord Goldsmith and the Prime Minister ...
>
> MB: Too bloody right![105]

On March 17th, Lord Goldsmith delivered a short so-called summary of his legal advice to Parliament, in which he declared that war against

---

104. Antony Barnett and Martin Bright, "War chief reveals legal crisis," *The Observer*, March 7, 2004.

105. Antony Barnett, "Interview: Admiral Sir Michael Boyce," *The Observer*, May 1, 2005.

Iraq would be legal and omitted all his earlier reservations.[106] Clearly Goldsmith was under enormous pressure during the ten days between giving his full advice on March 7th and his final acquiescence on March 17th. The fact that Boyce and 60,000 British troops in Kuwait had to wait five days for a two or three line assurance that they were not about to commit a war crime was a measure of his confusion.

But change it he did. Bush unconstitutionally declared war against Iraq on March 17th, and the United Kingdom joined the United States in this act of aggression. On the same day, the U.S., the U.K., and Spain withdrew their new resolution rather than submit it to a vote in the Security Council, where a clear majority were bound to vote against it. Many of these countries had been subjected to enormous pressure, and the French and Russian vetoes would have killed the resolution in any case, yet small countries in Africa and Latin America were willing to incur the wrath of the United States and Britain to uphold the legitimacy and the authority of the U.N. Security Council and the cause of peace to which it is dedicated. They understood that millions of people's lives and the very foundation of world order were at stake and that the consequences of appeasing the United States at this critical juncture would be a historical watershed with irrevocable consequences.

Earlier in the day, Robin Cook, the Leader of Britain's House of Commons, resigned in protest at the decision to declare war on Iraq. Cook had been Foreign Secretary during the U.S. and British attack on Yugoslavia in 1999, and was an advocate for the principle of military intervention in cases of humanitarian crisis. But now he challenged the case for war against Iraq:

> Iraq's military strength is now less than half its size than
> at the time of the last Gulf war. Ironically, it is only because

---

106. "A case for war," *The Guardian*, March 17, 2003.

Iraq's military forces are so weak that we can even contemplate its invasion. Some advocates of conflict claim that Saddam's forces are so weak, so demoralised and so badly equipped that the war will be over in a few days. We cannot base our military strategy on the assumption that Saddam is weak and at the same time justify pre-emptive action on the claim that he is a threat.

Iraq probably has no weapons of mass destruction in the commonly understood sense of the term—namely a credible device capable of being delivered against a strategic city target. It probably still has biological toxins and battlefield chemical munitions, but it has had them since the 1980s when US companies sold Saddam anthrax agents and the then British Government approved chemical and munitions factories.

Why is it now so urgent that we should take military action to disarm a military capacity that has been there for 20 years, and which we helped to create?

Why is it necessary to resort to war this week, while Saddam's ambition to complete his weapons programme is blocked by the presence of UN inspectors?

Cook contrasted the rush to enforce Security Council resolutions against Iraq with 30 years of international patience with Israel over SC resolution 242, which required Israel's withdrawal from the occupied Palestinian territories. He commended Blair's efforts to obtain a second resolution against Iraq, but pointed out that "the very intensity of those attempts underlines how important it was to succeed. Now that those attempts have failed, we cannot pretend that getting a second resolution was of no importance."

And he spoke out against the false accusations made by the warmongers against people who rejected their arguments: "It is entirely legitimate to support our troops while seeking an alternative to the conflict that will put those troops at risk. Nor is it fair to accuse those of us who want longer for inspections of not having an alternative strategy."

Cook concluded, "I intend to join those tomorrow night who will vote against military action now. It is for that reason, and for that reason alone, and with a heavy heart, that I resign from the government."[107]

Cook's speech received an unprecedented standing ovation in the House of Commons. And yet, the following day, the same House of Commons voted by 412 to 149 in favor of the invasion. In fact, the Commons vote had a wider relative margin than November's vote in the U.S. House of Representatives, in spite of being a more explicit declaration of war and despite greater public opposition and a more skeptical press than in the United States.

On the same day, Elizabeth Wilmshurst, the Deputy Legal Adviser at the British Foreign Office, also tendered her resignation. Two years later, the BBC obtained a copy of her resignation letter under Britain's Freedom of Information Act. Here is the full text of her letter, including a portion (emphasis added) that the Foreign Office withheld from its original response to the FOIA request:

> I regret that I cannot agree that it is lawful to use force against Iraq without a second Security Council resolution to revive the authorisation given in SCR 678. I do not need to set out my reasoning; you are aware of it.
>
> *My views accord with the advice that has been given consistently in this office before and after the adoption of UN security council resolution 1441 and with what the attorney general gave us to understand was his view prior to his letter of 7 March. (The view expressed in that letter has of course changed again into what is now the official line.)*
>
> I cannot in conscience go along with advice—within the Office or to the public or Parliament—which asserts the legitimacy of military action without such a resolution, particularly since an unlawful use of force on such a scale amounts to

---

107. http://news.bbc.co.uk/1/hi/uk_politics/2859431.stm

the crime of aggression; nor can I agree with such action in circumstances which are so detrimental to the international order and the rule of law.

I therefore need to leave the Office: my views on the legitimacy of the action in Iraq would not make it possible for me to continue my role as a Deputy Legal Adviser or my work more generally.

For example: in the context of the International Criminal Court, negotiations on the crime of aggression begin again this year.

I am therefore discussing with Alan Charlton whether I may take approved early retirement. In case that is not possible this letter should be taken as constituting notice of my resignation.

I joined the Office in 1974. It has been a privilege to work here. I leave with very great sadness.[108]

The italicized portion that the Foreign Office tried to withhold provides further confirmation of the unanimity of the British government's legal advice prior to March 7th, and undermines Goldsmith's claims regarding the British interpretation of SC resolution 1441. According to Wilmshurst's letter, all the British legal advisers, including Lord Goldsmith, were still insisting until March 7th that an explicit Security Council authorization for the use of military force was essential.

Wilmshurst makes no bones about the gravity of acting without that authorization. Having said, "I cannot agree that it is lawful to use force against Iraq without a second Security Council resolution," she goes on to say that "an unlawful use of force on such a scale amounts to the crime of aggression." The Chilcot inquiry revealed that Wilmshurst's boss, senior Legal Adviser Sir Michael Wood, used identical language in his warnings to Foreign Secretary Jack Straw in January 2003, and that he also considered resigning in March 2003.

---

108. http://news.bbc.co.uk/1/hi/uk_politics/4377605.stm

The British legal advisers were far from alone in their interpretation. We have already noted international law professor Michael Byers' rejection of the whole principle of revival based on the 1991 ceasefire resolution, and Kofi Annan's declaration that the invasion of Iraq "would not be in conformity with the Charter." On September 16th 2004, Annan elaborated on this when pressed by the BBC's Owen Bennett-Jones:

> OBJ: I wanted to ask you that—do you think that the resolution that was passed on Iraq before the war did actually give legal authority to do what was done?
>
> KA: Well, I'm one of those who believe that there should have been a second resolution because the Security Council indicated that if Iraq did not comply there will be consequences. But then it was up to the Security Council to approve or determine what those consequences should be.
>
> OBJ: So you don't think there was legal authority for the war?
>
> KA: I have stated clearly that it was not in conformity with the Security Council—with the UN Charter.
>
> OBJ: It was illegal?
>
> KA: Yes, if you wish.
>
> OBJ: It was illegal?
>
> KA: Yes, I have indicated it is not in conformity with the UN Charter, from our point of view and from the Charter point of view it was illegal.[109]

In December 2004, following the U.S. assault on Fallujah, I wrote an article about the illegality of the war titled "The Crime of War: from Nuremberg to Fallujah."[110] I cited the U.N. Charter, the relevant Security Council resolutions, the U.S. Constitution, the Nuremberg Judgment, the *Caroline* principle and Kofi Annan. I am not an international law-

---

109. http://news.bbc.co.uk/1/hi/world/middle_east/3661640.stm
110. Nicolas J. S. Davies, "The crime of war: from Nuremberg to Fallujah," *Z Magazine*, February 2005, 33 - 36.

yer, so I wanted to make sure that my analysis was correct and that I was not misrepresenting the legal situation. I therefore sent the essay to a few legal experts to review before I submitted it for publication. I was surprised and gratified when I received an e-mail back from Benjamin Ferencz, who was a Chief Prosecutor at the U.S. War Crimes Tribunal at Nuremberg in 1947. He told me, "You have written a clear, intelligent and accurate description of how we are involved in aggression in Iraq".

Ben Ferencz retains the distinction of having prosecuted the largest murder trial in history, obtaining convictions against 22 senior SS Einsatzgruppen officers for the murders of more than one million people. In a radio interview on December 22nd 2003, he called the invasion of Iraq "a crime of aggression, a crime against peace," and said that it would "qualify under the Nuremberg principles as a violation of international law." He has since suggested that George W. Bush should stand trial for war crimes.[111]

Phillippe Sands of University College, London, the author of *Lawless World*, is another international lawyer who has argued that the invasion was illegal. The occupants of the chairs of international law at both Oxford and Cambridge Universities, Vaughan Lowe and James Crawford, have both concurred.[112] And Britain's Solicitor-General in the 1970s, Lord Archer, declared before the invasion that it would be "flagrantly unlawful."[113]

The implications of the illegality of the invasion of Iraq by the United States and the United Kingdom are extremely serious. The judges at Nuremberg called aggression the "supreme international crime." They

111. http://www.benferencz.org/arts/75.html
112. Phillippe Sands, *Lawless World*, (New York: Viking, 2005); Michael Byers, *War Law*, (New York: Grove Press, 2005), 44.
113. Ben Russell, "Peers demand that Goldsmith explain the legal basis for war," *The Independent*, March 13, 2003.

treated it as a capital crime and imposed the death penalty on the twelve defendants who were convicted of waging a war of aggression. To explain why they took the crime of aggression more seriously than the individual war crimes committed in the course of the Second World War, they included this statement in the Nuremberg Judgment:

> The charges in the indictment that the defendants planned and waged aggressive wars are charges of the utmost gravity. War is essentially an evil thing. Its consequences are not confined to the belligerent states alone, but affect the whole world. To initiate a war of aggression, therefore, is not only an international crime; it is the supreme international crime differing only from other war crimes in that it contains within itself the accumulated evil of the whole.[114]

The crimes with which the German defendants were charged at Nuremberg took place before the signing of the U.N. Charter, and the court relied on the Kellogg Briand Pact as the treaty that had outlawed and criminalized the act of aggression. While the signatories to the Pact renounced "war as an instrument of national policy," it was not universally accepted that individual officials could be held criminally accountable for violating the treaty, let alone sent to the gallows upon conviction. The court therefore spelled out its reasoning on this question very carefully:

> The question is, what was the legal effect of this pact? The nations who signed the pact or adhered to it unconditionally condemned recourse to war as an instrument of policy, and expressly renounced it. After the signing of the pact, any nation resorting to war as an instrument of national policy breaks the pact. In the opinion of the Tribunal, the solemn renunciation of war as an instrument of national policy necessarily involves the proposition that such a war is illegal in international law; and that those who plan and wage such a war,

---

114. http://www.yale.edu/lawweb/avalon/imt/proc/judcont.htm

> with its inevitable and terrible consequences, are committing
> a crime in so doing.

The Tribunal also cited the statement by U.S. Secretary of State Henry Stimson in 1932 that, "War between nations was renounced by the signatories of the Kellogg-Briand Treaty. This means that it has become throughout practically the entire world ... an illegal thing. Hereafter, when engaged in armed conflict, either one or both of them must be termed violators of this general treaty law ... We denounce them as law breakers." I should add that the Kellogg-Briand Pact is still a treaty in force to which the United States is obligated in addition to its more recent commitments under the United Nations Charter.[115]

The plans for the International War Crimes Tribunal at Nuremberg were questioned at the time by many who regarded the tribunal as an instrument of victor's justice. It was the American representatives to the London Treaty negotiations who persuaded their British and Russian allies of the importance of granting the German defendants scrupulously fair trials based on universal principles of international law to ensure the legitimacy of the tribunal. U.S. Supreme Court Justice Robert Jackson, who was subsequently appointed as chief prosecutor at the Tribunal, told the London Conference on July 23rd 1945, "If certain acts in violation of treaties are crimes, they are crimes whether the United States does them or whether Germany does them, and we are not prepared to lay down a rule of criminal conduct against others which we would not be willing to have invoked against us."[116]

Justice Robert Jackson must have been turning in his grave in March 2003. It is clear that the United States and the United Kingdom violated the Kellogg-Briand Pact and the United Nations Charter and that the leaders responsible for those actions are criminally accountable for

---

115. http://www.state.gov/documents/organization/83046.pdf
116. "International Conference on Military Trials," Dept. State Pub. No. 3880, July 23 1945, 330.

their crimes. And, as the Nuremberg Judgment pointed out in relation to the *Caroline* principle, such matters "must ultimately be subject to investigation and adjudication if international law is ever to be enforced."

However, international tribunals play only a secondary role in the enforcement of international law. Unless a country has no functioning judicial system, or one that is structurally incapable of prosecuting such crimes, the primary responsibility for the prosecution of war crimes rests with the domestic courts of the country in question. In the case of war crimes committed by civilian officials of the United States, this grave responsibility rests with the U.S. Justice Department and the U.S. Federal Courts.

CHAPTER 7. SHOCK, AWE AND DEATH

About 86% of the people killed in the First World War were uniformed combatants. Military strategists and engineers have since devised ways to protect their own forces from the deadly effects of ever more powerful modern weapons. Those who fire the most destructive weapons are now well protected from their effects, even the psychological effects of seeing what they do to other human beings. Thus cruise missiles are fired from ships at targets far over the horizon; $2 billion B-2 bombers fly from Whiteman AFB in Missouri to hurt unknown people and break unknown things on the other side of the world; and now Hellfire missiles are fired from Predator and Reaper drones over Iraq, Afghanistan, and Pakistan by people sitting at computer terminals at Creech Air Force base, only an hour's drive from the bright lights of Las Vegas.

Enemy combatants, the nominal targets of these weapons, likewise make use of evolving defensive strategies, from high-tech armor to asymmetric warfare, to protect themselves from all this destructive power. This leaves tragically unlucky and defenseless civilians as the principal victims of modern warfare. The inevitable consequence is that about 90% of the people killed in modern wars are not combatants but civilians.[117]

The public perception of war in developed countries has not quite caught up with this reality. When Americans complained about censorship of the news from Iraq, they were generally asking to see more flag-draped coffins, not pictures of children dismembered by the weapons their tax dollars had paid for. The reality that children dismembered by "precision weapons" were a more common feature of the war in Iraq

---

117. Richard M. Garfield and Alfred I. Neugut, "The Human Consequences of War," *War and Public Health*, edited by Barry S. Levy and Victor W. Sidel, (Oxford: Oxford University Press, 1997).

than flag-draped coffins was still taboo, and neither politicians nor media executives were prepared to face the consequences of breaking the spell.

On January 24th 2003, *CBS News* reported some details of the U.S. government's military planning for the invasion of Iraq. The plans were based on a doctrine developed at the National Defense University in 1996 by Harlan Ullman and James Wade. They called it "Shock and Awe," and described it as an attempt to develop a post-Cold War military doctrine for the United States.[118]

Ullman and Wade advocated capitalizing on American military and technological superiority to launch a massive aerial bombardment which they explicitly compared to a German *blitzkrieg*. This would theoretically overwhelm, disorient, and incapacitate the military organization of a hypothetical enemy country to achieve what they called "rapid dominance." They also emphasized "jointness," using advanced technology to create greater coordination between ground and air forces. They wrote that "shutting the country down would entail both the physical destruction of appropriate infrastructure and the shutdown and control of the flow of all vital information and associated commerce so rapidly as to achieve a level of national shock akin to the effect that dropping nuclear weapons on Hiroshima and Nagasaki had on the Japanese."[119]

Ullman and Wade's theory fit perfectly into the perennial American quest for maximum destruction with minimum American casualties. However, since they relied so heavily on references to Hiroshima and Nagasaki, it is strange that they seemed to ignore the U.S. Strategic

---

118. "Iraq faces massive U.S. missile barrage," *CBS News*, January 24 2003.
http://www.cbsnews.com/stories/2003/01/24/eveningnews/main537928.shtml
119. Harlan K. Ullman and James Wade, *Shock And Awe: Achieving Rapid Dominance*, (National Defense University, 1996).
http://www.dodccrp.org/files/Ullman_Shock.pdf

Bombing Survey's report on the actual effects of those nuclear attacks. Otherwise they would have known that the effect they imagined was a myth even in those most extreme cases.

Although the American bombs obliterated several square miles in the centers of Hiroshima and Nagasaki and killed at least 100,000 people, Nagasaki's naval dockyard, just a few miles away, was almost undamaged by the nuclear explosion. The Mitsubishi works in Nagasaki, like many Iraqi factories in 2003, was already operating at a fraction of its capacity because of a shortage of raw materials, but could have been back at 80% capacity within four months. Rail access to Hiroshima was restored in forty-eight hours, and the main industrial plants on the outskirts of Hiroshima could have resumed normal production within 30 days. Only 29% of the survivors were convinced that Japan could not win the war following the bombings, and the impact on the rest of the country was minimal, precisely because nobody in Japan had any idea what a nuclear bomb was.[120]

In reality, aerial bombardment has nearly always had the effect of stiffening military and popular resistance rather than eliminating it. So "Shock and Awe" was really an insidious effort to rationalize a massive, use of expensive high-tech weaponry whose only guaranteed result would be massive devastation and loss of life. Expanding on their perverse application of nuclear mythology, Ullman and Wade promoted their theory as a way to minimize casualties by shortening a hypothetical war.

Now that Iraq and its people had been assigned the role of the targets in this murderous experiment, *CBS News* reported that "If Shock and Awe works, there won't be a ground war." Harlan Ullman echoed the wishful thinking of aggressors throughout history, "We want them

---

120. United States Strategic Bombing Survey, Summary Report (Pacific War), (Washington: Government Printing Office, 1946), 22 - 26.

to quit. We want them not to fight." He suggested that, because the plan relied on massive use of "precision" weapons, "you have this simultaneous effect, rather like the nuclear weapons at Hiroshima, not taking days or weeks but in minutes." *CBS* also quoted a more realistic U.S. official who "called it a bunch of bull, but confirmed it is the concept on which the war plan is based."

In the early hours of March 20th 2003, all the deadly fantasies concocted by people sitting behind desks in Washington and London emerged into the cold light of day, and the reality of American and British aggression was unleashed on the people of Iraq. The Strategic Studies Institute at the U.S. Army War College studied the relatively quick collapse of Iraqi defenses in a report published on August 18th 2003 and found that the theoretical claims of "Shock and Awe" had nothing to do with the result.[121]

Iraqi communications did not disintegrate as promised: "scouts in civilian clothes reconnoitered U.S. positions continuously; reported via cell/sat phones, landlines, couriers" and "reporting apparently reached high command." The Iraqi high command retained the ability to respond to the invasion: "Republican Guard redeployed elements of 4 divisions directly across V Corps axis of advance;" 10,000 Fedayeen were moved South undetected to engage U.S. forces in urban combat in Najaf and Nasiriyah; a captured Fedayeen command post in Nasiriyah had an accurate sand-table map of U.S. positions in the area; and, on April 4th, after two weeks of "Shock and Awe," the "Republican Guard reinforced [a] tank battalion in prepared positions on ground of [its] own choosing, eluded air attack, [and] met U.S. ground advance at full strength."

---

121. Stephen Biddle et al., *Iraq and the Future of Warfare*, (U.S. Army War College, August 18 2003). http://www.globalsecurity.org/military/library/congress/2003_hr/03-10-21warcollege.pdf

As in 1991, the decisive factor in tank battles was the superior range and accuracy of the guns on U.S. tanks, which were able to destroy Iraqi tanks before their own guns were in range. The relative losses of U.S. forces were actually greater than in 1991, when "less-joint Coalition offensive with smaller technology edge defeated Iraqis at *lower* loss rate" (my emphasis). And there was "little evidence that OIF low-cost victory is attributable to a significant increase in jointness."

As for the effect of "Shock and Awe" on Iraqi morale, the Army War College study found that, while the morale of most Iraqi forces was "largely broken before the invasion," that of the Special Republican Guards and Fedayeen was unaffected by the U.S. strategy. In town after town, morale was "broken only by defeat via close combat in urban centers." Iraqis retained sufficient morale to "reoccupy destroyed positions behind U.S. advance," so that, for example, a convoy bringing emergency resupply had to "fight through to advance position after nightfall, losing 2 fuel (trucks), 1 ammo truck, 2 killed in action, [and] 30 wounded in action en route."

Another significant factor was "Iraqi ineptitude," which included lack of training; poor marksmanship (e.g. less than 10% accuracy with RPGs at 100-500 meters in Baghdad); repeated, exposed frontal assaults by inferior forces; poor equipment maintenance; inability to "exploit potential of urban terrain" to inflict what could have been "possible U.S. losses of multiple thousands." The overall result was best explained by a combination of U.S. advanced technology and Iraqi failings, *"but requires advanced technology and skill mismatch: either alone insufficient"* (italics and underline in original).

The study concluded that "2003 technology punishes ineptitude very severely, but cannot guarantee similar results vs. adept enemies." The "Strategy and Policy Implications" of the study included the advice that it "would be dangerous to assume Iraqi-style scenarios as the future norm." It was equally foolish to think that this scenario would remain the norm in Iraq as conventional war gave way to protracted guerilla warfare.

Although "Shock and Awe" had little to do with the initial success of the invasion, it did provide the rationale for bombarding Iraq with 29,000 bombs and missiles in the first month of the war. As in 1991, the central feature of Centcom's propaganda operations was the claimed effectiveness of its "precision" weapons.

"Precision bombing" has occupied a central role in American war propaganda ever since World War II. According to a pamphlet titled "The Weapon of Ultimate Victory," the B-17 Flying Fortress was "the mightiest bomber ever built … equipped with the incredibly accurate Norden bomb sight, which hits a 25-foot circle from 20,000 feet." This triumphalist language faded quickly as "precision bombing" proved to be an oxymoron and became a central feature in the black humor of American bomber crews. As one airman told the U.S. Strategic Bombing Survey, "We made a major assault on German agriculture." In Britain in 1941, the Butt Report on RAF bombing of Germany found that only one in three bombs fell within five miles of its target. In the heavily defended Ruhr Valley, it was only one in ten. In practice, "precision bombing" was soon replaced by "area bombing," destroying German and Japanese cities to "dehouse" the civilian population, as Winston Churchill callously described it.[122]

During the Vietnam War, the United States developed "laser-guided smart bombs", but the Vietnamese quickly discovered that a bonfire with plenty of smoke was sufficient to confuse their guidance systems. As one American soldier described it, "They'd go up, down, sideways, all over the place. And people would smile and say, 'There goes another

---

122. Paul Fussell, *Wartime: Understanding and Behavior in the Second World War*, (New York: Oxford University Press, 1989), 13 - 19.

smart bomb!' So smart a gook with a match and an old tire can fuck it up!"[123]

The dog-and-pony show over "precision" weapons in 1991 concealed the fact that they only comprised 7% of the bombs and missiles used against Iraq. In 2003 they made up 65% of the American bombs and missiles unleashed on Iraq, and their accuracy had improved, but to nowhere near the extent conveyed by the Centcom press office and its partners in the Western media.[124]

Rob Hewson, the editor of *Jane's Air Launched Weapons*, made an assessment that 75-80% of these weapons were accurate, which is to say that they detonated within about 30 feet of their targets.[125] This was a significant improvement from the assault on Yugoslavia in 1999, when the accuracy was only 60-70%, and it was a real advance from the experimental prototypes used against Iraq in 1991. However, out of a total of 29,000 bombs and missiles detonated in Iraq in March and April 2003, more than 10,000 were not "precision weapons" at all, and, based on Hewson's assessment, about 4,000 of those that were "precision weapons" missed their targets completely.

So, overall, about half of the total 29,000 bombs and missiles dropped on or fired into Iraq were no more accurate than the carpet bombing or "area bombing" of past wars, wreaking death and destruction on civilians, their homes, and other inadvertent targets. Even those that did explode somewhere near their intended targets, especially in urban areas, certainly killed civilians and damaged civilian homes and

---

123. Douglas Valentine, *The Phoenix Program*, (New York: William Morrow, 1990), 196

124. Lt. Gen. T. Michael Moseley, *Operation Iraqi Freedom - By the Numbers*, (US-CENTAF Assessment and Analysis Division, April 30 2003), 11.
http://www.globalsecurity.org/military/library/report/2003/uscentaf_oif_report_30apr2003.pdf

125. "U.S. precision weapons not foolproof," Associated Press, April 1 2003.
http://nucnews.net/nucnews/2003nn/0304nn/030401nn.htm

infrastructure. A Mark 82 500 pound bomb, the smallest of these weapons, has a damage radius of anywhere from 30 to 300 feet depending on building construction, so that the explosion of even one bomb in an inhabited area is a horrific nightmare for its victims.[126]

A puzzled Rob Hewson concluded, "In a war that's being fought for the benefit of the Iraqi people, you can't afford to kill any of them. But you can't drop bombs and not kill people. There's a real dichotomy in all of this."

Some U.S. cruise missiles went so far off target that they detonated in other countries. Saudi Arabia and Turkey both withdrew permission for the Americans to fire missiles through their air-space. After Al-Jazeera dared to show its viewers throughout the Middle East the effects of U.S. bombing, its offices in Baghdad were targeted and hit by two U.S. missiles, killing Jordanian cameraman Tariq Ayoub.

The *Sydney Morning Herald* in Australia reported that U.S. forces incinerated Iraqi troop concentrations with a modern form of napalm. An American propaganda counter-offensive challenged the *Herald's* claims and blunted their impact, but the newspaper was eventually able to dismiss the denials as pure semantics. The Mark 77 fire bombs used in Iraq were an "improved" version of the Napalm-B used in Vietnam 35 years earlier, but American troops and aircrews still referred to them as napalm. They were designed to burn hotter and longer, leaving less environmental damage(!). The *Herald* tracked down an order from the U.S. Marine Corps to the Rock Island Arsenal in Illinois for 500 new Mark 77 fire bombs to replenish its stocks soon after the invasion.[127]

---

126. Yuna Huh Wong, *Ignoring the Innocent*, (Santa Monica: Rand Corp, 2006), 98 - 108.

http://www.rand.org/pubs/rgs_dissertations/2006/RAND_RGSD201.pdf

127. Ben Cubby, "Napalm by another name: Pentagon denial goes up in flames," *Sydney Morning Herald*, August 9 2003.

U.S. forces also used cluster munitions that released at least 2 million bomblets in Iraq, many of which fell in civilian areas. Human Rights Watch reported more than 500 civilian casualties from cluster munitions in Hilla alone. Even at the Pentagon's official cluster munitions "dud" rate of 16%, which is considered a low estimate, this left the country scattered with more than 300,000 unexploded bomblets, many of which killed Iraqi civilians later. One also killed Sergeant Troy Jenkins of California, 25, who heroically threw himself on a cluster bomblet handed to him by a child in a crowd in Baghdad on April 19th 2003.[128]

The Iraqi government reported more accurately than Western propaganda on the effects of American bombing, and indeed on much of the war, for as long as it was able to do so. Subsequently, and throughout the war, many efforts were made to estimate the civilian death toll. The People's Kifah, an Iraqi resistance group, conducted a nationwide survey of violent deaths as of October 2003. It counted more than 37,000 civilian deaths by that time, with the majority probably occurring during the invasion. It employed hundreds of academics and volunteers, who "spoke and coordinated with grave-diggers across Iraq, obtained information from hospitals and spoke to thousands of witnesses who saw incidents in which Iraqi civilians were killed by U.S. fire."[129]

An actual count of specific deaths in a war zone like the People's Kifah survey is by definition an undercount of actual deaths, as many are bound to be missed. In any case, the survey was never completed. One of its researchers, Ramzi Musa Ahmad, was seized by Kurdish *Peshmer-*

---

128. Corine Hegland, "Civilian death toll in Iraq," National Journal, May 29th 2004, 1704.
129. Ahmed Janabi, "Iraqi group: civilian toll over 37,000," *Al Jazeera*, October 29 2004. http://english.aljazeera.net/English/archive/archive?ArchiveId=5525

ga militiamen, reportedly handed over to U.S. forces, and never seen again. The survey was abandoned.

On July 1st 2004, the *New England Journal of Medicine* published the results of a survey of the experiences of U.S. invasion forces as part of a PTSD study. The participants were from the 3rd Infantry Division and the 1st Marine Expeditionary Force, the two divisions that led the invasion. These units comprised about 20,000 soldiers and 40,000 Marines respectively. The other combat division that took part in the invasion was the 101st Airborne with another 20,000 combat troops. The sample was designed to be representative of combat troops during the invasion and the first few months of U.S. occupation—the Marines had returned to the U.S. in July 2003, and the 3rd Infantry Division was withdrawn in September 2003.[130]

The survey found that 14% of the infantrymen and 28% of the marines reported that they had been "responsible for the death of a non-combatant" in Iraq, while 48% of infantrymen and 65% of marines reported "being responsible for the death of an enemy combatant." Even if the 101st Airborne and other "support" or "non-combat" forces killed no civilians at all, and if each of the respondents who answered affirmatively to these questions was responsible for the death of only one civilian or combatant, this means that at least 14,000 civilians and 35,000 Iraqi combatants were probably killed by U.S. ground fire during this period.

Such widespread killing of civilians corresponds to the many stories of civilians shot in their cars approaching American check-points; violent house raids; indiscriminate fire in response to Iraqi attacks on U.S. patrols; and deliberate decisions to conduct military operations in populated civilian areas. Camilo Mejia was a staff sergeant in the Florida

---

130. Charles W. Hoge et al., "Combat Duty in Iraq and Afghanistan, Mental Health Problems, and Barriers to Care," *New England Journal of Medicine*, Volume 351:13-22, July 1st 2004.

National Guard company from my neighborhood in Miami. He was stationed in Ramadi in late 2003. He told me that his company killed about 33 people and that only three of them were found to have been armed.

However, the evidence suggests that, for much of the war, U.S. air strikes killed more Iraqi civilians than ground fire by U.S. troops. This is consistent with the general pattern of modern warfare, but it was accentuated by American rules of engagement that emphasized the use of overwhelming force to avoid U.S. casualties, even at the cost of massive enemy and civilian casualties. U.S. ground troops operated under standing orders to "call for fire", meaning to call in an air strike, on any building where resistance fighters took cover, with little regard for the numbers of civilians also present. Air operations over Iraq declined immediately after the invasion, but they then increased thereafter throughout most of the occupation until the beginning of 2008, with the exception of a small decrease in 2006.

Official figures for air strikes by U.S. Air Force and Navy planes were recorded as "Strikes (munitions dropped)," or "Munitions expended", sometimes with an additional note that this "does not include 20 mm and 30 mm cannon or rockets." There were 285 of these strikes in 2004, 404 in 2005, 310 in 2006, a huge increase to 1,708 in 2007 and 915 in 2008. The maximum monthly total of 400 air strikes in January 2008 exceeded the annual totals for most previous years. Clearly, the "surge" or escalation of the war in 2007 included a far greater reliance on air power, even though the accompanying propaganda campaign instead highlighted new "counter-insurgency" tactics such as U.S. efforts to establish small outposts on the ground in Baghdad and the training of Iraqi forces recruited during the occupation.[131]

---

125. http://www.centaf.af.mil/shared/media/document/AFD-091103-001.pdf and http://www.afa.org/edop/2009/2004-08CFACCstats123108.pdf

But published figures on U.S. air strikes did not tell the full story. They did not appear to count strikes conducted by U.S. Marine Air Wings, which were the primary air force in Anbar province for most of the war. Nor did they include the hundreds of missile-firing, machine-gun-toting helicopters operating in Iraq, nor the increasing numbers of Predator and Reaper unmanned drones. By October 2007, Predators were flying more than 4,000 hours per month in Iraq. A hundred and twenty active duty Air Force pilots were grounded in late 2007 and sent to Las Vegas to fly the growing fleet of drones over Iraq and Afghanistan.[132]

Then there were the U.S. Special Forces' AC-130 Spectre gun-ships, adapted from an older model used in Vietnam known as "Puff the Magic Dragon." These modified cargo planes were equipped with machine-guns, howitzers, and every weapon in between "to provide surgical firepower or area saturation during extended loiter periods" according to the U.S. Air Force web site. In other words, they cruised over and around targets, pouring a torrent of bullets and shells into them for as long as necessary to completely obliterate them. The United States had thirteen of these planes operating in Iraq, Afghanistan, Somalia, and elsewhere. Incredibly, the Air Force touted their value in "urban operations."[133]

The number of close air support missions reached a new interim high in September and October 2007 with 60 to 70 missions flown each day. In each period of higher air activity, the greater reliance on air power was linked to efforts to reduce U.S. casualties and corresponded to news reports that civilians were being killed by air strikes. In October 2007, following at least 981 air strikes in 4 months, the U.N. Assistance Mission to Iraq protested continuing U.S. air strikes in civilian

---

132. Lolita C. Baldor, "Military's use of unmanned aircraft soars in Iraq," Associated Press, January 2 2008. http://biz.yahoo.com/ap/080102/unmanned_killers.html?.v=2
133. http://www.af.mil/factsheets/factsheet.asp?fsID=71

areas in a Human Rights Report and reminded U.S. authorities that these attacks violated international human rights laws. The U.N. demanded "that all credible allegations of unlawful killings by MNF forces be thoroughly, promptly and impartially investigated, and appropriate action taken against military personnel found to have used excessive or indiscriminate force." The report added that, "The initiation of investigations into such incidents, as well as their findings, should be made public."[134]

The interim Iraqi government's Health Ministry started collecting civilian mortality figures from hospitals in 2004, and in June that year, it started separating the figures for people killed by resistance forces from those killed by U.S. and other occupation forces. *Knight Ridder* correspondent Nancy Youssef was given the figures for the period between June 10th and September 10th 2004 and covered them in an article on September 25th 2004 that the *Miami Herald* titled "U.S. attacks, not insurgents, blamed for most Iraqi deaths."[135]

During this three month period, the Health Ministry counted 1,295 Iraqis killed by the occupation forces and 516 killed in what the ministry called terrorist operations, but it agreed with hospital officials who told Youssef that these figures only captured part of the death toll. The Centcom press office refused to provide her with an alternative estimate, although it admitted that the U.S. command did have one, and the International Committee of the Red Cross told her it didn't have sufficient staff in Iraq to compile such information.

Youssef questioned whether some of the Iraqis counted as killed by the occupation forces might have been resistance fighters, but Dr. Shihab Jassim of the Health Ministry's operations section told her the min-

---

134. http://www.uniraq.org/aboutus/HR.asp

135. Nancy Youssef, "U.S. attacks, not insurgents, blamed for most Iraqi deaths," *Miami Herald*, September 25 2004. http://www.commondreams.org/headlines04/0925-02.htm

istry was convinced that nearly all were civilians, because a family member wouldn't report it to the occupation-controlled Health Ministry if his or her relative died fighting for the Mahdi Army or other resistance forces. This view was corroborated by Dr. Yasin Mustaf, the assistant manager of al-Kimdi Hospital in Baghdad: "People who participate in the conflict don't come to the hospital. Their families are afraid they will be punished. Usually, the innocent people come to the hospital. That is what the numbers show."

Dr. Walid Hamed, another Health Ministry official told Youssef, "Everyone is afraid of the Americans, not the fighters. And they should be." Another doctor she spoke to had lost his own 3-year old nephew in a check-point shooting, and a doctor at the Baghdad morgue told her about a family of eight who were all killed by a helicopter gun-ship after they went up to sleep on their roof to escape the summer heat. Overall, officials attributed the high numbers of civilians killed by occupation forces primarily to air strikes rather than to shootings by ground forces.

Also in September 2004, an international team of epidemiologists, led by Les Roberts and Gilbert Burnham from Johns Hopkins School of Public Health and Drs. Lafta and Khudhairi of Al Mustansiriya University in Baghdad, conducted the first of two more scientific studies of mortality in Iraq. This one covered the first eighteen months of the war. Roberts had worked with a joint team from the Center for Disease Control and Doctors Without Borders in Rwanda in 1994, and had conducted similar studies in war zones around the world. Mortality estimates he produced in the Democratic Republic of Congo in 2000 were widely cited by American and British leaders, and the U.N. Security Council drafted a resolution demanding the withdrawal of all foreign forces from the DRC following that report.

In Iraq, the epidemiologists found that, "Violent deaths were widespread ... and were mainly attributed to coalition forces. Most individuals reportedly killed by coalition forces were women and children ... Making conservative assumptions, we think that about 100,000 excess deaths or more have happened since the 2003 invasion of Iraq. Violence accounted for most of the excess deaths and air strikes from coalition forces accounted for most violent deaths." Their report was published in the *Lancet*, the British medical journal, in November 2004.[136]

There was nothing surprising in their conclusions in light of the already existing evidence that "coalition" air strikes had killed thousands of civilians, both during and after the invasion. However, their report was quickly dismissed by the American and British governments. The American media, following their tradition of deference to U.S. officials, took their cue from the government and more or less ignored the study. Following the publication of the epidemiological team's second study in 2006, which garnered a bit more media attention, President Bush said only, "I don't consider it a credible report."

The cynicism of these official dismissals was eventually exposed by yet another set of leaked British documents. On March 26th 2007, the BBC published a memo from Sir Roy Anderson, the chief scientific adviser to Britain's Ministry of Defence, in which he described the epidemiologists' methods as "close to best practice" and their study design as "robust." These documents included memos sent back and forth between worried British officials saying things like, "Are we really sure the report is likely to be right? That is certainly what the brief implies." Another official replied, "We do not accept the figures quoted in the *Lancet* survey as accurate," but added, in the same e-mail, "the survey methodology used here cannot be rubbished, it is a tried and tested way of measuring mortality in conflict zones."[137]

---

136. Les Roberts et al., "Mortality before and after the 2003 invasion of Iraq: cluster sample survey," *The Lancet*, Vol 364, November 20 2004.

137. Owen Bennett-Jones, "Iraq deaths survey was robust," *BBC World Service*, March 26 2007. http://news.bbc.co.uk/1/hi/uk_politics/6495753.stm

The methodology that the British officials were referring to was a "cluster sample survey," the same type of study that Les Roberts had conducted in the Democratic Republic of Congo in 2000. Prime Minister Blair had publicly cited that study's figures to the 2001 Labour Party Conference to justify British policy in Africa, but he dismissed the study in Iraq, telling reporters in December 2004, "Figures from the Iraqi Ministry of Health, which are a survey from the hospitals there, are in our view the most accurate survey there is." This was interesting in light of Youssef's report. Blair dismissed the overall numbers in the *Lancet* report, but avoided the even more sensitive question of who killed all these people, on which the Health Ministry and the epidemiologists were in total agreement.

The Western media widely cited the Iraqi Health Ministry and *Iraqbodycount.org* as sources for civilian mortality figures, but these both used a passive methodology to count deaths, essentially adding up deaths that had already been reported either in hospital records or in Western media accounts. Epidemiologists working in other war zones over the past twenty years have typically found that such passive methods only capture between 5% and 20% of actual deaths. That is why they have developed the cluster sample survey method to obtain a more accurate picture of the deadly impact of conflicts on civilians, and thus to facilitate more appropriate responses by governments, U.N. agencies, and NGOs.

The cluster sample survey method used in war zones was adapted from epidemiological practice in other types of public health crises, surveying a representative sample of a population by clusters to estimate the full extent of a health problem that affects the whole population. As Les Roberts pointed out, "In 1993, when the U.S. Centers for Disease Control randomly called 613 households in Milwaukee and concluded that 403,000 people had developed *Cryptosporidium* in the largest outbreak ever recorded in the developed world, no one said that 613 households was not a big enough sample. It is odd that the logic of epidemiology embraced by the press every day regarding new drugs or health risks somehow changes when the mechanism of death is their armed forces."[138]

In Iraq in September 2004, the epidemiological teams surveyed 988 households in 33 clusters in different parts of the country, attempting to balance the risk to the survey teams with the size needed for a meaningful sample. Michael O'Toole, the director of the Center for International Health in Australia, said, "That's a classical sample size. I just don't see any evidence of significant exaggeration ... If anything, the deaths may have been higher because what they are unable to do is survey families where everyone has died."

Beyond the phony controversy in the media regarding the methodology of these epidemiological studies, there was one significant question regarding the numbers in the 2004 study. This was the decision to exclude the data from a cluster in Fallujah due to the much higher number of deaths that were reported there (even though the survey was completed before the final assault on the city in November 2004). Roberts wrote, in a letter to the *Independent*, "Please understand how extremely conservative we were: we did a survey estimating that 285,000 people have died due to the first 18 months of invasion and occupation and we reported it as at least 100,000."

The dilemma they faced was this: in the 33 clusters surveyed, 18 reported no violent deaths (including one in Sadr City), 14 other clusters reported a total of 21 violent deaths and the Fallujah cluster alone reported 52 violent deaths. This last number is conservative for the reason Michael O'Toole highlighted. As the report stated, "23 households of 52 visited were either temporarily or permanently abandoned. Neighbors interviewed described widespread death in most of the

---

138. Nicolas J. S. Davies, "Burying the Lancet report," *Z Magazine*, February 2006.

abandoned homes but could not give adequate details for inclusion in the survey."

Leaving aside this last factor, there were three possible interpretations of the results from Fallujah. The first, and indeed the one the epidemiologists adopted, was that the team had randomly stumbled on a cluster of homes where the death toll was so high as to be totally unrepresentative and therefore not relevant to the survey. The second possibility was that this pattern among the 33 clusters, with most of the casualties falling in one cluster and many clusters reporting zero deaths, was an accurate representation of the distribution of civilian casualties in Iraq under "precision" aerial bombardment. The third possibility, which effectively incorporated the other two, was that the Fallujah cluster was atypical, but not sufficiently abnormal to warrant total exclusion from the study, so that the real number of excess deaths fell somewhere between 100,000 and 285,000.

In each case, however, these figures were only the mid-point of a statistical range, leaving considerable uncertainty over the actual number of deaths. The epidemiologists found, with 95% certainty, that the excess number of deaths as a result of the war, excluding the 3% of the country represented by the cluster in Fallujah, was somewhere between 8,000 and 194,000. In itself, this was hardly a solid or satisfactory conclusion. However, it was very unlikely that the actual number of dead was close to either of those extremes, and there was a 90% likelihood that it was more than 44,000.

The Fallujah cluster, statistically representing the most devastated 3% of the country, reported 52 of the 73 total violent deaths in the survey. Even if this was not a perfect representation of the distribution of violent deaths, these parts of the country by definition suffered considerably worse than other areas, and yet the published estimate of about 100,000 violent deaths effectively counted zero violent deaths in these areas. The survey team that visited Fallujah reported that "vast areas of the city had been devastated to an equal or worse degree than the area they had randomly chosen to survey," so that the area chosen did in fact appear to be representative of many severely bombed areas.

One could therefore arrive at the estimate of "about 100,000 excess deaths or more" by looking at the survey data in a number of different ways, which made the authors very confident in their interpretation. There were other conservative biases built into the study, such as ignoring empty and bombed-out houses, as Michael O'Toole pointed out, but no serious criticisms were made that would account for a significant over-estimate of deaths resulting from these methods. The main criticism made by politicians and journalists was that these studies produced higher estimates than passive reporting, but that is exactly what one would expect.

One larger survey that did produce lower civilian mortality figures was the Iraq Living Conditions Survey (ILCS). This survey was conducted by the Coalition Provisional Authority's Ministry of Planning and Development Cooperation in April and May 2004 and it was published in May 2005 by the U.N. Development Program. The "UNDP" imprimatur and the large sample size gave credence to its reassuringly low figure of about 24,000 "war deaths."[139]

However, its estimate of war-deaths was derived from a single question posed to families in the course of a 90-minute interview on living conditions conducted by officials of the occupation government. By contrast, the mortality studies published in the *Lancet* were designed with the sole purpose of obtaining accurate mortality figures, and included extensive precautions to guarantee the anonymity of the respondents and to reassure them of the independence of the survey teams.

---

139. http://www.iq.undp.org/ilcs.htm

Jon Pederson, the Norwegian designer of the ILCS, said himself that its mortality figures were certainly too low. Survey teams that returned to the same houses and enquired only about child deaths found almost twice as many as in the main survey. This suggested precisely the reluctance to report violent deaths that Roberts and his colleagues sought to overcome by stressing their impartiality. And in April or May 2004, a question regarding "war-deaths" could still be interpreted to refer only to the invasion itself, as opposed to the long guerilla war that followed it. This interpretation is supported by the fact that more than half the deaths reported in the ILCS were in the southern region of Iraq, which bore the brunt of the invasion but was later more peaceful than other regions.

In January 2005, the health ministry provided the BBC with a summary of its hospital survey for the previous six months which painted a similar picture to the one given to Nancy Youssef of Knight Ridder in September. It counted 2,041 civilians killed by U.S. forces and their allies, and 1,233 killed by so-called insurgents. After the BBC broadcast these figures all over the world, it received a call from the Health Minister of the occupation government claiming that his ministry's report had been misrepresented and that the number of deaths attributed to the occupation forces was not accurate. The BBC issued a retraction, and the Health Ministry stopped providing breakdowns of its figures that attributed any responsibility for civilian deaths to the occupation forces.[140]

Another actual nationwide count of civilian deaths was published by a group called Iraqiyun on July 12th 2005. Iraqiyun was an Iraqi humanitarian group headed by Dr. Hatim Al-Alwani and affiliated with the political party of Interim President Ghazi Al-Yawer. It counted 128,000 actual violent deaths, of whom 55 percent were women and children

---

140. "BBC obtains Iraq casualty figures," *BBC News*, January 28 2005. Original report at http://www.informationclearinghouse.info/article7906.htm

under the age of 12. The report specified that it included only confirmed deaths reported to relatives, omitting significant numbers of people who had simply disappeared without trace amid the violence and chaos. It was highly unlikely that an effort like this to actually count every one of the dead could result in anything but a significant undercount, for the reasons already discussed.[141]

Then, between May and July 2006, Roberts, Burnham and Lafta led a second epidemiological study in Iraq to update their estimate of at least 100,000 deaths between March 2003 and September 2004. They increased their sample size to 1,849 households, comprising 12,801 individuals, in 47 clusters. They were now surveying the results of 40 months of war. These factors enabled them to narrow the statistical range of their results. This time they were able to say, with 95% certainty, that between 426,000 and 794,000 Iraqis had died violent deaths as a consequence of the war. Their best estimate was that there had been about 655,000 excess deaths, of which about 600,000 were violent deaths. The finding of the earlier survey that at least 100,000 Iraqis had been killed by October 2004 was validated, with a new estimate of 112,000 excess deaths for that period. This also validated the conservative assumption that the Fallujah sample was unusual but not irrelevant.[142]

They also found some changes in the pattern of violent deaths. Gunfire was now the most common cause of death overall, and "the proportion of deaths ascribed to coalition forces had diminished in 2006, although the actual numbers have increased every year." Their overall conclusion, however, was that, "The number of people dying in Iraq has continued to escalate."

---

141. "Iraqi civilian casualties," *United Press International,* July 12 2005. http://www.upi.com/Security_Terrorism/Analysis/2005/07/12/iraqi_civilian_casualties/2280/

142. Gilbert Burnham et al., "Mortality after the 2003 invasion of Iraq: a cross-sectional cluster sample survey," *The Lancet,* October 11 2006.

This overall trend was extremely disturbing, with each period accounting for more violent deaths than the one before and a proliferation in types of violence over time. Air strikes now accounted for only 13% of total violent deaths, but were still responsible for the deaths of about half of all the children killed in Iraq, underlining the inherently indiscriminate nature of powerful air-launched weapons. There had been huge increases in violent deaths among males between the ages of 15 and 44, now accounting for 59% of all violent deaths, but the epidemiologists decided not to try to differentiate between combatant and non-combatant deaths. With much of the population now involved in armed resistance to the occupation, they felt that asking questions about this could put the survey teams at greater risk, and that responses would not be reliable in any case.

Households attributed 31% of violent deaths to coalition forces, which would result in an estimate of at least 180,000 people killed directly by American and other foreign occupation forces. However, the report noted that, "Deaths were not classified as being due to coalition forces if households had any uncertainty about the responsible party; consequently, the number of deaths and the proportion of violent deaths attributable to coalition forces could be conservative estimates." Also, Iraqi forces recruited and trained by U.S. forces and under overall U.S. command played an increasing role in the war, in particular in the reign of terror launched in Baghdad in May 2005. These forces were responsible for the summary executions of thousands of young men and teenage boys, but those deaths were not attributed to "coalition" forces in this survey.

Two more studies of mortality in Iraq were published in January 2008. The first was the Iraq Family Health Survey, which was conducted by the same group (COSIT) that conducted the CPA's Iraq Living Conditions Survey in 2004. This study focused exclusively on the death toll, with some cooperation from the World Health Organization and was published in the *New England Journal of Medicine*. It surveyed deaths only up to June 2006, to provide a comparison with the second survey by Roberts, Burnham, and Lafta. Although it also found evidence of a huge increase in the death rate since the invasion, the IFHS produced a much lower estimate of about 150,000 violent deaths.[143]

Unfortunately, there are several reasons to doubt the accuracy of this lower figure. Like the ILCS in 2004, this survey was conducted by employees of a government that was taking part in the violence it was attempting to quantify. This predictably leads to underreporting. Secondly, its estimate of the pre-invasion death rate for 2002 is about one third of the official death rate recorded by the World Health Organization. Thirdly, it found no increase in the violent death rate from year to year between 2003 and 2006. Every other data set available, from mortality studies to the Pentagon's statistics on violence in Iraq, showed increases in violence each year. Fourth, it found that only one in six post-invasion deaths was due to violence, compared with a majority of deaths due to violence in the other epidemiological studies, and in independent surveys of graveyards.

A fifth factor that surely contributed to the IFHS's low mortality figure was that it was unable to survey mortality in the most dangerous 11% of the country. It attempted to compensate for this based on the regional distribution of violent deaths in *Iraqbodycount.org (IBC)*, a record of deaths compiled from international media reports. However, because the unsurveyed areas were also the most dangerous for Western reporters, *IBC* inevitably undercounted deaths in these same areas. And yet IFHS used this distorted distribution pattern based on passive reporting to estimate deaths in the deadliest parts of the country.

The other survey published in January 2008 was a survey conducted in August and September 2007 by Opinion Research Business, a British

---

143. Iraq Family Health Survey Study Group, "Violence-related mortality in Iraq from 2002 to 2006," *New England Journal of Medicine*, Vol 358: 484-493, January 31 2008.

polling firm, in conjunction with Iraq's Independent Institute for Administration and Civil Society Studies. They surveyed 2,414 households and asked them if they had lost a member or members of the household to violence since the invasion. They were unable to survey three provinces (Anbar, Karbala and Irbil), and most of the 8% of households who refused to answer were in Baghdad, where death-rates were among the highest. These factors contributed a conservative bias to their estimate. In spite of this, ORB found that about 20% of households surveyed had lost at least one member, and estimated that 1.03 million people had died in the war. Without compensating for the conservative biases mentioned above, their data and sample size gave them 95% certainty for a number of deaths between 946,000 and 1.12 million.[144]

After the publication of the second epidemiological study in the *Lancet*, the scale of violent death it revealed was gradually acknowledged among educated circles in the West, including in the United States. The ORB survey provided independent confirmation of the scale of the violence. It also suggested that deaths had continued to increase for at least another year after the publication of the second study in the *Lancet* and that the death toll probably now exceeded a million violent deaths.

The work of all these researchers showed that the United States and other modern governments could not unleash this kind of violence on another country without eventually facing the consequences of public awareness of the nature and magnitude of its effects. And, although U.S. officials may never publicly acknowledge it, the publication of these studies probably served to restrain some of their most violent impulses in the conduct of the war.

---

144. http://www.opinion.co.uk/Newsroom_details.aspx?NewsId=88

CHAPTER 8. MISLEADING THE TROOPS

In the last chapter, we examined the scale and nature of the cataclysm that descended on the people of Iraq in 2003. This chapter will explore some of the factors that made the U.S. occupation of Iraq particularly brutal and violent, with daily, systematic violation of the Geneva Conventions and international human rights laws. This brutality was not a reflection of any sort of widespread personality defect in American troops, nor was it simply a regrettable but inevitable feature of war and military occupation. Rather, there are specific factors in the way Americans live and are educated, U.S. troops are trained, and the occupation forces in Iraq were conditioned that combined to make occupation by *American* forces a unique threat to the lives of the people of Iraq. The responsibility for this lay primarily with American civilian and military leaders, rather than with the troops themselves.

Just as the nations of the world came together under American leadership to found the United Nations in 1945, to try and prevent future wars, they also met in 1949 and drafted or updated the four Geneva Conventions, agreeing to common rules of conduct for their armed forces, to mitigate some of the most dreadful aspects of war. The International Committee of the Red Cross was granted unique supranational authority to monitor compliance with the Conventions and to make confidential interventions regarding any mistreatment of prisoners of war.

The First Geneva Convention covers the treatment of battlefield casualties, the Second covers the conduct of war at sea, the Third relates to prisoners of war, and the Fourth Geneva Convention, which was the one newly drafted in 1949, covers the rights of civilians under conditions of war or military occupation. All four conventions share Common Article Three relating to "conflicts not of an international character," making it clear that its prohibition against "Violence to life and person, in particular murder of all kinds, mutilation, [and] cruel treatment and torture" applies across the board, regardless of whether an individual is a wounded soldier or sailor, a prisoner of war, or a civilian.[145]

Two additional protocols were added in 1977, clarifying certain "grey areas" such as the status of guerillas and other combatants who do not wear uniforms. 163 countries have signed and ratified both protocols, so that they are now considered to be part of customary international law and therefore binding on all countries. The United States has signed but not ratified these protocols, and this is the basis on which it has claimed that its prisoners in the so-called war on terror are not entitled to the protections of the Geneva Conventions. U.S. troops in Iraq were frequently instructed that prisoners they detained or guarded were not protected, leading to confusion and systematic use of torture.

Understanding that public awareness and acceptance of the Conventions is a primary factor in their effectiveness, the International Committee of the Red Cross marked the fiftieth anniversary of their signing in 1999 by conducting a survey of more than 17,000 people in 17 countries to "explore people's understanding and attitudes about the rules and limits of what is permissible in war." The project was called "People on War - civilians in the line of fire."[146]

The survey was conducted in twelve countries that had recently experienced war, in Switzerland where the ICRC is based, and in four countries that are permanent members of the U.N. Security Council and whose governments therefore play a special role in questions of war and peace.

---

145. http://www.icrc.org/ihl.nsf/CONVPRES?OpenView
146. Greenberg Research, *The People on War Report*: ICRC worldwide consultation on the laws of war, (Geneva: ICRC, 2000).
http://www.icrc.org/Web/Eng/siteengo.nsf/html/p0758

The "People on War" report noted, as I did in the last chapter, that about 90% of the people killed in modern wars are civilians, and, in the twelve war-torn countries, it found that 31% of the people surveyed reported losing an immediate family member. In the modern world, as the report said, "war is war on civilians." But it also found that:

> ... the more these conflicts have degenerated into wars on civilians, the more people have reacted by reaffirming the norms, traditions, conventions and rules that seek to create a barrier between those who carry arms into battle and the civilian population. In the face of unending violence, these populations have not abandoned their principles nor forsaken their traditions. Large majorities in every war-torn country reject attacks on civilians in general and a wide range of actions that by design or default could harm the innocent. The experience has heightened consciousness of what is right and wrong in war. People in battle zones across the globe are looking to forces in civil society, their own state institutions, and international organizations to assert themselves and impose limits that will protect civilians.

People in the United States, Great Britain, Russia, France, and Switzerland were also asked about the importance of protecting civilians in time of war. They were asked to choose between a firm statement that combatants "must attack only other combatants and leave civilians alone" and a weaker one that "combatants should avoid civilians as much as possible." In Great Britain (72%), Russia (77%), France (76%), and Switzerland (77%), about three quarters of those surveyed chose the absolute prohibition on attacking civilians, which in fact accords with international law under the Fourth Geneva Convention, while 17% in Russia and France, 16% in Switzerland, and 26% in Britain chose the weaker one.

In the United States, however, a different pattern emerged. Only 52% agreed that combatants "must leave civilians alone," while 42% chose the weaker option, roughly twice as many as in the other permanent member countries. The report added that, "Across a wide range of questions, in fact, American attitudes towards attacks on civilians were much more lax." Another question asked about military actions that put civilians at risk, and found that

> American respondents are far more likely than their Security Council counterparts to sanction actions that put civilians at risk. More than one-third (38 per cent) say it is part of war to attack "enemy combatants in populated villages or towns in order to weaken the enemy, knowing that many civilians would be killed." This compares with 29 per cent of respondents in the United Kingdom, 26 per cent in France and 20 per cent in the Russian Federation. This gap holds true when Security Council respondents are asked if they sanction attacks on civilians who provide enemy combatants with food and shelter.

A similar discrepancy emerged in response to questions about torture and the treatment of prisoners of war:

> Among the four Security Council countries surveyed, consciousness of the obligations owed to prisoners of war is strongest among the French, the British and the people of the Russian Federation. Once again, American respondents display a lower level of understanding of the rules of wartime conduct. Eight in ten of those surveyed in the three other Security Council countries surveyed say, for example, that an independent representative must be allowed to visit a prisoner of war; only 57 per cent of United States respondents agree. In the same vein, while fully 90 per cent of the French and 81 per cent of the British say that prisoners cannot be subjected to torture, only 65 per cent of Americans and 72 per cent of those surveyed in the Russian Federation agree.

The survey also asked questions about attitudes toward the Geneva Conventions themselves. Respondents were asked whether they believed that the Conventions can help prevent wars from getting worse or whether they "make no real difference." Only a minority (28%) of people in the twelve countries who had experienced war thought the conventions "make no real difference," along with 33% of Russians and

45% in France. But a majority of British (55%) and Americans (57%) agreed with the statement that the Conventions "make no real difference."

The difference in attitudes revealed by the "People on War" survey should be disturbing to Americans. Article VI of the United States Constitution enshrines treaties like the Geneva Conventions as part of the "supreme Law of the Land," so that, of all people, Americans should be leading the world in honoring these obligations. So why are "American attitudes towards attacks on civilians more lax" than the attitudes of people in other countries, as the *People on War* study found?

One factor could be that Americans have not experienced war on their own soil since the American Civil War and the wars against Native Americans in the 19th century, nor foreign military occupation since 1815, and therefore find it harder to empathize with the predicament of civilians in war-zones.

Or perhaps Americans have been gradually conditioned over time by deferential political and media responses to the killing of civilians by U.S. forces to regard it as regrettable but acceptable.

Or the elites who influence American education and public opinion may have chosen not to educate people about the laws of war for fear that it would weaken the United States' ability to commit military forces to combat or limit the ways in which they could be used. This would coincide with the general deterioration in the commitment of U.S. leaders to their constitutional obligation to comply with international treaties.

The history of U.S. covert action described in Chapter 1, including assassinations and proxy wars that have killed millions of people all over the world, must also be relevant. Covert forms of violence, by their very nature, violate both laws and moral codes. When the United States has already crossed legal and moral lines on such a scale since the signing of the conventions in 1949, perhaps it is unrealistic to expect a more responsible public attitude toward the conduct of its armed forces.

Some combination of these factors (isolation from the reality of war, the more deferential attitude of U.S. media, a deliberate lack of education in this area, and the corrosive effect of widespread covert action) may account for the unique results in the American portion of the "People on War" survey. This whole question certainly warrants further investigation and some serious national soul searching.

However, in more general terms, when the victims of war in the survey were asked to explain the breakdown in civilized norms that led to combatants killing civilians, they chose *the will to win at any cost* and *disrespect for the laws of war* as the two principal factors. Another reasonable explanation they offered placed greater responsibility with political and military leaders, and seems relevant to the case of the United States:

> Many people think the limits are breached because ordinary people have been ordered to harass, dislodge or even attack civilian populations, sometimes uncomfortably at odds with their own beliefs and prevailing norms. Political and military leaders, it is believed, have chosen to pursue the battle in ways that endanger civilians, but people are prepared to believe that the leaders have a plan or a good reason for their course of action. At the very least, they are ready to follow their orders, because as ordinary people they have little choice.

The survey questioned both civilians and present or former military personnel in the permanent member countries and found little difference between the responses of civilians and soldiers. So when we look at the conduct of U.S. troops in Iraq, we can safely start from the understanding that soldiers are first of all citizens and take with them to war the basic attitudes they have learned at home and at school. The results of the survey suggest that, without a special emphasis on the laws of war in their military training, American troops would be more likely than their French, British, Russian, or Swiss counterparts to kill civilians, torture prisoners, and otherwise violate the Geneva Conventions.

It is especially unfortunate in light of this that U.S. military personnel receive very limited education in the laws of war. The basic training of recruits includes a single fifty-minute lecture from a JAG officer on the Uniform Code of Military Justice, the Hague and Geneva Conventions, and other military law issues. Troops deploying to Iraq or another combat zone receive a refresher as part of their preparation for deployment. The lectures are typically conducted by a JAG officer addressing about a thousand troops with the aid of a Powerpoint presentation.

Article 144 of the Fourth Geneva Convention includes the provision that "Any civilian, military, police or other authorities, who in time of war assume responsibilities in respect of protected persons, must possess the text of the Convention and be specially instructed as to its provisions". And yet U.S. forces deploying to Iraq are not given a copy of the text, nor do they receive special instruction as to its provisions. An officer at the Centcom press office in Baghdad told me that he remembered the lecture dealing more with the treatment of prisoners and seemed unclear as to what the Fourth Geneva Convention was about.

There is no question that the Fourth Geneva Convention applied to the U.S. invasion and occupation of Iraq, at least until the formation of the interim and transitional governments. The nominal restoration of sovereignty led the ICRC to make a statement in 2004 that it "no longer considers the situation in Iraq to be that of an international armed conflict between the U.S.-led coalition and the state of Iraq and covered by the Geneva Conventions of 1949 in their entirety." But the U.S. Embassy in Baghdad clarified in a letter to the U.N. Assistance Mission in Iraq in December 2007 that its forces were still operating under the rules of the Fourth Geneva Convention. It would be interesting to know how many of them were aware of that or could describe any of its provisions.

In any case, international human rights law provides very similar protections to civilians via other treaties and customary law once a war is over. Iraq ratified the International Covenant on Civil and Political Rights in 1971 and the United States eventually ratified it in 1992. The U.N. mission in Iraq has reminded the U.S. government and its Iraqi allies that the ICCPR "is clear on the basic protections that must be afforded to persons and from which no derogation is permissible, even in times of emergency." Under both the Fourth Geneva Convention and the ICCPR, civilians are entitled to protection from indiscriminate or excessive use of force, including air strikes and military raids in predominantly civilian areas, and the collective punishment of civilian populations is always prohibited.[147]

The U.N. human rights report for the second quarter of 2007 included a reminder to U.S. military commanders in Iraq that "Customary international humanitarian law demands that, as much as possible, military objectives must not be located within areas densely populated by civilians. The presence of individual combatants among a great number of civilians does not alter the civilian nature of an area."

But inadequate training in their legal responsibilities toward Iraqi civilians was only the beginning of the problem for U.S. forces in Iraq. In fact, their attitude toward the people of Iraq was poisoned before the war had even begun by widespread rumors of secret evidence connecting Iraq to the terrorist attacks of September 11th 2001. To some extent, this was part of the propaganda operation directed at the general public, but there were additional factors at work in the military context that made the effects of this campaign more insidious and dangerous, as military leaders must have understood.

------

147. http://www.uniraq.org/aboutus/HR.asp

A PIPA poll published on July 1st 2003 found that 25% of Americans believed that Iraq was directly involved in carrying out the September 11th attacks, while only 7% understood that there was no connection at all between the Iraqi government and al-Qaeda. Most Americans knew that the administration had exaggerated the connections between Iraq and Al Qaeda to make its case for war, but 65% still believed either that Iraq gave substantial support to Al Qaeda or that there was at least some contact between Al Qaeda and Iraqi officials, as Secretary Powell had asserted to the U.N. Security Council.[148]

The strangest finding of this poll was that 52% of Americans believed that U.S. forces in Iraq had actually "found clear evidence in Iraq that Saddam Hussein was working closely with the Al Qaeda terrorist organization." This misperception was much stronger among certain segments of the population. For instance, 78% of "Republicans following Iraq news closely" subscribed to it, even more than among Republicans at large and a sad reflection on the quality of "Iraq news." There was a strong correlation with pre-war acceptance of the government's claims. Among those who believed the government had been fully truthful before the war, 84% shared the misperception that its claims of links between Iraq and Al Qaeda had been substantiated following the invasion. PIPA concluded that "this misperception may to some extent be motivated by a desire to avoid cognitive dissonance."

The theory of cognitive dissonance holds that, when someone is faced with incompatibility between their own actions or beliefs and some new information, they experience "dissonance" proportional to the difficulty of dismissing either the position they originally held or the new information. The effect is magnified enormously when one has taken important or irrevocable action based upon the preconception in question, or when one's personal identity or moral values are chal-

---

148. http://www.pipa.org/OnlineReports/Iraq/IraqWMD_Jul03/IraqWMD%20Jul03%20rpt.pdf

lenged by the dichotomy. If armchair warriors in the United States found it so difficult to let go of their earlier beliefs linking Iraq to September 11th, how much harder must this have been for soldiers preparing for combat and then fighting, killing, losing friends, and witnessing horror in Iraq?

In fact, the great majority of U.S. troops in Iraq not only believed widespread rumors circulating among them about Iraq's role on September 11th 2001, but actually saw this as the principal reason that they were being ordered to conquer and occupy Iraq. Speaker of the U.S. House of Representatives Nancy Pelosi spoke publicly of her confusion when she visited U.S. troops in Kuwait preparing for the invasion and asked them to tell her what they understood about the reasons for the invasion. They nearly all told her, "September the 11th, Ma'am!" But when she asked the general in command who was telling them this, he assured her that it was not him.

A full three years into the war, in February 2006, a Zogby International poll of U.S. troops in Iraq found that 85% of them believed their mission was to "retaliate for Saddam's role in the 9/11 attacks," and 77% believed that the primary reason for the war was to "stop Saddam from protecting Al Qaeda in Iraq." By this point, only 7% linked the war to "weapons of mass destruction," the official justification for the war.[149]

Whether senior officers actively promoted these beliefs to motivate their troops, or whether they only failed to correct them for fear of undermining morale, the effect was that, to an even greater extent than "Republicans following Iraq news closely," the troops in the U.S. invasion and occupation force in Iraq comprised a subset of the U.S. population that faced enormous cognitive dissonance if they accepted that the people they confronted every day in Iraq had nothing to do with the September 11th terrorist attacks in the United States.

---

149. http://zogby.com/news/ReadNews.dbm?ID=1075

And so this belief persisted in military circles, buoyed by rumors that "the higher-ups know things they can't tell us," as a junior Air Force officer told a host on *Air America* in 2006. This type of rumor is especially powerful in a military context. It is in the nature of a military organization that the "higher-ups" do know things they can't tell their subordinates, and the most essential component of military discipline is an implicit trust in one's superiors and the understanding that personal doubts cannot be allowed to interfere with obedience to their orders. When this trust broke down on a wide scale in Vietnam, the war was effectively lost.

As with the underlying issue of half-hearted education on the laws of war, confusion among U.S. troops about who did and didn't commit terrorism in the United States on September 11th 2001 is something that military leaders could have remedied at any time. But they did not do so. Instead, it remained official U.S. military doctrine that the American war in Iraq was part and parcel of the so-called "war on terror," America's response to September 11th. Political rhetoric preserved this link by implication and innuendo, without ever crystallizing it into something that could be confirmed or dismissed once and for all, allowing rumors to persist among those most threatened by cognitive dissonance, those who had killed and seen their friends die based on these lies. And of course, both public support for the war and military morale gradually disintegrated under the strains inherent in these contradictions.

The nature of the military occupation of Iraq was surely made far more dangerous from the outset by this insidious and irresponsible mis-seduction of the occupation forces. Not only were most of the troops oblivious to their obligations under the Fourth Geneva Convention and other international human rights laws, but they also believed that they were in Iraq to retaliate against the terrorists who had attacked the United States. When Iraqis began to resist the illegal occupation of their country, they were identified as terrorists, no different from Mohammed Atta and his Saudi Arabian companions. Every Iraqi the troops killed was one more terrorist who would never be able to attack Boise, Idaho, or Mobile, Alabama. "We can fight them there or fight them here," as a U.S. special forces NCO told me, repeating Bush's well-worn maxim.

In April 2007, four years into the war, a military Mental Health Advisory Team examined the ethics of U.S. soldiers and Marines in Iraq. In response to a survey question, 17% said that all Iraqi non-combatants should be treated as "insurgents," and there is evidence that this view was really more widely held than that. 36% of soldiers and 39% of Marines said that torture should be allowed "in order to gather important info about insurgents" (which would cover almost any situation short of sheer sadism). The torture numbers went 5 points higher if the troops were told that American lives were at stake.[150]

Less than half the troops surveyed said that they would report a member of their unit for stealing from an Iraqi civilian, hitting or kicking a civilian, violating rules of engagement (such as firing at civilians), or unnecessarily destroying private property. Only 55% of soldiers and 40% of marines said they would report a comrade for injuring or killing an innocent civilian.

How the miseducation of U.S. troops affected their attitude toward the civilian population of Iraq in practice is borne out by a host of anecdotal evidence. The Pentagon survey's results probably presented a sanitized view of reality. Aidan Delgado witnessed a scene in which a Sergeant lost patience with a group of children who were asking for candy, detached the steel antenna from a Humvee, and attacked the children with it. Later, Delgado's fellow soldiers fired into a crowd of unarmed prisoners at Abu Ghraib prison who were protesting their detention and conditions, killing four of them. He has a photograph of another soldier holding an MRE (meals ready to eat) spoon, pretending

---

150. http://www.armymedicine.army.mil/news/mhat/mhat_iv/mhat-iv.cfm

to eat the brains out of the shattered skull of one of the prisoners killed in that incident.[151]

At a court martial for murder at Camp Pendleton in California on July 14th 2007, a Marine Corporal testified for the defense that he did not see the cold-blooded killing of an innocent civilian as a summary execution. "I see it as killing the enemy," he told the court, adding that, "Marines consider all Iraqi men part of the insurgency." The same witness testified that "dead-checking," or the killing of wounded Iraqis, was a routine procedure during house raids. "If somebody is worth shooting once," he told the court, "they're worth shooting twice."[152]

"Dead-checking," the cold-blooded killing of wounded enemy combatants, is a flagrant violation of the First Geneva Convention, and yet it was standard procedure in many combat units in Iraq. "They teach us to do dead-checking when we're clearing rooms," a U.S. Marine told Evan Wright of the *Village Voice*. "You put two bullets into the guy's chest and one in the brain. But when you enter a room where guys are wounded you might not know if they're alive or dead. So they teach you to dead-check them by pressing them in the eye with your boot, because generally a person, even if he's faking being dead, will flinch if you poke him there. If he moves, you put a bullet in the brain."[153]

Defense attorneys representing three soldiers who were convicted of murdering three civilians in Iraq offered a defense that would be startling if it was not consistent with other accounts of military operations. The lawyers claimed that the soldiers were acting under explicit orders to "kill all military-age males" during the raid in question. The soldiers attacked an island on Lake Tharthar that had been used by resistance

151. Aidan Delgado, *The Sutras of Abu Ghraib*, (Boston: Beacon Press, 2007), 74 & 149-58.
152. "Marine: beating of Iraqis became routine," *Associated Press*, July 15 2007. http://www.huffingtonpost.com/huff-wires/20070715/marines-iraq-shooting/
153. Evan Wright, "Dead-Check in Falluja," *Village Voice*, November 24-30 2004.

forces, but they met no resistance. They shot dead one elderly, un-armed man and detained three other unarmed men. Based on court martial testimony, "a sergeant in the company asked over the radio why they had done so, instead of killing the Iraqis as they had been told to do." The soldiers then staged an attempted escape and shot the three men to death. They were also charged with threatening to kill another soldier if he reported the incident.[154]

The soldiers' lawyers said that the Colonel commanding the brigade admitted issuing the order to "kill all military-age males," but he was allowed to testify in secret and was not charged with a crime. The Colonel in question (who was also a senior commander in Somalia during the *Black Hawk Down* incident in 1993) kept "kill-boards" for each company in the brigade, on which he tallied how many Iraqis each soldier had killed. One of the kill-boards was inscribed, "Let the bodies hit the ground," a quote from a "Rambo" movie.

On the treatment of prisoners, Human Rights Watch has sworn statements in declassified documents that soldiers guarding prisoners not only lacked proper education on the Geneva Conventions, but were explicitly told by their superiors that the Conventions did not apply.[155]

Some of the most excessive and illegal violence in Iraq was committed by U.S. Special Forces, but most of their operations were secret and not widely reported. In recent years, Special Forces have performed a growing range of quasi-military operations that fit opportunistically somewhere between conventional military operations and covert CIA-type actions. This has been an integral part of the development of an American defense strategy that is not constrained by the laws of war and international behavior. These forces, now numbering at least 47,000 troops, operate in the shadows with very little public or media

---

154. Robert F. Worth, "Sergeant tells of plot to kill Iraqi detainees," *New York Times*, July 28 2006.
155. http://www.hrw.org/english/docs/2006/07/19/usint13767.htm

scrutiny, but, as early as December 2003, Seymour Hersh reported in the *New Yorker* that they were being assigned a special role in Iraq.[156]

Since the launch of the so-called "war on terror," Donald Rumsfeld had been pressing the military brass to approve what he called "manhunts" or "preemptive manhunts," assassination and kidnapping operations like those carried out by Israel in Palestine to destroy the Palestinian military, political, and civic leadership. However, General Charles Holland, the head of U.S. Special Forces, a former Spectre gunship pilot who flew 79 missions in Vietnam and other countries, refused to authorize operations that were not based on solid intelligence regarding specific individuals.

Holland's retirement in October 2003 gave Rumsfeld the chance to expand Special Forces operations further into the shadows. He had installed Stephen Cambone as Under Secretary of Defense for Intelligence just before the invasion of Iraq. Cambone saw eye to eye with Rumsfeld on everything from manhunts to the tactical use of nuclear weapons and was soon regarded as his right-hand man. After Holland's retirement, Cambone brought in General William Boykin as his military assistant. Boykin had led a U.S. Delta Force team in Colombia that took part in the assassination of Pablo Escobar, and he was the mission commander responsible for the *Black Hawk Down* fiasco in Mogadishu. Boykin immediately found himself under investigation by the Department's Inspector General over comments in which he characterized the "war on terror" as a Christian crusade against Muslims. Thomas O'Connell, a veteran of the Phoenix terror campaign, which killed about 41,000 people, mostly civilians, in Vietnam and Cambodia, was appointed Assistant Secretary for Special Operations.

With Rumsfeld's leadership team in place, the manhunts could begin. Israeli forces trained American Delta Force, Navy Seals, and CIA

---

156. Seymour M. Hersh, "Moving Targets," *The New Yorker*, December 15 2003.

paramilitary operatives in Israel and North Carolina in the methods developed by the *Mista'aravim* assassination squads in Palestine. *Mista'aravim* training focused on intensive classes in Arab language and culture, as well as in methods of assassination, so that the assassins could blend into the population in the Palestinian territories, kill their targets, and escape undetected.

This was the kind of training and the kind of operation that was being planned for the American *Mista'aravim* in Iraq. The U.S. had already succeeded in killing or capturing most of the senior officials of the Iraqi government but now feared that resistance was being coordinated by "mid-level" Baath Party members, essentially the middle class of the country, who would now become the targets of the American *Mista'aravim*. The assassins worked with an Iraqi Mukhabarat agent named Farouk Hijazi and former Iraqi exiles to identify targets, and prowled the streets of Iraqi cities at night to hunt and kill their prey.

Hersh's extensive contacts in the military and intelligence communities gave him a wide range of views on the possible effects of this campaign. He wrote, "There is much debate about whether targeting a large number of individuals is a practical—or politically effective—way to bring about stability in Iraq, especially given the frequent failure of American forces to obtain consistent and reliable information there."

An American advisor to the occupation government told him, "The only way we can win is to go unconventional. We're going to have to play their game. Guerilla versus guerilla. Terrorism versus terrorism. We've got to scare the Iraqis into submission." On the other hand, Scott Ritter, one of the few Americans with first-hand knowledge of contemporary Iraqi society and government, told him: "(Hussein) has released the men from his most sensitive units and let them go back to their tribes, and we don't know where they are. The manifests of those units are gone; they've all been destroyed. Guys like Farouk Hijazi can deliver some of the Baath Party cells, and he knows where some of the intelligence people are. But he can't get us into the tribal hierarchy."

The potential for widespread slaughter of innocents was obvious. A former Special Forces official questioned the knowledge and the motives of the Iraqis the U.S. was working with: "These guys have their own agenda. Will we be doing hits on grudges?" And the Special Forces' "Grey Fox" electronic intelligence service would be useless: "These guys are too smart to touch cell phones or radio. It's all going to succeed or fail spectacularly based on human intelligence."

An assassination program like this is inherently vulnerable to manipulation by the enemy. Navy SEAL Mike Beamon took part in the Phoenix campaign in Vietnam, but eventually realized it was out of control. "It is my feeling", he said, "that later on we were hitting people that the Viet Cong wanted us to hit, because they would feed information through us and other intelligence sources to the CIA and set up a target that maybe wasn't a Viet Cong, but some person they wanted wiped out. It might even have been a South Vietnamese leader. I didn't understand Vietnamese. The guy could've said he was President for all I knew. He wasn't talking with me. I had a knife on him. It was just absolute chaos out there. Here we are, their top unit. It was absolutely insane."[157]

Julian Borger of the *Guardian* interviewed U.S. intelligence officials who confirmed the essentials of Hersh's story, that the Israelis were training U.S. Special Forces assassination teams for deployment in Iraq. A U.S. intelligence source told Borger, "It is bonkers, insane. Here we are—we're already being compared to Sharon in the Arab world, and

---

157 Douglas Valentine, *The Phoenix Program*, (New York: William Morrow, 1990), 170.

we've just confirmed it by bringing in the Israelis and setting up assassination teams."[158]

An Israeli official warned Hersh that eliminating the command structure of Hamas had created a nightmare for Israel as popular resistance "now consists largely of isolated cells that carry out terrorist attacks against Israel on their own. There is no central control over many of the suicide bombers. We're trying to tell the Americans that they don't want to eliminate the center. The key is not to have freelancers out there." As with the larger American war on terror, the precise effects of all this were difficult to predict or control. The only outcome that anyone could be sure of was that a lot of people were going to be killed.

The illegitimacy of the invasion, the miseducation of the U.S. occupation forces, and the criminality and desperation of their leaders combined to present the people of Iraq with a classic case of hostile military occupation, enhanced by the most powerful weapons in military history. Examining each of the factors that contributed to the extreme brutality of the occupation makes it clear that moral and criminal responsibility rest with the leaders of American society, from the media and educational elite to the political and military command.

To finish this chapter on a redemptive note, many of the American service-members who have taken part in the invasion and occupation of Iraq have understood a great deal about the societal forces that conspired to make them accomplices in aggression and atrocities, and are facing the reality of what they have done with extraordinary honesty. A sailor named Andrea who served on a destroyer during the initial onslaught on Iraq wrote this in 2007:

---

158. Julian Borger, "Israel trains U.S. assassination squads in Iraq," *The Guardian*, December 9 2003.

On 19 March 2003, the day Operation Iraqi Freedom began, I was stationed on a destroyer in the Persian Gulf. My deployment should have ended 6 weeks before, but because of the war the entire battle group's deployment was extended. I was part of the Tomahawk launch team, and over the first four weeks of the war we emptied our launchers. The hours were brutal. We could and did launch missiles at all hours of the day and night. It became so commonplace to see them fly that CNN even stopped covering it. Since then, my personal year has revolved towards and away from the 19th of March. It is my own Ash Wednesday, a Yom Kippur that I mark with no one but myself.

In military circles, you don't speak of regretting your part in a war, and it feels disloyal besides. I know, I'm brainwashed. It happens. I am not overwhelmingly depressed this year, thanks be to God for small mercies that I probably don't deserve. I am mournful, I am contemplative. I wish for forgiveness from myself, I wish I could feel right with God again, but these things may take a while and for the most part, I am at peace.

Less than a year from now I will finally take off my uniform for the last time, and be out of it all for good. Next year on the 19th of March, I can go to one of the protests marking the anniversary of the start of the war, and not feel like a damned hypocrite or a spy. Next year when I renew my membership in Iraq Veterans Against the War, I will check the box that says "I am willing to speak publicly" and if they ask me to speak, I will go, and I will tell the audience about how all members of the military carry wounds and scars and scabs on the soul, not just the ground forces. I will speak of the choices you make, the things you do to stay out of prison and earn that honorable discharge and the benefits that come with it. I will speak of the nights I have woken up in a cold sweat, clutching a worried dog like a lifeline, with nightmares of the people I have killed arriving, one by one, at my front door in a line that stretches longer than I like to admit.

I wonder, sometimes, why I ended up like this and other people on my Tomahawk team did not. Firing Tomahawks is a triumph of military engineering, designed to kill a maximum number of the enemy while causing the least amount of potential trauma to the firing team. It includes any number of factors that will make it easier for a person to kill, including the extremely long range of the weapon, the shared responsibility (an average Tomahawk team includes at least seven people), and lack of decision-making (targets are selected for you). All of these factors should have buffered all of us, kept us safe from accepting personal responsibility for our choices.

Why did my brainwashing, so firm in other matters, fail me when I most needed it? I mean, I compulsively check to make sure the buttons on my shirt, the buckle of my belt, and the overlap of the zipper on my pants are neatly lined up throughout the day. My military bearing is rather impeccable when I'm in uniform, if I do say so myself. Bark at me in an authoritative voice and I am liable to follow the order first and think about it later. All the basics are there, but somehow the higher functions didn't install. DOS works, but the Windows-level brainwashing just failed to take, and while on the one hand I'm proud of my ability to retain some level of independent thought, on the other hand entirely I wish like hell I could just buy into the party line and not ... not think, not wonder, not accept that I made the choice to kill rather than to go to prison, even though I thought in 2003 that our reasons for going to war were complete rampaging bullshit dressed up like truth and sent out to walk the halls of the U.N.

It's different this year, at least, and for that I am grateful. This afternoon I played in the sunshine with my dogs, and came in and snuggled the kitties in a sunbeam in the library. I must pause, periodically, in my typing to massage the ears of a grey dog who keeps shoving her head in my lap. I have explained to her that I am a mass murderer in the service of the government. She doesn't much care and wants to know if more ear rubbing will be forthcoming. She doesn't understand why her doomed attempt to be a lap dog made me cry a little today. But maybe this is where being ok starts: with the one creature in this world who will forgive me any human failing at all. I'm not right with myself and I'm not right with God, yet, but I am right with Dog and that's a start, isn't it?[159]

159. Personal statement read aloud at *MoveOn* "Counter-filibuster to end the war" events at Republican Senators' district offices, July 17 2007.

CHAPTER 9. RESISTANCE

Lying is never without purpose. Even the most impudent lie, if repeated often enough and long enough, always leaves a trace. German propaganda subscribes to this principle, and today we have another example of its application. Inspired by Goebbel's minions, cheered on by the lackey press, and staged by the Militia, a formidable campaign has just been launched— a campaign which seeks, in the guise of an attack on the patriots of the underground and the Resistance, to divide the French once again. This is what they are saying to Frenchmen: "We are killing and destroying bandits who would kill you if we weren't there. You have nothing in common with them."

Although this lie, reprinted a million times, retains a certain power, stating the truth is enough to repel the falsehood. And here is the truth: it is that the French have everything in common with those whom they are today being taught to fear and despise. There is one France, not two: not one that is fighting and another that stands above the battle in judgment. For even if there are those who would prefer to remain in the comfortable position of judges, that is not possible. You cannot say, "This doesn't concern me." Because it does concern you. The truth is that Germany has today not only unleashed an offensive against the best and proudest of our compatriots, but it is also continuing its total war against all of France, which is exposed in its totality to Germany's blows.

Don't say, "This doesn't concern me. I live in the country, and the end of the war will find me just as I was at the beginning of the tragedy, living in peace." Because it does concern you. Take note. On January 29, in Malleval in the Isere, a whole village was burned by the Germans on the mere suspicion that refractaires (people fleeing deportation to slave labor camps) might have taken refuge there. Twelve houses were completely destroyed, eleven bodies discovered, fifteen men arrested. On December 18 at Caveroche in Correze, five kilometers from Ussel, where a German officer was wounded in murky circumstances, five hostages were shot and two farms put to the torch. On February 4 in Grole, in the Ain, Germans, after failing to find the refractaires they were searching for, shot the mayor and two leading citizens.

These dead Frenchmen were people who might have said, "This doesn't concern me." But the Germans decided that it did concern them, and on that day they demonstrated that it concerned all of us...

Don't say, "I sympathize, that's quite enough, and the rest is no concern of mine." Because you will be killed, deported, or tortured as a sympathizer just as easily as if you were a militant. Act: your risk will be no greater, and you will at least share in the peace at heart that the best of us take with them into the prisons.

Total war has been unleashed, and it calls for total resistance. You must resist because it does concern you, and there is only one France, not two. And the incidents of sabotage, the strikes, the demonstrations that have been organized throughout France are the only ways of responding to this war. That is what we expect from you. Action in the cities to respond to attacks in the countryside. Action in the factories. Action on the enemy's lines of communication. Action against the Militia: every militiaman is a possible murderer.

Albert Camus, writing in the underground newspaper Combat, Occupied Paris, March 1944[160]

The U.S. invasion and occupation of Iraq confronted every member of the Iraqi population with a classic, excruciating predicament: the life and death choice between collaboration and resistance to the hostile military occupation of their country. Although the invasion violated the U.N. Charter, the Security Council recognized the governments of the United States and the United Kingdom as occupying powers in Iraq in resolution 1483 on May 22nd 2003. The resolution was carefully worded

---

160. Albert Camus, *Camus at Combat*, (Princeton: Princeton University Press, 2006), 1 - 3.

not to provide after-the-fact legitimacy to the invasion, and, by placing the occupation under U.N. supervision, some members evidently hoped this might be a first step toward a restoration of legitimacy and sovereignty in Iraq. However, by acquiescing in the result of American and British aggression, the resolution instead served to consolidate their military occupation of the country.

In August 2003, S.C. resolution 1500 welcomed the establishment of the "broadly representative" Governing Council of Iraq as an "important step towards the formation by the people of Iraq of an internationally recognized, representative government that will exercise the sovereignty of Iraq." Five days later, the Iraqi Resistance let the world know what it thought of the U.N.'s effective support for the occupation by blowing up its headquarters in Baghdad. Then, in October 2003, SC resolution 1511 authorized a "Multi National Force" in Iraq, placing the lives and safety of the Iraqi people in the hands of the same U.S. and British forces that had illegally invaded the country, in spite of already abundant evidence of the violent, corrupt and unpopular nature of the occupation.[161]

There is no precedent for a U.N. mandate for an occupying power under such circumstances. In addition to being in the country illegally in the first place, the "MNF" consistently violated the Geneva Conventions, international humanitarian law, and its own mandate; and yet the Council extended this mandate several times, well beyond the formation of a nominally sovereign Iraqi government, when it was originally designed to expire. It was renewed each time at the request of the various Iraqi governments established under the occupation, but it was never approved by Iraq's Council of Representatives, which was constitutionally required to ratify international agreements before they could take effect.

---

161. http://www.un.org/Docs/sc/unsc_resolutions03.html

In April 2007, a majority of the Iraqi Council of Representatives (144 members) sent a letter to the U.N. Security Council asking it not to grant further renewals of the MNF's mandate without a firm timeline for its withdrawal. At the same time, it passed a law requiring the government to abide by the relevant clauses of its constitution and to send any further requests for renewal of the MNF mandate to parliament for ratification before submitting them to the Security Council. In spite of this, the Maliki government submitted a request for the renewal of the mandate in December 2007 without the parliament's approval, and, once again, the Security Council rode roughshod over the Iraqi constitution and Council of Representatives, and extended the MNF mandate.[162]

From the very beginning of the occupation, the U.N. Security Council's actions left the Iraqi people with no middle ground to stand on. The international community was not going to rescue them. The leaders of the appointed Iraqi Governing Council (IGC) were former exiles who had been flown in with the invasion forces. This was exactly what ordinary Iraqis had expected and feared, a corrupt puppet government of former exiles "who are coming to Iraq with empty pockets to fill," as a Baghdad taxi-driver told a Western reporter before the invasion. The only respect in which the IGC could be called "broadly representative" was that it included exiles from each of the major ethnic and sectarian groups in the country, the beginning of the political division of the country along those lines, pitting each group against the other with the occupying powers as mediators and kingmakers.

Article 51 of the U.N. Charter defines the right of self defense in the modern world as follows:

> Nothing in the present Charter shall impair the inherent
> right of individual or collective self-defence if an armed attack

---

162. http://www.globalpolicy.org/security/issues/iraq/mnfindex.htm

occurs against a Member of the United Nations, until the Security Council has taken measures necessary to maintain international peace and security. Measures taken by Members in the exercise of this right of self-defence shall be immediately reported to the Security Council and shall not in any way affect the authority and responsibility of the Security Council under the present Charter to take at any time such action as it deems necessary in order to maintain or restore international peace and security.

But what right do people have to resist the invasion and occupation of their country when the Security Council fails to take "measures necessary to maintain international peace and security," and instead places their fate in the hands of the powers that are violating their sovereignty and independence in the first place? International lawyers emphasize the use of the word "inherent" in Article 51 as the key to resolving difficult questions regarding the right of self defense. As international law professor Michael Byers wrote in *War Law*, " ... the content of Article 51 is greatly informed by customary international law, in part because of the explicit reference to the "inherent" character of the right of self-defence."[163]

Thus the U.N. Charter acknowledges that the right of self-defense is one that already exists in customary international law independently of U.N. actions. In the case of Iraq, just as the resolutions passed by the Security Council since the invasion of Iraq never directly addressed the central issue of the invasion of the country, neither did they directly address the Iraqi people's right to resist it. Instead, they sought to superimpose a format of legitimacy on top of the existing state of conflict in the hope that it might eventually supersede it.

This was arguably a doomed and disastrous appeasement of British and American aggression. Any hope for success depended on the Security Council's ability to gradually transfer power from the occupying

---

163. Michael Byers, *War Law*, (New York: Grove Press, 2005), 56.

powers to a sovereign government, but the Council had failed from the outset to assert the necessary authority to actually make this happen at any critical juncture in the coming years.

The resolutions contained frequent references to "the right of the Iraqi people freely to determine their own political future." They also contained condemnations of "terrorism," including specific condemnations of attacks against civilians and foreign diplomats. However, in spite of the deaths of thousands of American and other foreign troops in Iraq, none of the Security Council resolutions explicitly condemned acts of resistance against the U.S. and British occupying forces, even after they had granted them a mandate as a "Multi-National Force." The American and British governments must surely have wanted such language, and so its absence appears to signify that their Security Council partners would not agree to it: a small but significant diplomatic price paid by the invaders for the illegitimacy of their position.

Within Iraq itself, opposition to the occupation and to the Iraqi Governing Council was widespread and vocal, and was soon met with savage repression. Iraqis who spoke out publicly against the occupation were assassinated, often in ways that deliberately obscured responsibility. Iraqis blamed the exile groups and the IGC, but assumed American support for the assassinations, and Seymour Hersh's research suggests that direct U.S. involvement was more instrumental than the U.S. government will ever publicly acknowledge without strong public pressure for accountability.

Many of the people targeted for assassination were from the professional class of the country: academics, lawyers, and doctors; the leaders of civil society who could give voice to the concerns of the people. Assassinations of academics, doctors, and local leaders, and the resulting exodus of the professional class, seem to have been calculated to deprive Iraq of the intellectual and political resources to arrest the decomposition of the country. The suppression of avenues of non-violent political action reduced Iraq's fate to a bloody struggle in which the Americans believed their greater capacity for violence would ultimately prove decisive.

In spite of serious threats to their lives, Iraqis continued to organize politically to oppose the occupation. Democracy had spontaneously broken out on a local level in many parts of Iraq following the invasion. In Samarra, Hilla, Mosul and other areas, Iraqis started organizing local elections. U.S. forces even assisted in these efforts, taking President Bush's rhetoric about democracy at face value. But this didn't last for long. In June 2003, ten weeks after the invasion, the order went out to U.S. forces across the country to halt this process, leaving former Baathist military officers running local governments in collaboration with American forces in most areas. Paul Bremer candidly admitted to the *Washington Post*, "In a postwar situation like this, if you start holding elections, the people who are rejectionists tend to win."[164] And with good reason.

As the official transfer of power from the Coalition Provisional Authority to an interim Iraqi government drew near in May 2004, democratic groups from around the country held a conference in Baghdad under the auspices of *Iraq for the Iraqis*, a slogan coined by the opposition to the British-backed monarchy in the 1950s. Kofi Annan had appointed Algerian diplomat Lakhdar Brahimi to oversee the formation of the interim government. He attended the *Iraq for the Iraqis* conference and met with other representative groups all over Iraq. He indicated an apparently genuine desire that the interim government should represent "the right of the Iraqi people freely to determine their own political future," as the Security Council resolutions required.[165]

---

164. William Booth and Rajiv Candrasekaram, "Occupation forces halt elections throughout Iraq," *Washington Post*, June 28 2003, A20.

165. http://www.un.org/News/ossg/hilites/hilites_arch_view.asp?HighID=9

Tragically, the United States government was not prepared to relinquish its own goals in Iraq, and Brahimi was effectively sidelined by U.S. officials when the critical decisions were made regarding the composition of the interim government. Long-time MI6 and CIA asset Ayad Allawi became the interim prime minister, and the occupation continued. Iraq was sovereign in name only.

Brahimi held a press conference before leaving Iraq, at which he finally broke his diplomatic silence and expressed his frustration at the failure of his mission. He told reporters, "Bremer is the dictator of Iraq. He has the money. He has the signature." Pressed on who he would have chosen to lead the interim government, he made it clear who would remain in charge in any case, "I will not say who was my first choice, and who was not my first choice ... I will remind you that the Americans are governing this country."[166]

Another non-violent response to the occupation came from Iraqi trade unions, with the General Union of Oil Employees taking the lead in opposing the U.S.-backed petroleum law that aimed to reverse the nationalization of the Iraqi oil industry, and the Electricity and Energy Union opposing the privatization of utilities and public services. Iraqi union leaders even toured the United States to educate American union members on the U.S. government's privatization agenda in Iraq and to rally opposition to it.[167]

But, as always, violence breeds violence. It is probably too idealistic to imagine that the people of Iraq could have found entirely peaceful means to oppose the occupation of their country in the face of violent repression of peaceful demonstrations; assassinations of civic leaders;

---

166. Tom Lasseter, "Brahimi: Bremer the 'dictator of Iraq' in shaping Iraqi government," *Knight Ridder Newspapers*, June 2 2004.
http://www.mcclatchydc.com/staff/tom_lasseter/story/10386.html
167. David Bacon, "Iraqi workers strike to keep their oil," *Dollars & Sense*, September/October 2007.

mass detentions without charge or trial; widespread, arbitrary, indiscriminate violence; and, above all, in the face of American policymakers' brutal determination to pursue the goals of the invasion regardless of the cost to the Iraqi people. This is of course terribly tragic, and, as Camus described in France sixty years earlier, armed resistance is easily seized on to justify even greater violence by the forces who are responsible for all of the violence in the first place. The rhetoric of accompanying propaganda campaigns is equally well-worn and predictable, but can still be persuasive to the faraway domestic constituencies that sustain such policies.

The principal struggle in Iraq was not between Sunnis, Shiites, and Kurds, as American propaganda claimed, but between the United States and its allies on one side and the majority of Iraqis who opposed the U.S. occupation on the other. This was abundantly clear from the U.S. Defense Intelligence Agency's published data on "enemy-initiated attacks" in Iraq. This data showed that at least 75% of resistance operations targeted U.S. or other foreign occupation forces, while at least another 16% were against Iraqi forces under U.S. command.[168]

While attacks against civilians dominated Western media coverage, and were one of the most dreadful by-products of the occupation, they actually comprised less than 10% of total "insurgent" attacks. Even this small proportion included attacks against Iraqi civilians who were collaborating with the occupation, so that the proportion that were strictly acts of terrorism against innocent civilians was even smaller. Most terrorist attacks against civilians were carried out by small groups of religious extremists rather than by the larger nationalist groups that led the armed resistance to the occupation. But the occupation authorities presented these relatively isolated incidents as the principal form of violence in occupied Iraq, and as the justification for continued occupa-

---

168. http://www.brookings.edu/saban/iraq-index.aspx

tion rather than the result of it. Their partners in the Western media deferentially relayed this view to their readers and viewers.

On February 15th 2005, the "Anti-Occupation Patriotic Forces" held a meeting at the Umm Al-Qura mosque in Baghdad that "discussed proposals aiming at restoring Iraq's full independence, unity and sovereignty." The twenty-one groups and political parties who participated included Muqtada al-Sadr's Current party, the (Sunni) Association of Muslim Scholars, the Patriotic Front for the Liberation of Iraq (an umbrella group that included former Baath Party members), the Progressive Union of Iraqi Students, two women's groups, a communist party, a socialist party, and the Nationalist Democratic Party. The conference released a statement of principles that included a clear distinction between resistance and terrorism. All these groups agreed on:

> Acknowledgment of the principle of the right of the Iraqi people to reject occupation; recognition of the Iraqi resistance and its legitimate right to defend its country and its resources; rejection of terrorism which takes aim at innocent Iraqis, facilities and institutions of public utility, and places of worship—mosques, *husseiniyyat* [Shia religious centers], churches and all holy places.[169]

Many Iraqis blamed pro-U.S. forces and "false flag" operations for dramatic attacks on civilian targets like the bombing of the Golden Dome in Samarra in 2006.[170] The mainly Sunni tribe who were custodians of this Shiite shrine had faithfully protected and maintained the mosque for hundreds of years, and many Iraqis refused to believe that they or other Sunnis in Samarra could have been responsible for damaging it. The widespread Iraqi belief in "false flag" operations was

---

169. http://www.juancole.com/2005/03/achcar-allawis-offensive-gilbert.html
170. Dahr Jamail and Arkan Hamed, "Iraq: mosque outrage also brings solidarity," *Inter Press Service*, February 25 2006.

bolstered when two British SAS soldiers were arrested by police in Basra with bomb-making equipment in the trunk of their car.[71]

Most Americans are skeptical of such claims, but the history of U.S. "false flag" operations in Vietnam and elsewhere suggests that they warrant further investigation. Bill Taylor was a Marine Corps CID (Criminal Investigation Division) officer in Vietnam, who unwittingly found himself embroiled in a U.S. "false flag" operation. In July 1970, he personally witnessed a U.S. Army intelligence officer from the Phoenix program and a South Korean accomplice roll hand grenades under some bamboo skirting into an upscale café in Da Nang. Fourteen people were killed. Thirty were injured.

Taylor chased and arrested the perpetrators. Within hours though, the killers were set free, even as reports of the "Viet Cong" attack on the restaurant poured in to CID headquarters. Bill Taylor found himself placed under guard, "for his own safety", and was quickly flown out of Vietnam back to the U.S. He was relieved of his gun and accompanied on the flights by a succession of agents, one of whom was dressed as a U.S. Navy chaplain. He was debriefed at Camp Lejeune in North Carolina and ordered not to tell anyone about the incident. Twenty years later, he described his experience to Douglas Valentine, who included his story in a comprehensive history of the Phoenix program. [72]

Iraqi resistance during the first few months of occupation was characterized mainly by non-violent street demonstrations in many cities. The history of resistance in Fallujah began with a demonstration against U.S. forces who had commandeered a local school. On April 28th 2003, local residents marched to the school to demand its return so that their children could go to school again. They were confronted by armed paratroopers blocking their way, somebody threw a stone,

---

171. http://www.wsws.org/articles/2005/oct2005/basr-021.shtml

172. Douglas Valentine, *The Phoenix Program*, (New York: William Morrow, 1990), 357-361.

and all hell broke loose. The Americans killed at least 13 people and wounded many more.[173]

When Sami Ramadan, an Iraqi sociologist teaching in London, visited his native Baghdad in September 2003, he found people angry at the occupation and its brutality, and ready to support armed resistance. But he also found a common feeling that armed resistance was "premature," and that peaceful, political means could be more effective in ending the occupation. Ramadan believed that the growing violence in central Iraq, which the Americans now dubbed "the Sunni triangle," had been deliberately initiated by the Americans to send a message of terror to the larger populations in Baghdad and the South. As he noted, "They provoked conflict by killing civilians in cold blood in Fallujah, Mosul, Ramadi and elsewhere long before any armed resistance in those areas."[174]

By November 2003, even Paul Bremer accepted the conclusions of a CIA assessment that armed resistance was growing; that more and more Iraqis believed it could succeed in ending the occupation; and that greater violence by the occupation forces was likely to increase popular support for the Resistance rather than suppress it. The CIA also warned that resistance in mainly Sunni communities in central Iraq could easily spread to predominantly Shiite populations in Sadr City and the South, implying that stoking sectarian differences into mutual hostility was the only way to prevent unified resistance.[175]

This report from November 2003 sheds light on Seymour Hersh's reporting on the new U.S. Special Forces assassination campaign in December 2003. Clearly a high-level decision was made to take the risk of

---

173. Sarah Left, "U.S. troops kill 13 Iraqi protesters," *The Guardian*, April 29 2003.
174. Sami Ramadani, "Patriots and invaders," *The Guardian*, September 27 2003.
175. Jonathan S. Landay, "More Iraqis supporting resistance, CIA report says," *Knight Ridder Newspapers*, November 11 2003.
http://www.mcclatchydc.com/reports/intelligence/story/10108.html

escalating violence by launching an extremely widespread campaign of state-sponsored terrorism, to terrorize opponents of the occupation, but also to drive a wedge between people of different sects and ethnicities to forestall united resistance. And of course, the effect was as predicted, a deadly spiral of growing resistance and even more violent state terrorism. In fact, at the time of the CIA report in November 2003, attacks against occupation forces had only risen to 35 per day, as opposed to 150 per day over the next three years. And only 400 Americans had died in Iraq by November 2003. If the U.S. government had seriously weighed the CIA's report and been willing to cut its losses, the U.N. could have supervised a restoration of sovereignty and legitimacy before most of the bloodshed and destruction of the years that followed and before the occupation created gaping fissures in the fabric of Iraqi society.

During the first American attack on Fallujah in April 2004, the Shiite Mahdi Army sent a small unit to fight alongside the local Sunni Arab resistance, and people all over Iraq donated relief supplies to help the beleaguered people in the city. Muqtada al-Sadr hailed these shows of unity, "You are witnessing the union of Sunnis and Shiites toward an independent Iraq, free of terror and occupation. This is a lofty goal ... Our sentiments are the same, our goal is one, and our enemy is one. We say yes, yes to unity, yes to the closing of ranks, combating terror and ousting the infidel West from our sacred lands."[176]

Resistance to the occupation was not motivated by sectarianism, and local people of different sects fought together in many parts of the country. But after the American attack on Najaf in August 2004, American military operations concentrated on Sunni Arab areas, while permitting Shiite groups like the Mahdi Army to control Sadr City and much of southern Iraq. By choosing its own targets on a sectarian and

---

176. Anthony Shadid, *Night Draws Near*, (New York: Picador, 2007), 449.

regional basis, American strategy did succeed in one respect, and that was in preventing the whole country from uniting in a coordinated national resistance movement.

Another part of the U.S. response to growing armed resistance and rising American casualties was to withdraw its forces from the effort to occupy Iraqi cities, shifting instead to a strategy of punitive strikes and raids launched from fortified bases. When the Americans and British gave up the effort to occupy critical urban areas, local resistance groups took charge: the Mahdi Army in Sadr City, Amara, Najaf and Kufa; and other local resistance groups in Fallujah, Ramadi, Samarra, Mosul, Basra, and most of Baghdad.

March 25th 2004 was a critical turning point for the Iraqi Resistance. On that day, Paul Bremer announced that U.S. forces would not be leaving Iraq following the nominal transfer of power to an interim Iraqi government in June 2004. In addition, the U.S. would take control of any Iraqi forces recruited by the new government: "All trained elements of the Iraqi armed forces shall at all times be under the operational control of the commander of Coalition forces for the purpose of conducting combined operations." The U.S. would also retain control of all money appropriated for "reconstruction," and would retain fourteen military bases that were already under construction. Combined with effective control over the political process in the Green Zone, these measures were designed to ensure that the nominal transfer of power would not diminish the ability of the U.S. government to pursue its own goals in Iraq regardless of the interests and the will of the Iraqi people.[177]

If armed resistance seemed premature to many Iraqis in September 2003, this was no longer the case following this announcement six

177. John Burns and Thom Shanker, "U.S. officials fashion legal basis to keep force in Iraq," *New York Times*, March 26 2004.

months later. Resistance spread like wildfire. It was soon no longer safe for Westerners to travel through most of Iraq. Following the death and mutilation of four Blackwater mercenaries in Fallujah, the Americans launched a full-scale attack on the city. They also tried to capture Muqtada al Sadr in Kufa before the official end of the occupation, but they failed on both fronts. After installing Allawi as interim prime minister, they attacked Najaf and Fallujah again in August. U.S. forces drove the Mahdi Army out of Najaf but did not dare to challenge its control in Sadr City. Fallujah was subjected to heavy aerial bombardment in August, but this went largely unreported as the Western media focused on the battle in Najaf.

Much has been written about the composition of the Iraqi Resistance in the Western media, interpreting it through the lenses of sectarianism, Baathism, Islamism, factionalism, tribalism, and Middle Eastern politics. While the degrees and forms of resistance fluctuated among different sectors of Iraqi society over what became a lengthy period of American occupation, the central and consistent feature was resistance to foreign occupation. The American effort to exterminate Chomsky's "independent nationalism" with the products of Eisenhower's "military-industrial complex" was met by Camus' "total resistance."

In February 2005, I wrote, "The United States government is choosing to continue the war in an increasingly desperate effort to set up a government that will support U.S. interests, and to recruit forces that will fight for it against Islamists and other opponents. The greatest danger facing Iraq today is that the United States will be partially successful in building and arming such a force and that, with U.S. support, this force will continue to wage war against its own people, gradually destroying what is left of the country."[178]

---

178. Nicolas J. S. Davies, "Whose war is this anyway?," *Z Magazine*, April 2005.

Tragically, this is more or less what happened. The 60% unemployment rate caused by the dismantling of state industries and public institutions made it possible to recruit young men to the puppet government's armed forces and to *ad hoc* auxiliary forces under U.S. command. Many Iraqis recruited to these forces also used their weapons and training to take part in resistance operations, and U.S.-led Iraqi forces had high attrition rates, with large quantities of weapons and equipment transferred to the resistance and the black market. However, the partial success of U.S. recruitment efforts played a deadly role in the continuation and escalation of the war.

Both the creation of widespread unemployment and the recruitment of native occupation forces are classic techniques of military occupation that are prohibited by the Fourth Geneva Convention. Article 52 states, "All measures aiming at creating unemployment or at restricting the opportunities offered to workers in an occupied territory, in order to induce them to work for the occupying Power, are prohibited." And Article 51 includes the provision, "The Occupying Power may not compel protected persons to serve in its armed or auxiliary forces. No pressure or propaganda which aims at securing voluntary enlistment is permitted."

One can debate whether U.S. actions in Iraq fell strictly under these prohibitions, but it is more important to understand that U.S. tactics in Iraq fell clearly into patterns that are common to occupying powers throughout history and constitute behavior that the world has tried to outlaw, along with its deadly and dangerous consequences. The transient effects of U.S. political efforts to win over or exploit different sectors of Iraqi society at different times in order to divide and rule the country destroyed it both physically and socially. But they failed to decide the ultimate outcome of the war. By achieving the gradual, total and irreversible alienation of almost the entire population, they instead ensured the ultimate failure of the American adventure in Iraq.

Surveys of the views of people in Iraq made this obvious. The proportion of Iraqis who "supported the presence of coalition forces in Iraq" fell from 39% in February 2004 to 21% by September 2007. Amongst Sunni Arabs, it fell to 2%. There was no intermediate period when this trend was reversed—including during the 2007 "surge" of American troops and propaganda, which 70% of Iraqis said made their security worse rather than better. Approval for attacks on "U.S.-*led* forces" (not specifically excluding Iraqi forces) rose to 61% by September 2006. Amongst Sunni Arabs, it rose to 92%.

Already in January 2006, 87% of Iraqis agreed with the position later adopted by the Iraqi Council of Representatives that foreign troops should only remain in Iraq if there was a firm timeline for their withdrawal. And yet 78% of Iraqis told a PIPA poll in September 2006 that they did not believe the United States would comply with an order by the Iraqi government to withdraw all its forces. In another survey in March 2007, only 4% of Shiites and 7% of people in central Iraq believed that the security situation in Iraq would get worse in the weeks following a withdrawal of U.S. forces. In the September 2006 PIPA poll, 78% of Iraqis agreed with the statement that "the U.S. military in Iraq is currently provoking more conflict than it is preventing."[179]

In fact, the only periods of peace that most cities in Iraq enjoyed during the first five years of occupation were when the Iraqi Resistance succeeded in expelling American and other occupation forces from Fallujah, Sadr City, Basra and elsewhere. While resistance forces were unable to gain access to funding from the central government that would have enabled them to rebuild the areas under their control, they were at least able to provide law and order, to restore basic levels of local government and public services, and to defend their communities

---

179. http://www.globalpolicy.org/security/issues/iraq/pollindex.htm

against American attacks by organizing local resistance and mining roads.

If only one thing is clear as I write this in 2010, it is that, for as long as U.S. forces and officials remain in Iraq, they will meet resistance. There is no political or military "solution" that can reconcile the people of Iraq to their invasion, subjugation, and subservience to American interests. Any Iraqis who ally themselves with the Americans will always be seen as collaborators or traitors by most of their countrymen and be unable to live safely in Iraq. Former Iraqi Governing Council member Ali Allawi, who kept his day-job as a lecturer at Oxford University, told Terry Gross of *National Public Radio* in January 2008 that he could not travel inside Iraq without at least fifteen bodyguards. And neither Ayad Allawi nor Ibrahim al-Jaafari ever risked moving their families back to Iraq, even as they served as Prime Ministers in the interim and transitional occupation governments. Both of them soon rejoined their families in London.

A common complaint about the Iraqi Governing Council was that it couldn't accomplish anything because its members were always scattered around the world cutting business deals with foreign companies looking for a piece of the action in the new Iraq. The new Iraqi Council of Representatives elected in 2005 was likewise hamstrung by the fact that so many of its members were exiles who did not really live in Iraq. Since it could barely make a quorum on a good day, a walk-out by one party could usually shut it down completely. Many of America's Iraqi allies behaved even worse than the taxi-driver predicted—they came and filled their pockets, but they didn't even stay in Iraq to spend the profits. In effect, they used the hostile foreign occupation of their own country to feather their nests in exile.

The tragedy of all such situations throughout history is that so many people who did nothing to bring about this crisis were forced to confront it by forces far beyond their own control. Like the *refractaires* in

France in 1944 who joined the Resistance as an alternative to being passively rounded up and enslaved, Iraqis who chose resistance over collaboration were making a rational choice. They could face misery and death either as passive victims or as active combatants, but the latter course at least offered them some measure of dignity and autonomy. The rest of the world owes such people the only kind of support and protection that can invalidate the rationale for armed resistance—the genuine restoration of legitimacy, sovereignty, independence and self-determination to them and their country.

CHAPTER 10. TORTURE AND IMPUNITY

In February 2006, Rear Admiral John D. Hutson, the former Judge Advocate General of the United States Navy, wrote a preface to "Command's Responsibility," a report by Human Rights First on 98 deaths in U.S. custody in Iraq and Afghanistan:

> Command's Responsibility documents a dozen brutal deaths as the result of the most horrific treatment. One such incident would be an isolated transgression; two would be a serious problem; a dozen of them is policy. The law of military justice has long recognized that military leaders are held responsible for the conduct of their troops. Yet this report also documents that no civilian official or officer above the rank of major responsible for interrogation and detention practices has been charged in connection with the torture or abuse-related death of a detainee in U.S. custody. And the highest punishment for anyone handed down in the case of a torture-related death has been five months in jail. This is not accountability as we know it in the United States."[180]

As a military lawyer, when Admiral Hutson refers to "accountability, as we know it in the United States," he is referring to the Uniform Code of Military Justice, which applies to Americans serving in the U.S. military and to U.S. Federal Law, which is binding on all Americans, civilian or military. In 1996, the United States Congress passed the War Crimes Act, which codifies the consequences of violating the Geneva Conventions in U.S. Federal Law. Here is the text of the War Crimes Act:

> Sec. 2441. War crimes
>
> (a) Offense.— Whoever, whether inside or outside the United States, commits a war crime, in any of the circumstances described in subsection (b), shall be fined under this title or imprisoned for life or any term of years, or both, and if

---

180. Human Rights First, *Command's Responsibility*, February 2006. http://www.humanrightsfirst.info/pdf/06221-etn-hrf-dic-rep-web.pdf

death results to the victim, shall also be subject to the penalty of death.

(b) Circumstances.— The circumstances referred to in subsection (a) are that the person committing such war crime or the victim of such war crime is a member of the Armed Forces of the United States or a national of the United States (as defined in section 101 of the Immigration and Nationality Act).

(c) Definition.— As used in this section the term "war crime" means any conduct—

(1) defined as a grave breach in any of the international conventions signed at Geneva 12 August 1949, or any protocol to such convention to which the United States is a party;

(2) prohibited by Article 23, 25, 27, or 28 of the Annex to the Hague Convention IV, Respecting the Laws and Customs of War on Land, signed 18 October 1907;

(3) which constitutes a violation of common Article 3 of the international conventions signed at Geneva, 12 August 1949, or any protocol to such convention to which the United States is a party and which deals with non-international armed conflict; or

(4) of a person who, in relation to an armed conflict and contrary to the provisions of the Protocol on Prohibitions or Restrictions on the Use of Mines, Booby-Traps and Other Devices as amended at Geneva on 3 May 1996 (Protocol II as amended on 3 May 1996), when the United States is a party to such Protocol, willfully kills or causes serious injury to civilians.[181]

Whether prisoners of U.S. forces in Iraq are defined as prisoners of war or as prisoners in a "conflict not of an international character," the Geneva Conventions directly address their status, and provide very similar protections in either case. Article 17 of the 3rd Geneva Convention

---

181. http://assembler.law.cornell.edu/uscode/18/2441.html

states that "No physical or mental torture, nor any other form of coercion, may be inflicted on prisoners of war to secure from them information of any kind whatever. Prisoners of war who refuse to answer may not be threatened, insulted, or exposed to unpleasant or disadvantageous treatment of any kind."[182]

Common Article 3 of the Geneva Conventions, which covers "conflict not of an international character" states that, "the following acts are and shall remain prohibited at any time and in any place whatsoever" with respect to detainees and most other people:

> (a) violence to life and person, in particular murder of all kinds, mutilation, cruel treatment and torture; (b) taking of hostages; (c) outrages upon personal dignity, in particular, humiliating and degrading treatment; (d) the passing of sentences and the carrying out of executions without previous judgment pronounced by a regularly constituted court affording all the judicial guarantees which are recognized as indispensable by civilized peoples.

The passage of the 1996 U.S. War Crimes Act was in fact a tardy fulfillment of America's obligations under these Conventions. Article 146 of Fourth Geneva begins: "The high Contracting Parties undertake to enact any legislation necessary to provide effective penal sanctions for persons committing, or ordering to be committed, any of the grave breaches of the present Convention defined in the following article." It goes on to require each party to "bring such persons ... before its own courts" or "hand such persons over for trial to another."

The reference to "grave" breaches of the Conventions in the U.S. War Crimes Act and in this article refer to definitions in Article 130 of the Third Geneva Convention and Article 147 of the Fourth Geneva Convention. These articles designate certain violations as "grave" breaches of the Conventions: "torture or inhumane treatment, includ-

---

182. http://www.icrc.org/ihl.nsf/CONVPRES?OpenView

ing biological experiments, willfully causing great suffering or serious injury to body or health, unlawful deportation or transfer or unlawful confinement of a protected person, compelling a protected person to serve in the forces of a hostile Power, or willfully depriving a protected person of the rights of fair and regular trial prescribed in the present Convention, taking of hostages and extensive destruction and appropriation of property, not justified by military necessity and carried out unlawfully and wantonly."

While the public revelations of abuse and torture at Abu Ghraib prison in Baghdad created a brief and localized furor in the United States in 2004, the International Committee of the Red Cross, Human Rights First, Amnesty International, Human Rights Watch, and other human rights groups documented far more widespread and systematic crimes committed by U.S. forces against people they extra-judicially detained in Iraq. In numerous human rights reports, they established that command responsibility for these crimes extended to the highest levels of the U.S. government and its armed forces.

The forms of torture documented in these reports included death threats; mock executions; near-drowning or "water-boarding"; "stress positions," including excruciating and sometimes deadly forms of hanging; hypothermia; sleep deprivation; starvation and thirst; withholding medical treatment; electric shocks; various forms of rape and sodomy; endless beatings; burning; cutting with knives; injurious use of flexi-cuffs; suffocation; sensory assault and/or deprivation; and more psychological forms of torture such as sexual humiliation and the detention and torture of family members.

The International Committee of the Red Cross attempted to fulfill its legitimate function by inspecting detention facilities, interviewing prisoners, and intervening in a confidential manner with the U.S. government to end abuses it discovered in Iraq. However, by February 2004, ICRC personnel were so shocked by the treatment they found and the failure of U.S. forces to grant access as required and to correct problems they identified, that somebody, presumably an ICRC employee, took the extraordinary step of leaking one of its reports to the *Wall Street Journal*.[183]

Based on 27 visits to 14 facilities, the ICRC had established that the violations of international humanitarian law that it recorded were systematic and widespread. In spite of the infrequency of its visits, its staff personally witnessed two incidents in which guards shot Iraqi prisoners with live ammunition. They documented four more such incidents, including the one reported by Aidan Delgado at Abu Ghraib. It seems likely that many other similar incidents were not reported to the ICRC. The American and British authorities did investigate each of these six incidents, but "concluded in all cases that a legitimate use of firearms had been made." The ICRC disagreed: "In all cases, less extreme measures could have been used to quell the demonstrations or neutralize persons deprived of their liberty trying to escape." The exoneration of all involved in these incidents demonstrated that such behavior was, as Admiral Hutson suggested, a matter of policy rather than a series of isolated transgressions.

Military intelligence officers told the ICRC that "between 70% and 90% of the persons deprived of their liberty in Iraq had been arrested by mistake," which was consistent with many other reports. Nevertheless, the ICRC found a common pattern of abuse and torture, in which the abuse of arrested Iraqis began during their arrest and transport to the prisons and continued throughout their detention. Many suffered death or injury during their arrest or transportation. Most were not informed of the reason for their arrest, and it often took their families many frightful months to find out whether they were still alive and where they were being held. In 2010, tens of thousands of Iraqi families

---

183. http://www.informationclearinghouse.info/pdf/icrc_iraq.pdf

still had no news of loved ones arrested years ago by U.S. or Iraqi occupation forces. Many had their homes ransacked and vandalized, or were threatened with death, transfer to Guantanamo, or sexual abuse of their female relatives. Standard practices included taking people away in pajamas or underwear; confiscating or stealing their belongings, including cars and large sums of money; hooding; tight flexi-cuffing to the point of injury; severe beating and kicking; verbal abuse; and all kinds of humiliation.

During interrogation, these abuses were accentuated. For as long as four days on end, prisoners were kept naked, hooded, blindfolded, in flexi-cuffs, "which were sometimes made so tight and used for such extended periods that they caused skin lesions and long-term after-effects on the hands (nerve damage), as observed by the ICRC." Prisoners were "attached repeatedly over several days, for several hours each time, with handcuffs to the bars of their cell door in humiliating (i.e. naked or in underwear) and/or uncomfortable position[s] causing physical pain."

Techniques of interrogation included "pressing the face into the ground with boots;" "food or water deprivation;" death threats; "beatings with hard objects (including pistols and rifles), slapping, punching, kicking with knees or feet on various parts of the body (legs, sides, lower back, groin);" "solitary confinement combined with threats;" and "prolonged exposure while hooded to the sun over several hours, including during the hottest time of the day when temperatures could reach 50 degrees Celsius (122 degrees Fahrenheit) or higher." Also, "a 61-year-old person deprived of his liberty alleged that he had been tied, hooded and forced to sit on the hot surface of what he surmised to be the engine of a vehicle, which had caused severe burns to his buttocks. The victim had lost consciousness. The ICRC observed large crusted lesions consistent with his allegation."

The ICRC cited specific articles of the Geneva Conventions and other international humanitarian law that the occupation forces were violating and concluded, "The practices described in this report are prohibited under International Humanitarian Law. They warrant serious attention by the CF (coalition forces). In particular, the CF should review their policies and practices, take corrective action and improve the treatment of prisoners of war and other protected persons under their authority."

As with the CIA report on popular resistance in Iraq in November 2003, heeding this ICRC report after less than a year of war could have prevented a great deal of additional death, pain, and suffering. However, as later eyewitnesses and human rights reports demonstrated, torture continued at Abu Ghraib until at least the end of 2005. The U.S. government's response to the scandal was to confront it as a public relations problem, while refining and even expanding the atrocities it revealed, delegating a significant role in the escalation of torture and terror to its Iraqi allies. The American reign of terror in Iraq was just beginning and it was not to be derailed by what U.S. leaders perceived primarily as a public relations problem.

At the time of the ICRC report in February 2004, General Antonio Taguba was already conducting an internal inquiry into atrocities at Abu Ghraib for the U.S. Army.[184] On May 6 2004, he met with Secretary Rumsfeld, Under-Secretary Cambone and senior officers at the Pentagon. Asked whether what he had found constituted torture or merely abuse, Taguba described, "a naked detainee lying on the wet floor, handcuffed, with an interrogator shoving things up his rectum," and told them, "That's not abuse. That's torture."[185]

184. http://www.humanrightsfirst.org/us_law/800th_MP_Brigade_MASTER14_Mar_04-dc.pdf
185. Seymour M. Hersh, "The General's report," *The New Yorker*, June 25 2007.

Taguba also obtained "a video of a male American soldier in uniform sodomizing a female detainee," which was not made public or discussed in any subsequent inquiries. In fact, in spite of Taguba's actual video and photographs of sodomy taking place at Abu Ghraib, an inquiry into allegations of atrocities by U.S. special forces at Camp Nama at Baghdad Airport conducted by General Richard Formica in November 2004 concluded that detainees who reported being sodomized were seeking sympathy and better treatment and therefore were not credible. An interrogator who worked for several months at Camp Nama in 2004 told Human Rights Watch that neither the Army's Criminal Investigation Division nor the ICRC were ever given access to that facility. When he asked the colonel in charge about the ICRC, the colonel told him that he "had this directly from General McChrystal (Commander, Joint Special Operations Command) and the Pentagon that there's no way that the Red Cross could get in." In spite of being responsible for facilities where torture was documented in Iraq, General McChrystal was later placed in command of all U.S. forces in Afghanistan."[186]

Human Rights First's "Command's Responsibility" report made it clear that, in spite of the great variety of torture techniques used in U.S. prisons and camps in Iraq, most of the people who were tortured to death in those facilities were killed by a variant of the same method: the combined effects of broken ribs and other injuries from savage beatings followed by asphyxiation caused by some form of hanging or suffocation.

The court martial of Chief Warrant Officer Eric Welshofer for the murder of Major General Abed Mowhoush is the most thoroughly documented case in the report.[187] Mowhoush surrendered to U.S. forces on November 10th 2003. U.S. forces had detained his four sons a week

---

186. Human Rights Watch, *No Blood No Foul: Soldiers' Accounts of Detainee Abuse in Iraq*, July 2006. http://www.hrw.org/reports/2006/us0706/
187. *Command's Responsibility*, 6.

or two earlier, and their interrogators explicitly told them that they were being held as hostages to force their father to turn himself in. Mowhoush was told that they would be released when he surrendered, but they were not, and Welshofer even staged a mock execution of his 15-year-old youngest son as part of his interrogation. CWO Welshofer supervised most of Mowhoush's interrogation, but also brought in CIA and special forces personnel to "interrogate Mowhoush and beat the crap out of him" with sledgehammer handles, according to court martial testimony.

Welshofer testified at length to orders that he could ignore the Geneva Conventions, even in the case of this Iraqi general who was clearly either a prisoner of war or a protected person under the Fourth Geneva Convention. In late August 2003, a memo from a captain in his chain of command stated that there were no specific rules of engagement for interrogations and that Centcom officials "were still struggling with the basic definition of a detainee." In the meantime, detainees were to be considered "unprivileged combatants," not entitled to Geneva Convention protections.

On September 10th 2003, Lieutenant General Ricardo Sanchez, the U.S. Army commander in Iraq, specifically authorized sleep and environmental manipulation as well as the use of aggressive dogs and "stress positions." Welshofer explained at his court martial that nothing in his training gave any definition to the term "stress positions," so he relied on techniques that he had been taught to resist during SERE (survival, evasion, resistance, escape) training, based on the experiences of American prisoners of war in North Korea and Vietnam.

After other techniques were unsuccessful, he received permission from Major Jessica Voss to use a technique that they had already used on at least 12 other detainees. On November 26 2003, he stuffed Mowhoush headfirst into a sleeping bag, tied him with electrical cord, sat on his chest and blocked his nose and mouth. After clinching and kicking his legs "almost like he was being electrocuted," Mowhoush died of "asphyxia due to smothering and chest compression." The autopsy found that he also had five broken ribs. The MNF press release the following day stated that he had died of natural causes.

Welshofer was convicted of negligent homicide and negligent dereliction of duty. He was issued a written reprimand, ordered to pay a $6,000 fine and was restricted to home, base, and church for 60 days.[188] Neither Major Voss nor her superior, Colonel David Teeples, commander of the 3rd Armored Cavalry, who also approved the sleeping bag technique, were charged in Mowhoush's death, while General Sanchez has yet to face charges for any of the many crimes committed on his orders in Iraq.

Neither was Colonel Teeples charged with a crime in the death of Lieutenant Colonel Abdul Jameel. Teeples' men tried a different stress position on Jameel, hanging him by his arms from the top of his cell door with a gag in his mouth. They'd already broken twelve of his ribs, and fractured his throat, to say nothing of internal bleeding and numerous lacerations and contusions all over his body. Once he was "lifted to his feet by a baton held to his throat" and hung in the doorway, it only took five minutes for him to die.[189]

Manadel al-Jamadi died under CIA interrogation at Abu Ghraib on November 4 2003. He had six broken ribs and a bullet wound to the spleen, but was killed by an Israeli technique known as a "Palestinian hanging." He was detained by Navy SEALs and CIA personnel and taken to the "Romper Room" at Baghdad Airport, where he was doused with cold water, beaten, and tortured. At Abu Ghraib, he was a "ghost" prisoner, hidden from the ICRC. The Palestinian hanging involved a sort of crucifixion, hanging from a window frame with his arms out-

---

188. Josh White, "Army Interrogator Reprimanded in Iraqi's Death," *Washington Post*, January 24 2006, A2.

189. *Command's Responsibility*, 10.

stretched so that he could neither stand, sit, nor kneel without pain. His body was found with his arms "almost coming out of their sockets" and blood gushing from his mouth. Navy SEAL Lieutenant Andrew Ledford was acquitted of all charges in his death, and Mark Swanner, Jamadi's CIA interrogator at Abu Ghraib, was not charged and was still working for the CIA in 2006. Indeed, no CIA personnel have ever been charged in the deaths of prisoners in Iraq in spite of the CIA's leading role in many of these cases.[190]

Nagem Hatab also had six broken ribs when he died at a U.S. Marine prison camp near Nasiriyah in June 2003. After being badly beaten, including "karate kicks" to his body as he stood hooded and handcuffed, he was left lying in the sun covered in his own feces until he died. Hatab's body was so abused following his death that the autopsy findings and other medical evidence were ruled inadmissible to court martial proceedings against his killers, who all went free. Parts of his body were destroyed or lost, along with his medical records. His internal organs were destroyed by hours of exposure to the sun and heat on an airport runway.[191]

Dilar Dababa, 45 years old, also had a broken rib, 22 bruises and at least 50 abrasions, in addition to the brain hemorrhage that killed him, officially a "closed head injury with a cortical brain contusion and subdural hematoma." The autopsy record noted that "physical force was required to subdue the detainee, and during the restraining process, his forehead hit the ground." There is no official cause of death listed in military records, and nobody was charged with a crime in his death.[192]

Altogether, Human Rights First investigated 98 deaths in U.S. custody in Iraq and Afghanistan. Official U.S. records acknowledged that eight of these people were tortured to death, but only four of their

190. *Ibid.*, 11.
191. *Ibid.*, 12.
192. *Ibid.*, 22.

deaths resulted in punishment of any kind. Human Rights First identified four more confirmed torture deaths, making a total of at least twelve. Another 26 deaths were classified in official records as suspected or confirmed homicides. A total of 48 deaths in which the cause of death was "undetermined" or "unannounced" essentially escaped investigation, including the death of Dilar Dababa.

This pervasive lack of investigation was in spite of rules that require the Army's Criminal Investigation Division to take victim and eyewitness testimony within 24 hours of any death in military custody, to send out requests for lab work and coordination with other agencies within five days, and to keep extensive records. And yet, in 16 cases, evidence was simply not collected, resulting in no prosecution. In at least 12 cases, key witnesses were never interviewed. The shooting deaths of four prisoners at Abu Ghraib described earlier were not reported to CID for eight days. The death of Hadi al-Zubaidy at Camp Bucca was not reported for a year.

When cases did come before courts martial, the "astonishing" lack of evidence, as senior medical officer Brigadier General Stephen Xenakis called it, made conviction extremely difficult. But adjudicating officers faced another even more troubling dilemma: because the lower ranks charged with these crimes were acting under orders, it would have been unfair to punish them too harshly; and yet the more senior officers who gave the orders and were ultimately responsible for these crimes were never charged. These two factors, the lack of evidence and the failure to charge senior officers, largely accounted for the impunity and injustice that is abhorrent to military lawyers like Admiral Hutson.[193]

Going one step further, the "Command's Responsibility" report revealed that this failure to charge higher ranking officers was the direct

---

193. *Ibid.*, 35.

result of the "key role" that those same officers played "in undermining chances for full accountability." By delaying and undermining investigations of deaths in their custody, senior officers compounded their own criminal responsibility in a common pattern of torture, murder, and obstruction of justice. Senior officers abused the enormous power they wield in the military command structure to place themselves beyond the reach of the law, even as they gave orders to commit terrible crimes. It was in recognition of the terrible potential for exactly this type of criminal behavior that the Geneva Conventions were drafted and signed in the first place, and it is why they are just as vital today.

But responsibility for these crimes was not limited to Americans attempting or claiming to serve their country in uniform. The public record also includes documents in which senior civilian officials of the U.S. government approved violations of the Geneva conventions, the 1994 Convention against Torture and the 1996 U.S. War Crimes Act. These include memos, letters, and reports written and signed by Secretary of Defense Rumsfeld, Assistant Attorney General Jay Bybee, White House Legal Counsel Alberto Gonzalez, Deputy Assistant Attorney General John Yoo, Assistant Attorney General Jack Goldsmith, and a working group of Defense Department lawyers. And President Bush himself issued a directive on February 7th 2002 to treat "Al Qaeda and Taliban detainees" according to the standards of the Geneva Conventions only "to the extent appropriate and consistent with military necessity," claiming that absolute prohibitions on the torture and mistreatment of prisoners under U.S. and international law did not apply.

Documents in which other officials contradicted President Bush, Secretary Rumsfeld, and their cohorts of corrupt lawyers have also been made public. These include memos from Secretary of State Powell, State Department Legal Adviser William Taft, an FBI legal adviser, the Judge Advocate Generals of the U.S. Army, Navy and Marine Corps, and the Deputy JAG of the Air Force, all of which warned the U.S. government of the illegality and inadvisability of the policies that it was adopting.[194]

Human Rights First and the ACLU brought a civil suit in a U.S. Federal Court against Secretary Rumsfeld on behalf of nine torture victims in Iraq and Afghanistan, but it was dismissed on March 28 2007. The judge's ruling stated, "the facts alleged in the complaint stand as an indictment of the humanity with which the United States treats its detainees." The judge called the facts of the case "lamentable" and "appalling," but threw it out on grounds of lack of jurisdiction and official immunity from civil suits.[195]

One can only hope and demand that more of the crimes that resulted from these policies will eventually be adjudicated. Investigators must be permitted to follow the chain of command and to prosecute those who issued the illegal orders that led to crimes of murder and torture by American forces in Iraq. That is command responsibility as it was established at Nuremberg and as it has been codified in U.S. and international law for more than sixty years.

U.S. officials have argued that the more widespread existence of terrorism in the world today provides a justification for torture, ignoring the inevitable effect of these policies as a motivation for people all over the world to take up arms against the United States. In fact, by authorizing and committing torture, American officials undermined their own ability to gain the cooperation of other countries to apprehend suspected terrorists. Article 3 (1) of the 1984 Convention Against Torture states that, "No State Party shall expel, return or extradite a person to another country where there are substantial grounds for believing that he would be in danger of being subjected to torture."

---

194. Karen J. Greenberg, Joshua L. Dratel & Anthony Lewis, *The Torture Papers: The Road to Abu Ghraib*, (Cambridge: Cambridge University Press, 2005). Also http://www.humanrightsfirst.org/us_law/etn/gov_rep/gov_memo_intlaw.htm
195. http://www.humanrightsfirst.org/media/etn/2007/alert/321/index.htm

Thus any state that apprehends terrorism suspects is prohibited by international law from extraditing them to the United States, undermining precisely the kind of international cooperation that would be the cornerstone of any legitimate international counter-terrorism campaign. This raises familiar questions as to the real purpose of the so-called "war on terror". Is it really to counter terrorism by non-state actors or is it an opportunistic pretext for extreme forms of state terrorism by the United States? These two purposes are clearly at odds, linked only by a vicious cycle of violence and the war psychosis identified by Michael Howard.

Chapter 11. Massacre in Fallujah

Like the torture of Iraqi detainees, indiscriminate and excessive use of force in violation of international law was part and parcel of U.S. war policy in Iraq. This was documented by U.N. officials and human rights groups and supported by the eyewitness accounts of Iraqi civilians, journalists, and American soldiers. In November 2004, this policy climaxed in a desperate holocaust of collective punishment against the city and people of Fallujah.

There was a common pattern to the tactics used by American forces against cities and towns that successfully resisted the U.S. occupation. These tactics were not improvised. They were based on "rules of engagement" and "standard operating procedures." The fact that many of these tactics were prohibited by international treaties and customary international law did not prevent them from being used repeatedly and systematically. However, as with American torture policy, the pervasive and systematic nature of these crimes made it clear that criminal responsibility lay primarily with senior military and civilian officials who made these tactics an integral part of their overall strategy.

The assault on Fallujah in November 2004 was preceded by the aborted attack on the city in April 2004 and assaults on Najaf in August, Tal Afar in September and Samarra in October. In each case, cities were sealed off with concrete walls, earthen berms, and razor wire. In preparation for a later attack in 2005, Tal Afar was completely surrounded by an eight foot high, twelve mile long dirt wall.[196] Delivery of food, water, medicine, electricity, and communications to the besieged cities were either severely restricted or completely cut off. These restrictions were explicitly used as bargaining chips to try to persuade townspeople to hand over resistance fighters, as in a medieval siege. Civilians were told to leave, but those who did so risked arbitrary and indefinite extra-

---

196. http://www.whitehouse.gov/news/releases/2006/03/20060320-7.html

judicial detention when they passed through American checkpoints. The fact that civilians had been told to leave was then used as a justification for the use of excessive and indiscriminate force against those who remained.

Article 14 of the Second Protocol to the Geneva Conventions states that, "Starvation of civilians as a method of combat is prohibited. It is therefore prohibited to attack, destroy, remove, or render useless for that purpose objects indispensable to the survival of the civilian population such as food-stuffs, agricultural areas for the production of food-stuffs, crops, livestock, drinking water installations, and supplies and irrigation works." As I explained before, the United States has signed but not ratified the 1977 protocols to the Geneva Conventions and they constitute binding customary international law because 167 other countries have signed and ratified them.

And yet, such illegal tactics are an acknowledged part of U.S. military doctrine. As U.S. forces prepared to attack Fallujah, a professor at the Naval Postgraduate School in Monterey told the *San Francisco Chronicle* that civilians were being "encouraged" to leave Fallujah "by cutting off water and other supplies" as well as by aerial bombardment.[197] Thus starvation, deprivation, and aerial bombardment were used both as illegal means of forced evacuation from Fallujah and other resistance-held cities and then as forms of collective punishment against civilians who were unable or unwilling to leave. All of these tactics violated the laws of war.

In October 2005, Jean Ziegler, the U.N.'s Special Rapporteur on the Right to Food, declared, "A drama is taking place in total silence in Iraq, where the coalition's occupying forces are using hunger and de-

---

197. Matthew B. Stannard, "U.S., Iraqi troops mass for assault on Fallujah," *San Francisco Chronicle*, November 6, 2004.

privation of food or water as a weapon of war." He called this "a flagrant violation of international humanitarian law."[198]

The *Washington Post* reported that electricity and water were cut off to Fallujah in conjunction with a new wave of air strikes on October 14th 2004, the day before the beginning of Ramadan. The *Post* noted that the embargo was consistent with preparations for previous attacks against Najaf and Samarra. It also reported that Interim Prime Minister Ayad Allawi had approved the imminent U.S. assault on the city.[199]

U.S. forces ordered unembedded journalists to leave Fallujah. Reporters Without Borders had protested "the totally unacceptable imposition of an information blackout" in Najaf in August, pointing out that "the presence of journalists on the spot is indispensable, as the worst atrocities are always committed in the absence of witnesses."[200]

The U.S. bombardment of Fallujah continued for three weeks after the beginning of Ramadan. Civilians streamed out of the city, but males between the ages of 15 and 55 were not allowed to leave. They were either detained at check-points or turned back to remain trapped in the killing zone of the besieged and bombarded city. "We assume they'll go home and just wait out the storm or find a place that's safe," an American officer told the Associated Press. Colonel Michael Formica, the commander of the 2nd Brigade of the 1st Cavalry, instructed his soldiers to tell the men, "Stay in your houses, stay away from windows and stay off the roof and you'll live through Fallujah." U.S. officials did not offer

---

198. "UN food envoy says coalition breaking law in Iraq," *Reuters*, October 14 2005. http://www.globalpolicy.org/security/issues/iraq/attack/consequences/2005/1014food.htm

199. Karl Vick, "Fallujah strikes herald possible attack," *Washington Post*, October 16 2004.

200. *Reporters Without Borders*, "News blackout in Najaf deplored," August 15 2004.

any explanation for this policy. The apparent purpose of sending men and boys back into Fallujah was to kill them.[201]

On November 6th, U.N. Secretary General Kofi Annan told journalists that he had sent a letter to the American, British and Interim Iraqi governments, warning them of the probable consequences of a major assault on Fallujah. He expressed "increasing concern at the prospect of an escalation in violence, which I fear could be very disruptive for Iraq's political transition ... I have in mind not only the risk of increased insurgent violence, but also reports of major military offensives being planned by the multinational force in key localities such as Falluja. I wish to express to you my particular concern about the safety and protection of civilians. Fighting is likely to take place mostly in densely populated urban areas, with an obvious risk of civilian casualties ... The threat or actual use of force not only risks deepening the sense of alienation of certain communities, but would also reinforce perceptions among the Iraqi population of a continued military occupation ... This is the moment for redoubling efforts to break the cycle of violence and open a new chapter of inclusiveness and national reconciliation ... " Ayad Allawi called Annan "confused."[202]

At the same time, Matthew Stannard of the *San Francisco Chronicle* interviewed military experts about the coming assault. A U.S. Marine urban warfare expert, a marksmanship instructor at Camp Pendleton, and John Pike of *Global Security* all agreed that U.S. Marine snipers were to play a special role in the attack. "If we simply pulverize the city, it would look bad on TV," said John Pike. "If we can just get the people that can reconcile themselves to the new dispensation out of the way and then kill the few thousand people who can't reconcile themselves, then we can let the remaining 98% come back and live out their lives. If

---

201. "U.S. won't let men leave Fallujah," *Associated Press*, November 13 2004.
http://www.foxnews.com/story/0,2933,138376,00.html
202. http://news.bbc.co.uk/1/hi/world/middle_east/3987641.stm

we bomb the place to the ground, those peace-loving people won't have a home to live in."[203]

Perhaps John Pike failed to understand the scale of the aerial and artillery bombardment that was "shaping the environment," as another military expert put it, for the U.S. invasion of Fallujah. The city had been bombed intermittently since April. In September, an epidemiological survey team found large numbers of deaths from otherwise unreported air strikes in August. This suggested that the media's focus on Najaf was exploited to escalate the bombing of Fallujah while it was out of the spotlight. By the end of November's assault on Fallujah, only about 40% of its homes were inhabitable. John Pike must have been relieved that it did not "look bad on TV," but this was the result of censorship, not of restraint in the use of air strikes and artillery. Five years later, many of the peace-loving people of Fallujah still don't have a home to live in.

On the other hand, Pike was right that U.S. Marine snipers had been assigned a special role in the American strategy. The *Chronicle* reported that U.S. planners were dividing Fallujah into small sectors. Two to four man sniper teams would cover each sector. As marines went house by house, they would flush people out into the snipers' field of fire to be shot in the street. Pike said that a similar tactic had been used with "considerable success" during the aborted assault on the city in April, and the marksmanship instructor told the Chronicle that snipers were trained to distinguish civilians from "insurgents."

However, journalists and other witnesses to the first "Battle of Fallujah" had already provided a more realistic view of what the residents of Fallujah could expect at the hands of U.S. Marine snipers. Journalist Dahr Jamail and human rights activist Jo Wilding accompanied a medi-

---

203. Matthew B. Stannard, "U.S., Iraqi troops mass for assault on Fallujah," *San Francisco Chronicle*, November 6 2004.

cal relief mission into Fallujah during that attack. They stayed at the Nazzal emergency clinic, one of the only two functioning medical facilities in the city. They witnessed a heartbreaking stream of wounded and dying people arriving at the clinic. Most of them told very similar stories of being shot by American snipers when they left the safety of their homes to seek food, water, or other necessities.[204]

The clinic had run out of anesthetics. While Jamail and Wilding were there, the generator ran out of fuel, leaving the doctors to perform operations without anaesthetics and lit by flashlights and cigarette lighters. Without electricity or many needed medicines, many of the victims were beyond the help of the small medical team. A brother and sister, aged ten and eighteen, were brought in with internal injuries and a head-wound from shots fired by an American sniper. They were dispatched in an ambulance to a hospital in Baghdad, but they both died on the way. A grandmother and her grandson were both shot by a sniper as she tried to escort a group of children to safety. She lay in a bed in the clinic, still clutching the white flag she had been carrying.

When Jamail finally had a chance to sit down and interview Maki al-Nazzal, the director of the clinic, he told him, "They say there is a cease-fire. They said twelve o'clock, so people went out to do some shopping. Everybody who went out was shot and this place was full, and half of them were dead." Twenty bodies were brought to the clinic during the twenty-four hours of the "cease-fire." Wilding went out to try and distribute medical supplies and was fired on twice by American snipers, once while on foot and once in an ambulance.[205] One of the ambulance drivers refused to go out again after a sniper's bullet grazed his head inside his ambulance. Attacks on ambulances are serious war-

---

204. Dahr Jamail, *Beyond the Green Zone*, (Chicago: Haymarket Books, 2007), 127 - 141.
205. Jo Wilding, "Getting aid past US snipers is impossible," *The Guardian*, April 17, 2004.

crimes under the First and Fourth Geneva Conventions and other international humanitarian laws.

On November 6th, the Nazzal emergency clinic, where Jamail and Wilding had stayed in April, was bombed to the ground, killing doctors, staff, and patients, and leaving only the front wall of the building standing.[206]

As U.S. Marines prepared to invade the city on November 8th, there was a night of even heavier aerial and artillery bombardment, destroying a railway station and an apartment complex among other targets.

Fallujah Hospital, across the river from the city, was seized early that night by U.S. forces, accompanied by members of the 36th Commando Battalion, an Iraqi "political" unit recruited and trained by the Americans. This battalion was originally comprised of about 220 Kurdish Peshmerga militiamen, and about 110 members each from three exile groups: the Iranian-trained Badr Brigades, Ayad Allawi's Iraqi National Accord and Ahmed Chalabi's Iraqi National Congress. By November 2004, about half the exiles had abandoned the unit, leaving it dominated by Kurdish militiamen. The role of this predominantly Kurdish force in the American attack on Fallujah quickly led to retaliatory violence against Kurds in Mosul as new fighting broke out there.[207]

American military statements justified the occupation of the hospital on the basis that it was under the control of the Resistance and "was being used as a center for enemy propaganda to inflate the number of civilian casualties." But the occupation forces met no resistance as they moved in to occupy it, and hospital officials assured journalists that they had been operating without interference until the arrival of U.S. forces. The hospital staff saw the occupation of the hospital as an

---

206. "US strike razes Fallujah hospital," *BBC*, November 6 2004.
http://news.bbc.co.uk/1/hi/world/middle_east/3988433.stm
207 ."Who are Iraq's 36th?," *Defense Tech*, November 8 2004.
http://www.defensetech.org/archives/001189.html

American psychological warfare operation to prevent the reporting of civilian casualties. Cutting off access to the city's main hospital for the civilian population was an apparently acceptable consequence of this operation for the Americans.

Another medical facility, the Central Health Centre, was destroyed by three American bombs at 5:30 a.m. on November 9th. Dr. Sami al-Jumaili, one of the survivors of the attack, had escaped from Fallujah Hospital when it was occupied, and was working at the clinic that morning. He reported that 35 out of about 60 patients were killed in the attack, including five children under the age of ten. Twenty-four of the staff were killed, including at least four doctors, Doctors Abbas, Rabia, al-Kubaissy and Sheriff. Dr. al-Ani, who also worked at Fallujah Hospital, arrived at the clinic soon after the attack and corroborated Dr. al-Jumaili's story that the entire structure had collapsed on the patients.[208]

Dr. al-Jumaili told Reuters, "There is not a single surgeon in Fallujah. We had one ambulance hit by U.S. fire and a doctor wounded ... There are scores of injured civilians in their homes whom we can't move. A 13-year-old child just died in my hands."[209] Hamid Salaman of Fallujah Hospital confirmed the attack on the ambulance and told the Associated Press that the driver and five patients were killed in that attack.

On November 11th, an Emergency Working Group convened by the U.N. in Amman issued its first report on the crisis in Fallujah. It reported that about 50,000 civilians were still trapped in the city when the attack began. No humanitarian relief convoys were getting into Fallujah, and the nationwide Emergency Law had closed border crossings to Red Cross shipments from abroad. The U.N. Assistance Mission for

---

208. Miles Schuman, "Falluja's Health Damage," *The Nation*, December 13, 2004.
209. "Fallujah residents say clinic bombed," *Associated Press*, November 9 2004.

Iraq had eventually negotiated the entry of 50,000 blood bags at the Jordanian border, and the EWG demanded that U.S. forces permit delivery of these and other medical aid to Fallujah.[210]

The Red Cross reported on November 9th that 2,000 to 3,000 families were now stranded in the open in the city with neither shelter, food, water, nor protection from bombardment and ground fire. The EWG assumed that this number had increased by the 11th and would continue to do so. A secondary humanitarian crisis was already developing amongst the hundreds of thousands of people displaced from the city, most of whom were now in refugee camps in Saqlawiyah, Amiriyah, and Nieamiyah. They needed at least 4,000 tons of food. A lot of food had been stockpiled inside Fallujah, but this was now either destroyed or inaccessible. The refugees were also suffering from severe shortages of water and sanitation.

Fallujah Hospital was still functioning, albeit under military occupation, but the numbers of wounded reaching it through the gauntlet of fire was very small, and its occupation by hostile forces obviously discouraged people from seeking refuge there. According to Dr. Chiad, the hospital's director, U.S. authorities denied repeated requests to send doctors, ambulances, and medical supplies into the city. The hospital remained virtually empty as thousands of people died in the streets of Fallujah just across the bridge.[211] The EWG stated that "agencies report their stocks of emergency items are good, and their principal concerns relate to security, access, and International Humanitarian Law issues."

On November 16th, Louise Arbour, the U.N. High Commissioner for Human Rights and the former Chief Prosecutor of the War Crimes Tribunal for Yugoslavia, issued a statement that "There have been a num-

---

210. "Emergency Working Group - Falluja Crisis Update Note," *United Nations Assistance Mission for Iraq,* November 11 2004.
http://www.uniraq.org/documents/Falluja%20Bulletin%2011%20November.pdf
211. Miles Schuman, "Falluja's Health Damage," *The Nation,* December 13 2004.

ber of reports during the current confrontation, alleging violations of the rules of war designed to protect civilians and combatants." She demanded an investigation of alleged abuses, including the disproportionate use of force and the targeting of civilians and that those responsible for these violations "should be brought to justice."[212]

As in other cities under attack, allegations of flagrant violations of the laws of war were directly linked to the "rules of engagement" issued to U.S. forces. Embedded journalist Kevin Sites of *NBC News* reported that most of Fallujah was declared a "weapons-free" zone and explained that, "Weapons-free means the marines can shoot whatever they see—it's all considered hostile."[213] Sites' interpretation of this seemingly ambiguous term was confirmed by Matt Howard of the 1st Marine Division, who took part in the invasion of Iraq in 2003. He told a town hall meeting in Burlington, Vermont, "You can only shoot someone under certain terms, if they were wearing a uniform or carrying a weapon. Weapons-free meant you could shoot anyone."[214]

During the U.S. War in Vietnam, the American public became familiar with the term "free-fire zone." It became widely known that thousands of civilians had been killed and wounded by American forces operating under these flagrantly illegal rules of engagement. The U.S. military responded to evidence of criminal rules of engagement in Vietnam, not by reforming its policies, but by changing its terminology. U.S. officials can claim that there are no free-fire zones in Iraq, but a "weapons-free" zone means exactly the same thing. It's the same difference as the one between Mark 77 fire bombs and Vietnam-era Napalm-

212. "Human rights chief calls for probe of abuses in Fallujah," *United Nations Radio*, November 16, 2004. http://www.un.org/radio/detail/899.html

213. Kevin Sites, "Marines let loose on streets of Fallujah," *NBC News*, November 10, 2004. http://www.msnbc.msn.com/id/6450268/#storyContinued

214. Victoria Welch, "Vermont vets speak out against Iraq war," *Burlington Free Press*, January 20, 2007. http://soc.mailarchive.ca/culture.usa/2007-01/12063.html

B. The names are different, but the human and legal consequences are the same.

An Italian documentary film crew obtained evidence of the use of white phosphorus against civilians in Fallujah. "Willy Peter" has a distinct yellow flame, it is very hard to extinguish, and it burns the bodies of its victims in a particularly gruesome way. The 1980 UN Convention on Certain Weapons bans the use of incendiary weapons, including WP and all forms of napalm, against civilians or "inside a concentration of civilians except when such military objective is clearly separated from the concentration of civilians." And of course, military attacks against civilians are prohibited regardless of what weapons are used under the Geneva Conventions and the International Covenant on Civil and Political Rights.[215]

Both Kevin Sites of *NBC* and an embedded reporter from *Channel Four* in the U.K. independently collected evidence of marines killing wounded Iraqis in cold blood—"dead-checking" them, to use another military code-word.[216] Like most other violations of the laws of war by U.S. forces, this was something that they were trained and ordered to do. It had nothing to do with "bad apples," unless this meant the ones at the very top of the command structure.

The consequences of indiscriminate killing under weapons-free rules of engagement in Fallujah were also documented by two unembedded Iraqi journalists who survived the massacre. Burhan Fasa'a worked for the *LBC* television network in Lebanon. He spent nine days in a house in Fallujah with a growing population that eventually numbered 26 people. As people were wounded or their houses were damaged or destroyed, there were no means of evacuation, so they took

---

215. Andrew Buncombe, Kim Sengupta and Colin Brown, "Incendiary weapons: the big white lie," *The Independent*, November 17 2005.

216. "U.S. war crimes in Fallujah," *Democracy Now*, November 19 2004. And see Chapter 8.

shelter with neighbors or just huddled in the ruins and often died of their wounds. Eventually, a squad of U.S. Marines burst into Fasa'a's house, yelling orders in English that most of the people could not understand. If people were too slow to understand and follow the marines' instructions, they shot them on the spot. "Americans did not have interpreters with them," Fasa'a explained, "so they entered houses and killed people because they didn't speak English .... Soldiers thought the people were rejecting their orders, so they shot them. But the people just couldn't understand them."[217]

Bilal Hussein won a Pulitzer Prize as an AP photographer working in his native Fallujah. In November 2004, he hunkered down at his home in the Jolan district as the city came under attack, hoping to keep working. Then, as Jolan came under intense attack and his house was hit by shells and bullets, he panicked and tried to flee. He had a plan to swim across the river to safety. When he reached the Euphrates, he found that other people had the same idea but that they were being shot in the water by marine snipers and helicopters. He saw a family of five machine-gunned as they tried to swim across. Hussein paused to bury a body with his bare hands and then continued down the river for five hours until he found shelter at a farmhouse. Bilal Hussein was detained by U.S. forces in Ramadi on April 12th 2006 and was held without charge or trial for nearly two years. Military spokesmen made various accusations against him, but the AP and other journalists vigorously defended him. His detention seemed to be part of an effort to intimidate journalists and to discourage independent journalism in Iraq. Bilal Hussein was eventually brought before an Iraqi court and then released on April 16th 2008.[218]

---

217. Dahr Jamail, "Fallujah refugees tell of life and death in the kill zone," *The New Standard*, December 3 2004.
http://dahrjamailiraq.com/hard_news/archives/hard_news/000145.php
   218. http://www.ap.org/bilalhussein/

William Kay of *The Republic* in Vancouver wrote an excellent summary of the American assault on Fallujah based on U.S. military sources. He wrote that the U.S. invasion plan for the city was to leap-frog between predetermined "lily-pads." These were specific buildings to be taken over as bases within the city, from which raids and patrols could then be launched and air strikes called in on strongholds of resistance. However, this played into the hands of the Resistance in many ways. Guerilla tactics always depend on avoiding major confrontations and attacking the most vulnerable enemy units, such as infantry patrols and supply convoys. In Fallujah, after four or five days of fighting, U.S. forces had leap-frogged from one end of the city to the other and set up hundreds of lily-pads, giving them control of the city center and major intersections, and plenty of snipers' nests. But even after they declared victory several days later, they had not defeated the Resistance at all.[219]

There was apparently a decision by the Resistance to evacuate about half their number from the city before the assault. There may have been as few as 1,000 trained and organized resistance fighters in the city when the assault began, and more of these slipped out during the first few days of fighting. In spite of the virtual destruction of the city and a civilian death toll of at least four thousand, there were still about four hundred resistance fighters roaming 60% of the city after two weeks of fighting. A renewed American bombing campaign destroyed more of what was left of the city, but bombed-out cities provide excellent cover for guerilla fighters, and air power becomes ineffective against rubble. The Americans still met resistance whenever they strayed too far from their lily-pads.

Two U.S. Stryker battalions that had been dispatched from Mosul to Fallujah to take part in the attack were withdrawn on November 12th. Some of the resistance fighters who had evacuated from Fallujah had

---

219. William Kay, "The Second Battle of Fallujah," *The Republic*, November 25 2004. http://www.republic-news..org/archive/102-repub/102_kay.htm

reorganized in Mosul and driven the police out of much of Iraq's third-largest city, so the Stryker battalions could no longer be spared. This left about 6,500 marines bearing the brunt of combat in the ruins of Fallujah, which they had destroyed but by no means pacified. The 2nd Brigade of the 1st Cavalry, on loan from Baghdad, manned the porous cordon around the city. Despite American declarations of victory, U.S. forces were still preventing relief convoys from entering the city, and officials were warning that water and electricity might not be restored until February.

On November 19th, a U.S.. Marine blogger named hEKle, who witnessed the renewed air raids from the outskirts of Fallujah, posted this description of what he saw on the "Fight to Survive" blog:

> Even as the sun was setting over the hazy orange horizon, artillery was pounding away at the remaining twelve percent of the already devastated Falluja. Many units were pulled out for the evening in preparation of a full-scale air strike that was scheduled to last for up to twelve hours. Our squad was sitting on top of our parked humvees, manning the crew served machine guns and scanning the urban landscape for enemy activity ...

> As the evening wore on and the artillery continued, a new gruesome roar filled the sky. The fighter jets were right on time and made their grand appearance with a series of massive air strikes. Between the pernicious bombs and fierce artillery, the sky seemed as though it were on fire for several minutes at a time. First you would see a blaze of light in the horizon, like lightning hitting a dynamite warehouse, and then hear the massive explosion that would turn your stomach, rattle your eyeballs, and compress itself deep within your lungs. Although these massive bombs were being dropped no further than one kilometer away, it felt like it was happening right in front of your face. At first, it was impossible not to flinch with each unexpected boom, but after scores of intense explosions, your senses became aware and complacent towards them.

At times the jets would scream menacingly low over the city and open fire with smaller missiles meant for extreme accuracy ... These air-deployed missiles make a banshee-like squeal, sort of like a bottle rocket fueled with plutonium, and then suddenly would become inaudible. Seconds later, the colossal explosion would rip the sky open and hammer devastatingly into the ground, sending flames and debris pummeling into the air. And as always, the artillery—some rounds were high explosive, some were illumination rounds, some were reported as being white phosphorus (the modern day napalm). Occasionally, on the outskirts of the isolated impact area, you could hear tanks firing machine guns and blazing their cannons. It was amazing that anything could survive this deadly onslaught. Suddenly a transmission came over the radio approving the request for "bunker-busters." Apparently, there were a handful of insurgent compounds that were impenetrable by artillery. At the time, I was unaware when these bunker-busters were deployed, but I was told later that the incredibly massive explosions were a direct result of these "final solution" type missiles.

I continued to watch the final assault on Falluja throughout the night from atop my humvee. It was interesting to scan the vast skies above with night vision goggles. Circling continuously overhead throughout the battle was an array of attack helicopters. The most devastating were the Cobras and Apaches with their chain gun missile launchers. Through the night vision I could see them hovering around the carnage, scanning the ground with an infrared spotlight that seemed to reach for miles. Once a target was identified, a rapid series of hollow blasts would echo through the skies, and from the ground came a "rat-a-tatting" of explosions, like a daisy chain of supercharged black cats during a Fourth of July barbeque. More artillery, more tanks, more machine gun fire, ominous death-dealing fighter planes terminating whole city blocks at a time ... this wasn't a war, it was a massacre![220]

---

220. http://ftssoldier.blogspot.com/2004/11/holiday-in-falluja_19.html

On November 22nd, the U.N.'s Emergency Working Group issued another report on the Fallujah Crisis. A Red Crescent team had been able to enter Fallujah for the first time, but it had quickly withdrawn again. It reported continued fighting, water still turned off, and no distribution of food and other supplies to Fallujah or the surrounding area. The report said it might be months before people could return to the city. Access to 12,000 refugees around Saqlawiya was also restricted because of ongoing military operations.[221]

A month later, on December 19th, when the EWG issued another report, the situation had hardly improved. The original plan to start allowing people to return by December 15th had been abandoned. There was still only "sporadic access to the various IDP (internally displaced persons) locations due to military activities/checkpoints and insecurity; whereas Falluja itself remains strictly inaccessible due to the ongoing conflict." The Iraqi Red Crescent had once again withdrawn from the city on December 5th "due to security issues" and had not been able to return. The EWG could not confirm whether standing water and sewage had been cleared by December 15th as planned.[222]

The final scale of the bloodshed and destruction in Fallujah were hard to assess. U.S. troops disposed of bodies before relief workers were allowed into the city, and no independent survey of the number of people killed was permitted. Survivors saw U.S. troops collecting bodies and dumping them in the Euphrates, and burying others in mass graves on the outskirts of the city. A team from Fallujah Hospital went through six of the city's twenty-eight residential districts to collect bo-

---

221. "Emergency Working Group - Falluja Crisis Update Note," *United Nations Assistance Mission for Iraq*, November 22 2004.
http://www.uniraq.org/documents/Falluja%20Bulletin%2022%20November.pdf
222. "Emergency Working Group - Falluja Crisis Bulletin Update," *United Nations Assistance Mission for Iraq*, December 19 2004.
http://www.nrc.ch/8025708F004CE90B/Country_Sources?ReadForm&country=Iraq&sort=date&count=10000

dies on December 25th and 26th 2004. According to the director of the hospital, it removed 700 bodies, of which at least 550 were of women and children and the rest were mostly of elderly men. The Study Centre for Human Rights and Democracy in Fallujah reported that 4,000 to 6,000 people were killed in November's assault and that the vast majority were civilians.[223]

Hafid al-Dulaimi, the chairman of the Fallujah Compensation Committee, reported on March 23rd 2005 that about 36,000 houses had been demolished as well as 9,000 shops, 65 mosques, and 60 schools. He added that, "The American forces destroyed one of the two bridges in the city, both train stations, the two electricity stations, and three water treatment plants" as well as "the whole sanitation system and the communication network." Other local authorities reported that 60% of all houses in the city were either completely destroyed or sufficiently damaged to be uninhabitable. By March 2006, less than 20% of these had been repaired, and much of the electricity, water, and sanitation infrastructure was still not working. Bassel Mahmoud, appointed by the Iraqi government to oversee reconstruction, said that only $103 million had been paid in compensation out of $500 million in claims. Only 24 of 81 public reconstruction projects had been completed, and many others were being cancelled for lack of funding.[224]

The refugee crisis resulting from the American siege and attacks on Fallujah was the beginning of the much larger displacement crisis that swept much of the country over the ensuing years of war and occupation. As with this larger crisis, its real impact was distorted and understated by imprecise population figures cited in the Western media. Most Western sources cited the pre-war population of Fallujah as 250,000 or

---

223. Dahr Jamail, "Life goes on in Fallujah's rubble," *Inter Press Service*, November 23 2005; "Death toll in Fallujah rising, doctors say," *IRIN*, January 4 2005.

224. Oxford Research Group, *Learning from Fallujah*, 2005. http://www.oxfordresearchgroup.org.uk/publications/books/pdf/fallujah.pdf ; "Fallujah situation improving slowly," *IRIN*, March 21st 2006.

300,000. Thus, the *Washington Post* reported in April 2005 that about 90,000 of Fallujah's 250,000 residents had returned, albeit "to find wide swaths of the town in ruin." This would have meant that more than a third of the residents had returned. *IRIN* reported in March 2006 that "The entire population of the city was estimated to be 300,000 and to-day it stands at roughly 230,000." This suggested that 70% of the population had returned within a year and a half.

However, the United Nations' official figure for the pre-war population of Fallujah was not 250,000 or 300,000, but 435,774. Iraqi Government figures put it even higher, at about 600,000. Patrick Cockburn of *The Independent*, who had worked in Iraq since 1978, found the higher number credible and cited it in his reports. The Study Centre for Human Rights and Democracy reported on December 27th, 2004 that there were 350,000 refugees from Fallujah in the surrounding towns and ref-ugee camps, many more than the 217,000 estimated by the UN Emergency Working Group. Neither of these totals included those who had fled farther afield. These higher population figures clarified the scale of the destruction of Fallujah. They also made it clear that hundreds of thousands of survivors remained scattered to the wind in other parts of Iraq, Syria, and Jordan.[225]

The American destruction of Fallujah and the killing of thousands of its citizens constituted another serious war crime within the greater crime of the U.S. war in Iraq. As with the crimes discussed in other chapters, the most difficult issues for future war crimes prosecutors would be to find precise answers to questions regarding the origin of each of the critical orders issued. Who made the determination that Fallujah should be a "weapons-free" zone? Who authorized the use of air-strikes, hunger, and thirst to force the evacuation of the city? Who made the decision to send all adult males back into the killing zone?

---

225. http://en.wikipedia.org/wiki/Fallujah ; and *Learning from Fallujah*.

Who authorized the use of napalm, white phosphorus, and cluster-bombs in a civilian area? And, above all, who gave the order to the United States armed forces to lay waste to a city of 435,000 to 600,000 people?

CHAPTER 12. SUNNIS AND SHIITES—HISTORY VERSUS PROPAGANDA

The primary conflict taking place in Iraq was always the guerilla war between the foreign army that invaded the country and the popular resistance forces fighting to free it from occupation. But, as the war dragged on, American propaganda increasingly portrayed the secondary "sectarian" conflict between Sunni and Shiite Arabs as the main conflict taking place in Iraq, with the foreign occupation forces that had invaded the country and plunged it into chaos and violence acting as well-meaning but frustrated peacekeepers or referees.

Western media drew attention to horrific acts of violence, in which thousands of civilians were killed by suicide bombers, car bombs, and seemingly random violence. But the media downplayed the U.S. Defense Intelligence Agency's data that more than 90% of "enemy-initiated attacks" in Iraq were against military targets, not against civilians.

In fact, as noted earlier, 75% of attacks by Iraqis targeted U.S., British, and other foreign occupation forces, while another 16% were directed against U.S.-led Iraqi forces. The remaining 9% of attacks, which did target civilians, included Resistance attacks against Iraqi occupation officials and other collaborators, so a very small proportion of attacks could possibly be attributed to "sectarian violence" or indeed to any other purpose than resistance to Western occupation. The DIA's data provided clear evidence that the principal dynamic of the war throughout all its phases was one of invasion, occupation and popular resistance.[226]

So any serious discussion of terrorism or violence between ethnic and sectarian groups and political parties in Iraq should have been

---

226. http://www.brookings.edu/saban/iraq-index.aspx

framed by the larger context of invasion, occupation, and popular resistance. But this context was conspicuously lacking in Western reporting on the war. The Western media instead cooperated in the U.S. government's efforts to portray the war as a sort of peacekeeping mission; to blame its Iraqi victims for the violence it unleashed in their country; and to explain the violence to Western audiences through a mythical narrative of an ancient, long-running conflict between Sunnis and Shiites in Iraq.

From the outset, U.S. "information warfare" operations sought to justify the violence of the occupation by delegitimizing and demonizing the Iraqi Resistance. Mr. Rumsfeld blamed early resistance on Baathists or "dead-enders." Then the Pentagon adopted a new term: "anti-Iraqi forces," an Orwellian formulation based on the presence of a few volunteers from other Arab countries fighting with the Iraqi Resistance against the occupation. But it soon became known that these volunteers comprised only a very small proportion of the Resistance, about 2% of the people detained by U.S. forces in Fallujah for example. And the term "anti-Iraqi forces" drew attention to the fact that there were foreign forces fighting Iraqis in Iraq and that most of them were wearing American uniforms.

So the next phase in U.S. propaganda operations was a campaign to link the Iraqi Resistance to Al-Qaeda and the American "war on terror," personified by the mythical figure of the Jordanian "terrorist mastermind," Abu Musab al-Zarqawi. This was the same Zarqawi who had figured in a claim by Colin Powell to the U.N. Security Council that Saddam Hussein was working with Al-Qaeda in northern Iraq. Zarqawi's role as the supreme leader of the Iraqi Resistance was equally fictitious. A U.S. military intelligence officer described his key role in American propaganda to a British reporter in March 2004:

> We were basically paying up to $10,000 a time to opportunists, criminals and chancers who passed off fiction and supposition about Zarqawi as cast-iron fact, making him out

as the linchpin of just about every attack in Iraq ... Back home this stuff was gratefully received and formed the basis of policy decisions. We needed a villain, someone identifiable for the public to latch on to, and we got one.[227]

Zarqawi's mythical presence in Fallujah was used to justify the American attack in November 2004, and the American propaganda machine linked him to almost every act of barbarity in Iraq for two or three years until either the man, the myth, or both were finally killed in September 2006. Although most of this narrative was dismissed by credible figures in Iraq, people were disoriented and terrorized by the inexplicable violence the occupation had unleashed in their communities. Identifying the Iraqi Resistance with a bloodthirsty foreign Wahhabi terrorist supported American efforts to divide and rule Iraq by exploiting the very real fear that was gripping the population.

But the Zarqawi campaign was mainly for American domestic consumption. The identification and demonization of Zarqawi and "Al Qaeda in Iraq" as America's new enemy fulfilled several important functions. As Iraq became the "central front in the war on terror," Zarqawi and Al-Qaeda in Iraq took the role of public enemy number one that neither Osama Bin Laden nor Saddam Hussein could credibly fill in occupied Iraq. The emphasis on terrorism and sectarian bloodshed as the new narrative of the war also fulfilled a vital function in bolstering flagging American support for the war effort. It assigned responsibility for the escalating violence to the Resistance and cast the forces that had invaded and occupied the country as its well-intentioned guardians. With all the previous public justifications for the war now discredited, it also provided a badly needed new reason to stay the course: to prevent a hypothetical "bloodbath" between Sunnis and Shiites.

---

227. Adrian Blomfield, "How US fuelled myth of Zarqawi the mastermind," *The Daily Telegraph*, March 10 2004.

The American media swallowed whole the myth that U.S. forces had become embroiled in an intractable centuries-old blood feud. The stereotype of Iraqis consumed by ancient sectarian rivalries was soon so well established in America's public imagination that it became a common theme for commentators and comedians. Even Americans who opposed the war in Iraq accepted this perverted caricature. A Doonesbury comic strip depicted the exasperation of an American soldier as a Shiite he was working with sought revenge against a Sunni over the murder of a family member. The punch-line was that the murder in question had taken place in 1387.[228]

This fabricated and racist Western stereotype could not have been farther from the truth. In Iraq, people of the same tribe often belonged to different sects, and social interaction and intermarriage between Sunni Arabs, Shiites, and Kurds was commonplace among the secular majority of Iraqis. In other countries and contexts, American sociologists treat intermarriage as a prime indicator of social integration.[229]

In reality, until the 19th century, the Arab tribes of southern Iraq, like other Arabs throughout the region, were mainly nomadic herders and adherents of Sunni rather than Shia Islam. The existence of small Persian colonies and *madrasas* or religious schools around the Shiite shrines in Najaf and Karbala had little impact on the beliefs and culture of the surrounding Arab tribes. The Ottoman government permitted these small, distinct Persian communities to retain Persian citizenship and immunity from Ottoman law. Their success in converting a majority of the surrounding Arab population to Shia Islam during the late 19th century was a striking historical phenomenon, but it did not begin in earnest until after 1831. That was when the Ottoman government

---

228. http://www.doonesbury.com/strip/dailydose/index.html?uc_full_date=20080113

229. Peter Blau and Joseph Schwartz, *Crosscutting Social Circles*, (Edison, New Jersey: Transaction, 1997), 13.

reestablished direct rule over Iraq after an 85-year period of relative autonomy under a dynasty of Georgian Mamluks. But somehow, by the time the British conducted the first census of Iraq in 1919, 53% of the population had come to identify themselves as Shiite Muslims.[230]

The last major conflict between Sunnis and Shiites in what is now Iraq was not between Arabs at all but between Turks and Persians in the 17th century. The Persian Empire occupied Baghdad for two brief periods (1508-1533 and 1622-1638). When the Ottomans recaptured Baghdad in 1638, they massacred 1,700 Persians, and the Persian colonists in the Shiite shrine cities of Najaf and Karbala fled to Persia. The Ottoman army recaptured Basra in 1668.

An Afghan army captured Isfahan, the capital of Persia, in 1722. Persia's new Afghan ruler, Nadir Shah, a Sunni, expropriated much of the wealth of the Persian Shiite clergy. The Mamluk rulers of Iraq permitted Persian Shiite clerics to reestablish colonies in Karbala and Najaf. In 1776, Basra came under Persian rule again for three years before being recaptured by the Mamluks. The Persian community in Iraq continued to grow, and numbered about 80,000 by 1919.[231]

Also in the 18th century, Shiites around Lucknow in northern India established a Shiite state called Awadh or Oudh, and wealthy Indian pilgrims from Awadh came to settle in the shrine cities of Iraq. The government of Awadh financed the construction of the Hindiyya canal between 1790 and 1803, which provided Najaf with a reliable source of drinking water for the first time in its history, and permitted its eventual growth from a small town around a pilgrimage site into a wealthy city. The resulting development of new agricultural land around Najaf

---

230. Yitzhak Nakash, *The Shi'is of Iraq*, (Princeton: Princeton University Press, 1994), 4-5 & 13.
231. Nakash, *ibid.*, 15-17.

led to the settlement of local nomadic tribes as farmers, which in turn facilitated their conversion to Shiism.[232]

In the early 19th century, Karbala remained a larger town than Najaf, attracting greater numbers of immigrants from Persia. Local Arab tribal leaders formed alliances with the Persian clerics. By 1831, the Ottomans became alarmed by the growing autonomy of many parts of Iraq under the Mamluks and re-established direct rule. Resistance to Ottoman rule in Karbala led to its occupation by Turkish forces in 1843. Ironically, because Karbala's Persian population was effectively under Persian protection and immune from submission to Ottoman authority, Karbala became an even more autonomous Persian colony. The Arab tribes who had been affiliated with the Persians shifted their base to Najaf, which then emerged as the center of Arab Shiism in Iraq, while Karbala's population of about 50,000 remained 75% Persian until the turn of the 20th century.[233]

The Iraqi tribes began to settle down to an agricultural and eventually an urban way of life in the early 19th century, but this process was slower in southern Iraq than in areas around Baghdad. By 1867, only 23% of the population of central Iraq still led nomadic lives, while 50% of the population in the south remained nomadic. This had changed dramatically by 1905, with the proportion of agricultural workers in the south increasing from 41% to 72% of the population and the nomadic population shrinking to 19% of the total.[234]

In 1869, the Ottomans passed a sweeping property law that institutionalized and accelerated the revolution in settlement and land ownership in Iraq. Like the Inclosure Acts in England, the highland clearances in Scotland, the appropriation of Native American land and sub-

---

232. Nakash, *ibid.*, 16 & 31.

233. J.G.. Lorimer, Gazetteer of the Persian Gulf, Oman and Central Arabia (Calcutta, 1908-1915), 2A:976; and Nakash, *ibid.*, 21-23.

234. Nakash, *ibid.*, 33-36.

sequent privatizations of communal land all over the world, this process spelled the beginning of the end of their traditional way of life for most of the nomadic tribes of southern Iraq. The tribes-people gradually settled down and became peasant farmers, while their tribal leaders acquired title to most of the land they farmed and became wealthy landlords. This process continued under successive regimes until the revolution against the monarchy in 1958, by which time 55% of the agricultural land in Iraq was owned by less than 1% of the population.[235]

This sweeping change in the way of life of the Iraqi tribes was the essential context for their conversion to Shiism, but the Persian clerics in the shrine cities had reasons of their own for wanting to convert them. Following the spread of fundamentalist Sunni Wahhabism in Arabia, the shrine cities came under successive attack by bands of Saudi tribesmen, who sacked Karbala in 1801. The Mamluk rulers of Iraq raised an army of Iraqi tribesmen to fight the Saudis, but it was largely ineffective and had no particular loyalty to the shrine cities or their Persian clerics. Saudi marauders were a constant threat until an Egyptian army eventually defeated and contained the Saudis in 1811. But then the shrine cities were threatened again by a rising of Iraqi tribes against the Mamluks in 1814. As a result of this succession of threats, the Persian clerics came to see the conversion of the local tribes to Shiism as essential to the defense of the shrines and to their own survival. They also badly needed a new economic base as a result of being cut off from Persian government funding and from their other traditional sources of income in Persia.[236]

The construction of the Hindiyya and other canals produced newly fertile agricultural land around Najaf and Karbala while unintentionally drying out the formerly fertile agricultural area around Hillah. Najaf

235. Phebe Marr, *The Modern History of Iraq*, (Boulder: Westview Press, 1985), 135.
236. Nakash, *ibid.* 28-33 & 207.

and Karbala displaced Hillah as major regional market towns and as the centers of these newly fertile agricultural regions. The shrine cities became the center of community life for the newly settled local populations, who came increasingly to identify with the shrines, their history, and their religious significance at the same time that their former tribal identities were eroded by their new way of life. The active efforts of the clerics to convert the Arabs to Shiism were accepted by Ottoman officials, who had their own interests in settling and "civilizing" the tribes, such as taxing them and conscripting them into the army. It was only after the mission succeeded beyond all expectations that the Ottoman government established new Sunni *madrasas* to try and stem the tide of Shiism.[237]

Despite its position on the frontier of the Ottoman and Persian empires, the relatively peaceful history of Iraq in the 18th and 19th centuries stands in stark contrast to the bloody and contentious history of Europe and North America during the same period. But the catastrophic climax of European militarism eventually overflowed into Iraq during the First World War. The British captured Basra, then suffered a humiliating surrender to Ottoman forces at al-Kut in 1915. They eventually captured Baghdad in 1917 and held a mandate over Iraq until 1932.

Arab nationalism was a powerful force at the end of the Ottoman Empire, and popular nationalist groups throughout Iraq rose against the British in a major rebellion in 1920. The British were able to put down the rebellion with 130,000 British and Indian troops, in part because the population of Iraq at that time was only about three million, compared to about thirty million today. Thousands of British, Indians, and Iraqis were killed, and the rebellion forced the British to rethink their strategy for governing the country. They had begun to establish a civil administration based on the model of British India, with political

---

237. Nakash, *ibid.* 44-45.

officers attached to tribal leaders throughout the country. Instead they installed Faisal, who had led the Arab Revolt against the Turks, as King of Iraq.

Former Ottoman officers had played an instrumental role in the 1920 rebellion, but the British secured their support for Faisal by restoring their role in the army, which became the dominant political institution in the new country. Both Faisal's circle and the Ottoman officer class were mainly Sunni Arabs. Shiite political and religious leaders in Najaf and Karbala, who welcomed their liberation from the Turks but then rose in revolt against the British, were either deported to Persia or politically marginalized.[238]

British administrators were determined to set up a more efficient tax system than the Ottomans. The widespread new territory would be difficult to police with the forces available to them, especially with growing pressures at home over the cost of the Empire after the First World War. Britain's new Royal Air Force (RAF) had already played a major role against local resistance forces in Iraq. As a British official reported in April 1919, "Bombing still continues to be carried out. No sooner has one area been subdued than another breaks out in revolt and has to be dealt with by aeroplane ... all these tribal disturbances have been dealt with from the air ... thus the Army has been saved from marching many weary miles over bad country and sustaining casualties."[239]

The RAF was also instrumental in suppressing the major rebellion in 1920, so it was then given the prime responsibility for policing the country and enforcing tax collection. The RAF kept four squadrons of bombers in Iraq. It punished tribes that did not pay their taxes with air raids, using fire bombs to destroy villages and burn their people. Tribes that were too poor or drought-ridden to pay taxes before they were

---

238. Charles Tripp, "Iraq: the imperial precedent," *Le Monde Diplomatique*, January 2003.

239. Peter Sluglett, *Britain in Iraq: 1914-1932*, (London: Ithaca Press, 1976), 262-270.

bombed were certainly unable to do so after their villages had been burned to the ground, but that was hardly the point. The express purpose of the policy was to make an example of the punished tribes and thereby terrorize others into paying their taxes.

One British officer who led an RAF squadron in Iraq was Squadron Leader Arthur Harris. He is better known to history as Air Chief Marshall "Bomber" or "Butcher" Harris, the Commander-in-Chief of RAF Bomber Command during the Second World War. He implemented Britain's policy of area bombing against Germany after the Butt Report concluded that precision bombing did not work. He expressed his core belief in fire-bombing civilian targets as an effective weapon during the Arab Revolt in Palestine in 1936. He wrote that, based on his experience in Iraq and on the Afghan frontier, "one 250 lb. or 500 lb. bomb in each village that speaks out of turn" would solve Britain's problems in Palestine. This strategy evolved into mass murder on a far greater scale in Cologne and Dresden. In Iraq, Afghanistan, and Palestine, where Harris developed this strategy, people are still "speaking out of turn" seventy years later, casting doubt on his thesis and bearing out the now generally understood principle that bombing civilians tends to stiffen resistance rather than discourage it.[240]

Historian Peter Sluglett believed that British reliance on bombing in the 1920s contributed to the instability of the Iraqi monarchy and the subsequent history of repressive governments in Iraq. "Perhaps the most serious long term consequence of the ready availability of air control was that it developed into a substitute for administration," he wrote. "Several incidents during the Mandate period indicate that the speed and simplicity of air attack was preferred to the more time consuming and painstaking investigation of grievances and disputes. With

---

240. Ian Gilmour & Andrew Gilmour, "Terrorism Review," *Journal of Palestine Studies 17:2, 1988.*

such powers at its disposal the Iraqi government was not encouraged to develop less violent methods of extending its control over the country."

The British Labour government elected in 1924 reconsidered British policy in Iraq, but made little change. George Lansbury led the opposition in Parliament to "this Hunnish and barbarous method of warfare against unarmed people." But the new Colonial Secretary, Leo Amery, concluded, "If the writ of King Faisal runs effectively throughout his kingdom, it is entirely due to British aeroplanes. If the aeroplanes were removed tomorrow, the whole structure would inevitably fall to pieces." The British granted formal independence to Iraq in 1932, but the British Embassy continued to play an advisory role in the government and the RAF retained two of its bases.[241]

Opposition to the monarchy grew in the 1940s and 1950s, leading to its bloody overthrow in 1958. Throughout Sunni-led regimes from the Ottomans to the British mandate to the succession of governments under the monarchy, the Shiite clerical establishment in Iraq never developed the kind of political influence that it had historically enjoyed in neighboring Persia, where its roots were older and deeper. Successive Persian regimes up to and including the Western-backed Pahlavis used the clerics as a counterweight to secular opposition parties like the Tudeh communist party, and the Shah sealed his fate when he broke openly with Khomeini and the clerics in the 1970s.

Secular Shiites developed significant roles in Iraqi society under the monarchy, as Iraq developed and urbanized. Concentrated land ownership and the exploitation of agricultural workers combined with the growth of Baghdad to draw millions of Shiites from the south to the capital. By 1947, 25% of Iraqis born in Amara province, where land ownership was most concentrated, had migrated to other provinces, two thirds of them to Baghdad. Most of these new urbanites were poor

---

241. Sluglett, *ibid.*

slum-dwellers, but others joined the urban upper and middle classes. Baghdad's old Jewish business class had constituted 43% of the membership of the Baghdad Chamber of Commerce in 1939, but when the Jews emigrated from Baghdad after 1948, the vacuum was filled by a new Shiite business class of landlords, businessmen, and professionals, including the families of tribal leaders. By 1958, Shiites comprised 50% of Baghdad's population, but their exposure to education, city life and the Iraqi Communist Party had eroded both their religious observance and their sectarian identity.[242]

While the population of Iraq mushroomed, the populations of Najaf and Karbala stagnated and declined. Najaf only grew from 45,000 to 58,000 between 1918 and 1947, while Persian-dominated Karbala actually shrank by half, from 50,000 in 1908 to 25,000 in 1928. Successive laws passed between 1924 and 1950 gradually forced Persians in Iraq to adopt Iraqi nationality or return to Persia. The number of students enrolled at *madrasas* in Najaf declined from about 8,000 in 1900 to less than 2,000 by 1957, while influential new schools at Qum in Iran attracted at least 5,000 students. The very same links to Persia and foreign Shiite communities that had preserved the shrine cities' independence from Ottoman control and facilitated the growth of Shiism in Iraq in the 19th century resulted in a lack of local support which undermined their position in the emerging Iraqi state of the 20th century.[243]

Control of the Ministry of Education by influential Shiites in the 1930s led to the expansion and decentralization of the educational system. By the 1940s, a large number of Shiites were educated and competing for top jobs in the Iraqi government. Salih Jabir, a Shiite from Nasiriyah, became Prime Minister in 1947. By 1950, five out of twelve ministerial positions in the government of Prime Minister Tawfik al-Suwaidi were held by Shiites, including Salih Jabir as Interior Minister

---

242. Nakash, *ibid.*, 96-97 & 233.
243. Nakash, *ibid.*, 97-98, 237, 254 & 261.

and the ministers of finance and economics. The backlash of the traditional governing elite to the growing power of Jabir and his colleagues forced him to start a new party, the Popular Socialist Party (PSP). He called for direct parliamentary elections to replace the anti-democratic electoral system based on official "lists" of candidates, a system also used later in elections held under U.S. occupation. New elections were held in 1953 under a semi-democratic hybrid electoral system, but the PSP was successfully marginalized. Many of Jabir's young educated supporters felt excluded from the political system and joined the Iraqi Communist Party.[244]

Jabir and the PSP began to work with two other opposition parties that attracted the support of secular, educated Iraqis: the National Democratic Party, essentially a liberal democratic party that supported land reform and a more equitable distribution of wealth; and the Arab nationalist Independence (Istiqlal) Party. The newer Arab nationalist, socialist Baath Party also began as a small but well-organized opposition party under the monarchy. It partially overcame the traditional Shiite suspicion of pan-Arabism, and many of its early leaders in the 1950s were Shiites, including its leader, Fuad al-Rikabi, a young engineer from Nasiriyah. In 1957, these five opposition parties came together to form the United National Front. The catalyst for united opposition was not so much domestic as foreign policy. Most Iraqis opposed the Baghdad Pact, the Iraqi government's pro-Western alliance with Turkey, Iran, and Pakistan. The Suez crisis brought the contradictions between Iraq's foreign policy and the loyalties of its people to a head.

Unlike the Kurds in northern Iraq, the political aspirations of the Shiite population in Iraq were never for autonomy but always for full integration into the Iraqi state and society, as expressed by their leading role in the opposition to the monarchy. Forty-five percent of the

---

244. Nakash, *ibid.*, 125-134.

members of parliament under the monarchy were landlords and tribal sheiks, including many wealthy Shiites who were pro-monarchy and pro-Western. The opposition to the monarchy likewise crossed sectarian lines and drew primarily on the new urban middle and working classes who were unrepresented and alienated from the oligarchic political system.[245] These civilian parties were united by a determination to free Iraq from British and Western influence and to shape the destiny of their own country, but it ultimately required a mutiny in the army to overthrow the monarchy, placing General Qasim and a new cadre of mainly Sunni Arab officers at the head of the revolutionary government.

Between 1958 and 1979, successive governments succeeded in gaining control of and expanding Iraq's oil industry and using its revenues to develop the country. The Baath regime of the late 1970s was particularly successful in its goals of eliminating the former privileges of the upper class, distributing and expanding public services on an egalitarian basis, nationalizing basic industries, and achieving rapid economic development. By 1983, this succession of revolutionary governments had succeeded in increasing enrollment in primary school from 400,000 to 2.6 million, secondary school enrollment from 50,000 to a million, and university enrollment from 6,000 to 120,000. In the same period, the number of doctors in Iraq increased from 1,190 to 4,661. All this progress was gradually squandered by the subsequent years of dictatorship, war, and sanctions under Saddam Hussein, until it was finally destroyed by the American invasion and occupation.[246]

Although Hussein's inner circle was made up to a great extent by a small group of his own relatives and associates from around Tikrit, and the officer corps of the army remained dominated by Sunni Arabs, the wider leadership of the Baath Party and government was more diverse.

---

245. Marr, *ibid.*, 123-125.
246. Marr, *ibid.*, 240-243 & 261-264.

Writing in 1990, Library of Congress researcher Helen Chapin Metz made this assessment of the role of Shiites in the Baath Party and the Iraqi government:

> Although the Shias had been underrepresented in government posts in the period of the monarchy, they made substantial progress in the educational, business, and legal fields. Their advancement in other areas, such as the opposition parties, was such that in the years from 1952 to 1963, before the Baath Party came to power, Shias held the majority of party leadership posts. Observers believed that in the late 1980s Shias were represented at all levels of the party roughly in proportion to government estimates of their numbers in the population. For example, of the eight top Iraqi leaders who in early 1988 sat with Husayn on the Revolutionary Command Council—Iraq's highest governing body—three were Arab Shias (of whom one had served as Minister of Interior), three were Arab Sunnis, one was an Arab Christian, and one a Kurd. On the Regional Command Council— the ruling body of the party—Shias actually predominated. During the war, a number of highly competent Shia officers have been promoted to corps commanders. The general who turned back the initial Iranian invasions of Iraq in 1982 was a Shia.[247]

The Revolutionary Command Council was expanded to nineteen members in 2001. The secular pre-invasion government did not record the sectarian affiliation of its officials or their families, and not all were publicly linked with any sect. But it appears that the Council was still about equally divided between Sunni and Shiite Arabs. Saddam and Qusay Hussein, Izzat Ibrahim, Ali al-Majid, Adil Mahdi, Rashid Kazim, and probably Uklah Sakr and Samir al-Najm were from Sunni families. The family origins of Mizban Hadi, Latif Jasim, Muhammad al-Razzaq, Abd al-Sadun, Aziz al-Numan, Fadil Gharib, Muhsin Khafaji, Huda

---

247. Helen Chapin Metz, "Sunni-Shia relations in Iraq," *Iraq: a country study*, (Washington, D.C.: Federal Research Division, Library of Congress, 1990). http://lcweb2.loc.gov/frd/cs/iqtoc.html

Ammash, and probably Yahia al-Abbudi, were Shiite, giving Sunnis and Shiites roughly equal numbers on the Council. Of the two vice presidents, Taha Yasin was a Kurd, and Tariq Aziz was a Chaldean Catholic.[248]

Various people have examined the sectarian affiliations of the 55 Iraqis depicted on the "Most Wanted" deck of cards distributed to U.S. invasion forces in 2003, and concluded that about 35 of the Iraqi leaders that the Americans targeted for death or capture were Shiites. The greater proportion of Shiites that this indicated in the broader leadership of Iraq than in the Revolutionary Command Council was consistent with the pattern described by Ms. Chapin Metz in 1990.[249]

Iraqis were baffled by post-invasion propaganda that conflated Baathism with Sunnism, because most of the local Baathist officials they had personal contact with were Shiites. The Iraqi blogger Riverbend wrote in a posting about Saddam Hussein's execution, "Through the constant insistence of American war propaganda, Saddam is now representative of all Sunni Arabs (*never mind most of his government were Shia*)."[250]

Since the majority of Baathist officials were Shiites, it is worth examining why American propaganda went to such lengths to identify Sunni Arabs in Iraq with Baathism. As in other neo-colonial ventures, occupation officials scrambled ethnic, sectarian, tribal, class, economic, political, and geographic groups and interests in a complex society to create schisms that could be exploited to facilitate a "divide and rule" strategy. The Americans installed Kurdish and exile groups in a succes-

---

248 Edmund A. Ghareeb, *Historical Dictionary of Iraq*, (Lanham, Maryland: Scarecrow Press, 2004), p385-8. Also see BBC Monitoring Newsfile for *Iraqi TV (Baghdad)*, May 17 2001.

249. Raed Jarrar, "Iraq's "hidden" conflict," *Foreign Policy in Focus*, March 18 2008. http://www.fpif.org/fpiftxt/5078

250. http://www.riverbendblog.blogspot.com/ 2006_12_01_riverbendblog_archive.html

sion of occupation governments in the Green Zone and mobilized the historically disadvantaged southern Shiites as a majority population with links to some of these exile groups, notably the Dawa Islamist party and its SCIRI (Supreme Council for the Islamic Revolution in Iraq) offshoot. The southern Shiite working class had historically provided the rank and file of the Iraqi army and could be recruited into military and police forces along with the Kurdish *peshmer*ga militia. The clergy in Najaf also had aspirations that could be manipulated, specifically to revive its role as a trusted mediator between the government and the Shiite population that it had developed in the 19th century but had lost in secular 20th century Iraq.

Writing in 1985, Iraq scholar Phebe Marr warned of the vulnerability of southern Shiites to precisely this kind of exploitation by a foreign power, although she did not appear to be thinking of the United States. "In the south, which is less affected by secularism and urbanization, traditional leaders retain a tighter hold over the population, and *shi'i* identification is stronger," she wrote. "This makes the southern *shi'i* population a likely target for foreign powers interested in stirring up dissidence in Iraq, as Syria did in the mid 1970s and Iran in the 1980s."[251]

The educated secular middle class in Baghdad and the Sunni population in Anbar and other provinces were bound to be marginalized by the American strategy, but U.S. officials believed that they could ultimately impose their will upon them and were prepared to use as much force as necessary to do so. Identifying the Sunnis and the middle class with the old regime, and then with Al-Qaeda, provided the necessary rationale for unleashing unlimited violence against them.

During the occupation, the United States gradually allied itself with the Dawa and SCIRI Shiite Islamist parties. These parties' claim to represent a majority of Shiite Iraqis was based on the two carefully ma-

---

251. Marr, *ibid.*, 284.

naged elections conducted by the occupation authorities in 2005. Ayatollah al-Sistani issued a *fatwa* to Shiites to vote for the Dawa-SCIRI
"list" of candidates in the January election. Voters were not told who
was on the list until the day of the election. The only secular alternatives in either of these tightly controlled elections were parties led by
Ayad Allawi and other U.S.-backed, Western-based exiles, who had
even less legitimacy in Iraq than the Islamists.

The sudden apparent widespread popularity of these Islamist parties
had no precedent in Iraqi history. During the Iran-Iraq War, when Dawa supported Iran and ordered its members not to fight for the Iraqi
government, it was largely ignored. Seventy-five percent of the Iraqi
conscripts on the Basra front were Shiites, and they were led by a Shiite
general. Iranian forces conducted a propaganda campaign with louds-
peakers and leaflets calling on Iraqi Shiites to desert and join the Islamic Revolution, but Iraqi nationalism and Arab identity were a much
stronger force among Shiite Iraqis than any foreign notion of Shiite unity.[252]

Following the U.S. invasion, most Iraqis continued to believe strongly in secular nationalist politics. An Oxford Research International survey in February 2004 found that only 21% of Iraqis wanted an Islamist
state, and only 14% preferred religious politicians and parties to secular
ones.[253] Although various factions of the Islamist Dawa party won 89 of
the 230 seats awarded by proportional representation by province in
the December 2005 election, 55 of those 89 seats were won by indigenous factions of Dawa that opposed the occupation and stood for Iraqi
nationalism and independence. The "victory" of the United Iraqi Alliance at the polls did not by any means demonstrate a public prefe-
rence for sectarian or religious politics, or for the American occupation,

---

252. Metz, "The Iran-Iraq Conflict," *ibid.*
253. Oxford Research International, *National Survey of Iraq*, February 2004, page 20.
http://news.bbc.co.uk/nol/shared/bsp/hi/pdfs/15_03_04_iraqsurvey.pdf

and the alliance soon fell apart in any case. The role of Shiite and Sunni Islamist parties in the American occupation and in attacks on civilians by both sides in fact produced growing disillusionment with religious politics in Iraq and a popular reaffirmation of secular nationalism. This was eventually exploited by Ayad Allawi to engineer a political come-back in 2010, despite his unpopular role as an American puppet in the interim government. To what extent Washington was still pulling his strings in 2010 remained unclear at the time of writing.

The Dawa Party was founded in October 1957 to counter secularism and atheism in Iraq, in response to the Iraqi Communist Party's grow-ing popularity among middle- and working-class Muslims. After the 1958 revolution, General Qasim began a land reform program that threatened the revenues of mosques and tribal leaders, and granted equal inheritance rights to women. This brought Dawa increasing sup-port from religious and tribal leaders who were threatened by Qasim's reforms. Dawa originated in Najaf, at the heart of Shiism, but it also sought to include Sunnis. It succeeded in winning the support of Sunni mullahs who shared its concerns about the diminishing role of religion in Iraqi society and were equally threatened by land reform and wom-en's rights. In the 1980s Dawa claimed that 10% of its members were Sunnis.[254]

Muhammad Baqr al-Sadr, Muqtada al-Sadr's father-in-law, was the early leader of Dawa who wrote the party's manifesto in 1960. The Baathist government deported and imprisoned some Dawa members in 1969, beginning a crackdown that intensified over the next decade. Al-Sadr became an Ayatollah, the highest rank of Shiite cleric, and the government imprisoned him briefly in 1972. The government executed five Dawa leaders in December 1974. In 1975, it banned the annual Shiite procession from Najaf to Karbala. When Shiites defied the ban

---

254. http://www.middleeastreference.org.uk/iraqiopposition.html

and marched in 1977, they were attacked by the police. Dawa leader Muhammad Baqr al-Hakim was arrested and imprisoned for two years. Al-Sadr was placed under house arrest in 1979. Dawa began to call for the violent overthrow of the government, and Dawa members made two assassination attempts against Saddam Hussein. Two or three hundred members were executed and several thousand imprisoned. Ayatollah Al-Sadr and his sister were executed in April 1980, after Dawa claimed responsibility for an assassination attempt against Deputy Prime Minister Tariq Aziz.

Dawa was banned in Iraq in 1980, and established its principal base in Tehran for the next 23 years. In 1983, members of Dawa carried out the first recorded suicide bombing in the Middle East, targeting the U.S. and French embassies in Kuwait. Three Americans and three French citizens were killed. Dawa supported Iran's Islamist government, but a new faction that was even more closely aligned with Iran was formed while it was in exile: the Supreme Council for the Islamic Revolution in Iraq or SCIRI.

The elder Al-Sadr and Ayatollah Khomeini had been close associates in Najaf, but they had always presented different models for Islamic government. The original Dawa Party stuck to al-Sadr's model of a democratic government, with religious leaders providing only constitutional and regulatory oversight to ensure compliance with Islamic law. SCIRI advocated an Iranian-style Islamist government for Iraq with final authority in all matters of state and government resting with religious leaders. SCIRI's paramilitary militia, the Badr Brigade, became powerful within the party and received military and police training in Iran.

During the 1990s, the Dawa Party was split between semi-independent branches in Iraq, Iran, Syria, and the U.K. It had some contact with Ahmad Chalabi's Iraqi National Congress (INC) in the early 1990s, but formally broke with it in 1995. Ibrahim al-Jaafari, its spokesman in London, had at least four meetings with U.S. officials beginning in October 2002, including a meeting with Zalmay Khalilzad in January 2003. Dawa at first refused to participate in the U.S. occupation government and organized demonstrations during a meeting between General Garner and other Iraqi groups in Nasiriyah on April 15th 2003. But it joined what became the Iraqi Governing Council on May 7th 2003, and played a major role in the occupation government from then on.

SCIRI was established in Tehran in November 1982. It supported placing the government of Iraq under the direct authority of the Iranian religious leadership. The two countries would have separate legislatures, but they would both answer to the same *faqih* or Council of Guardians. It negotiated with and played a role in the INC in the 1990s but withdrew from it in 1999. Its Badr Brigades paramilitary militia claimed at times to have anywhere from 10,000 to 70,000 members, but the higher number was probably exaggerated.

SCIRI refused funding offered by the United States following the passage of the Iraq Liberation Act in 1998. It voiced support for a U.S. invasion of Iraq in 2001, but withdrew its support after President Bush threatened Iran along with Iraq in his "Axis of Evil" speech in 2002. SCIRI took part in several meetings with U.S. officials before the invasion. It opposed a U.S. occupation of Iraq or any U.S. role in a post-Baathist government, but it ordered its forces not to fight the Americans. It eventually joined the Iraqi Governing Council and held critical power in the United Iraqi Alliance that won the election in January 2005. Its control of the Interior Ministry in that government increased the role of its Badr Brigades militia in Special Police Commando units recruited by the Americans and the interim government. These forces conducted a brutal campaign of summary execution, torture and ethnic cleansing in Baghdad beginning in 2005 (see Chapter 13).

The Americans permitted the Islamist parties a large role in the transitional government, hoping at first to use Ayad Allawi and other secular exiles to mediate the competing interests of narrowly sectarian and ethnic Shiite, Kurdish, and Sunni parties. But Allawi's brutal performance as interim president had alienated the public, earning him the nick-name "Saddam without the mustache." He was so clearly identified as an American puppet that he won almost no support in the 2005 elections. Despite extensive reported stuffing of ballot boxes in his favor, he won only 14% of the votes in the first poll in January. Deprived of a role in managing the election in December, his share of the votes fell to 8%. Like many of the exiles who were flown in with the U.S. invasion forces in 2003, he returned to rejoin his family in London, undoubtedly richer and wiser, but disillusioned with his American allies.

With no legitimate domestically-based secular, nationalist parties included in the political process, American strategy depended on managing and exploiting the Dawa, SCIRI, and Kurdish parties they had placed in power in the Green Zone. By using aggressive military force against Sunni and secular Arab communities, the Americans presented themselves as the allies and protectors of these Islamist and Kurdish parties.

Before the election in January 2005, violence between Iraqis began to dominate the news from Iraq. American commentators enthusiastically grasped the prospect of "civil war" as a new reason to "stay the course." I took the trouble to break down the reports of violence from that month, to look for evidence that there might really be a sectarian or ethnic motivation behind at least some of it.

Here's what I found: out of 169 reported attacks by Iraqis on other Iraqis in January 2005, 43% were against U.S.-led Iraqi security forces; 36% were directly election-related, either targeting polling places, election workers, or voters; 11% targeted officials of Allawi's interim government; another 5% of the victims worked for the occupation in other capacities; and the remaining 5% were insufficiently documented to identify any motive at all. Not one attack was legitimately ascribed to sectarian or ethnic hatred. On closer examination, even the bombing of a Shiite mosque in Baghdad turned out to be election-related, following a local campaign threatening violence if people in the neighborhood took part in the election. So, even though the collaboration of Shiite Islamist parties in the electoral process placed Shiite communities in a compromised and vulnerable position, there was no evidence at that point that election-related violence had metastasized into anything that could legitimately be described as "sectarian violence."[255]

Following the election, the continuing role of these Shiite parties in the transitional government certainly led some Sunnis to regard all Shiites as collaborators and to attack Shiite civilians. Communities of all ethnicities formed local militias, often linked to larger organizations such as the Mahdi Army and Sunni resistance groups, to protect their residents from attacks by U.S. forces, Interior Ministry death squads, criminal gangs, and violence of all kinds amid the chaos of occupied Iraq. The Centcom press office eagerly seized on every act of violence between Iraqis to shape Western news coverage, and the Western media quickly embraced the mythical history of Sunni and Shiite conflict as the primary source of violence in Iraq.

By clinging to the myth of the occupation forces as protectors of the population and resistance forces as "terrorists" targeting civilians, Western media coverage never presented a coherent explanation of the conflict. Precisely who was attacking who and why was explained away by a narrative of "sectarian" or "random" violence. Reports of seemingly inexplicable violence and barbarity exploited the racism of Western audiences and became a justification for even greater violence by the occupation forces. The sad truth is that every society contains fault-

255. Nicolas J. S. Davies, "Whose war is this anyway?," *Z Magazine*, April 2005.

lines within it that an unscrupulous occupying power could exploit as part of a "divide and rule" strategy. It does not take a great deal of imagination to grasp what sort of horrific violence a beleaguered occupying power could unleash in the United States by exploiting racial differences in American society. But most Iraqis consistently, and correctly, blamed the occupation for all of the violence it inflicted on their country.

The question of religion as a motivation for Iraqis resisting the U.S. occupation was examined in a news report in March 2008. It found that only one third of the resistance fighters in U.S. custody claimed to be fighting a religious war. Among juvenile detainees, the proportion of self-identified *jihadis* fell to less than 10%. Major General Douglas Stone, in charge of all U.S. prison camps in Iraq, confirmed that, "As a group, they are not religious. When we ask if they are doing it for *jihad*, the answer is no." So although the American invasion confronted the Iraqis with the same enemy as Al-Qaeda and Islamist groups operating in other countries, and religious groups that found common cause with them did play some role in resistance to the occupation, the Iraqi Resistance maintained a primarily secular and nationalist orientation. The roles of religious parties in the occupation government and in violence against civilians by both sides ultimately only further undermined popular support for religious politics in Iraq.[256]

American promotion of sectarian and ethnic parties was a deliberate effort to undermine the strong tradition of secular, nationalist politics that had endured in Iraq since 1958 and which posed the greatest challenge to the U.S. occupation. As we shall see in a later chapter on American plans for Iraq's oil, no nationalist or independent Iraqi government was ever going to agree to the terms that the United States wanted to impose for the privatization of Iraq's oil industry and subser-

---

256. Sabrina Tavernise, "Violence leaves young Iraqis doubting clerics," *New York Times*, March 4 2008.

vience to American strategic interests. The overblown but nonetheless destructive sectarian divisions were a direct result of this U.S. strategy to divide and rule the country, not a new phase in some imaginary, long-running conflict between Sunnis and Shiites.

American officials exploited the ambitions of long-marginalized parties led by former exiles to establish an occupation government that was too weak and too illegitimate to survive beyond the walls of the Green Zone or without the protection of American forces even within its walls. An unemployment rate that rose to 60% permitted the recruitment of young men to new security forces linked to the Green Zone government, but their loyalty was nearly always either to a paycheck or to a party militia rather than to the government itself, and many were also active in the Resistance. For several years, as we shall see in the next chapter, the only Iraqi forces that the United States could rely on to follow its orders in Iraq were formed by combining the most brutal and unscrupulous elements of the Baathist security apparatus with Iranian-trained Badr Brigades and other exile groups.

The weakness of this government, its corruption by U.S. interests and its dependence on U.S. support were all essential to American policy, to prevent a reemergence of secular, nationalist Iraqi politics. However, as Gabriel Kolko has written, "The notion of an honest puppet is a contradiction Washington has failed to resolve anywhere in the world since 1945." The American false presumption of legitimacy for the occupation of Iraq blinded U.S. officials to the reality that whoever they placed in power in Iraq would face the same inevitable conflict between the self-serving interests of his American advisers and the insistent demands of the Iraqi people for sovereignty and independence. The prospect that U.S. interests could ultimately prevail was remote from the outset. But the narrative of "sectarian violence" obscured the violence of the occupation and provided a new way to explain the war to the folks back home after every other rationale had been discredited. It thus created an environment in both Iraq and the United States that permitted U.S. officials to order unrestrained escalations of violence against the people of Iraq in pursuit of their elusive goals.

CHAPTER 13. LAUNCHING THE DIRTY WAR IN IRAQ

In earlier chapters, we explored the role of Iraqi exile groups in the failed CIA coup in 1996; in fabricating evidence to support the American case for war with Iraq; and in the occupation government following the U.S. invasion. As these exile groups worked with U.S. occupation authorities to try to consolidate their positions and take control of the country, they naturally faced opposition from Iraqis who had remained in Iraq under the Baathist government, and who now saw the Americans and the exile groups cruelly stealing their long-denied hopes for democracy and self-determination.

The Americans were not going to allow independent domestic constituencies in Iraq to claim the right to govern their own country and deny them the fruits of victory. The U.S. government and its Iraqi allies were determined to retain instrumental control of the political process and to stifle dissenting voices that challenged their dominance. As we have seen, the U.S. government responded to peaceful protests, the beginning of armed resistance, and the CIA's warnings of more widespread resistance with an escalation of deadly force and a campaign of assassination by Israeli-trained U.S. Special Forces that continued throughout the occupation.

It soon became clear that the Iraqi exile groups were also slated to play an important role in the violent response to dissent in occupied Iraq. On January 1st 2004, Robert Dreyfus reported in the *American Prospect* that the U.S. government planned to create paramilitary units comprised of militiamen from Iraqi Kurdish and exile groups including the Badr Brigades, the Iraqi National Congress and the Iraqi National Accord to wage a campaign of terror and extra-judicial killing. Dreyfus called his article "Phoenix Rising." Former CIA counter-terrorism chief Vincent Cannistraro told him, "They're clearly cooking up joint teams to do Phoenix-like things, like they did in Vietnam," referring to the assassination and terror campaign that killed tens of thousands of civilians as that war similarly spiraled out of American control.[257]

The $87 billion supplemental appropriation for the war in November 2003 included $3 billion for a classified program headed by an Air Force brigadier-general, most of which would be used to fund the paramilitaries for the next three years. Over that period, the news from Iraq gradually came to be dominated by reports of death squads and ethnic cleansing, usually couched in the language of "sectarian violence" discussed in the last chapter. However, while some of this violence may eventually have taken on a spontaneous, local character in some areas, there is overwhelming evidence that most of it was the fruition of the plans described by Cannistraro and other American experts in December 2003.

Despite subsequent American efforts to distance U.S. policy from the horrific results of this campaign, it was launched with the full support of conservative opinion-makers in the United States. Having apparently learned nothing from the pre-war intelligence fiasco, the *Wall Street Journal* declared in an editorial that, "The Kurds and the Iraqi National Congress have excellent intelligence operations that we should allow them to exploit ... especially to conduct counterinsurgency in the Sunni Triangle." Gary Schmitt of the Project for a New American Century wrote a paper proposing the CORDS program in Vietnam, which included the Phoenix campaign, as an excellent model for Iraq.

On March 15th, 2004, the *New Statesman* published an article by Stephen Grey titled "Rule of the Death Squads." The results of Grey's investigation into the murder of Professor Abdul-Latif Ali al-Mayah in Baghdad on January 19th 2004 suggested that the Phoenix campaign in Iraq was already under way. Professor al-Mayah was the director of the Baghdad Centre for Human Rights and the fourth professor from al-

---

257. Robert Dreyfus, "Phoenix rising," *American Prospect*, January 1st 2004.

Mustansiriya University to be killed. Twelve hours before he died in a hail of gunfire, he had denounced the corruption of the occupation's Iraqi Governing Council on Al-Jazeera television. Men with red keffiyehs covering their faces stopped his car on his way to work, and ordered him to get out. As he opened the door to do so, they shot him three times in the head. They then fired another seventeen shots into his body as it lay in the street.[258]

Abdul-Latif al-Mayah was born in Basra, and he spent his life as a poorly paid academic. Al-Mayah joined the Baath Party as a young man, but he quit the party in 1991. He was imprisoned in 1996, after calling publicly for elections in Iraq. He credited his escape from torture and long imprisonment to the lucky coincidence that one of his interrogators was a former student. After the invasion, he predicted that he would be assassinated by the CIA or the Mossad. He told his brother that he had received an e-mail from a member of the Iraqi Governing Council suggesting that "it would be safer if he left the country."

A senior American military spokesman blamed al-Mayah's death on "the guerillas," saying that "Silencing urban professionals .. works against everything we're trying to do here." But a senior Iraqi police officer gave Stephen Grey a very different explanation of who killed Professor al-Mayah and why. "Dr. Abdul-Latif was becoming more and more popular because he spoke for people on the street here," the officer told him. "He made some politicians quite jealous." He told Grey that al-Mayah's was the eighth apparent political assassination in a month in the small district where he lived.

Then, wrote Grey, "the leather-clad commander, tightly gripping his new Motorola police radio, looked at me sternly and demanded that his name never be printed." The commander continued, "You can look no

---

258. Stephen Grey, "Rule of the death squads," *New Statesman*, March 15 2004.

further than the Governing Council. There are political parties in this city who are systematically killing people. They are politicians that are backed by the Americans and who arrived to Iraq from exile with a list of their enemies. I've seen these lists. They are killing people one by one."

Other Iraqi officials told Grey that many of the dead were victims of "death by Google." If their names appeared on lists of Baath Party members or supporters on the internet, they were automatically added to the death squads' lists. By some accounts, the internet lists were originally published by the Iranian secret service, with the intention that they would be used by death squads whenever Saddam Hussein's regime was eventually overthrown. They included much of the civic leadership of the country, from military officers to scientists and academics to writers and artists. As in any country ruled by a single political party, joining the Baath Party was an important step in many peoples' careers and did not necessarily signify support for its repressive policies.

By the end of 2004, Dr. Isam al-Rawi, a geologist who was the head of Iraq's Association of University Lecturers, had collected details of about 300 academics and university staff who had been assassinated. He estimated that another 2,000 more had fled the country to avoid meeting the same fate. Professor al-Rawi chose to remain. He was assassinated outside his home in Baghdad on October 30th, 2006.[259]

At the end of 2005, the Minister of Education of the occupation's transitional government reported that another 296 university faculty and staff had been murdered that year. The Brussels Tribunal on Iraq sent a list of assassinated academics to the UN's Special Rapporteur on Summary Executions. The tribunal pointed out that the victims came

---

259. Charles Crain, "Approximately 300 academics have been killed," *USA Today*, January 16 2005.

from many different backgrounds, and had diverse ethnic and political affiliations. The only common factor was that they were all vocal opponents of the U.S. occupation.

On February 28th, 2006, Iraqi novelist Haifa Zangana, herself a victim of Saddam Hussein and a long-time exile in London, wrote an article for the *Guardian* about the "systematic campaign to assassinate Iraqis who speak out against the occupation." "Like many Iraqis," she concluded, "I believe these killings are politically motivated and connected to the occupying forces' failure to gain any significant social support in the country. For the occupation's aims to be fulfilled, independent minds have to be eradicated. We feel that we are witnessing a deliberate attempt to destroy intellectual life in Iraq."[260]

Following the formation of Ayad Allawi's interim government and John Negroponte's appointment as U.S. Ambassador in June 2004, Allawi declared a "state of emergency" and President Bush said that Allawi would have to "take tough measures." An Iraqi-American named Falah al-Naqib was appointed to head the Interior Ministry of the interim government. He was the son of General Hassan al-Naqib, the former Chief of Staff of the Iraqi army who defected to the United States during the 1970s and was one of the founders of the Iraqi National Congress in 1992. Both Naqibs had long-term contacts with the CIA while in exile. In September 2004, Falah al-Naqib appointed his uncle, another former Iraqi general and Baath Party official named Adnan Thavit to lead a new paramilitary force called the Special Police Commandos.[261]

These forces were formed under the direct supervision of Falah al-Naqib and Steven Casteel, who had run the interior ministry for the Coalition Provisional Authority. He stayed on in Iraq as Naqib's Senior Adviser, reporting directly to Ambassador Negroponte. General David

---

260. Haifa Zangana, "Death of a professor," *Guardian*, February 28, 2006.
261. Sgt. Jared Zabaldo, "Iraq interior ministry forms police commando battalions," *American Forces Press Service*, October 20, 2004.

Petraeus, who was officially in charge of training new Iraqi security forces, was reportedly not informed of the Special Police Commandos' existence until the new force was already established in the ruins of an old army base on the edge of the Green Zone, but he went along with Naqib and Casteel's plans.

Retired Colonel James Steele took charge of training the commandos, and he continued to work with them and to accompany them on deployments until he left Iraq in April 2005. Steele was a veteran of previous dirty wars in Cambodia and Central America who had later become a vice president at Enron and was officially sent to Iraq following the invasion as an "energy consultant." Now he was appointed as Counselor for Iraqi Security Forces to Ambassador Negroponte.

By October 2004, two battalions of Special Police Commandos were operational, a third was in training, two more had been recruited, and a sixth was planned. General Thavit described some of the recruits as "police who have previous experience fighting terrorism and also people who received special training under the former regime." However, one of the first brigades formed, called the Wolf Brigade, consisted mainly of Badr Brigade militiamen and was commanded by a Shiite general called Mohammed Qureshi, more commonly known as Abu Walid. The Wolf Brigade fought alongside U.S. forces and Kurdish militiamen in Mosul in November 2004 to suppress the rebellion that broke out during the U.S. assault on Fallujah. This Badr-dominated commando brigade later provided the model for the expansion of the Special Police Commandos under the Dawa and SCIRI transitional government in 2005 and it played a leading role in the subsequent reign of terror in Baghdad.

By November 2004, Reuters reported that U.S. and British special forces operating around Iskandariya operated "almost exclusively alongside commandos from the Ministry of Interior and a SWAT team from the provincial capital Hilla." None of the Iraqi commandos would speak to reporters, but their American commander told Reuters, "The hardest fighters we have are the former special forces from Saddam's days." Across the country, American and British forces were blending ideologically committed exile and Kurdish militias with the most brutal forces from the Baathist regime to create new organs of state terror to suppress resistance to the occupation.[262]

In January 2005, more than a year after Hersh, Borger, and Dreyfus had first exposed the Pentagon's planning for assassination and paramilitary operations in Iraq, the "Salvador Option" hit the pages of *Newsweek*: "One Pentagon proposal would send Special Forces teams to advise, support and possibly train Iraqi squads, most likely hand-picked Kurdish Peshmerga fighters and Shiite militiamen, to target Sunni insurgents *and their sympathizers* (italics mine)." While Special Forces would conduct raids into Syria, "... activities inside Iraq itself would be carried out by Iraqi paramilitaries," U.S. officials told *Newsweek*.[263]

The idea that the U.S. military adviser mission to El Salvador in the 1980s could provide a model to be emulated in Iraq must have seemed strange to many Americans. But, in military circles, the low budget and low public profile of the U.S. forces in El Salvador, and the outsourcing of state terrorism to local proxy forces, were regarded as key components of a policy that had succeeded in preventing the total defeat of the U.S.-backed government. In fact, in 2004, two senior U.S. Army officers published a favorable review of the American proxy war in Colombia based precisely on its similarities to the El Salvador model.

They wrote, "Presidents Ronald Reagan and George H. W. Bush supported a small, limited war (from a U.S. perspective) while trying to keep U.S. military involvement a secret from the American public and

---

262. Alastair Macdonald, "U.S. sends in secret weapon: Saddam's old commandos," *Reuters*, November 27 2004.

263. Michael Hirsh and John Barry, "The Salvador option," *Newsweek*, January 8 2005.

media. Present U.S. policy toward Colombia appears to follow this same disguised, quiet, media-free approach." While most Americans would regard this as a highly disturbing aspect of U.S. military involvement in either country, Major General Valenzuela and Colonel Rosello, who wrote the article, saw this "disguised, quiet, media-free approach" as a tactic that worked from a military point of view. As we will see, the Salvador Option in Iraq incorporated precisely these features into yet another American military horror story.[264]

The underlying views of Pentagon officials who backed these policies were once more exposed to public scrutiny by *Newsweek*'s Salvador Option article. An American officer acknowledged that the problem facing U.S. forces in Iraq was not limited to the armed Resistance but extended to the active and passive support that the population was giving the resistance fighters. "The Sunni population is paying no price for the support it is giving to the terrorists," he said. "From their point of view, it is cost-free. We have to change that equation."

This officer's statement unwittingly revealed the fundamental nature of "dirty war." He expressed precisely the rationale that lay behind previous American dirty wars in Latin America and the worst excesses of the Vietnam War. The purpose of dirty war is not to identify and then detain or kill actual resistance fighters. The target of dirty war is the civilian population, rather than the resistance fighters it supports, and this is what distinguishes it from any conceivably legitimate form of counter-insurgency. Dirty war is a strategy of state terrorism and collective punishment against an entire civilian population with the objective of terrorizing it into submission.

---

264. Major General Alfred A. Valenzuela and Colonel Victor M. Rosello, "Expanding roles and missions in the war on drugs and terrorism: El Salvador and Colombia," *Military Review*, March-April 2004.
http://usacac.army.mil/CAC/milreview/English/MarApr04/MarApr04/valenzuela.pdf

Newsweek implied that these operations were still being debated at the Pentagon and the CIA, and were not yet under way in Iraq. It essentially ignored Hersh, Dreyfus, and Borger's articles a year before; Grey's evidence that the campaign was already operational by January 2004; and subsequent reports on the recruitment, training, and deployment of the Special Police Commandos. What really seems to have been in contention in early 2005 was an expansion, under the Pentagon's authority, of a campaign already launched in Iraq by the CIA, U.S. special forces and Iraqi exile groups. The Kurdish and exile groups that had worked with the Americans to launch this dirty war in the early days of the occupation had come to form the core of successive governing institutions established by the United States in Iraq. Their role in its campaign of state terrorism was becoming institutionalized, and their victims would eventually number in the hundreds of thousands, or even the millions if we include all the people forced to flee the reign of terror.

While there had been virtually no official response to Hersh, Borger, Dreyfus, or Grey's articles, one aspect of the *Newsweek* article received a direct challenge from one of its most prominent subjects within two days of its publication. *Newsweek* had alluded to the strange coincidence that John Negroponte, the former Political Officer in Saigon during the Vietnam War and the U.S. Ambassador to Honduras in the 1980s, was once again at the heart of U.S. policy just as an American war was taking a turn to the dark side.

Negroponte told *Newsweek* that the use of his name in its Salvador Option story was "utterly gratuitous" and that he was not involved in military strategy in Iraq. And yet James Steele and Steven Casteel, the two senior American advisers working with the Interior Ministry's Special Police Commandos, both reported directly to Ambassador Negroponte. Within a few months, Steele, Casteel and their Iraqi trainees and associates would be linked to a growing wave of atrocities that fit precisely the model *Newsweek* had described.

Also hidden in plain sight were the resumes that James Steele and Steven Casteel brought with them to Iraq. Like Negroponte, they were both veterans of other American dirty wars. Between 1984 and 1986, Steele was the commander of the U.S. Military Advisor Group in El Salvador. He and his subordinates were responsible for training and working with Salvadoran forces that killed tens of thousands of civilians in their own country. Steele was also deeply implicated in the Iran-Contra affair, overseeing flights from Ilopango air-base in El Salvador that delivered weapons and supplies to the U.S.-backed "Contras" in Nicaragua. The FBI found that he had lied to Iran-Contra investigators and to the Senate Intelligence Committee to help cover up the scandal, but he eventually confessed to his role in the affair after failing an FBI polygraph test. Steele then provided incriminating evidence against senior officials, including U.S. Ambassador Corr, and was not charged with a crime.[265]

The only personal price Steele appears to have paid for his part in Iran-Contra is that Senator Harkin blocked his promotion to Brigadier General. It certainly did not prevent the U.S. government, perhaps via the CIA, from calling on him to establish a similar program in Iraq to the one he oversaw in El Salvador. The common pattern of atrocities committed by Steele's trainees in El Salvador and Iraq is ultimately at least as disturbing as his role in Iran-Contra and equally deserving of thorough investigation.

Before joining the CPA in Iraq, Steven Casteel was the Chief of Intelligence for the U.S. Drug Enforcement Agency (DEA). He worked for the DEA in Peru, Bolivia, and Colombia, where he was involved in the campaign to track and kill drug lord Pablo Escobar. This campaign brought together many of the same elements as the dirty war in Iraq:

---

265. Lawrence E. Walsh, "Final report of the independent counsel for Iran/Contra matters," *United States Court of Appeals for the District of Columbia Circuit*, August 4 1993.

the CIA, U.S. special forces, local police forces, and paramilitaries. In particular, it saw the birth of Los Pepes (People Persecuted by Pablo Escobar), a death squad formed by rival drug dealers, including the leaders of the Cali cartel, to hunt down and kill Escobar and his associates. Los Pepes conducted joint raids with American DEA agents and received U.S. funding. In 1997, the leaders of Los Pepes joined the core leadership of the AUC paramilitary force, which was responsible for about 75% of civilian deaths in the Colombian civil war over the next decade. Diego Murillo-Bejarano or "Don Berna," one of the leaders of Los Pepes, became the Inspector General of the AUC.

As news of atrocities by interior ministry forces in Iraq hit the newsstands in 2005, Casteel would play a critical role in blaming extrajudicial killings on "insurgents" with stolen police uniforms, vehicles and weapons. He also claimed that torture centers were run by rogue elements of the Interior Ministry, even as accounts came to light of torture taking place inside the ministry headquarters where he and other Americans worked. The deference of the Western media to American officials like Steven Casteel preserved the essential factor of "plausible denial" that prevented a worldwide popular and diplomatic outcry over the massive escalation of the dirty war in Iraq in 2005 and 2006. This was consistent with the "disguised, quiet, media-free approach" that General Valenzuela and Colonel Rosello admired in El Salvador.

In January 2005, even as *Newsweek* broke its Salvador Option story, U.S. forces were busy setting up a high-tech operations center for the Special Police Commandos at an "undisclosed location" in Iraq. American technicians installed satellite phones and computers with uplinks to the internet and U.S. forces networks. The command center had direct connections to the Iraqi Interior Ministry and to every U.S. forward operating base in the country. A Special Police commander explained, "This is the first Iraqi force created in the organization of the Ministry of the Interior to fight the insurgency. The Americans have provided the equipment, supplies, munitions, phones, and training."[266]

As the *Newsweek* story broke, General Downing, the former head of U.S. Special Forces, appeared on NBC's *Today Show*. He explained to the host, Katie Couric, "I think what they're considering is to use a special—or more special Iraqi units trained and equipped and perhaps even led by U.S. special forces to conduct strike operations against this insurgency, against the leaders of it, which of course is a very valid strategy, a very valid tactic. And it's actually something we've been doing since we started the war back in March of 2003."[267]

A worried Katie Couric asked, "But is this going to be used more, or in greater numbers? According to *Newsweek*, they're going to—the U.S. special forces will train specially chosen Kurdish forces and Shiite militiamen ... So does this signal a—I guess an escalation of this technique at least?"

Downing responded, "I think what we're looking at is—there are already some special units formed. We have Special Police Commandos now of the Iraqi forces which conduct these kind of strike operations ... But, Katie, I really want to emphasize what they are going after here. These insurgent leaders, these are terrorists ... These are very, very legitimate targets, and actually part of the overall strategy for countering the insurgency."

Couric, to her credit, did not give up: "But in El Salvador many innocent civilians were killed when these kind of tactics were employed. Are you concerned about that or the possibility that this will increase anti-American sentiment in the general Iraqi population?"

---

266. Sgt. Matt Murphy, "Iraqi police commandos get connected," *DefendAmerica News*, February 11 2005.

267. "The Today Show," *NBC*, January 10 2005; quoted in Stephen R. Shalom, "Phoenix Rising in Iraq?," *ZNet Commentary*, February 11 2005. http://www.zmag.org/znet/viewArticle/6895

In the face of Couric's persistence, Downing fell back on a well-worn fiction about the American role in El Salvador. "Katie, this has nothing to do with El Salvador. Those operations that were conducted down there were conducted by renegade military leaders," he claimed. In fact, the U.N. Truth Commission in El Salvador identified the Atlacatl Battalion and the other Salvadoran units that worked most closely with Steele and other U.S. advisers as the ones primarily responsible for thousands of cases of torture and extra-judicial killing. Two-thirds of the officers linked to atrocities were graduates of the U.S. School of the Americas, where Latin American officers were explicitly trained to torture and summarily execute suspected guerillas.[268]

Downing insisted to Couric that, *"This is under the control of the U.S. forces, of the current interim Iraqi government.* There's no need to think that we're going to have any kind of a killing campaign that's going to maim innocent civilians" (my emphasis). Within months, Iraq was swept by exactly that "kind of a killing campaign." But Downing was correct that the forces involved, namely the Special Police Commandos he referred to in the interview, were "under the control of the U.S. forces," like all Iraqi forces recruited under U.S. occupation.

A few days later, General Boykin, the Deputy Under-Secretary of Defense for Intelligence, testified to Congressional intelligence committees. He was asked point-blank whether the U.S. government should re-establish an assassination program like Operation Phoenix in Iraq. He responded that U.S. forces in Iraq and Afghanistan were "doing a pretty good job of that right now." "We're going after these people," he said, "Killing or capturing these people is a legitimate mission for the

---

268. http://www.usip.org/library/tc/doc/reports/el_salvador/
tc_es_03151993_toc.html; also Lisa Haugaard, "Torture 101 in the US School of the Americas (SOA)," *In These Times,* October 14th 1996.
http://www.thirdworldtraveler.com/SOA/torture101_SOA.html

department ... I think we're doing what the Phoenix program was designed to do, without all the secrecy."[269]

Meanwhile, the *Wall Street Journal* interviewed General David Petraeus about the Special Police Commandos and other "irregular" forces recruited by the occupation government in Iraq. General Petraeus told the *Journal*, "There is a tension between on the one hand encouraging and fostering initiative and on the other executing the plan for the Iraqi Security Forces everyone has agreed on. To be candid, I would err on the side of fostering initiative. I want to get the hell out of here."[270]

The *Journal* made it clear that the Special Police Commandos were in a different category than other irregular and militia units. The commandos had already fought against the Resistance alongside U.S. forces and had lost 43 killed and about 300 wounded during deployments in Samarra, Mosul and elsewhere. U.S. officers praised them as "the toughest force we've got." General Petraeus credited Generals Thavit and Abu Walid and other Commando leaders. "The reason the Commandos are so special is that a couple of great leaders at the top have just flat out put their imprint on that organization," Petraeus said.

On April 4th 2005, the Interior Ministry announced a plan to expand the recruitment of commando and special forces units to a total of 24 battalions. Generals Thavit and Abu Walid were by now household names thanks to a grotesque form of "reality" TV show called "Terrorism in the Grip of Justice," which displayed badly beaten Iraqis confessing to resistance activities and horrible crimes on U.S.-backed al-Iraqiya television. To accentuate their humiliation, some were also forced to confess to being homosexuals. The show was soon linked directly to atrocities. The body of an Iraqi policeman accused on the

---

269. Douglas Jehl and Thom Shanker, "Congress is reviewing Pentagon on intelligence activities," *New York Times*, February 4 2005, Page A4.
270. Greg Jaffe, "New factor in Iraq: irregular brigades fill security void," *Wall Street Journal*, February 16 2005.

show of killing two other policemen was delivered to his family a few days after his confession was broadcast.[271]

As the new U.S.-backed Islamist government prepared to take office in May 2005, the *Los Angeles Times* reported that it was planning "to crack down on Sunni-led insurgents and purge suspected infiltrators and corrupt officers from the nation's security forces ... A likely tactic, authorities say, is unleashing well-trained Iraqi commandos in Baghdad and other trouble spots. The special forces units have a reputation for effectiveness and brutality ... The plan for Iraqi commandos' wider deployment is indicative of how the raging guerilla conflict here is increasingly a war pitching Iraqis against Iraqis, leading to a decline in U.S. casualty rates as the number of Iraqi dead soars."[272]

Steven Casteel remained in place to work with the incoming Interior Minister of the transitional occupation government, a senior Badr Brigades militia commander by the name of Bayan al-Jabr. Jabr told Lebanon's al-Hayat newspaper that, "The recent acceleration in terrorist attacks is posing a serious challenge on the ground. We must take immediate action."

Meanwhile, *Knight Ridder Newspapers* reported that the CIA was still in firm control of the "intelligence" functions of the Iraqi puppet government. "Right after Saddam's ouster, the U.S.-led coalition took the top intelligence agents from each of the main opposition parties and trained them in how to turn raw intelligence into targets that could be used in operations," an Iraqi intelligence expert who took part on the program explained. "The CIA recruited agents from SCIRI, the two main Kurdish factions, and two secular Arab parties: the Iraqi Na-

---

271. "Iraq Ministry to enlist ex-army officers into commando units - official," Al-Sharqiyah, April 4 2005.
http://www.globalsecurity.org/wmd/library/news/iraq/2005/04/imm-050405-unami.htm
272. Patrick J. McDonnell and Solomon Moore, "Iraq to purge corrupt officers," *Los Angeles Times*, May 1 2005.

tional Congress led by Ahmed Chalabi and the Iraqi National Accord led by Iyad Allawi who later became the interim prime minister."[273]

Now, faced with a nominally independent Iraqi "transitional" government, "The CIA has refused to hand over control of Iraq's intelligence service to the newly elected Iraqi government." Without naming him, *Knight Ridder* noted that the director of Iraq's secret police had been handpicked and paid by the U.S. government, and still reported directly to the CIA according to Iraqi politicians and intelligence officers.

The new Shiite Islamist government had conceded that the post of Defense Minister would go to a Sunni Arab, although it could not find one it liked. The *Los Angeles Times* article reported therefore that

> The new Shiite leadership appears determined to use its control of the Interior Ministry as a spear point in coming offensives. Tens of thousands of police officers and other troops are under its command. Authorities plan increased deployment of the Interior Ministry's special commandos, known as Maghawir (Fearless Warrior) brigades. The units are largely composed of well-trained veterans of Hussein's military who worked closely with U.S. forces during pitched battles last year in Najaf, Fallouja, and the northern city of Mosul ... The special forces units sport provocative titles—including the Wolf, Scorpion, Tiger and Thunder brigades. Many Sunni Arabs view the squads suspiciously as largely composed of Shiite and Kurdish rivals eager to exact revenge for decades of suppression under Hussein.

The commandos had already raided some Sunni mosques in Baghdad and Baquba in April 2005, killing at least one imam. Another Sunni cleric, Sheik Abdul-Salam Kubaysi of the Muslim Scholars' Association, told the *Times*, "I blame the Maghawir for this outrage. All of these

---

273. Hannah Allam and Warren Strobel, "CIA won't turn over spy info to Iraqis," *Knight Ridder Newspapers*, May 9 2005.

people arrested are not terrorists. They are wise, simple and humble people." General Abu Walid of the Wolf Brigade gave a good indication of what he and his American partners had in store for Baghdad in the coming months: "We are studying Baghdad now, to be ready for any mission we are assigned. Baghdad is filled with terrorists."

Then, on May 6th 2005, amid other reports of violence in Iraq, the *BBC*'s Jim Muir noticed an incident that did not fit the pattern of insurgent activity he was accustomed to reporting. "When the insurgents kill people they regard as collaborators, they publicize it," Muir noted. "Bodies are thrown in the street, often with signs attached to them, warning that others will share the same fate." But this new incident involved fourteen bodies of Sunni Arab execution victims discovered in shallow graves in the Kasra-Wa-Atash industrial district at the edge of a predominantly Shiite area. The bodies showed signs of torture, including broken skulls, other fractures, and burns. Many had their right eyeballs removed. They were identified as the bodies of fourteen farmers who had been arrested at a vegetable market. Another eight bodies were found a week later in the al-Shaab area of Baghdad in a similar condition.[274]

By May 15th 2005, the Wolf Brigade was directly implicated in this wave of extra-judicial execution in Baghdad. As well as the eight bodies found in al-Shaab, seven more were found behind a mosque in Ore at about the same time. But two of the victims survived, and they identified their assailants as a unit of the Wolf Brigades. "They arrested us and fired bullets at our heads after having our mouths muzzled and hands tied behind our backs," according to one of them. The two survi-

---

274. "Baghdad 'execution victims' found," *BBC News*, May 6 2005. http://news.bbc.co.uk/2/hi/middle_east/4520389.stm

vors were taken to a hospital, but one of them was recaptured from the hospital by interior ministry forces and was never seen again.[275]

Hareth al-Dari of the Muslim Scholars' Association told *Islam Online*, "The mass killings and the crackdown and detention campaigns in northeastern Baghdad over the past two days by members of the Iraqi police or by an Interior Ministry special force known as the Wolf Brigade are part of a state terror policy." Al-Dari also spoke at the funeral of one of those killed, a cleric named Hassan al-Naimi who was abducted from his mosque in al-Shaab on May 16th by Special Police Commandos and Badr militiamen. Al-Dari told the congregation, "This is state terrorism by the Ministry of the Interior," and called for the resignation of the new Interior Minister. A large crowd outside the mosque chanted, "We will take revenge on the brigade of shame."

Al-Dari also accused the occupation government of "trying to hide the truth and cover up those behind the killings." But even the commander of the Iraqi National Guard confirmed the identity of the units conducting these raids, "Iraqi National Guardsmen have no connection with the detention campaigns in the area over the past two days. The detention campaign was conducted by the Wolf Brigades, which was responsible for taking the slain Iraqis to a camp in central Baghdad."

Muqtada al-Sadr made a rare public appearance to prohibit his followers from taking part in this campaign. "Any action targeting unarmed civilians is forbidden under any circumstances," he said in Najaf. "All Sunnis cannot be held responsible for the terrorist deeds of the occupiers and Nawaseb (Wahabis)." As he reiterated two months later, "The occupation itself is the problem. Iraq not being independent is the

---

275. Samir Haddad, "Sunnis complain of "state terror" in Iraq," *Islam Online*, May 17 2005. http://www.islamonline.net/English/News/2005-05/17/article02.shtml

problem. And other problems stem from that—from sectarianism to civil war. The entire American presence causes this."[276]

On May 19th 2005, the Arab League discussed the new pattern of atrocities in Iraq at a meeting in Cairo. Secretary General Amr Moussa urged "all Iraqi parties to show restraint and act responsibly in the face of those who try to sow the seeds of discord between Iraq's communities," a veiled reference to the American role in these developments. A group of about 1,000 Sunni Arabs meeting in Baghdad issued the following statement: "We ask for the creation of an independent investigation team to look into the murders, the torture of detainees, and we demand the Interior Minister's dismissal."[277]

American reporting on this new crisis in Iraq quickly took an Orwellian turn. On May 21st 2005, *Knight Ridder Newspapers* ran a feature on the Wolf Brigade by Hannah Allam that didn't even mention its already widely acknowledged links to this new wave of extra-judicial killings. Instead it was titled "Wolf Brigade the most loved and feared of Iraqi security forces," and it presented them as the real-life heroes of al-Iraqiya's "Terrorism in the Grip of Justice."

Here's an excerpt: "Standing outside their ramshackle barracks one recent day, members of the Wolf Brigade preferred to focus on their adoring public. With pride, they described the reaction they get when they don ski masks and zip through Baghdad streets with rocket-propelled grenade launchers and machine guns in the backs of their trademark blue-and-white pickups .... Even when Iraqis first shrink at the sight of armed men tooling around the city, there is a palpable change when they notice the unique logo of the Wolf Brigade. Drivers honk, children cheer, and street vendors ply them with falafel and bot-

---

276. Patrick Cockburn, "Iraq's top Shia cleric warns of 'genocidal war'," *The Independent*, July 19 2005.

277. "Arab League concerned over targeting Iraqi Sunnis," *Islam Online*, May 19 2005. http://www.islamonline.net/English/News/2005-05/19/article03.shtml

tles of water. A 35-year-old commando named Majed Bilal put it simply: "Because we love them, they love us."[278]

In early June, *Knight Ridder* ran another piece by Tom Lasseter, Allam's colleague in Baghdad, about the role of the Badr Brigade in the terror campaign. Lasseter interviewed Mohammed Jassim Mohammed, a torture victim who told him that Iraqi soldiers had kidnapped him from his home in Baghdad in April and tortured him for more than twelve days. Mohammed said that they had not tried to conceal their affiliation with the Badr Brigade. "When we were tortured, they said 'How dare you fight against the Badr Brigade?' " Mohammed told Lasseter, sobbing over the phone. Lasseter reported that many of the victims of extra-judicial killings appeared to have been tortured before being killed. Like many of them, the cleric al-Naimi had holes in his head, neck, and shoulder that appeared to have been made by an electric drill.[279]

A U.S. Embassy official in Baghdad told Lasseter, "People are killed in Iraq for various reasons. It's not always clear why people are killed or who killed them. Sometimes it's clear, sometimes it's not clear. But I don't want to go any further." A number of Iraqi Interior Ministry officials were more candid. A Sunni brigadier-general told Lasseter, "There is no real difference between the Badr Brigade and the former special forces we had. If you talked badly about them in the past, you could be killed. And it is still the same. If you talked about the Badr Brigade, you might be killed."

Firas al-Nakib, another Sunni who was a senior legal adviser at the Interior Ministry, told Lasseter that 160 senior officials had been dismissed by the new transitional government and that many police

---

278. Hannah Allam, "Wolf Brigade the most loved and feared of Iraqi security forces," *Knight Ridder Newspapers*, May 21 2005.

279. Tom Lasseter, "Sunnis claim Shiite militia carries out campaign of threats, murder," *Knight Ridder Newspapers*, June 8 2005.

commanders had been replaced by SCIRI or Badr Brigade loyalists. When Nakib asked at work about a raid on a mosque in his neighborhood, other officials told him to stay out of the matter. The bodies of five of the thirty people arrested that day turned up mutilated and tortured at the morgue. The other twenty-five disappeared without a trace. Nakib gave no credence to a spokesman's statement that the ministry's forces were not involved in the raid and that it might be connected to the theft of some police uniforms. Lasseter asked Nakib who he thought was behind the abductions and killings. Nakib paused, and then said, "Badr, of course."

But *Knight Ridder* failed to mention that the specific Badr force blamed for most of these atrocities was the very same Wolf Brigade that it had heaped praise on two weeks earlier. And it positioned the American officials who had recruited, trained, equipped, and continued to work with these forces as being concerned and puzzled by reports of atrocities. In all their reporting on the reign of terror in Baghdad, *Knight Ridder* and other U.S. media outlets never connected it to the well-known plans for precisely such a "Phoenix" or "Salvador" operation that present and former U.S. policymakers like Downing, Boykin, Cannistraro, and Schmitt had discussed quite openly before the horrific results of the operation started appearing at the morgue in Baghdad, and that had been clearly telegraphed by al-Jabr and Abu Walid before it began.

This failure to connect the dots between related events that were already a matter of public record pervaded American reporting on the war in Iraq and U.S. foreign policy in general. It facilitated a process by which events, actors, and issues became artificially separated and compartmentalized in the minds of readers. This fed a public discourse that was divorced from reality and was baffling to people in other countries where the media were not so deeply complicit in government propaganda operations.

The effect of simply not pointing out the connection between the Badr Brigade militia and the U.S.-backed Wolf Brigade and other Special Police Commando units, or the extent of American recruitment, training, command, and control of these units, was far-reaching. It distorted American perceptions of events in Iraq throughout the ensuing escalation of the war, creating the impression of senseless violence initiated by the Iraqis themselves and concealing the American hand in the planning and execution of the most savage forms of violence. By providing cover for the crimes committed by the U.S. government, American news editors played a significant role in avoiding the public outrage that might have discouraged the further escalation of this campaign.

CHAPTER 14. ATTACKERS IN POLICE UNIFORMS

> *Days after Iraq's new Shiite-led government was announced on April 28, the bodies of Sunni Muslim men began turning up at the capital's central morgue after the men had been detained by people wearing Iraqi police uniforms.*
>
> *from "Sunni men in Baghdad targeted by attackers in police uniforms," Tom Lasseter and Yasser Salihee (deceased), Knight Ridder Newspapers, June 27 2005.*

In contrast with the complicity of American media in "plausible denial" for atrocities in Iraq, one very brave Iraqi was determined to investigate and report on the reality behind the wave of torture and extra-judicial executions that began to terrorize much of Baghdad in May 2005. Yasser Salihee was an Iraqi doctor who worked as a translator for *National Public Radio* and *Knight Ridder*. He was interested in journalism and wanted to help tell the world what was happening to his country. He could also earn more working for the Western media than practicing medicine in occupied Iraq. So, while his wife Ragha continued to care for the occupation's victims as an emergency room doctor at Yarmouk Hospital, Yasser set out to investigate who was really responsible for the escalating dirty war as a special correspondent for *Knight Ridder*.[280]

Dr. Yasser Salihee was killed with a single shot to the head by a sniper from the U.S. 3rd Infantry Division on June 24th 2005. He was driving to a garage to get gas and an oil-change before taking his children to a swimming pool on his day off. His editor, Steve Butler, told me he had no reason to think Yasser's death was connected to his work. A military investigation concluded that this was a random shooting, a tragic case of one more Iraqi who was in the wrong place at the wrong time. But U.S. military investigations of civilian deaths in Iraq were not

---

280. Jacki Lyden, "Dr. Yasser Salihee, translator and friend," *NPR Weekend Edition*, July 2 2005. http://www.npr.org/templates/story/story.php?storyId=4726759

reliable, as the Italian government found in its own inquiry into the killing of its intelligence agent Nicola Callipari. The links between the forces Yasser Salihee was investigating and the ones that killed him cast a long dark shadow over his death.

Three days after Yasser Salihee's death, *Knight Ridder* posthumously published a report on his investigation into the Interior Ministry's Special Police Commandos and their links to torture, extra-judicial killings, and disappearances in Baghdad. Although Dr. Salihee was silenced so quickly and so close to the beginning of this operation, this remains one of the most thorough investigations conducted into the reality behind the horrors of the dirty war in Iraq. In fairness to later investigators, Salihee's death and the growing climate of terror in Baghdad certainly had the effect of making subsequent investigations increasingly dangerous for reporters.

Salihee and his colleagues investigated at least thirty separate cases of abductions leading to torture and death. In every case, witnesses to the abductions gave him consistent accounts of raids by large numbers of police commandos, in uniform, in clearly-marked police vehicles, with police weapons and bullet-proof vests. And in every case, some or all of those detained were later found dead, with almost identical signs of torture, and they were usually killed by a single gunshot to the head.[281]

Salihee provided more background on the abduction and murder of 14 farmers that had first brought these operations to public attention. He interviewed two market vendors who had witnessed the abductions on May 5th. Ali Karim, a fruit vendor, told him, "A patrol of more than ten police vehicles drove up and parked. They were running through

---

281. Tom Lasseter and Yasser Salihee, "Sunni men in Baghdad targeted by attackers in police uniforms," *Knight Ridder Newspapers*, June 27, 2005.

the street with their guns, saying that the farmers had a car bomb with them."

Ahmed Adil independently corroborated his story: "We were sitting, and the police cars pulled up and spread in different directions. A neighborhood guard asked the police what they were doing—he said these are just farmers—and the police said don't get involved, they have a car bomb with them." Of course, there was no car bomb, but the farmers were arrested, tortured and killed. They were from Maidan, the scene of earlier fighting between Sunni resistance fighters and occupation government forces, so the apparent motive was to send a graphic message to people in that area about the price they should expect to pay for their opposition to the occupation.

A brigadier-general at the Interior Ministry told Salihee he had conducted a personal investigation into the detention and killing of his own brother. Every witness gave the same description of the abductors: men in police commando uniforms, flak vests and helmets, in white police Toyota Land Cruisers, carrying the Glock pistols that the Americans had issued to the Special Police Commandos. When the general tried to find out exactly which unit had been in his brother's neighborhood in west Baghdad when he disappeared, he was warned by colleagues that his inquiries were putting his own life in danger.

A grocer named Abu Ahmed was detained in south Baghdad and later released, but he was able to provide Salihee with some information about one of his neighbors, a welder named Anwar Jassim, who was not so lucky. Both men were detained by large groups of police commandos and were held in the same facility. Other men in Abu Ahmed's cell were periodically taken out of the cell and badly beaten with long wooden staffs. He could hear other prisoners screaming. Before he was released, his guards told him they had killed Jassim.

A group of police commandos delivered Jassim's body to the morgue at Yarmouk Hospital with a bullet wound to the back of his neck and cuts and bruises on his abdomen, back and neck. The commandos told Abu Amir, the director of the morgue, to keep the body outside where the dogs could eat it, "because he's a terrorist and he deserves it."

The last case that Yasser Salihee investigated before he was killed himself was that of Mohammed and Saadi Khalif, two brothers taken from a home in western Baghdad on June 10th 2005. Their family told him that about thirty uniformed policemen drove up in pickup trucks with police markings, radios, flak vests, and helmets. Ten of them came into the house. When the family went to the Yarmouk morgue to retrieve their bodies, Mohammed Khalif still had metal police hand-cuffs on his wrists. Their brother Ahmed described the condition of Saadi Khalif's body to Salihee, "The doctor told us he was choked and tortured before they shot him. He looked like he had been dragged by a car."

Yasser Salihee also interviewed Dr. Faik Baqr, the director and chief forensic investigator at the central morgue in Baghdad. He had noticed the new pattern of killing that was revealed by the state of the bodies he examined. Before the U.S. invasion, he examined an average of 16 bodies with gunshot wounds each month. The number had now sky-rocketed to about 500 per month. But it was not just the numbers that caught his attention. These men had been killed methodically. They had their hands tied or handcuffed behind their backs. They were blindfolded. They showed signs of electric shocks, beatings with cords and blunt objects, and were killed by a single gunshot to the head. The signs of torture on their bodies matched those seen on two groups of 32 and 67 prisoners rescued from Interior Ministry jails by representatives of the Ministry for Human Rights.

Asked who was responsible for this wave of torture and extra-judicial executions, Dr. Baqr said only, "It is a very delicate subject for society when you are blaming the police officers ... It is not an easy issue. We hear that they are captured by the police and then the bodies are found killed ... it's obviously increasing." Dr. Baqr eventually fled the country after receiving threats against his own life, which he of all people could hardly ignore.

Knight Ridder asked the Interior Ministry's senior adviser Steven Casteel about the reign of terror being conducted by his Iraqi partners. "The small numbers that we've investigated we've found to be either rumor or innuendo. You can buy a police uniform in twenty different places in the market," Casteel claimed. He said he knew of only one case in which Interior Ministry forces had falsely detained an Iraqi and beat him, and that both the troops and the commander had been convicted and jailed for that crime. Questioned about Interior Minister and Badr commander Bayan al-Jabr's role in torture and extra-judicial killings, he said that members of Jabr's family had been killed by the Baathist regime and that he therefore had "little patience for human rights violations."

So, after a whole career's experience with drug cartels, paramilitaries and corrupt police forces, the former chief of intelligence of the U.S. Drug Enforcement Administration claimed that the murders committed by his Iraqi partners were the work of "insurgents" posing as policemen. *Knight Ridder* acknowledged that Casteel's explanation raised "troubling questions about how insurgents are getting expensive new police equipment. The Toyotas, which cost more than $55,000 apiece, and Glocks, at about $500 each, are hard to come by in Iraq, and they're rarely used by anyone other than Western contractors and Iraqi security forces."

Based on the facts revealed by Salihee's investigation, *Knight Ridder* could have added that none of the eyewitness accounts were consistent with Casteel's hypothesis. None of these cases involved a small group of men with police uniforms and one or two police vehicles. On the contrary, they all involved well-organized raids by large groups of police commandos with ten to thirty clearly-marked police vehicles and the full complement of equipment issued to the commandos by their American trainers. This included radios connected to U.S. military networks via their high-tech U.S.-equipped command center, which was staffed by American as well as Iraqi personnel. And yet Casteel's absurd explanation became the party line of U.S. and Iraqi occupation officials throughout the escalation of this crisis in the coming months, until even complicit Western news editors demanded a better one.

When the smokescreen became too transparent even for the Western media, it gradually gave way to a new narrative of "sectarian violence," in which the perpetrators' links to the occupation government were more widely acknowledged but were treated as being irrelevant to their crimes. The term "Shiite militia" obscured the fundamental difference between Special Police Commando units and local Mahdi army militiamen, and the Centcom press office naturally blamed the anti-occupation Mahdi army for most of the atrocities. The Western media continued to ignore the mounting evidence that the U.S.-backed Special Police Commandos were the principal perpetrators of horrific violence against innocent civilians, and that this was the result of explicit and well-documented U.S. policy decisions.

After Yasser Salihee's death, Knight Ridder did not follow up on his investigation into the chain of command of the Special Police Commando death squads. American journalists continued to present Casteel's disingenuous and calculated efforts to confuse them with all the deference the American media traditionally reserve for U.S. government officials. They never even examined them in the context of Casteel's own interest in covering up the crimes of the Iraqis he supervised. The serious implications of the instrumental role played by Casteel, Steele, Petraeus, Negroponte, and other American officials in every phase of the recruitment, training, equipping, deployment, command, and control of these forces made this story either too dangerous for American journalists to examine or too explosive for their editors to print.

Admittedly, while Iraqi journalists faced the greatest dangers in occupied Iraq, Western reporters were not untouchable. Steven Vincent was an award-winning art critic from New York, who went to Iraq as a freelance journalist and reported for *National Review*, the *Wall Street Journal*, and *Harpers*. He wrote a book called *In the Red Zone* about life in occupied Iraq. On July 29th 2005, the *New York Times* published a piece by Vincent about police death squads that had killed hundreds of people, mostly Sunnis, in Basra where he was living. Four days after the article was published, Vincent was abducted by a group of men in a brand new white Chevrolet pick-up with police markings. His corpse was found by the side of a road outside the city with three gunshot wounds to the head.[282]

The British press were a little more forthright than their American counterparts. The *Financial Times* on June 29th 2005 reported on Operation Lightning, a huge sweep in Baghdad in which the Wolf Brigade arrested 474 people. All but 22 were reportedly released a month later, but they told tales of terrible torture. Wolf Brigade commandos gave a painter named Mustafa Mohammed Ali electric shocks to his ears and genitals from a hand-cranked telephone, and his descriptions of his treatment and torture were corroborated by other detainees.[283]

In an article in the *Observer* on July 3rd 2005, Peter Beaumont made no bones about the Interior Ministry's responsibility for torture and extra-judicial killings. He gave graphic descriptions of methods of torture described to him, from burning with irons to "being sat on the bottle," a brutal form of sodomy. Anonymous international officials inter-

---

282. Jenny Booth, "Basra blogger is abducted and murdered," *The Times*, August 3 2005.

283. Awadh al-Taee and Steve Negus, "Sunnis feel full force of Lightning strike," *Financial Times*, June 29 2005.

viewed by Beaumont in Iraq acknowledged the extent of the atrocities and the Interior Ministry's responsibility for them.[284]

Beaumont identified six Interior Ministry facilities in Baghdad where torture was taking place: the seventh floor of the Interior Ministry headquarters, al-Hadoud prison in the Kharkh district, the basement of a clinic in Shoula, the Nissor Square headquarters of the Wolf Brigade (understandably reputed to be one of the worst), al-Muthanna airbase, and the old National Security headquarters. An Iraqi official told him, "There are places we can get to and know about. But there are dozens of other places we know about where there is no access at all."

One international official told Beaumont, "What is so worrying is that allegations concerning the use of drills and irons during torture just keep coming back. And we have seen precisely the same evidence of torture on bodies that have turned up after they have been arrested. There is a dirty counter-insurgency war, led on the anti-insurgency side by groups responsible to different leaders. People are not appearing in court. Instead, what is happening to them is totally arbitrary."

On June 25th 2005, Beaumont attended a party at the Iraqi Ministry of Human Rights, coincidentally near one of the new Iraqi torture centers, to commemorate the U.N.'s International Day for the Victims of Torture. At the party, he spoke to Aida Ussayran, a British-Iraqi woman who was now the Deputy Human Rights Minister. She acknowledged that the abuses were getting worse not better, in spite of her efforts. Eating chocolate cake and drinking soda under a sign that read "No to Torture," another official told Beaumont, "There are people in the ministry (of interior) who want to use these means. It is in their ideology. It is their strategy. They do not understand anything else. They believe that human rights and the Convention against Torture are stupid."

---

284. Peter Beaumont, "Revealed: grim world of new Iraqi torture camps," *The Observer*, July 3 2005.

Beaumont also questioned the U.S. and British role in all this, given their relationship with the Iraqi forces committing these atrocities. "British and U.S. police and military officials act as advisers to Iraq's security forces," he wrote. "Foreign troops support Iraqi policing missions." In fact, all Iraqi "security" forces were still under the overall command of the "multi-national force," and the history of the recruitment, training, and deployment of the police commandos and the establishment of their command center in January 2005 had already revealed the extent and the sophistication of U.S. command and control of the Special Police Commandos.

The glaring question raised but unanswered by the *Observer* article was that, if its correspondent in Baghdad could identify at least six Interior Ministry facilities where torture and extra-judicial killings were taking place day in and day out, and if the forces committing the atrocities were under overall U.S. command and working closely with American and British trainers and advisers, why did U.S. forces not intervene to stop the atrocities? U.S. advisers to the Interior Ministry had their offices on the eighth floor, directly above a jail on the seventh floor where torture was taking place. At the very least, policy decisions were made at the highest level to turn a blind eye to the torture and murder of thousands of people.

The degree of U.S. initiative in the recruitment, training, equipping, deployment, command and control of the Special Police Commandos made it clear that American trainers and commanders established the parameters within which these forces operated. How explicitly these parameters were established, and who exactly determined what they should be has yet to be thoroughly investigated.

On July 6th 2005, the *Associated Press* obtained a report by an Iraqi lawyers' association that documented more abuses by the Wolf Brigade. In particular, it challenged the farcical and gruesome parade of "confessions" broadcast on the U.S.-backed "Terrorism in the Grip of Justice"

TV show. The association had located and identified 27 people who were still alive in spite of televised confessions by their alleged murderers, and the *AP*'s Mariam Fam spoke to a number of people who had been forced to record confessions following brutal torture and humiliation.[285]

In particular, Fam investigated the case of Khalida Zakiya, a 46-year-old housewife in Mosul. She was detained for nearly three months, tortured, and publicly humiliated by the Wolf Brigade as a means of pressuring her brother to turn himself in, presumably to receive even worse treatment than her. When the Wolf Brigade finally left Mosul to transfer its reign of terror to Samarra and Baghdad, it turned Zakiya over to the local police. The police saw no reason to hold her, and the police chief later came to her house and apologized for her treatment.

Khalida Zakiya had confessed on national television to providing money and explosives to insurgents. But what led up to her appearance was eleven days of solitary confinement punctuated with threats of public nudity and of being "sat on the bottle." This treatment climaxed in a bizarre confrontation with another detainee, who accused her of having sex with him and then giving him money and explosives for the Resistance. Left alone with him for a minute, she asked him how he could say such things. He pulled up the legs of his pants, and showed her streams of blood running down both his legs. Being "sat on the bottle" was more than an idle threat. Zakiya was then whipped with electric cables by six men for about fifteen minutes, and thrown back in her cell. Two days later she was placed in front of a TV camera and forced to read a scripted confession.

On July 13th 2005, another police commando raid in northern Baghdad detained 13 people, including a Sunni cleric named Dia Mohammed

---

285. Mariam Fam, "Iraqis say security forces use torture," *Associated Press*, July 6 2005.

al-Janabi. Twelve of their tortured bodies were recovered the following day in Sadr City. The families collected the bodies, and one who was a Shiite was taken to Najaf for burial. Then came another report that 10 Sunni men had suffocated inside a police vehicle a few days earlier. The *Gulf Daily News* placed both incidents in the context of "rising tension between Sunnis and the Shiite-dominated government." But the killing of a Shiite in one of the incidents and the newspaper's emphasis on the role of the government in the rising tension made it clear that this was not "sectarian violence" as it was being portrayed in the West, but rather a dirty war by the occupation government against its opponents.[286]

On September 8th 2005, the Human Rights Office of the U.N. Assistance Mission for Iraq issued the first of a long series of Human Rights Reports on the deteriorating state of human rights in Iraq. In diplomatic language, the summary of the report expressed "continuing concern for the lack of protection of civilians in regard to their civil, cultural, economic, political and social rights," as well as "deficiencies in the administration of the justice system, and in particular the handling of the circumstances and conditions for detention ... Corpses appear regularly in and around Baghdad and other areas. Most bear signs of torture and appear to be victims of extrajudicial executions."[287]

The body of the report was more explicit, linking the campaign of detentions, torture, and extra-judicial executions directly to the Interior Ministry and indirectly to the U.S.-led "multi-national force:"

> There are serious allegations of extra-judicial executions taking place which underline a deterioration in the situation of law and order. The bodies of 36 men, blindfolded, handcuffed, bearing signs of torture and summarily executed, were found on 25 August near Badhra. Families of the victims reported to

---

286. "13 tortured do death by police," *Gulf Daily News*, July 14 2005. http://www.iraqfoundation.org/news/2005/july/14_tortured.htm
287. http://www.uniraq.org/aboutus/HR.asp

the Human Rights Office that the men had been detained on 24 August in the Al Hurria district of Baghdad following an operation carried out by forces linked to the Ministry of Interior. A similar incident was reported to the Human Rights Office involving 11 males who had been allegedly detained by forces linked to the Ministry of Interior on 10 July in Seba' Abkar district of Baghdad and who were found dead three days later at the Medico Legal Institute.

UNAMI received consistent reports of excessive use of force with regard to persons and property as well as mass arrests carried out by Iraqi police and special forces acting alone or in association with the MNF. Reports of ill-treatment of detainees and inadequacies in judicial procedures have continued. Furthermore, first and second hand accounts from Baghdad, Basra, Mosul, Kirkuk and the Kurdish governorates, as well as corroborating information from other credible sources, consistently point to the systematic use of torture during interrogations at police stations and within other premises belonging to the Ministry of Interior.

A human rights organization reported to UNAMI that many detentions took place during the month of July in Adhamiya neighbourhood and that on many occasions the family of the detainees cannot find their relatives in any recognized detention facility. Others have complained that they have found their relatives dead or that they have suffered torture while in detention.

The U.N. report was written by John Pace, the director of the human rights office at UNAMI in Baghdad and the former Secretary of the U.N. Commission on Human Rights. He finished his assignment in Iraq in February 2006 and returned to his regular job at the University of New South Wales in Sydney, Australia. After leaving Iraq, he gave several interviews in which he spoke more frankly about the Iraqi death squads and about American complicity in their campaign. He told the *Times* in his native Malta that U.S. officials were aware that torture was taking place in Iraqi prisons and that 80 to 90% of the prisoners involved were innocent of any crime, making their plight even more frightful.[288]

Pace told the *Associated Press* that the atrocities he investigated were comparable to those under Saddam Hussein. "It is certainly as bad," he said, "It extends over a much wider section of the population than it did under Saddam." He said that Badr Brigade commanders held key posts in Interior Ministry commando units. "They have caused chaos. They do basically as they please. They arrest people, they execute people, they detain people, they negotiate ransom and they do that with impunity."[289]

John Pace also gave an extensive interview to *Democracy Now*. Amy Goodman asked him about the role of militias in Iraq. "With the procedure for the transition of reintegration of the country to more representative forms of government, a number of these militias who were armed wings of political entities found themselves in government," Pace explained. "And therefore they—many of them now, are actually acting as official police agents as a part of the Ministry of Interior ... And regrettably, the Minister of Interior, at least up to now, was himself the head of one of the main militias ... They have been very closely linked with numerous mass executions, at least mass arrests of people who later turned up showing signs of execution. And so they constitute a major destabilizing factor in the sense that they are responsible for a large degree of the lack of protection of Iraqis in their own country."[290]

---

288. Herman Grech, "US aware of Iraq torture," *The Times of Malta*, February 20 2006.

289. Ed Johnson, "Ex-official: Iraq abuses growing worse," *Associated Press*, March 2 2006.

290. "Exclusive: former UN human rights chief in Iraq says US violating Geneva Conventions, jailing innocent detainees," *Democracy Now*, February 28 2006. http://www.democracynow.org/2006/2/28/exclusive_former_un_human_rights_chief

Goodman asked Pace about the roles of James Steele and Steven Casteel in Iraq and for his reaction to comparisons with El Salvador. Pace was non-committal on specifics but agreed in general: "And so I would say yes, there are death squads. They do follow a pattern in Iraq of a sort." He went on,

> But I prefer to look at the situation in Iraq on its own, on its own merits as it were, rather than compare it to other situations because the particularities of the situation in Iraq are quite unique in that respect, especially for the U.N., where you have a process of re-stabilization of the country at the political level without a corresponding serious effort at re-stabilization at the security level of the country. If you look at this schizophrenic situation ... you see nothing on the security side except further deterioration, including as a result of government intervention, further deterioration of security of people in Iraq. And that, of course, neutralizes completely any serious effort at re-stabilizing the country. Unless you have a police force that's acting in the interests of society and the interests of the country at large and efficiently so, and therefore as a corollary to that, the withdrawal and the nonexistence of military intervention, then you cannot have a serious political resolution in the country.
>
> And this is the problem in Iraq today. You have a disparity between the political dialogue on the one hand and the dialogue of violence and murder on the other. They are both going in different directions. I would personally much prefer to ... focus on the fact that Iraq itself presents and refrain from comparing it to behavior patterns and other situations. Having said so, it is correct and my observations would confirm that at least at a certain point last year ... , we saw numerous instances where the behavior of death squads was very similar, uncannily similar to that we had observed in other countries, including El Salvador.

Pace also told *Democracy Now* that he had warned American authorities that their detention practices in Iraq violated the Geneva Conventions. He compared U.S. efforts at policing the country by military force to "trying to swat a fly with a bomb." And he noted that "if there is any element that unites the Iraqis in spite of their several internal differences, it is the desire to see the end of the occupation."

He concluded by emphasizing the essential contradiction: "there's very little place for a military intervention in a situation, if you want to have normalization again, that is. There is a remarkable absence of serious attention to the need to have a civil police element and a judiciary that can work. These elements do not exist at the moment. On the contrary, in regards to the police … , a large number of them have been associated with being perpetrators, rather than protectors, of human rights problems."

The situation Pace described in his reports and in these interviews reinforces the view that American recruitment and training of "security" forces in Iraq was not really designed to accomplish re-stabilization or normalization, but rather to complete their own conquest of the country. The dirty war was part of a continuing, desperate effort to reduce Iraq to a state of shock, to render the population powerless to resist the efforts of the United States and its allies to impose their will on the country.

As Naomi Klein has described in *The Shock Doctrine*, combinations of political repression and economic shock treatment have succeeded in imposing "disaster capitalism" on other countries, from Indonesia to Chile to Central America to Eastern Europe in the 1990s. But this model depends on a willingness to use greater and greater amounts of repression and violence to overcome resistance, and it always runs the risk of simply destroying a society without ever reaching the idealized "clean slate" on which a new capitalist system can be built. It has never worked as cleanly as imagined by proponents like Milton Freedman and Jeffrey Sachs, and every society that has been subjected to this process has suffered long-lasting trauma. The shock doctrine may have finally met its match, even its undoing, in Iraq.[291]

On October 9th 2005, the *Times* of London reported on another incident in which 22 men from the district of Iskan were arrested in a large raid involving about 40 police vehicles. They were taken away by masked Badr Brigade militiamen accompanied by police officers. General Thavit denied all knowledge of the raid and claimed that "fighters were dressing in police uniforms to inflame sectarian divisions." Like the victims of the incident documented by the U.N. Human Rights Office, the corpses of the men from Iskan were found near Badhra, seventy miles away, near the border with Iran. The *Times* correspondent spoke to many family members of the dead and discovered that every single one of them was a Sunni man who was married to a Shiite woman. Iskan was a mixed but predominantly Shiite district. A Shiite neighbor who was himself married to a Sunni woman explained the secular roots of Iskan's local culture: "In the 1970s no one talked about Shiites or Sunnis—I don't think my father knew which sect he belonged to."[292]

Some of the victims' families were planning to leave the district, but, because of the mixed composition of the families, most did not see this as a solution and were staying put. Instead, the community had come together under the umbrella of Muqtada al-Sadr's Mahdi army to "set up an armed force of their own to defend themselves against future raids." This report contrasts sharply with the later campaign by U.S. officials to blame the Mahdi army for "sectarian violence," and to divert responsibility from Interior Ministry and Badr Brigade forces allied with the occupation. American media companies collaborated in the Pentagon's efforts to confuse the diametrically opposing roles of the

---

291. Naomi Klein, *The Shock Doctrine*, (New York: Metropolitan Books, 2007).
292. Hala Jaber, "Iraqi police linked to ethnic cleansing," *The Sunday Times*, October 9 2005.

two Shiite militias, consistently supporting the narrative of "sectarian violence" and downplaying the primary nature of the conflict between pro- and anti-occupation forces. It was only in 2008, when U.S. and Badr forces began a new assault on Shiite areas, that this fundamental distinction between the U.S.-backed Badr Brigade and the anti-occupation Mahdi army was finally made clear in American news reports.

In September 2005, Khalid Jarrar, an Iraqi blogger, gained first-hand experience of arbitrary detention and interrogation on the seventh floor of the Interior Ministry. He and his family had already fled to Amman, Jordan, but he returned to Baghdad to complete his engineering degree. While waiting at the university for an official to sign some paperwork so that he could pay his tuition, he went to an on-campus internet cafe, where he checked his brother Raed's *Raed in the Middle* blog. On his way back to the financial department, he was stopped by a security officer, who accused him of visiting "terrorist" web sites. After a brief interrogation, he was hooded, tightly handcuffed, and thrown into a van. He soon found himself in a small cell with 34 other prisoners on the seventh floor of the Interior Ministry, one floor below the offices of the ministry's American advisers, reputedly the headquarters of the CIA in Baghdad.[293]

Jarrar spent eleven days in detention. Unlike most of his fellow prisoners, who were unable to contact their families, he was able to get a message out to his family on the third day and this may have saved him from far worse treatment. He endured long interrogations, during which he was slapped on the face and neck. He was accused of a wide range of offenses, from a role in the recent bombings in the London Underground to hating Shiites (his mother is a Shiite). He was brought

---

293. http://secretsinbaghdad.blogspot.com/2005_07_01_archive.html

before a judge after eight days of detention and released a few days later.

Most of his cell-mates were not so lucky. Some of them had been there for months. He told the story of two brothers, Maysam and Nathom. Nathom was hung upside down and beaten until he "confessed" that his brother Maysam had killed 300 people. Then Khalid and Nathom wept together as they listened to Maysam's screams as he was interrogated. Incredibly, later that night, the three of them laughed together at the absurdity of it all.

A second U.N. Human Rights Report in November 2005 reiterated the same concerns as the previous one. It described "a general breakdown of law and order," including "extrajudicial execution-style killings" and widespread impunity for human rights violations, as well as "ongoing military operations" that "have a devastating effect on the civilian population." It also cited a report from the World Health Organization that "during military operations in Al Anbar Governorate in October, medical doctors were detained and medical facilities occupied by armed forces." The report added, "Such actions are contrary to international law governing armed conflict ... The price paid by civilians, including women and children, during military activity currently under way calls for further reflection on the nature and conduct of the conflict and on the proportionality of the use of force."[294]

At about the same time, in November 2005, the horrors of one of the Interior Ministry's torture centers were exposed to the world. A U.S. army unit was called by Iraqi police to assist in the search for a missing boy, and this led them to al-Jadiriyah prison. At least one hundred and one out of the 168 prisoners in the prison had been horribly tortured, and the inmates provided the names of 18 more who had already died. According to a U.N. report, the prisoners "presented wounds and signs

---

294. http://www.uniraq.org/aboutus/HR.asp

of abuse consistent with electric shocks, beatings and stabbing." Ten inmates were so badly injured that the American troops who raided the prison immediately took them to a hospital.[295]

Among the inmates hospitalized was Professor Tareq Sammaree (Ph.D. Kansas), the former director of Baghdad University's School of Education. After eight months in prison and a dozen torture sessions, Sammaree was missing his front teeth and three toenails, had a wound on his shin caused by a hot skewer, and his spine was damaged by blows with electric cables. His torturers also told him that they had his daughters in captivity and would rape them if he did not talk. Sammaree could have revealed the locations of other academics the Interior Ministry was searching for. But he remained silent under intense torture because he was convinced that his captors would kill him once they thought he had told them what he knew.[296]

At the hospital, he gave his son's phone number in California to an American soldier named Jackson and begged him for help. The soldier returned to the hospital the next day after speaking to his son, led Sammaree and two fellow prisoners to an unguarded exit, and told them "Go! Go! Don't look back!" They all escaped, and Sammaree paid a smuggler to take him and his family to Syria. He eventually sought political asylum in Europe.

The prison was run by the Interior Ministry's Special Investigative Directorate, under the command of a colonel who reported directly to Interior Minister al-Jabr. As usual, the American press treated this as an isolated incident, and U.S. officials expressed shock at the discovery. But prisoners who escaped or were eventually released from al-

---

295. Solomon Moore, "Killings linked to Shiite militias in Iraqi police force," *Los Angeles Times*, November 29 2005.

296. Max Fuller, "Ghosts of Jadiriyah: a survivor's testimony," *Brussels Tribunal*, November 14 2006. http://www.brusselstribunal.org/FullerJadiriyah.htm

Jadiriyah insisted that this was far from the first or last time that U.S. troops visited the prison.

Abbas Abid, from Fallujah, was the chief engineer at the Science and Technology Ministry in Baghdad. U.S. and Iraqi occupation forces raided his brother's house on August 28th 2005. Abid went over to help his brother's family and try to sort things out. He was ordered to report to the al-Muthanna Brigade headquarters for questioning. Once there, he was detained, beaten, electrocuted, and threatened with death by a team of Iraqis and one American, who seemed to be in charge. After a month, he was transferred to al-Jadiriyah.[297]

At al-Jadiriyah, the torture continued. Abid was forced to drink a diuretic solution, while his penis was tied with a rubber band to prevent him from urinating; he was hung from a wall with heavy weights attached to his penis; he was electrocuted, also on the penis; he was hung with his hands handcuffed behind his back, so that his shoulders were dislocated and he was beaten in that position until the handcuffs broke on several occasions; his finger nails were pulled out; he and his family were threatened with rape; he was starved; and he was hooded for two months straight. Conditions in the prison were unsanitary and horrific, and it was rife with disease, from TB to scabies. Abid named eight prisoners who had been tortured to death.

Eventually, on September 5th 2006, Abbas Abid was brought before a court, his case was dismissed, and he was set free on October 2nd 2006. Three other prisoners freed at the same time were followed and killed, but Abid's brother had hired some local police to escort and protect him until he could reach safety and leave the country.

Abbas Abid gave sworn testimony to a tribunal in Malaysia that U.S. troops were frequent visitors at al-Jadiriyah throughout his detention,

---

297. "Statutory Declaration - testimony of Abbas Abid in Kuala Lumpur," *Brussels Tribunal*, February 7 2007. http://www.brusselstribunal.org/ArticlesIraq3.htm#Abbas

before and after the widely reported raid in November 2005. He rejected American denials of complicity. A U.N. human rights report confirmed that U.S. forces had visited the prison prior to November 2005, and that al-Jabr and other senior officials knew about it. A U.S. official corroborated the fact that American forces were only pretending to be surprised by the "discovery" of the jail in November 2005, confirming to the *Los Angeles Times* on July 9th 2006 that, "The military had been at the bunker prior to the raid in November, but they said nothing." The U.N. report revealed that the prison functioned as a central interrogation center, receiving prisoners from several different police agencies.[298]

Assigning responsibility for the concerted campaign of extra-judicial killing and torture that engulfed Baghdad in 2005 is complicated by the parallel chains of command that appeared to govern the forces responsible. Many of the Special Police Commandos and other death and torture squads were affiliated both with factional militias and with the U.S.-backed Iraqi government, but this distinction is not as critical as it seems. The same people were involved in both militias and the government all the way to the top, as exemplified by Bayan al-Jabr. And all the forces involved had close working relationships with U.S. forces throughout this period. This included Allawi's Iraqi National Accord, the SCIRI party and its Badr Brigade militia, the Ministry of the Interior, the Wolf Brigade, and other Special Police units.

In the wake of the al-Jadiriyah story, the *New York Times* spoke to Falah al-Naqib, the former interim Interior Minister who, together with Steven Casteel, had created the Special Police Commandos in 2004. The *Times* reminded Naqib that reports of torture and prisoner abuse had

---

298. Solomon Moore, "Police abuses in Iraq detailed," *Los Angeles Times*, July 9 2006.

begun during his tenure, and he acknowledged that "there were some mistakes made."[299]

It was widely reported that al-Jabr had purged these forces when he succeeded Naqib as Interior Minister in May 2005 and integrated his Badr Brigade militia into the police commandos. In the context of al-Jadiriyah in November 2005, this gave Naqib a credible basis to distance himself from the atrocities committed by the Wolf Brigade and other commando units following his departure from the Interior Ministry. He had every interest in blaming the abuses on later infiltration by al-Jabr's Badr militia. But Naqib did not do this. Instead he acknowledged that he had recruited many members of the Badr Organization to the police commandos himself, although "not nearly as many as Mr. Jabr." In fact, despite Jabr's expanded recruitment of Badr militiamen, Naqib admitted to the *Times* that "the majority of commando officers working in the ministry now were appointed by him."

Naqib had no motive to associate himself with torture and extra-judicial executions, so his statements appear to be credible. They provide confirmation that, although the infiltration of greater numbers of Badr militiamen into the Special Police by Bayan al-Jabr may have expanded the scale of their atrocities, the nature and composition of these forces was largely consistent from their inception under Negroponte, Casteel, Steele, Naqib and Petraeus in 2004 through the depths of the reign of terror in Baghdad in 2005 and 2006.

On December 13th, 2005, U.S. Ambassador Zalmay Khalilzad held a news conference at which he promised a thorough investigation of Iraqi prisons and arrest procedures. However, a U.N. human rights report a full year later in December 2006 noted that neither U.S. nor Iraqi au-

---

299. Edward Wong and John F. Burns, "Iraqi rift grows after discovery of prison," *New York Times*, November 17 2005.

thorities had conducted the investigations into al-Jadiriyah and other Iraqi prisons that they had promised with such fanfare a year earlier.[300]

Khalilzad also announced a decision to start embedding U.S. troops with Interior Ministry forces. The *New York Times'* John Burns was puzzled by this announcement, because he had understood that this was already a long-standing practice. He wrote:

> The ambassador's statement that the American command had decided to embed officers with Interior Ministry units suggested that the practice of having American officers attached to commando units like the Wolf Brigade, common when they were established over the last year, had fallen away as the buildup of Iraqi forces accelerated. Although American policy has been to assign "military transition teams" of up to 10 soldiers to each brigade-level Iraqi army unit, the free-wheeling police commandos appear to have had little American oversight in recent months. Mr. Khalilzad acknowledged as much when he said of the plan to embed Americans with the Interior Ministry units, "It's a new phenomenon."[301]

But Khalilzad's claim that the Wolf Brigade and other Interior Ministry forces had been operating without American supervision was belied by contemporary accounts of their operations. One such account described an operation that was conducted in Baquba on November 12th 2005, the day before the "discovery" of al-Jadiriyah. It was called Operation Knockout.

Colonel James Greer, the Chief of Staff of the Multi-National Security Transition Command in Iraq, wrote a glowing report on this operation for the November-December 2005 edition of *Military Review*. He stressed the high degree of coordination between the MNF command and the Interior Ministry commandos who conducted most of the

300. http://www.uniraq.org/aboutus/HR.asp
301. John F. Burns, "To halt abuses, U.S. will inspect jails run by Iraq," *New York Times*, December 14 2005.

house raids in the Baquba operation, and he identified the units in question as the same ones who had been operating in and around Baghdad. He cited the leading role being played by the Special Police Commandos and their coordination with U.S. forces as evidence of the advances that had been made in U.S. "counter-insurgency" strategy in 2005.[302]

He explained that, in 2003 and 2004, "coalition" forces had conducted most "cordon and search operations," but that in 2005 most of these operations were taken over by Iraqi "security" forces. He claimed that Operation Knockout succeeded in rounding up "377 suspected insurgents without destroying one house or harming one civilian" (not counting the "suspected insurgents"). No one was killed during the operation, although "three Iraqi Special Police were wounded."

He went on: "More remarkable was that the Iraqi Special Forces Police Forces of the Iraqi Ministry of Interior had planned, prepared, and executed the entire operation." But he did not claim they had done it alone:

> Simultaneously, Multi-National Force-Iraq was notified through its cell in MOI (Ministry of Interior) National Command Center. Planning and coordination continued with an MOI/Multinational Command-Iraq meeting on 9 November to address deconfliction of routes, battlespace, and access to Coalition medical evacuation and effects. The 3rd Brigade Combat Team of Multi-National Division-North Central hosted the meeting and conducted detailed coordination with Public Order Division units to prepare for supporting the Iraqi operation.
>
> Throughout the planning and coordination stage of Operation Knockout, Special Police Transition Teams (SPTTs) under Colonel Gordon B. "Skip" Davis and Colonel Jeffrey Bu-

---

302. Colonel James K. Greer, "Operation Knockout: COIN in Iraq," *Military Review*, November-December 2005.

chanan advised the Iraqis and planned and coordinated their own support to the operation. *These teams of 10 to 12 soldiers lived, trained and fought alongside the Iraqi Special Police 24 hours a day and contributed significantly to the Iraqis' development. For several months before Operation Knockout, Davis and Buchanan's teaching, coaching, and mentoring helped the Iraqi Special Police plan, coordinate, and develop the operational skills necessary for success.* At the small unit level, the SPTTs did not just train the Iraqi Special Police to fight; they helped develop noncommissioned officers and junior leaders who could lead the fight.

At 5 a.m. on November 12th 2005, "seven battalions of Iraqi Special Police struck their main objectives nearly simultaneously." In order to prevent the targets from being tipped off, the Baghdad-based commandos were not told the real target of the operation until the night of the operation: "Special Police commanders briefed their troops on potential operations in southern Baghdad and then employed deception as to the timing and magnitude of the coming operation." Then, "Special Police units staged in Baghdad at various (U.S.) Forward Operating Bases [and] moved the approximately 40 kilometers to the Baquba area along multiple routes in the middle of the night." After the operation, the commandos "returned to their protected compounds near Baghdad."

Greer also mentioned that the division headquarters of the Iraqi Public Order Division was at U.S. Forward Operating Base Justice, and that that Colonel Davis trained the division commander to perform command and control functions from a mobile van during the operation. The van also had "operational communications back to Ministry of Interior National Command Center and division headquarters." During the operation, American "Special Police Transition Teams at each level accompanied their assigned units, (and) observed and ensured that Coalition forces had situational awareness of the operation."

The presence of U.S. troops working with Iraqi Interior Ministry forces in Special Police Transition Teams and in cells at the Special Police's National Command Center revealed a higher degree of coordination, ongoing training and supervision, and command and control than U.S. officials ever discussed with journalists in the context of atrocities committed by these same Iraqi forces. And they made nonsense of Ambassador Khalilzad's description of embedding U.S. forces with the Special Police after al-Jadiriyah as "a new phenomenon."

After a smaller "cordon and search" raid in Medain, south of Baghdad, on September 24th 2005, Major Rick Ackerman of the Special Police Transition Team described his team playing an identical role to their counterparts in the later operation in Baquba. The team was attached to the Iraqi 2nd Public Order Brigade and provided a liaison with the 3rd Squadron of the U.S. 7th Cavalry, which created an "outer cordon" for the operation. Ackerman's account of the raid emphasizes that his Iraqi charges were just beginning, in September 2005, to plan and lead their own operations with less American oversight. Ackerman's Special Police Transition Team had "worked extensively with the 2nd POB in Baghdad for the past six months." The unit was based out of Fort Drum in New York State, and it specialized "in training and advising the Special Police in combat." Other military reports show that the Special Police Transition Teams took over in April 2005 from the team headed by James Steele that had worked with the Special Police Commandos until that time.[303]

And an American special forces officer from the 160th Special Operations Aviation Regiment, known as the "Nightstalkers," wrote about a

___

303. Specialist Ben Brody, "Iraqi police conduct Baghdad raid without U.S. oversight," *American Forces Press Service*, October 1 2005.
http://www.defenselink.mil/news/newsarticle.aspx?id=18182; William H. McMichael, "Navy awarding Bronze Stars to Marines," *Navy Times*, January 25 2007.
http://www.navytimes.com/news/2007/01/ntmarinebronze070125/; and Laurence Lessard, "Interview with Maj Scott Schumacher," *Operational Leadership Experiences Project*, (Fort Leavenworth, Kansas: Combat Studies Institute, November 17 2006).
http://cgsc.cdmhost.com/cgi-bin/showfile.exe?CISOROOT=/p4013coll13&
CISOPTR=642&filename=643.pdf#search=%22we%22

joint operation with the Wolf Brigades on November 10th on his personal weblog. He described a battalion-sized operation in southern Baghdad in which his Iraqi partners captured "vehicle after vehicle of blindfolded detainees."[304]

Based on Naqib's statement, Greer's and multiple other accounts of the Special Police Transition Teams, and the evidence that accumulated day by day in Iraq, the succession of cover stories to distance American officials from "situational awareness" or responsibility for Special Police operations and atrocities in Baghdad deserved to be challenged very seriously. Neither stolen uniforms, rogue elements, militia infiltration, nor sectarian hatred could account for the organized campaign of detention, torture, and extra-judicial killing that terrorized the people of Baghdad through most of 2005 and the following years.

As in other countries where U.S. forces have engaged in what they refer to as "counter-insurgency," American military and intelligence officials recruited, trained, equipped, and directed local forces which engaged in a campaign of state-sponsored terror against the overwhelming proportion of the local population who continued to reject and oppose the invasion and occupation of their country. The "disguised, quiet, media-free approach" noted by General Valenzuela and Colonel Rosello is considered one of the keys to the success of all such operations, but it relies for its success on significant cooperation from nominally independent Western news organizations. Many Iraqis were clearly guilty of terrible crimes in the conduct of this campaign. But the prime responsibility for this policy, and for the crimes it involved, rests with the individuals in the civilian and military command structure of the U.S. Department of Defense, the Central Intelligence Agency and the White House who devised, approved and implemented the "Phoenix" or "Salvador" terror policy in Iraq.

---

304. Gareth Porter, "US military still runs with dreaded Wolf Brigade," *Inter Press Service,* January 2nd 2006.

CHAPTER 15. TOGETHER FORWARD: THE ETHNIC CLEANSING OF BAGHDAD

In the course of 2006, the scale of the U.S.-backed campaign of arbitrary detention, torture, and extra-judicial execution in Iraq expanded and proliferated, leaving tens of thousands more people dead in Baghdad alone. The numbers of men and boys killed in cold blood by death squads linked to the U.S.-backed puppet government increased throughout 2006, even as U.S. forces became more directly involved in attacks on Sunni and mixed districts in Baghdad.

The U.N.'s human rights reports provided a baseline minimum of civilian deaths for the year. By combining the figures from the central morgue in Baghdad with the Health Ministry's numbers from hospitals in other parts of the country, the U.N. was able to publish total figures for each month, adding up to a total of 34,452 civilian deaths for the year. The U.N. noted that only about 5 or 6% of these were non-violent deaths. The caveats on passive reporting of civilian casualties in war-torn countries mentioned in Chapter 7 still applied, of course, and epidemiological studies indicated that the numbers of dead counted by morgues and hospitals were only a fraction of the actual victims. Many more people disappeared without a trace after being arrested by Interior Ministry death squads.[305]

Death squad violence proliferated beyond what could conceivably be blamed on stolen police uniforms, even by the most credulous Western journalists. American officials and the Western media embraced "sectarian violence" as the new central narrative of the war, and the principal justification for continued occupation. The myths discussed in Chapter 12 became common currency, and even many Americans who opposed the war now believed that the continuing violence

---

305. http://www.uniraq.org/aboutus/HR.asp

was the result of an imaginary "centuries-old blood feud" between Iraq's Sunnis and Shiites.

However, other reports made it clear that the primary instrument of violence in Baghdad remained the U.S.-backed Interior Ministry and its Special Police forces, operating partly under the parallel command structure of the SCIRI party's Badr Brigades. In April 2006, an Iraqi group called the Organization for Follow-Up and Monitoring matched thousands of morgue records with reports of arrests and abductions. It found that 92% of the bodies of execution victims brought to morgues matched the names and descriptions of people who had been detained by forces working for the Interior Ministry.[306]

American officials and media ignored the death squads' origins within the U.S.-backed government, and therefore reported atrocities linked to government forces as the result of their infiltration by militias with independent agendas. They ignored even more fastidiously all the evidence that the reign of terror was in fact the result of decisions by American policy-makers to recruit and train counter-insurgency forces to torture and kill beyond the rule of law, as they had done in Latin America and in the Phoenix operation in Vietnam. The campaign in Iraq exemplified the "disguised, quiet, media-free approach" noted by Valenzuela and Rosello in El Salvador and Colombia.

Western news reports increasingly linked the detentions and extra-judicial killings to Muqtada al-Sadr's Mahdi Army militia. U.S. propaganda operations naturally seized on the opportunity to blame extra-judicial executions on anti-occupation groups. To the extent that local police forces and communities were drawn into the violence, there were certainly Mahdi Army members who took part in detentions and killings, just as Sunni resistance forces also kidnapped and killed civi-

---

306. Dirk Adriaensens, "Foxes in the hen-house, Iraqi puppet government submits candidacy for the UNHRC and other tales," *Brussels Tribunal*, May 6 2006. http://www.brusselstribunal.org/IraqUNHRC.htm

lians. But the media's silence on the institutional roots of the reign of terror in CIA and Pentagon plans developed during the rule of the Coalition Provisional Authority and the Negroponte-Allawi period served to disguise fundamental distinctions between primary and secondary forms of violence. Western journalists consistently failed to distinguish between the killing of Sunnis or Shiites by local groups desperate to defend their own neighborhoods and the orchestrated campaign by the occupation government that created the terror in the first place.

Making such distinctions was not always easy. As a U.N. human rights report pointed out, "The distinction between acts of violence motivated by sectarian, political, or economic considerations was frequently blurred as a multitude of armed groups claimed responsibility for numerous acts of terror." In this environment, with Western reporters an increasingly captive audience trapped inside the Green Zone, Centcom's information operations successfully shaped news reports to conform to its own narrative.

In March 2006, however, the U.S. State Department's annual global human rights report acknowledged the U.S.-backed Iraqi government's widely recognized role in arbitrary detentions, torture, and extrajudicial executions: "Reports increased of killings by the government or its agents that may have been politically motivated ... Members of sectarian militias dominated police units to varying degrees and in different parts of the country ... Police abuses included threats, intimidation, beatings, and suspension by the arms or legs, as well as the reported use of electric drills and cords and the application of electric shocks. Reportedly, police threatened or, in fact, sexually abused detainees."[307]

But the killing continued. On the day before the State Department report became public, an American patrol found the dead bodies of 18 men inside a truck in the Amariya district of Baghdad. They had all

---

307. http://www.state.gov/g/drl/rls/hrrpt/2005/61689.htm

been garroted and were still wearing police-issue flexicuffs. And on the day that the human rights report was issued, 50 employees of al-Rawafid, a private security firm in the mixed Zayouna district in eastern Baghdad, were abducted by a large squad of police commandos in at least seven police vehicles. But the Interior Ministry denied any part in the raid or any knowledge of the fate of the victims.[308]

On the following day, Solomon Moore of the *Los Angeles Times* filed an update on the purported U.S. efforts to transform the Interior Ministry's forces into a legitimate police force following the revelations about al-Jadiriyah in November. U.S. officials now echoed John Pace's concern that the paramilitary role of the Interior Ministry's forces in the U.S.-led war against the Iraqi Resistance was antithetical to the establishment of a police force that could actually earn the respect of the population and restore law and order to the country.

"U.S. officials have revamped and expanded training programs for Iraqi police units amid mounting concern that their focus on fighting insurgents, and not protecting citizens, has created an unaccountable force plagued by corruption and rights abuses," Moore wrote. "The police units are under the Iraqi Interior Ministry, led by Bayan Jabr, a Shiite Muslim with ties to a sectarian militia. The predominantly Shiite force has become highly politicized and is accused of torture and death squad operations against Iraq's Sunni Arab minority."

Moore's discussions with U.S. officials revealed their suspicions that the Iraqi torturers at al-Jadariyah had in fact received training in American torture practices. There was a great deal of consistency between the experiences of victims of torture by the Special Police Commandos in Iraq and the victims of American torturers in Iraq, Afghanistan, Guantanamo and elsewhere.

---

308. Jonathan Steele, "Baghdad rocked by kidnappings and mass killings," *The Guardian*, March 9 2006.

Moore reported that the 27 brigades of Special Police had been re-named the National Police and that the Wolf Brigade had been im-probably re-branded the Freedom Brigade. Four brigade commanders had been fired. Major General Peterson, in charge of police training op-erations in Iraq, told Solomon Moore, "It's about changing images. We're trying to create the new culture, new representations." But not all Americans subscribed to this approach. Many officers in combat units were still more interested in seeing the Iraqis take the lead in counter-insurgency operations, to take the heat off their own troops, and were still willing to turn a blind eye to horrific crimes. One of the police trainers, who insisted on remaining anonymous, told Moore,

> If we're going to leave the country at some point, the Ira-qis are going to have to know how to fight crime—not just terrorists. But we've got a lot of military guys who just want to kill terrorists. You could kill all the terrorists today, but if the police are too heavy-handed, the populace is just going to re-sent and fear them. And tomorrow, you're going to create more insurgents.[309]

In April 2006, evidence emerged of new, more open operational coordination between U.S. and Iraqi Interior Ministry forces. Residents of Adhamiya in Baghdad reported a new wave of attacks on their dis-trict by Special Police Commandos backed up by significant U.S. ground and air support. After months of abductions, torture, and extra-judicial killings, the residents had reached a deal with the Americans and the puppet government that Iraqi National Guards could patrol the district, as long as they did not try to disarm residents, and as long as the Interior Ministry's Special Police Commandos and Shiite militia-men were kept out. Relations between the residents and the National Guards had been very good. In a previous incursion by Special Police Commandos, a National Guard commander had tipped off the Resis-

---

309. Solomon Moore, "U.S. expands training to address Iraqi police woes," *Los Angeles Times*, March 9 2006.

tance and provided weapons for the residents to defend themselves. Residents had also barricaded streets with tires and tree trunks to protect their community from a return of the death squads.

Then, on the night of April 16th 2006, a large force in about 40 police vehicles broke through into Adhamiya from three directions, including through a U.S. checkpoint on a bridge. American helicopters circled overhead. "We'd had sporadic fighting for several nights before, but nothing like this," a resident told *Inter Press Service*. "My family and I thought a war was happening because so many heavy guns, mortars and rocket propelled grenades were being used."

But the community was ready to resist. Local residents said that at least six police vehicles were destroyed and torched, and at least one commando was killed in addition to ten residents, who included one woman. Another resident told *IPS*, "Men in police uniforms attacked the neighborhood. The Ministry of Interior claimed the uniformed men don't belong to the puppet forces, but local residents are quite sure they are special forces from the Ministry of Interior, probably Badr brigades. The neighborhood was sealed off and the mobile phone network was disconnected until 10:45 p.m. Electricity was cut off from 10 a.m."

He went on, "When the uniformed forces entered the neighborhood, the National Guards that are usually patrolling the streets left. Young armed men from the neighborhood fought side by side with mujahedin against the attacking forces to protect al-Adhamiya. Several residents have been killed in the streets, but there are currently no figures available. U.S. troops also entered the neighborhood. At first, they only stood by and watched; later on they too fired at the locals, who tried to repel their attacks." Other residents confirmed that U.S. forces had played an active supporting role in the attack.[310]

---

310. Dahr Jamail, "Baghdad slipping into civil war," *Inter Press Service*, April 20 2006.

Several elements of this report indicated that U.S. forces played a greater role than had been reported in previous attacks by Interior Ministry forces. Cutting off electricity and cell phone service were standard procedures for U.S. forces attacking towns and cities in Iraq, and required the cooperation of Iraqi utilities and government agencies. The National Guard units in the area were apparently warned of the attack, using communications networks that were also under U.S. control. The Centcom press office did not dispute the fact that U.S. forces took part in the fighting. The Associated Press carried a report that "Army officials said they had suffered no casualties, and planned to raid homes to search for the gunmen," as if the residents of Adhamiya who resisted the attack were to blame for it.

An Iraqi blogger in Adhamiya, a dentist named Zeyad, provided a more comprehensive account of the battle. He wrote that the assault by forces from the Interior Ministry began at 1 a.m., but was repelled by the Resistance and the residents within 2 hours. U.S. forces then entered Adhamiya accompanied by Iraqi National Guards and started a fire-fight with local forces at the Adhamiya police station. The fighting continued sporadically until noon the next day, when local leaders negotiated a cease-fire with the National Guard commander. He claimed that it had all been a misunderstanding, and that he and the Americans had believed "insurgents" were attacking the police station.

The following morning, at 6:45 a.m., somebody drove by and fired at a National Guard unit stationed at an intersection, perhaps seeking revenge for an earlier incident. The National Guards returned fire indiscriminately, and this escalated into a fire-fight with the local guards of the al-Anbia mosque. U.S. forces again charged into Adhamiya, also firing indiscriminately and producing "an inferno of machine-gun fire," but things calmed down again by 1 p.m. If the Interior Ministry attack was designed to undermine the previously good relations between the residents and the National Guard, it was partially successful. It clearly also served as a probing mission to gauge the strength and disposition of resistance forces in Adhamiya, and this would explain the constant presence of American helicopters observing the attack.[311]

This was consistent with a new strategy being developed as the new Dawa-led government prepared to take office. Each new government established in the Green Zone collaborated in some new U.S. offensive: Allawi approved the destruction of Fallujah and the formation of the Special Police Commandos; Jaafari and Jabr unleashed them on Baghdad; and Maliki would oversee an escalation of military force and ethnic cleansing that would kill thousands more Iraqis and drive millions from their homes and into exile. By the end of 2006, half the population of Adhamiya had fled to live as refugees, mostly in Syria. By 2008, this once thriving multi-ethnic secular community was a sparsely populated impoverished ghetto, surrounded by concrete walls, razor wire and check-points.

Just as the Special Police Commandos were storming into Adhamiya on the night of April 16th, Britain's *Sunday Times* published an article by Sarah Baxter titled, "US plots new liberation of Baghdad." It began, "The American military is planning a 'second liberation of Baghdad' to be carried out with the Iraqi army when a new government is installed. Pacifying the lawless capital is regarded as essential to establishing the authority of the incoming government and preparing for a significant withdrawal of American troops." The term "second liberation of Baghdad" was coined by Daniel Goure, the vice-president of the Lexington Institute and a senior adviser to the Pentagon. As it turned out, of course, this policy did not lead to "a significant withdrawal of American troops," but instead to the "surge" or increase of troop levels and the further escalation of the war in 2007.

Lieutenant General David Petraeus, who had overseen the establishment of the Special Police Commandos in 2004 and was considered

---

311. http://healingiraq.blogspot.com/2006_04_01_healingiraq_archive.html

an expert in "counter-insurgency," was drawing up the plans for this next phase of the war at Fort Leavenworth in Kansas. "The battle for Baghdad is expected to entail a 'carrot-and-stick' approach, offering the beleaguered population protection from sectarian violence in exchange for rooting out insurgent groups and al-Qaeda," wrote Baxter. "Sources close to the Pentagon said Iraqi forces would take the lead, supported by American air power, special operations, intelligence, embedded officers and back-up troops. Helicopters suitable for urban warfare, such as the maneuverable AH-6 'Little Birds' used by the marines and special forces and armed with rocket launchers and machine guns, are likely to complement the ground attack."[312]

The Adhamiya attack appears to have been an early probing mission to test these tactics and to gather intelligence on resistance forces in the district. The planned offensive described in the *Sunday Times* was subsequently unleashed on Adhamiya and other parts of Baghdad, including Dora, Mansour and Ghazaliya, in the coming months. While these districts continued to be targeted by Interior Ministry death squads, these forces were now backed up by U.S. ground and air support, up to and including air strikes, artillery fire, and obliteration by Special Forces Spectre gun-ships.

After a year of horrific death squad violence, the goals of the terror campaign were as far as ever from being realized. The population of the targeted areas was not terrorized into submission and was organizing increasingly effective resistance, often with the cooperation of Iraqi Army and National Guard units stationed among them. Sabrina Tavernise of the *New York Times* reported from Adhamiya on May 10th 2006 that "neighborhoods across Baghdad have begun forming citizen groups to keep the paramilitary forces out of their areas entirely."

---

312. Sarah Baxter, "US plots new liberation of Baghdad," *Sunday Times*, April 16 2004.

And the composition of these groups cut across the American narrative of sectarian violence. Yusra Abdul Aziz, a teacher in Adhamiya, told Tavernise that the people on her block organized a "watch group" after four neighbors were killed in March. A mixed group of seven men, both Sunnis and Shiites, were now positioned on rooftops and street-corners from midnight until 6 a.m. every night to protect their neighbors.[313]

In response to the neighborhood watch groups, the National Police were changing their tactics. Night-time raids on homes were giving way to raids on places of business, on groups of people on their way to or from work, and even on hospitals. In April, 14 young men driving home in a minibus from Sinek to the Slekh district were stopped by National Police and detained. Their bodies were all found at the morgue a few days later, some bearing the marks of torture with electric drills.

A new occupation government took office in the Green Zone in May 2006, following elections for the National Assembly in December 2005. With Bayan al-Jabr and the Badr Brigades indisputably linked to atrocities, a lengthy power struggle ensued for the control of the Interior Ministry in the new government. Control of ministries was negotiated based on the respective strength of the various parties in the Council of Representatives.

The United Iraqi Alliance won the election with 128 out of 275 seats. The Alliance comprised five main parties and some independent candidates. The five main parties were SCIRI (or the Badr Organization), Muqtada al-Sadr's Current party, the Basra-based Fadhila or Islamic Virtue Party; the original Islamic Dawa Party, and the Iraq Organization of the Dawa Party (the rump of the Dawa Party that had remained

---

313. Sabrina Tavernise, "Alarmed by raids, neighbors stand guard in Iraq," *New York Times*, May 10 2006.

in Iraq when other Dawa leaders went into exile). All five were off-shoots of the original Dawa Party founded in 1957.

The seats won by the UIA were divided among its component parties in a way that favored SCIRI, which had been the most powerful party in the transitional government. Based on proportional representation in each province, Sadr's Current party won twenty-seven seats, SCIRI won twenty-one, Fadhila won fourteen, Dawa won thirteen and the Dawa Iraq Organization won twelve. Because proportional representation by province did not reflect proportional representation for the whole country, forty-five of the 275 seats in parliament were "compensatory" seats, awarded to achieve proportional representation for the whole country. Nineteen of these were awarded to the UIA, but they were not divided among its component parties based on their share of the vote. Instead, fifteen were awarded to SCIRI, two to the Sadrists and one each to Fadhila and Dawa.

By the end of this process, SCIRI retained thirty-six seats in the Assembly, only twenty-one of which were based on their actual votes by province. The Sadrists had only recently joined the Alliance after boycotting the January election, but won more votes and elected seats than any of their new partners. A smaller group of Sadrists (the Upholders of the Message) who refused to join the Alliance won an additional two seats.

Most Sunnis had boycotted the January election, and the Association of Muslim Scholars organized a less successful boycott of the December one too. However, the three main Sunni parties who did take part won 20.3% of the votes and fifty-eight of the 275 seats. The Sadrists, Fadhila and the Sunni parties formed a sizable bloc of 104 seats in the Assembly that was firmly opposed to the U.S. occupation, and provided solid leadership against U.S.-backed legislation. If necessary, these parties were ready to walk out and effectively shut down the parliament, as they did on several occasions.

Dawa and SCIRI held only fifty seats between them despite the by-zantine electoral system. Even with the Kurdish parties' fifty-eight seats and Allawi's Iraqi National List's twenty-two seats (at least three former members broke with Allawi's list in 2007), parties allied with U.S. inter-ests controlled only 130 out of 275 votes in the Assembly. In August 2007, after every other party had quit the government, these members formed a new alliance, the so-called "Moderates Front" (see Chapter One for a discussion of the term "moderate" in American propaganda). The next legislative election, originally scheduled for 2009, could hard-ly result in anything but a huge defeat for this coalition of Kurds and American-and-Iranian-backed Shiite Islamists. Efforts began in early 2008 to disqualify anti-occupation parties like Fadhila and Current from taking part in future elections.

The December 2005 election was certified on February 10th, 2006. Under the Iraqi constitution, the first meeting of the Assembly should have taken place within thirty days, a speaker should have been elected at that meeting, a prime minister should have been appointed within another thirty days, and a cabinet by May 11th. If any of these condi-tions was not met, the constitution required that the election be an-nulled and a new one held. So, when the new Assembly failed to meet until March 16th, and then failed to elect a speaker, this should have led to nullification and a new election.

Instead, the various parties wrangled over the important posts in the government, until Jalal Talibani of the Kurdish PUK was appointed as President on April 14th, Dawa's Nouri al-Maliki became Prime Minister on April 21st, and Mahmoud al-Mashhadani, a Salafi or religious fun-damentalist from the largest Sunni party, was elected as Speaker of the Assembly the following day. The Ministries of Defense, Interior and National Security were not finally awarded until June 8th.

The eventual Interior Minister, Jawad al-Bulani, was an independent from Amarah who had lived in Iraq his whole life. He entered politics after the U.S. invasion, working first with the Sadrists, and later with Iraqi Hizbollah and Ahmad Chalabi. He then joined Fadhila, and was a member of its General Secretariat during and after the December 2005 election. Fadhila quit Maliki's coalition in May 2006 during negotiations over the allocation of ministries. Fadhila had been negotiating for the position of Oil Minister based on its dominance in the oil-producing province of Basra. The party walked out on the grounds that American advisers were playing an inappropriate role in these negotiations. Jawad al-Bulani remained in the government as an independent and was eventually appointed Interior Minister.

The replacement of Bayan al-Jabr by Jawad al-Bulani was widely seen as a move to clean up the Interior Ministry and its record of atrocities against the population. During the next few months, Bulani signed 52 arrest warrants for Interior Ministry officials for crimes related to torture and extra-judicial killing. However, in an update on the situation in Iraq on September 1st 2006, UN Secretary General Kofi Annan noted that none of these warrants had actually been served.[314] It was widely understood that Jabr's former deputy, Adnan al-Asadi, another Badr Brigade commander, had retained effective control of the Special or National Police.[315]

As the U.N.'s figures demonstrated, there was no let-up in the tide of tortured bodies of victims of extra-judicial execution at the morgue in Baghdad. In fact the tide only swelled as U.S. forces launched their promised new offensives. The first, Operation Together Forward, was announced on June 24th 2006. The second, dubbed Operation Together Forward II, began in August. These operations increased U.S. combat strength in Baghdad to 15,000 troops. By October, it was clear that they

---

314. http://daccessdds.un.org/doc/UNDOC/GEN/N06/484/95/PDF/N0648495.pdf?OpenElement
315. Edward Wong and Paul von Zielbauer, "Iraq stumbling in bid to purge its rogue police," *New York Times*, September 17 2006.

had raised the level of violence in the city rather than reduced it. They also accelerated the ethnic cleansing of Baghdad that had begun with the deployment of the Special Police in 2005.

American military officials presented the two Operation Together Forwards as efforts to restore security to Baghdad, targeting both Sunni resistance fighters and Shiite death squads. However, when General Thurman announced the districts to be targeted, four out of five were the same Sunni or mixed neighborhoods that had been under attack by Interior Ministry death squads for more than a year: Adhamiya, Dora, Mansour, and Ghazaliya.

American units were teamed up with Iraqi Army and Interior Ministry forces, and the Americans were dependent on their Iraqi partners for the "intelligence" they needed to plan house raids and patrols. American junior officers and troops assigned to work with Iraqi forces in Operation Together Forward soon realized that there were strong links between their Iraqi partners and the death squads who were one of the nominal targets of the operation. But individual units on the ground had little choice but to follow the leads their Iraqi allies provided and take on whatever resistance they encountered.

The predictable result of the operation was that thousands more young men and boys from these areas were either killed or detained on suspicion of resistance activities, while the death squads continued to ply their gruesome trade in an even more favorable environment, effectively supported by the heavier American presence. The overall effect of Operation Together Forward I and II was to provide greater American support for the death squads, not to suppress or disband them. Perhaps the best illustration of this was the fact that the numbers of civilians killed in Baghdad swelled during these operations to their highest level in October 2006, and then declined in November and December after Operation Together Forward was called off.[316]

Extra-judicial executions in Baghdad had reached a new high in July 2006 after Operation Together Forward began. The coroner's office reported that 90% of the 1,800 bodies brought to the morgue that month were victims of summary execution. The death squads claimed twice as many victims in July as they had in February, just a few months earlier. And yet a Pentagon report to Congress in August showed that the Iraqi Resistance was more active than ever, conducting 800 operations per week against U.S. and auxiliary forces, collaborators and infrastructure. The two years of the interim and transitional governments, the recruitment and deployment of the Special Police and, the U.S. assaults on Fallujah and other Resistance-held cities, now including Baghdad, had only succeeded in doubling the scale of the resistance. "Coalition" forces were still the target of 60% of Resistance attacks, but the delegation of occupation, detention, torture, and killing to Iraqi auxiliary forces meant that they were now suffering 200 attacks per week as well.[317]

By the end of June 2006, the U.N. estimated that 150,000 people had been newly internally displaced since the bombing of the Golden Dome in Samarra in February. By the end of August, after Operation Together Forward I, its estimate doubled to 300,000. By the end of Operation Together Forward II in October, it rose to 433,000. By February 2007, the U.N. High Commission for Refugees estimated that 800,000 people had been internally displaced in the past year, in addition to 150,000 already displaced by the previous three years of war. The internally displaced were in addition to 1.6 million exiles outside the country—about 600,000 each in Jordan and Syria, and 436,000 further afield. The num-

---

316. http://www.uniraq.org/aboutus/HR.asp
317. "Measuring stability and security in Iraq," *U.S. Department of Defense*, August 29 2006. http://www.defenselink.mil/pubs/pdfs/Security-Stabilty-ReportAug29r1.pdf

ber of exiles outside the country rose to at least 2 million by May 2007. At least 40% of Iraqi professionals joined the exodus, leaving the population without healthcare, education, legal or political representation, or a functioning physical infrastructure.[318]

As the U.N. came to grips with the full scale of the refugee crisis in Iraq over the next two years, it would raise its estimate of the total number of refugees, both internally displaced and in exile, to 5 million. But this number grew most dramatically in the course of 2006, as a result of the escalation of death squad activities under Operation Together Forward, in addition to the pressure of excessive military force used by American forces in Anbar province and other parts of the country.

In Ramadi, according to the U.N., "Civilians are reported to be severely affected by heavy MNF (multi-national force) bombing in the districts of Al-Orphally, Al-Soufiya, Al-Katana, Al-Mala'ab, Al-Andalus, 30 July and Al-Azeeziya. Ongoing disruption in the supply of basic services, including water and electricity, and increasing militarization of the sectors of the town have forced residents to leave their homes and relocate to neighboring areas for fear of military attacks."[319]

The next U.N. human rights report two months later sounded a now familiar theme: "The new Iraqi Government established in May 2006, although strongly committed to the promotion and protection of human rights, is currently facing a generalized breakdown of law and order which presents a serious challenge to the institutions of Iraq ... there is a growing perception of impunity for current and past crimes committed which risks further eroding the rule of law."

This report also noted that more than a hundred journalists had been killed in Iraq since the invasion. Some of them appeared to have

318. http://www.uniraq.org/documents/UN-Iraq%20Humanitarian%20Briefing%20Fact%20Sheet%20May%2007.pdf
319. http://www.uniraq.org/aboutus/HR.asp

been detained and killed by the police. Seven journalists were detained while covering anti-government demonstrations in Sulaymaniyah governorate, but they were later released.

And meanwhile, UNAMI had "continued to receive reports of MNF-I involvement in incidents of excessive force ... " For instance, "On 28 August, it was reported that snipers shot thirteen civilians for breach of the curfew, killing six and injuring seven, in the district of Al-Eskan Al-Jadida in Ramadi."

In July, UNAMI officials and Iraqi torture victims met with Manfred Nowak, the U.N.'s Special Rapporteur for Torture, in Amman, Jordan. He told *ARD* public broadcasting's *Tagesschau* program in Germany, "Many of them credibly reported that in their view the situation is now worse than it was under Saddam Hussein. Under his dictatorship there was also terrible torture, but one could at least still predict who would have to fear being tortured. Today, on the other hand, the security situation is out of control to such an extent that in the final analysis every person can become a victim of abductions, summary executions, and the worst methods of torture: people's limbs are being amputated, their fingers are missing, their eyes have been put out."[320]

As people in the United States marked the fifth anniversary of the September 11th attack, the U.S. General Accounting Office (GAO) released a report on the situation in Iraq. It described attacks on U.S.-led forces as "still the primary source of bloodshed in Iraq," eclipsing the "sectarian violence" now highlighted by the Pentagon. It failed to note that resistance to occupation was by definition a secondary source of bloodshed, and that the invasion and military occupation of the country was therefore still the primary cause of all the bloodshed.

In other respects, the GAO report was unusually frank in its assessment of the situation. It acknowledged that resistance to the occupa-

---

320. http://www.juancole.com/2006/10/100-tortured-each-day-in-iraq.html

tion had increased throughout every phase of the war and that "insurgents continue to demonstrate the ability to recruit new fighters, supply themselves, and attack coalition security forces." And it cited a DIA finding that "the December 2005 elections appeared to heighten sectarian divisions and polarize sectarian divides," instead of representing real political progress as previous U.S. statements had claimed.

The GAO posed a number of serious questions for the U.S. government, notably, "Why have security conditions continued to worsen even as Iraq has met political milestones, increased the number of trained and equipped forces and increasingly assumed the lead for security?"[321] After reading the last two or three chapters, readers can hopefully answer this question more clearly than the GAO. Essentially, the United States government was still determined to militarily defeat political opposition in Iraq by any means available, and the terrible damage to the security of the civilian population was a principal component of this campaign rather than an unintended consequence of it.

As the grim results of this policy continued to overwhelm the Baghdad morgue, the Iraqi Health Ministry announced in October that it was building two new morgues, to increase its capacity in Baghdad by 250 bodies per day. And a U.S. military spokesman admitted that the 8th Iraqi Police Unit had been found responsible for the disappearance of 26 workers from a food factory in Amil in southwest Baghdad on October 1st. Ten of their bodies were later found in the Abu Chir district. Interior Minister Bulani suspended the unit from its duties pending an investigation. But General Thavit, who was still in military command of the now 24,000 strong National Police force, told *Inter Press Service*

---

321. David M. Walker, Comptroller General of the United States, "Stabilizing Iraq: an assessment of the security situation," *United States General Accounting Office*, September 11 2006. http://www.gao.gov/new.items/d061094t.pdf

that the police involved would not be charged with crimes. "They are going to be rehabilitated and brought back to service," he said.

In the wake of this incident, on October 17th, two senior National Police commanders, Rasheed Fleyah and Mahdi Sabeh, were finally removed from their posts. A communique from the largest Sunni bloc in the Assembly raised an obvious but unanswered question regarding this and other such crimes: "The Iraqi Islamist Party asks how could 26 people, women among them, have been transported from Amil to Abu Chir through all those Iraqi and U.S. army checkpoints and patrols?"

An officer in the Iraqi Army, Major Amir Jassim, challenged the public perception that the infiltration of the Interior Ministry by Shiite militias was responsible for its death squad activity. He had been deployed to Fallujah alongside Interior Ministry forces during the U.S. assault in November 2004, and he contrasted their behavior there with that of his own troops. When asked by *IPS* about the role of General Mahdi al-Gharrawi, now the overall commander of Interior Ministry "public order" forces, he told IPS, "All criminals who survived the Fallujah crisis after committing genocide and other war crimes were granted higher ranks. I and many of my colleagues were not rewarded because we disobeyed orders to set fire to peoples' houses after others looted them. Now they want to do the same things they did in Fallujah in all Sunni areas so that they ignite a civil war in Iraq. A civil war is the only guarantee for them to stay in power, looting such incredible amounts of money."

Major Jassim clearly took the view that the roots of death squad violence lay in the interim government's original recruitment and deployment of the Special Police, not in the later ascendancy of the Badr Organization. And a police officer at the Ministry of Defense told *IPS*, "This is a country that will never stand back on its feet as long as these killers are in power. And the Americans are supporting them by allowing their convoys to move during curfew hours."[322]

Iraqi officials who dared to challenge the reign of terror placed themselves and their families in grave danger. Mohammed al-Dini, a member of parliament, was one of a group of officials who made an unannounced visit to Site Four, an Interior Ministry prison, in the summer of 2006, exposing the detention and torture of hundreds of prisoners in conditions similar to those at al-Jadiriyah. Three days later, ten of his relatives came to visit him in Baghdad. At the end of their visit, he watched them climb back into a minivan for the return journey. The next time he saw his relatives, their bodies were lying in pools of blood next to the minivan, with flyers scattered around them reading, "Congratulations to those who killed these Sunni extremists." Mr. al-Dini had no doubt about who killed his relatives. "They were militiamen operating as death squads inside the police. And the attack was ordered by those people I exposed for running the prison."[323]

After Operation Together Forward II was called off on October 24th, the U.N. reported that violent civilian deaths in Baghdad declined by 18% in November. However, on November 14th, Interior Ministry forces launched one of their largest raids ever in Baghdad, abducting about 150 people from the Scholarship Department at the Ministry of Higher Education. This occurred on a day when the ministry was hosting teaching staff from universities in Anbar, Salahaddin and Mosul governorates, all predominantly Sunni Arab areas. The police opened fire on a group lined up at the department, wounding a female professor from Mosul. They then separated the men from the women, forced the men into vehicles, and drove them away. The presence of so many visitors at

322. Ali al-Fadhily and Dahr Jamail, "Government death squads ravaging Baghdad," *Inter Press Service*, October 19 2006.
323. Deborah Davies, "War on terror: Iraq's death squads," *Channel 4 News*, November 7 2006. http://www.globalresearch.ca/index.php?
context=viewArticle&code=DAV20061115&articleId=3879

the ministry that day made a precise count of the disappeared impossible. Nine men who were Shiites were released immediately. The tortured bodies of Dr. Abdil Salam al-Suwaydan, the head of the Scholarship Department and Abdil Hameed Hamadani, another employee, were found on November 23rd. Seventy more detainees were eventually released after being interrogated and tortured. About seventy more, including 56 employees of the Ministry of Higher Education, mostly Sunnis, were still unaccounted for five months later.[324]

The precise extent of U.S. complicity in different aspects and phases of death squad operations, torture, and disappearances deserves thorough investigation. It is not credible that American officials were simply innocent bystanders to thousands of these incidents. As frequently pointed out by Iraqi observers, Interior Ministry death squads moved unhindered through American as well as Iraqi checkpoints as they detained, tortured, and killed thousands of people.

The nature and extent of involvement by different individuals and groups within the U.S. occupation infrastructure has remained a dirty, dark secret, but there are many leads that could be followed by any serious inquiry. As with the "disguised, quiet, media-free approach" that American policy-makers have adopted elsewhere, witnesses and whistle-blowers would come forward if Congressional committees or the U.S. Justice Department launched serious investigations. The alternative is that it will be Iraqi and international investigators who will gradually shed light on these events, leaving U.S. officials in the familiar position of attempting to defend the indefensible against waves of international outrage.

Unfortunately, at the time of writing, the Obama administration has shown no desire to expose any of the crimes committed by U.S. officials in Iraq, nor to turn over a new leaf in the history of U.S. foreign policy

---

324. http://www.uniraq.org/aboutus/HR.asp

that would prevent the perpetuation or repetition of these crimes in Afghanistan, Pakistan or anywhere else.

In terms of U.S. policy in Iraq, it is clear that, while publicly subscribing to a "political solution" and to "winning the hearts and minds" of the Iraqi people, the United States in fact unleashed the most savage dogs of war to destroy countless human lives and the fabric of an entire society. The American response to the continuing failure of this strategy was only to escalate the intensity of the campaign and to provide greater direct military support to its Iraqi death squads.

The brutal reasoning behind this campaign seems to have stemmed from the American need to establish a subservient government that would be strong enough to survive with American help, but too weak to become independent of U.S. military support. The struggle for Iraq had to be reduced to a violent one in which the American capacity to commit greater violence than its adversaries would be the decisive factor. A purely political dialogue between different sectors of Iraqi society could not achieve the desired result, as it would lead only to a polite thank you to the Americans for overthrowing Saddam Hussein and a farewell parade for U.S. occupation forces.

The violence and corruption of U.S. policy in Iraq prevented this worst possible outcome, from the U.S. government's point of view, by providing power and wealth to Iraqis who were willing to collaborate, while neutralizing, marginalizing and often killing anyone that represented independent, nationalist or democratic forces in Iraqi civil society. At the same time, like any other organized crime operation, the U.S. occupation held onto power by selectively offering protection from the very violence it unleashed. But the people of districts targeted for destruction, like Adhamiya, Mansour, Dora, and Ghazaliya in Baghdad as well as Fallujah and Ramadi, were faced with an impossible choice: to submit to the most brutal forms of state terrorism, to resist or to flee. Their resistance was used to justify even greater violence by U.S.

forces wielding even more deadly weapons than the Glock pistols and electric drills of the Special Police, leaving flight as the only choice for 5 million Iraqis.

The final U.N. Human Rights Report of 2006 described the consequences of these policies for the people of Baghdad, while downplaying their institutional roots in American policy. "Baghdad is at the centre of the sectarian violence. Sunni and Shiite armed groups are attempting to establish territorial control of Baghdad's many predominantly mixed neighborhoods by intimidating and killing civilian populations and forcing them into displacements to parts of the city inhabited or controlled by members of their ethnic group. Reports suggest the existence of large movements of populations primarily within the city boundaries, as the neighborhoods become increasingly divided among Sunni and Shi'a armed groups, and are consequently grouped together based on their sect and ethnicity. This forced displacement has been achieved by means of large scale attacks targeting civilians, kidnappings, extrajudicial killings, dropping of threatening leaflets, destruction of properties, and intimidation."

But the "sectarian violence" that engulfed Iraq in 2006 was not an unintended consequence of the U.S. invasion and occupation but an integral part of it. The United States did not just fail to restore stability and security to Iraq. It deliberately undermined them in a desperate effort to "divide and rule" the country and to fabricate new justifications for unlimited violence against Iraqis who continued to reject the illegal invasion and occupation of their country.

CHAPTER 16. BRING THE CIVILIANS HOME

Exactly three years into the American war in Iraq, on March 21st 2006, the U.S. government's failure to offer any serious or credible justification for the war led veteran White House correspondent Helen Thomas to ask Mr. Bush directly at a press conference:

> I'd like to ask you, Mr. President, your decision to invade Iraq has caused the deaths of thousands of Americans and Iraqis, wounded Americans and Iraqis for a lifetime. Every reason given, publicly at least, has turned out not to be true. My question is, why did you really want to go to war? From the moment you stepped into the White House, from your Cabinet—your Cabinet officers, intelligence people, and so forth—what was your real reason? You have said it wasn't oil—quest for oil, it hasn't been Israel, or anything else. What was it?

Bush had pointedly avoided calling on Thomas at White House press conferences, so she had had years to think about what she would ask him if and when she finally got the chance. Predictably, when the time came, Bush did not answer her question, but she has explained in subsequent interviews why she chose to ask this particular question. She told Amy Goodman:

> I think the astounding thing, if you were in a room with many people and you went to ten people and asked them why we're in this war, you would get ten different answers, and that's no way to go to war. So I asked the President, what is the real reason, when every reason turned out to be untrue? Weapons of mass destruction, no. Ties to al-Qaeda, no. A threat from a third world country, no, to the world's only military superpower. So I asked him, what was his real reason? And then he said the Taliban. I said, "I'm talking about Iraq, Mr. President." Then he said 9/11. I said, "But the Iraqis had nothing to do with 9/11." And on it went. The thing is, I certainly didn't get a clear-cut answer. It isn't for me. It's for the world. It's for the country. Why are you being asked to die?

What is the valid reason? There are reasons. We have been in wars that I think people feel were—it was the right cause. Certainly World War II. But to send people to war, and under what pretenses now?[325]

The justifications for their decisions cited by senior U.S. officials turned out to be a shifting smoke-screen designed to disguise their real motives. But the question remained and still remains: what were the real objectives of the U.S. invasion and occupation of Iraq?

Part of the value of hiding real motives behind boilerplate political rhetoric and widely repeated lies is that it enables those responsible for decisions to harbor and conceal their actual purposes, avoiding debate on serious questions even among colleagues. This is obviously one of the dangers of a debased political culture and of subservient media that only echo "administration story-lines." Phil Donahue's film *Body of War* brilliantly collated clips of U.S. Senators of both parties justifying their pro-war votes in 2002 by glib repetition of catch-phrases created by the White House's public relations consultants. Behind this facade, institutional and corporate interests outweighed the popular opposition voiced in up to 90% of their constituent correspondence, as in the case of Senator Nelson of Florida.

The sustained support of America's political and business leadership for a war that probably killed a million people should lead Americans to question the very foundations of the U.S. political economy. To some extent it has. But it is important to recognize that different people and institutions are motivated by different interests, so that it takes a sort of "perfect storm" involving a confluence of interests to produce such a catastrophic result. The only meaningful context in which to understand American goals in Iraq is in relation to the interests that drove

---

325. "Veteran White House correspondent Helen Thomas on the Iraq War etc..," *Democracy Now*, January 22 2007.
http://www.democracynow.org/2007/1/22/veteran_white_house_correspondent_helen
_thomas

the country to war in the first place and have sustained the war effort ever since. The refusal of American policy-makers to relinquish or substantially alter their goals even as they destroyed an entire country and killed a million people is devastating evidence of their unswerving commitment to the interests at stake.

In the 1970s, following the total defeat of American military power in Vietnam, Donald Rumsfeld played an instrumental role in undermining detente with the Soviet Union, increasing military spending, and reinvigorating the Cold War military industrial complex. Rumsfeld gradually displaced Henry Kissinger at the helm of U.S. foreign policy, first as President Ford's Chief of Staff and then as Secretary of Defense.[326]

Rumsfeld's role in launching and conducting the American war in Iraq was consistent with his past role managing the post-Vietnam rehabilitation and expansion of the U.S. military industrial complex. If aggression against Iraq was successful, the American war machine would be firmly established as a dominant force in world affairs for another generation. American big business would "follow the flag" to the ends of the Earth, as it did in the 20th century. Even in the context of military failure in Iraq, U.S. military spending more than doubled to its highest level since the Second World War. The basic premises of this military expansion met no serious challenge from U.S. political or business leaders. Bipartisan support in Congress for redoubled American militarism fueled a new gravy train for the wide array of American corporations that benefit from contracts with the Pentagon, even as these policies exacerbated the underlying crisis in the U.S. economy.

Rumsfeld's protege, Richard Cheney, replaced him as Chief of Staff in Ford's White House and was also Ford's campaign manager in 1976.

---

326. James Mann, *The Rise of the Vulcans: The History of Bush's War Cabinet*, (New York: Viking Press, 2004).

He was then elected to Congress and served several terms. He was a member of the Intelligence Committee and Minority Whip. Cheney supported all of President Reagan's most dangerous military initiatives, including Iran-Contra, CIA operations in Afghanistan, and Star Wars.

Cheney emerged as an advocate for the more aggressive and direct use of U.S. military force following a Congressional visit to post-invasion Grenada in 1983. This was the first openly aggressive and un-ilateral use of U.S. military force to directly overthrow a foreign government since the 1960s. Opinion polls in both Grenada and the United States after the invasion revealed widespread public approval for the regime change. Cheney returned from Grenada to tell his hometown paper, the *Casper Star Tribune*, on November 6th 1983, that the international image of the United States would be bolstered when it demon-strated a willingness to "support its allies" through the use of military force. U.S. forces would be welcomed with open arms by the local pop-ulation following such invasions, and the global spread of Communism would be stopped.

This view ran counter to contemporary American military doctrine, which more cautiously emphasized the use of proxies to fight wars in the Third World, under the influence of Reagan's Defense Secretary Casper Weinberger. After Cheney was appointed Secretary of Defense by the first President Bush, he put his advocacy of direct use of U.S. military force to the test by invading Panama. James Baker and Brent Scowcroft, the Secretary of State and the National Security Adviser, were more involved with the opportunities presented by the collapsing Soviet empire in Eastern Europe at the time, making Cheney and Pow-ell the principal advisers to President Bush on Panama. The invasion of Panama was a critical step in the development of the doctrine that led to the war in Iraq and the so-called war on terror. It strengthened the beliefs of Cheney and many of his colleagues that the aggressive use of U.S. military force would be an effective means by which to preserve and expand America's commercial and military empire in the 21st century.[327]

The application of a doctrine of aggression to the Middle East seems a far cry from invading Grenada and Panama or directing covert and proxy forces against small countries in the Caribbean basin. But the fall of the Soviet Union and the results of the first Gulf War encouraged Cheney, Rumsfeld, and their colleagues to imagine that the extent of the new military imbalance between the United States and any potential competitors provided a window of opportunity to militarily seize control of this strategically and commercially critical region. I will write more about U.S. goals for Iraq's oil industry in the next chapter.

The post-Cold War period saw a gradual reorientation of long-term U.S. military strategy and overseas bases from the regions that were relevant to confronting the Soviet Union, like Western Europe and Korea, to wherever oil was produced and shipped around the world. This still included the periphery of the former Soviet Union, but the largest expansion of U.S. bases was in and around the Persian Gulf. The positioning of U.S. forces to gain effective control over the world's oil supply was an overarching component of U.S. strategy. These forces simultaneously protected and implicitly threatened the supply of oil to China, Japan, Western Europe and much of the world.

The weakness of Iraq as a result of war and sanctions, combined with the second or third largest oil reserves in the world, provided an irresistible target for American military action, a temptation that was ultimately too powerful for the critical decision-makers in Washington to resist, and that fit squarely within their larger strategy. While Cheney, Rumsfeld, and the neo-conservative ideologues led the charge, the entire business and political leadership of the United States fell in line behind this murderous adventure, ultimately undermining the very as-

---

327. Kevin Buckley, *Panama*, (New York: Touchstone, 1992).

pirations to extend America's position of global leadership into the twenty-first century that its architects had hoped to fulfill.

By the same token, once the U.S. government had seized control of the Green Zone, established a quasi-government with access to Iraqi oil revenues, and invested billions of dollars to build military bases, they were not going to be cheated of their prize by popular opposition in Iraq. Everything I have described in previous chapters, from air strikes to death squads, should be understood in this context. When faced with a conflict between the relative values of American wealth and power on the one hand and the lives of millions of Iraqis on the other, American leaders consistently chose to escalate the level of violence.

By examining the projects that the United States clung to most stubbornly in Iraq, we can gain some insight into its priorities and better understand the principal goals of the invasion and occupation. One part of its plans in Iraq that the United States refused to modify or scale down despite all the setbacks of the occupation was the construction of a huge "embassy" inside the Green Zone in Baghdad. During the 2008 presidential election in the United States, Senator Obama took the position that he would "keep some troops in Iraq to protect our embassy and diplomats," even as he promised to begin a gradual withdrawal of combat troops. Among the major party candidates for President, only Members of Congress Kucinich and Paul and Governor Richardson were committed to a full withdrawal of U.S. occupation forces without such a "residual force."

The controversial role of American diplomats in Iraq and the construction of the so-called embassy in Baghdad occupied a central position in American policy but, like air strikes and death squads, this aspect of U.S. policy was pursued with the now familiar "disguised, quiet, media-free approach." In reality, the United States was building a headquarters for a long-term American presence in the heart of the Iraqi government, from which U.S. State Department officials could play a dominant role in the administration of a nominally independent country.

During its construction, the media were explicitly prohibited from photographing the massive "embassy" as it rose over the banks of the Tigris in Baghdad. Its architects were accused of compromising its security when they posted the architectural plans on the internet, but they pointed out that its details were already visible to prospective attackers in greater detail on Google Earth. The same would have applied to pictures in the media. The shroud of secrecy covering the project was not intended to protect it from attack but from public scrutiny.

The Iraq Study Group (ISG) report that was published in December 2006 as a "bipartisan, independent, 'fresh-eyes' assessment of Iraq" likewise failed to challenge the construction of this gigantic colonial headquarters disguised as an embassy. The report did note some of the shortcomings of the project, such as the fact that only six of the 1,000 U.S. Embassy staff in Iraq were fluent in Arabic. It also noted that, "Civilian agencies have little experience with complex overseas interventions to restore and maintain order—stability operations—outside the normal embassy setting."

But rather than questioning the legitimacy of the role that U.S. foreign service officers were being assigned in Iraq, the report instead recommended that, "The State Department should train personnel to carry out civilian tasks associated with a complex stability operation outside of the traditional embassy setting ... Other key civilian agencies, including Treasury, Justice, and Agriculture, need to create similar technical assistance capabilities."[328]

In effect, the ISG recommended that American foreign service officers should be trained to run a colonial administration, like Britain's

328. http://www.usip.org/isg/iraq_study_group_report/report/1206/index.html

former Colonial Service, but it failed to recognize that this raised some fundamental, probably irreconcilable problems. This writer's grandfather retired from the British Colonial Service as Deputy Treasurer of Kenya in the 1940s, following a then common career track that kept him in Africa for much of his life, a long period of overseas service broken up only by a home leave every five years.

But Britain ultimately found colonialism, government by foreigners for the principal benefit of their home country, to be unsustainable in the 20th century. The British discovered that their interests were better served by maintaining commercial relations within a structure of political independence. There was no rational reason to believe that the United States could resurrect the corpse of colonialism in the 21st century, and this was tragically borne out by its experience in Iraq. Britain's Colonial Office and Foreign Office were in any case distinct services with very different training and experience. The effort to draft American foreign service officers as ersatz colonial administrators only made the failure of the American experiment in Iraq more certain than ever. And of course it was always going to be the luckless Iraqis who would bear the effects of this disaster while the Americans and British and their Iraqi exile allies returned to reflect on their adventures from the comfort of their homes in Washington and London.

The so-called U.S. Embassy in Baghdad occupied 104 acres, about ten times the size of the largest legitimate embassy in the world, the U.S. Embassy in Beijing. This prime piece of Baghdad real estate was once a nice public park on the bank of the Tigris, but was given as a gift to the United States by its Iraqi allies after the Americans captured Baghdad for them. It was completely cut off even from the surrounding 4-square mile Green Zone by 15-foot thick, 9-foot high concrete walls, and a razor-wire-enclosed kill zone. It had plush residences for senior officials, 619 one-bedroom apartments for the rest of the staff, office space for 1,000, a separate marine barracks, a social club, and a swimming pool—a total of 21 buildings altogether. As Iraqis struggled with power outages, contaminated drinking water, and sewage in the streets, the Americans had their own self-sufficient power, water, and sewage plants. The complex took several years to build, and cost $736 million by the time personnel began to move into the offices and living quarters in June 2008. Construction was nine months behind schedule, and $144 million over budget. But the fact that it was built at all was more galling to Iraqis as they watched it rise over their capital city while everything else in their country was progressively destroyed by the occupation.[329]

The billions of dollars that the United States spent to build its headquarters in the Green Zone and 265 bases around the country stood in sharp contrast to its record on "reconstruction," which served as a central component of American propaganda during the early years of the war. The U.S. Congress budgeted $18.4 billion in reconstruction funding for Iraq in 2003, but less than a billion had actually been spent a year later. As conditions in Iraq worsened, another $3.4 billion of this money was spent on "security," effectively diverted to the Pentagon and its contractors. The bulk of the money was never spent at all. By 2008, the GAO reported that only 24% of all U.S. funds budgeted for "reconstruction" in Iraq had been disbursed. As with many American foreign assistance programs, most of the money was in any case designed to wind up back in the United States one way or the other through contracts with American firms.

In fact, rather than spending American money to rebuild Iraq, the American occupation authorities joined their Iraqi allies in the looting of Iraqi oil revenues. U.N. Security Council resolution 1483 established the Development Fund for Iraq (DFI), intending that Iraqi oil revenues, previously seized assets and $6 billion remaining in the U.N.'s "oil-for-

329. Daniel McGrory, "In the chaos of Iraq, one project is on target: a giant US embassy," *The Times*, May 3 2006; William Langewiesche, "The mega-bunker of Baghdad," *Vanity Fair*, November 2007.

food" program would be used to restore the country's infrastructure. Subsequent audits by KPMG and a special inspector general found that a huge proportion of this money was stolen or embezzled by American officials. $8.8 billion of this money, nine months spending by the occupation government between the fund's establishment and the end of the Coalition Provisional Authority (CPA), was completely unaccounted for. The KPMG auditors hired by the U.N. had great difficulty tracking the missing funds, and were at first even refused passes to enter the Green Zone.

These audits and other reports provided details of at least some of the theft, embezzlement and mismanagement of DFI funds:

- $13 million found by customs officials in Lebanon aboard Iraqi-American interim Interior Minister Falah Naqib's plane;

- A $600 million slush fund maintained personally by Paul Bremer with no paperwork;

- A ministry that was paid for the wages of 8,206 guards but only had 602 on its books;

- An American army officer who doubled the price on a contract for work on an Iraqi hospital. He told the hospital's director that the extra money, more than a million dollars, was his "retirement package;"

- A contract to repair a cement factory in Samarah was signed for $20 million, but the American contractor billed the Iraqi government for $60 million—when the Iraqis complained, the contractor told them they should be grateful that the U.S. had saved them from Saddam Hussein;

- An American oil pipeline contractor was paid $3.4 million for "personnel not in the field performing work" and "other improper charges;"

- Oil exports were deliberately not metered, so that an estimated $4 billion worth of Iraqi oil may have been sold on the black market with the cooperation of the occupation government;

- Out of $3 billion in contracts awarded during the last few weeks of the CPA, but payable by the new Iraqi interim government, there were discrepancies of over $100 million each in both payments issued and amounts owed;

- Out of 198 contract files reviewed by the special inspector general, 154 contained no paperwork to document that any of the goods or services contracted for had actually been provided;

- And American "paying agents" disbursing Iraqi funds around Hillah, the only region examined by the special inspector general, provided no accounting for $96.6 million in cash they claimed to have disbursed. One agent did not account for $25 million and another accounted for only $6.3 million of $23 million disbursed. The CPA used agents like these all over the country. Many only submitted paperwork right before they left Iraq and huge amounts were simply "cleared" by the CPA—one agent who was challenged over a $1.9 million discrepancy returned the next day with the exact amount in cash, begging the question as to how much more he and others took home for their "retirement funds."[330]

While some Americans were stealing Iraqi development funds and other Americans were dropping bombs and firing artillery to demolish more Iraqi homes and infrastructure, the only places where construction was booming in Iraq were at the American occupation headquarters in the Green Zone and on U.S. military bases around the country. By 2008, the Global Security web site listed 265 U.S. military bases in Iraq. When the U.S. government began negotiating a Status of Forces Agreement with the Green Zone Iraqi government in 2008, it reportedly wanted to retain 200 of them, before scaling its demands down to 58 bases. These included major air bases where it had invested billions of

330. Ed Harriman, "Where has all the money gone?," *London Review of Books*, July 7 2005.

dollars in permanent structures, as well as Forward Operating Bases and Camps. The Iraqis insisted on a timetable for the withdrawal of all U.S. forces, eventually setting the date for the end of 2011.[331]

Between 2004 and 2008, the U.S. Department of Defense spent $5.6 billion on military construction in Iraq and Afghanistan. Aside from a decrease in 2006, the amount appropriated increased every year. The Democratic-run Congress appropriated an additional $1.83 billion in its war supplemental for Fiscal Year 2009, only a small decrease from the $2 billion appropriated for 2008.[332] The steady increases in appropriations for military construction in Iraq and Afghanistan made it clear that U.S. forces were gradually building more permanent and extensive facilities on many of their bases. Various Congressional resolutions prohibited the construction of "permanent" U.S. bases in Iraq, but, as Assistant Defense Secretary Mary Beth Long explained to the Senate Foreign Relations Committee in April 2008, the Department of Defense had no legal definition for the term "permanent base." Senator Webb suggested to her that, in that case, "It doesn't really mean anything," and she responded, "Yes, Senator, you're completely right. It doesn't."[333]

Unfortunately for the people of Iraq, hardly any of this money trickled down to them. Iraqis posed a security risk at U.S. bases in Iraq, so the American contractors who received Defense Department military construction contracts instead brought in workers from India, Pakistan, the Philippines, and elsewhere in Asia. On the Embassy project in the Green Zone, the contractor, First Kuwaiti General Trading and Contracting, told newly hired workers flown in from other parts of Asia that they would be working in Dubai. At the airport in Kuwait, they confiscated their passports and plane tickets, and loaded them onto

---

331. http://www.globalsecurity.org/military/facility/iraq.htm

332. http://www.fas.org/sgp/crs/natsec/RL33110.pdf, p.44; http://www.defenselink.mil/comptroller/defbudget/fy2009/Supplemental/FY2008_Global_War_on_Terrorism_Pending_Request/FY_2008_GWOT.pdf

333. "What basis for 'permanent' bases?," *Washington Post*, April 11 2008.

unmarked, aging chartered planes bound for Baghdad. When John Owen, a foreman from Florida, found himself on a plane with about fifty new hires from India and the Philippines, they all thought they were on the wrong plane. "I thought there was some sort of mix-up," he said. Owen resigned after seven months on the job. In his resignation letter to the State Department, he described up to 2,500 workers living in squalid conditions with poor sanitation, cases of medical malpractice and managers who beat them regularly. Another supervisor said the construction workers were "treated like dogs."

The health of the workers was entrusted to a Washington "procurement planning" firm called MSDS. It had no previous experience in healthcare, but enjoyed a good relationship with Jim Golden, the State Department official approving contracts on the embassy project. MSDS hired Rory Mayberry, a retired army medic who worked as a funeral director in Oregon, and put him on another bogus flight from Kuwait to Baghdad, with another planeload of Filipinos with tickets for Dubai.

After four days trying to treat the workers at the embassy, Mayberry found out that two of them had died immediately before his arrival, and he requested that the contractor investigate their deaths. He recommended that the clinic where he was working be closed because of unsanitary conditions. In a report to the State Department, he listed dozens of problems, from a lack of clean bedding, hot water, disinfectant and ambulances to a "candy store" of often mislabeled but powerful drugs. He wrote that injured workers were routinely given painkillers and sent back to work.

"People were walking around intoxicated on pain relievers with unwrapped wounds and there were a lot of infections," he recalled. "The idea that there was any hygiene seemed ridiculous. I'm not sure they were even bathing ... Some were on the construction site climbing scaffolding 30 feet off the ground. I told First Kuwaiti that you don't give painkillers to people who are running machinery and working on heavy construction and they said 'that's how we do it.'"[334]

Beyond the abuse and negligent homicide of construction workers, the lack of language skills among the embassy staff, the contradictions in the U.S. State Department's mission in Iraq and the massive expense of it all, lies the glaring significance of the United States' decision to build and staff this complex in the heart of Baghdad. As the International Crisis Group pointed out in 2006, the scale of the embassy "is seen by Iraqis as an indication of who actually exercises power in their country."

But who did exercise power in occupied Iraq? By the time State Department personnel began moving into their folly on the Tigris, the futility of their role in Iraq was already becoming clear. After six years of occupation, the United States only exercised certain kinds of power in Iraq, while more important kinds of power had completely eluded it. Although the United States demonstrated the ability and the will to unleash almost unlimited destructive power against the people of Iraq, and to build military bases all over their country, the Iraqi people were neither pummeled nor hoodwinked into granting their consent to be governed by an American occupation government or by Iraqi exiles they saw as its puppets. Like Napoleon's forces in Spain, nothing the United States did in Iraq could make up for the authority that it lacked from the outset. The failure of American leaders to grasp this critical factor lay at the root of all their problems, and was ultimately irreconcilable.

American military bases placed U.S. forces, air forces in particular, within easy striking distance of all parts of Iraq, as well as Iran and Syria. But, unlike the older generation of U.S. military bases in other parts

---

334. David Phinney, "Baghdad Embassy Bonanza," *CorpWatch*, February 12 2006. http://www.corpwatch.org/article.php?id=13258

of the world, these bases were not connected to the local communities in which they were built. They were designed as self-sufficient islands or "lily-pads," supplied either from the air or by heavily armed convoys. As it became expedient, they could destroy the country beyond their walls and razor-wire fences, like islands in a sea of their own destruction.

The extensive construction projects at sites from which Iraqis were excluded and which the United States clearly had no intention of returning to Iraq in the near term, provide a practical indicator of its actual goals in Iraq. The so-called Embassy was the jewel in the crown of the American network of bases, the headquarters of the U.S. occupation, from which American advisers planned to maintain their influence over the current and subsequent Iraqi governments on a long-term, if not "permanent" basis.

The political debate over war policy in Washington tacitly accepted this part of U.S. policy as a given. The establishment of the occupation headquarters was a central and non-negotiable part of U.S. policy because it fulfilled one of the original, primary goals of the invasion, to establish a puppet Iraqi government supervised by American officials. Incredibly, the historic disaster that followed did not result in any substantial modification of this goal. Even as the U.S. Congress voted for timetables for the withdrawal of combat brigades, not one of these resolutions required the U.S. government to scale back or give up the plans for its colonial headquarters in Baghdad. The United States might be prepared to "bring (some of) the troops home." But, unless it was forced by the Iraqis, the American public, or by diplomatic pressure, it had no intention of "bringing the civilians home." The defense of the U.S. "embassy" in Baghdad would be a vital national interest for which American troops, like it or not, could be fighting and dying for years to come, and with bipartisan support in Washington.

CHAPTER 17. BLOOD FOR OIL

Until the Second World War, the Anglo-Persian Oil Company, which later changed its name to British Petroleum or BP, held a monopoly on oil production in Persia. Anglo-Persian paid a 16% royalty to the Persian government, leaving it with an 84% share of Persian oil revenues. Anglo-Persian also owned a 50% stake in the Turkish Petroleum Company (TPC), which was granted an exclusive concession to explore for oil in what is now Iraq in 1912. The other shareholders were Shell, a German company, and Armenian businessman Calouste Gulbenkian, whose 5% share made him the richest man in the world and earned him the nickname, "Mr. Five Percent." Gulbenkian insisted on a clause that prevented his partners from operating independently of the TPC anywhere in the Ottoman Empire. This was known as the Red Line Agreement.

When the former Ottoman Empire was carved up at the San Remo Conference in 1920, TPC was reconstituted, with France forming the Compagnie Francaise de Petrole (CFP—now Total) to take over the German share and American companies also holding shares for the first time. Iraq itself was granted a 20% share. All of this maneuvering preceded the first gusher of oil north of Kirkuk on October 15th 1927, which led to the beginning of actual oil production in Iraq. In a new agreement in July 1928. Gulbenkian kept his 5%, and the other shares were equally divided four ways, between Anglo-Persian, Shell, CFP and an American entity called the Near East Development Corporation, a joint venture by Exxon and Mobil. This gave the American companies a share of Iraq's oil production, while the Red Line Agreement prevented them from operating independently elsewhere in the former Ottoman Empire. This effectively limited Exxon and Mobil to their 11.9% shares in the TPC. Each company refined, marketed and distributed its share of the oil, while TPC itself did the same within Iraq. Anglo-Persian received an additional 10% royalty on all production in exchange for its reduced share in the new company.

TPC was renamed the Iraq Petroleum Company (IPC) in 1929. The British and American partners wanted to hold back on production to keep up the price of the oil they were producing in other parts of the world, while the French and Dutch wanted badly to increase production. Amid these disagreements, the Iraqi government cancelled IPC's concession because it had failed to build pipelines and terminals as agreed in its contract. A new 70-year concession was negotiated in 1931, and pipelines were built to British-controlled Haifa in Palestine, and French-controlled Tripoli in Lebanon. The Iraqis were increasingly frustrated with the lack of production and granted a separate concession for exploration east of the Tigris to a new British-Italian consortium, the British Oil Development Company, which was later bought out by IPC and renamed the Mosul Petroleum Company.[335]

IPC did not produce significant quantities of oil until 1938, when production finally reached about 55,000 barrels per day. This was soon curtailed by dangers to shipping in the Mediterranean during the Second World War. The history of wrangling between foreign companies over Iraq's oil forms the background to Iraq's nationalization of its oil industry, and to the continuing and perennial lack of production from some of the world's largest and most accessible oil-fields. It was no coincidence that the five Western oil companies involved in U.S.-backed negotiations with Iraq in 2008 were none other than the five former partners in the Iraq Petroleum Company. These deals would have fulfilled their long-standing desire to get back into Iraq, and were intended as the second step in the process of reversing the nationaliza-

---

335. Helen Chapin Metz, ed., "The Turkish Petroleum Company," *Iraq: A country study*, (Washington: GPO for the Library of Congress, 1988). http://countrystudies.us/iraq/53.htm

tion of Iraq's oil industry. The first step was the American and British invasion of Iraq.

By the time the monarchy was overthrown in 1958, oil production accounted for 28% of Iraq's GNP. Iraq had become increasingly dependent on this single source of revenue, which was still under the control of the largely foreign-owned Iraq Petroleum Company.[336] Iraq expropriated 95% of the IPC's concessions in 1961, and completed the nationalization of its oil industry in 1972, prohibiting future concessions to foreign companies.

Neighboring Iran nationalized its oil industry in 1948. A new concession was granted after the Western-backed coup in 1953 (BP 40%; a U.S. consortium 40%; Shell 10%; CFP/Total 10%) but this was terminated by Iran's renationalization of its oil industry in 1979. Saudi Arabia nationalized its oil industry in several steps between 1973 and 1980, ending a 50-50 deal with Chevron, Texaco and Exxon. Kuwait nationalized in 1975, ending a concession to BP and Gulf. Venezuela took control of its oil industry between 1971 and 1976. The Abu Dhabi National Oil Company was created in 1971, and controls 90% of oil production in the UAE. State-owned oil production in Russia was privatized in the 1990s, but the government has since reasserted domestic and state control.

Following their sudden loss of direct access to most of the world's oil reserves in the 1970s, the Western oil "majors" suffered through the 1980s and 1990s as OPEC dominated the market and prices remained low. The majors' distribution, refining, and retail operations, the "downstream" portion of the oil business, profited from increases in global consumption, and they retained "upstream" operations in the Gulf of Mexico and other areas. However, as a new century greeted them in 2000, the majors found OPEC sitting on 77% of the world's oil

---

336. Charles Issawi and Muhammed Yeganeh, *The Economics of Middle Eastern Oil*, (New York: Praeger, 1962), 143 & 147.

reserves and Russia on another 26% of non-OPEC reserves. Many of the non-OPEC fields that the oil companies did have access to were at or past their peak and facing inevitable declines in production, even as global consumption kept growing year after year. Two decades of exploration in other parts of the world had failed to find any new oilfields on the scale of the ones that they had lost to nationalization.

In April 2001, the U.S. Council on Foreign Relations (CFR) published a report that warned of a projected shortfall in global oil supplies. It was imperative that "political factors do not block the development of new oil fields in the (Persian) Gulf." The CFR called on "the Department of State, together with the National Security Council" to "develop a strategic plan to encourage reopening to foreign investment in the important states of the Middle East."[337]

But the thesis that privatization held the promise of more efficiently tapping the world's oil reserves had little empirical support. The petroleum sectors of the major oil-producing countries lacked neither capital nor expertise. The urgency of the supply shortfall was driven more by the failure of Western companies to develop substantial new sources of oil in recent years than by any deficiencies in state-owned oil companies. The only major exporting country that had continued to find sufficient new reserves to replace its current production was Iran, which relied mainly on its own resources and expertise. In reality, the most serious barriers to greater production in 2001 were the sanctions imposed on Iraq and Iran by or at the behest of the United States.

Pressure was increasing at the U.N. to lift the sanctions on Iraq, as the world thirsted for its reserves, the second or third largest in the world. The new regime of George Bush and Richard Cheney in Washington found itself at the nexus of several currents that Cheney himself

---

337 Edward L. Morse and Amy Myers Jaffe, *Strategic Energy Policy Challenges for the 21st Century*, (New York: Council on Foreign Relations, 2001). http://www.downingstreetmemo.com/docs/energycfr.pdf

had helped to foster: the desire to use American military force more aggressively; the commercial pressure from the oil industry to get back into Iraq; and the unsustainable U.N. sanctions regime. Once a possible invasion of Iraq was placed "on the table," its potential to reverse state control of the global oil industry was tantalizing. It could be followed up with a similar threat or use of force against Iran, it could break the power of the OPEC cartel, and it could build pressure on Saudi Arabia and other producing countries to reopen to Western investment, as advocated in the CFR report.

But even if Iraq alone was affected, the potential profits to Western oil companies could be astronomical. The production cost of Iraqi oil was about $1 per barrel, among the cheapest, easiest oil to extract from the ground anywhere in the world. Industry analysts believed that, in the absence of sanctions and war, Iraq could easily produce 6 to 8 million barrels per day, once its infrastructure was repaired and upgraded and new fields were brought into production. If the long-term price of crude oil averaged around $70 per barrel on world markets, this level of production would generate net revenues of about $175 billion per year. If Western oil companies received only a 20% share of these revenues, this would earn them additional profits of more than $35 billion per year. To put this into perspective, the total profits of the five largest oil companies from all of their worldwide operations in 2002 were: $35 billion. The oil companies could earn as much from operations in Iraq as from the rest of their worldwide business combined, demonstrating the prime value of the "upstream" portion of the global oil market. And, in part due to reduced production under war and sanctions, Iraq still had sufficient proven reserves to maintain this flow of oil and money for at least 25 years, possibly much longer.[338]

---

338. James A. Paul, "The Iraq oil bonanza: estimating future profits," *Global Policy Forum*, January 28 2004.
http://www.globalpolicy.org/security/oil/2004/0128oilprofit.htm

The former head of Exxon's Persian Gulf operations told Ian Rutledge, the author of *Addicted to Oil*, that a group of Iraqi exiles approached him with an offer he couldn't refuse. They told him, "You can have our oil if we can get back in there."[339] In 2001 and 2002, Vice President Cheney held secret "Energy Task Force" meetings with the oil companies, and the State Department assembled a working group to plan the re-privatization of the Iraqi oil industry. The working group decided that Iraq "should be opened to international oil companies as quickly as possible after the war." "Production sharing agreements" between a new Iraqi government and Western companies would be the most promising vehicle to achieve this objective.[340]

Production sharing agreements (PSAs) are long-term contracts under which "upstream" or production revenues are shared between the national government and a foreign oil company. They offer considerable contractual protection to the oil company involved, and are difficult for a subsequent government to change. Walter van der Vijver, the head of Exploration and Production at Shell, explained why Western oil companies favored PSAs over other possible contractual agreements with the Iraqi government at a conference in Abu Dhabi in 2003:

> ... International oil companies can make an ongoing contribution to the region ... However, in order to secure that investment, we will need some assurance of future income and, in particular, a supportive contractual framework. There are a number of models which can achieve these ends. One option is the greater use of production sharing agreements, which have proved very effective in achieving an appropriate balance of incentives between governments and oil companies. And

---

339. Ian Rutledge, "U.S. appears to have fought war for oil and lost it," *Financial Times*, April 11 2005.

340. US State Department, Future of Iraq Project, Oil and Energy Working Group (Oil Policy Subgroup), "Iraqi oil policy recommendations after regime change," *Middle East Economic Survey*, May 5 2003, pp.D1-D11; cited in Greg Muttitt, *Crude designs: the rip-off of Iraq's oil wealth*, (London: Platform, 2005). http://www.carbonweb.org/documents/crude_designs_large.pdf

they ensure a fair distribution of the value of a resource while
providing the long term assurance which is necessary to secure the capital investment needed for energy projects.[341]

However, by more objective standards, PSAs would be an extraordinary and opportunistic device by which to gain a share of Iraq's oil
wealth. Elsewhere in the world, PSAs are only used to protect oil companies working in difficult conditions with specific technical challenges, and generally only in small countries that lack their own resources and expertise. A classic example would be a small, poor African
country wanting to develop a newly discovered offshore oil-field. In
that case, the country lacks the necessary expertise and resources, and
the Western oil company wants some protection for the risk it is taking. The only major oil producer with any PSAs is Russia, which was
persuaded to sign three PSAs in the mid-1990s. These were a bad deal
that quickly became controversial, and Russia unilaterally cancelled
one of them in 2008. Large oil producing countries don't need PSAs
and can make more beneficial arrangements. None of the usual conditions for PSAs existed in Iraq.

If Iraq's disputed Hydrocarbon Law had ever passed, it would have
opened the door to PSA contracts, negotiated by a severely weakened
Iraqi state, that would have lasted up to 35 years, and that would have
been very difficult to change later. Iraq's foreign partners would have
controlled decisions on oil output. If OPEC required Iraq to limit production and its corporate partners refused, Iraq's only recourse would
be to make drastic production cuts in its state-owned oil-fields, with
severe consequences for its public sector operations, personnel, and
revenues. The PSA contracts would also have prevented Iraq from introducing new regulations or higher taxes on oil production. Lastly,
PSA contracts are very complicated and permit the oil companies to

---

341. Walter van der Vijver, "A new era for international oil companies in the Gulf:
opportunities and challenges" (speech to ECSSR conference, Abu Dhabi), October 19
2003; cited in Muttitt, *ibid.*

deduct all sorts of expenses before sharing any profit at all with the host country. This can lead to cost inflation, known as "gold-plating." In the now cancelled Sakhalin II project in Russia, cost over-runs of $2.5 billion by a consortium led by Shell were paid entirely out of the Russian government's share of the revenues. In another form of gold-plating, oil companies can hand out lucrative sub-contracts to their own subsidiaries in order to create additional revenue streams that are not subject to sharing with the host government.

Following the invasion, war and sabotage crippled the Iraqi oil industry and Iraqi trade unions vigorously opposed privatization. U.S. officials were forced to adopt an incremental approach to the State Department working group's recommendations. In September 2003, the Coalition Provisional Authority (CPA) appointed a member of the State Department working group, an Anglo-Iraqi named Ibrahim Mohammed Bahr al-Ulloum, as Iraq's new Oil Minister. Under the CPA, Ulloum worked with a team that included senior officials from Shell, Exxon, ConocoPhillips, and BP; three officials from the U.S. Department of Energy; and an Australian government energy official.

In December 2003, the U.S. Agency for International Development commissioned a report by privatization specialists Bearing Point that compared the situation in Iraq to the privatization of the oil industry in Azerbaijan. Bearing Point noted that, in that case, additional risks relating to instability and corruption had been factored in to justify a sweeter deal for the oil companies, implying that the same approach would work in Iraq. Bearing Point remained involved in subsequent negotiations and in the drafting of Iraq's Hydrocarbon Law. Explaining that privatization would have to wait until after elections in January 2005, Bahr al-Ulloum told the *Financial Times*, "The Iraqi oil sector needs privatization, but it's a cultural issue. People lived for the last 30 to 40 years with this idea of nationalism."[342]

But the basic outlines of the privatization scheme were made public several months before the January 2005 election by interim prime minister Ayad Allawi. He instructed his Supreme Council for Oil Policy to develop a plan to open up the Iraqi oil industry to foreign companies. Under Allawi's guidelines, the Iraq National Oil Company would retain control of the seventeen oil-fields that were already in production, while another sixty-three oil-fields that were already explored and mapped would be developed by private companies through production sharing agreements. Allawi's guidelines remained the framework for oil privatization in Iraq throughout subsequent negotiations and legislation. Additional details in Allawi's guidelines included a partial privatization of the INOC itself and would have barred the INOC completely from contracts on previously untapped oil-fields. He also urged that PSAs be signed quickly in order to get work started on the new fields and suggested that problems could be worked out later. In reality, the PSA contracts would have made that impossible.[343]

Al-Ulloum stepped down as oil minister in June 2004, but was reappointed by the new transitional government in May 2005. The Supreme Council for Oil Policy was replaced by an Energy Council, headed by Ahmad Chalabi. The Energy Council wrote the first draft of the Hydrocarbon Law within a month, following the guidelines established by Allawi. The new Constitution approved in October 2005 declared that Iraq's oil and gas wealth would be developed "relying on the most modern techniques of market principles and encouraging investment."[344]

---

342. Nicolas Pelham, "Iraqi minister sees oil privatisation obstacles," *Financial Times*, September 4 2003.

343. "Iraq: Puzzling over the future," *Energy Compass*, October 1 2004; "Allawi outlines new Iraqi petroleum policy: INOC for currently producing fields/IOCs for new areas," *Middle East Economic Survey*, September 13 2004, pA1-A4; cited in Muttitt, *ibid.*

344. http://meria.idc.ac.il/journal/2005/issue3/Iraqiconstitution/constitution.html

When the International Monetary Fund issued loans to Iraq in December 2005, they were conditional on passage of the Hydrocarbon Law by the end of 2006.[345]

After Husayn al-Shahristani was appointed Oil Minister in May 2006, he announced that finalization of the Hydrocarbon Law would be one of his top priorities. In the coming months, Shahristani reviewed drafts of the law with U.S. Energy Secretary Samuel Bodman and representatives of nine major oil companies, including Shell, BP, Exxon, Chevron, and ConocoPhillips.

Iraq's cabinet finally approved the Hydrocarbon Law in May 2007, and submitted it to the National Assembly. But the National Assembly refused to pass it. The insidious nature of PSAs and other provisions of the law gradually became more widely understood, making eventual passage of the law increasingly unlikely as time went on. For a country like Iraq, PSAs would mean handing over a substantial share of its oil revenues to foreign companies in exchange for work it could be doing itself or just contracting out as necessary.

PSAs would also protect the oil companies from future political developments, notably the hopes of the Iraqi people for sovereignty, democracy, and control of their own resources. At some point in the future, Iraqis could vote overwhelmingly for public ownership of their resources, but there would be no escape clauses in the PSAs. Since the PSAs would mandate arbitration of disputes by international arbitrators, not Iraqi courts, Iraq could be forced to compensate the oil companies for hundreds of billions of dollars in lost future revenues as a consequence of re-nationalization. By insisting on PSAs as the vehicle for privatization, the U.S. government was trying to ensure that the oil

---

345. Dennis Kucinich, "Question of Personal Privilege," *Congressional Record*, May 7 2007, H5638-H5644.

companies, once they were back in Iraq, would never be kicked out again.

Another important feature of the Hydrocarbon Law submitted in 2007 was that "chief executives of important related petroleum companies" would be represented on a Federal Oil and Gas Council. This body would approve all oil and gas contracts, including PSAs, for the 63 untapped oil-fields. The law would give temporary control of oil pipelines and export terminals to the Iraq National Oil Company, but the oil and gas council could later hand over pipelines and terminals to foreign companies as it saw fit. Contracts approved by the council would not become public until 60 days after their approval, protecting the whole scheme from public scrutiny and outrage.

At the end of June 2008, with the Hydrocarbon Law no closer to passage in the National Assembly, the Iraqi government announced negotiations for the first contracts with major Western oil companies since Iraq took public ownership of its oil industry in the 1960s. Demonstrating the important role of the new U.S. occupation headquarters in Baghdad and its State Department staff, U.S. officials told the *New York Times* on June 30th 2008 that, "A group of American advisers led by a small State Department team played an integral part in drawing up contracts between the Iraqi government and five major Western oil companies to develop some of the largest fields in Iraq."[346]

Without PSAs or any legal basis for them, Exxon, Chevron, BP, Shell, and Total (the five former partners in the Iraq Petroleum Company in 1928) were instead prepared to sign two-year "technical service agreements" to perform oil-field services on several of the largest undeveloped fields in Iraq. The first extraordinary thing about these contracts was that these companies were not oil-field service providers. In fact,

---

346. Andrew E. Kramer, "U.S. advised Iraqi ministry on oil deals," *New York Times*, June 30 2008.

they usually outsourced technical service functions for their own operations to more specialized firms, such as Schlumberger or Baker Hughes. A spokesman for Total explained the anomaly to the *New York Times*, "This is necessarily a transitory stage, not a proper way to work over the long term."[347]

Public statements by U.S., Iraqi, and oil company officials linked the negotiation of the TSAs with these five companies to the fact that they had been advising the Iraqi oil ministry *pro bono* under "memoranda of understanding" since 2006. Nearly all of the new contracts were for the same oil-fields where the company in question had already been operating *pro bono*. However, there were actually 46 international oil companies doing work for the Iraqis on this basis, including Chinese, Russian, and Indian companies, but only the big five from the West were involved in these negotiations. In the West Qurna field, near Basra, a new contract was being negotiated with a consortium of Chevron and Total even though the Russian firm Lukoil had been providing training to Iraqi engineers there at no charge, and had an existing contract with the pre-invasion Iraqi government.

Another oddity in these contracts was that the Iraqi government would not be paying the oil companies for their services in cash but in oil. Leila Benali, an oil analyst with Cambridge Energy Research Associates, explained, "These are not actually service contracts ... They were designed to circumvent the legislative stalemate." In other words, these contracts were a foot in the door, a way to get into Iraq and get some of its oil on a transitional basis in the hope that the Hydrocarbon Law or some other legal basis would be in place by the time new contracts were issued in 2010.

---

347. Andrew E. Kramer, "Deals with Iraq are set to bring oil giants back," *New York Times*, June 19 2008.

In another deviation from normal practice, these contracts were not written by the Iraqi government. They were written by lawyers working for the oil companies and then modified in the course of negotiations with the Iraqis, with the State Department's amateur colonial officials at their elbows. This stood the usual procedure for such contracts on its head, and it begs the question: was there something in these contracts that would have put these companies in a favorable position to win the real prize, the PSAs they wanted, when the transitional contracts expired in 2010?

A great deal about these contracts was kept secret, but the critical provision was this. At the end of two years, the oil-fields would be opened to bidding for new contracts, but the previous contract holder on each oil-field would have the right of refusal to match the winning bid. The catch is that bidding on a PSA involves a great deal of work for the companies involved, and that no company is likely to do all this work when the previous contract-holder can simply match their bid and win the contract anyway. If everything worked according to plan, the companies holding the TSAs in 2008 would get their coveted PSAs in 2010, and on terms that would effectively eliminate competitive bidding.

Of course, this would be contingent on the National Assembly passing the Hydrocarbon Law or on the development of some other legal basis. If this did not happen, the oil companies would simply be working for the Iraqi Oil Ministry on a contract basis, as they do in other Persian Gulf countries. Either the Iraqis were using the carrot of possible PSAs in the future to string the oil companies along and get some work out of them, or the companies were taking steps that would ultimately gain them a share of Iraq's oil wealth, with the assistance of the U.S. State Department. The wannabe colonialists at the U.S. Embassy would have their work cut out in the interim, but it remained unclear at that point whether the puppet-master or the puppet would ultimately end up pulling the strings.

However, by the end of August 2008, no contracts had been signed, and the draft contracts had been revised in response to Iraqi concerns about giving too much away to the Western firms. The TSAs would now only last for one year and the companies involved would no longer get preferential treatment on future contracts, the most valuable element in the entire deal.

Then the Iraqi Embassy in Beijing stunned the global oil industry with the news that the Iraqi government was renegotiating a contract between the pre-invasion government of Iraq and the China National Petroleum Company. The renegotiated contract with the Chinese was approved by the Iraqi cabinet on September 2nd and signed the following week.

CNPC could earn up to $3 billion over 22 years for developing the al-Ahdab field south of Baghdad, but it would be paid in cash, not in oil, and this was hailed as a sign of what other oil companies could expect at the end of their negotiations with the Iraqi government. In announcing the deal with China, Oil Minister Shahristani said, "The Oil Ministry refused anything but a service contract. Iraqis will not share their oil, which belongs to the whole nation." This was a dramatic reversal since 2004, when the interim government had been only too eager to share its country's oil wealth with foreign companies.

June 30th, 2009 was a national holiday in Iraq and a day of celebration as U.S. occupation forces finally withdrew from Iraqi cities. But there was one important piece of business that was not postponed for the holiday. Extensive negotiations had finally resulted in a compromise on oil contracts, and, in stark contrast to the secret process outlined in the stalled Hydrocarbon Law, the bids were to be opened and deals negotiated on live television. The Iraqi government had agreed to negotiate service contracts under which foreign companies could receive per-barrel fees for oil produced in Iraq, but the fees were a tiny fraction of what they would have gained under PSA contracts.[348]

In the only successful deal of the day, the Iraqi government awarded a joint venture comprised of BP and China's National Petroleum Company the right to drill for oil in the giant Rumaila oil field, estimated to contain 17.8 billion barrels of oil, more than in all of China, Mexico or the North Sea, but still only 15% of Iraq's proven reserves. The firms were to receive only a $2 fee for each barrel of oil they produced, and this would apply only after they surpassed previous levels of production. The BP-CNPC consortium had submitted a bid of $3.99 per barrel, but it accepted the $2 offered by the Oil Ministry. Most of the Western companies bidding for these contracts did so in partnership with Asian companies that could provide cheaper labor and equipment and were more welcome in Iraq.

A consortium formed by Exxon-Mobil and Petronas of Malaysia made a bid of $4.80 per barrel for another contract on the Rumaila field. They rejected the ministry's offer of $2 and so remained shut out. Bids by foreign consortiums on other oil and gas fields were also rejected as too expensive. Under pressure from the Iraqi public and the National Assembly, the Iraqi Oil Ministry was now playing hardball, while the National Assembly was asserting its right to approve or reject any deals it made. At an OPEC meeting in Vienna in March 2009, Mr. Shahristani once again dangled the carrot of future PSAs, but he explained that they would in any case be limited to the most speculative operations. "This will most likely be for exploration fields that have not been discovered and assessed yet," he said.

In October 2009, two more contracts were allocated at the Oil Ministry's predetermined price of $2 per barrel. One was a service contract

---

348. Sinan Salaheddin, "Iraqi oil licensing runs into trouble," *Associated Press*, June 30 2009.

on the Zubair oil-field (4 billion barrels of proven reserves) to a consortium of Italy's ENI, Occidental Petroleum and Korea Gas. Another on Phase One of the West Qurna oil-field (8.7 billion barrels) went to a consortium of Exxon-Mobil, Conoco-Phillips and Russia's Lukoil, the same company that had been excluded from the negotiations with the former partners in the Iraq Petroleum Company only a year earlier.

In December 2009, Lukoil won another service contract on the even larger West Qurna Phase Two oil-field (12.9 billion barrels), in a joint operation with Statoil of Norway, but for an even lower fee of $1.15 per barrel. This second round of bidding also awarded a service contract on the Majnoon field (12.8 billion barrels) in southern Iraq to a consortium of Shell, Petronas of Malaysia and the Iraq National Oil Company (INOC) for $1.39 per barrel. The state-owned INOC's 25% share in the contract would effectively reduce the amount paid to its foreign partners even further. The third contract awarded in this round was on the Halfaya field (4.1 billion barrels), which went to a consortium of China NPC, Total and Petronas.

In 2008, as Iraq began to recover from the "surge", commerce of all kinds began to flow again. Oil production increased slightly to 2.4 million barrels per day, up from 2.1 million barrels per day in 2007. This was still well short of the immediate pre-invasion level of 2.8 million barrels per day, let alone the much higher levels attained in the late 1970s and late 1980s. Total Iraqi imports grew from $25.7 billion in 2007 to $43.5 billion in 2008. But there was one big loser in the world's restored trade with Iraq: the United States. Even as overall imports grew, imports from the United States remained flat at a meager $2 billion per year, and the bulk of that was through preexisting contracts with the U.S.-backed government.

By contrast, Turkey, which had refused to support the U.S. invasion, became one of Iraq's largest trading partners, with exports of $10 billion to Iraq in 2008. At a trade fair in Baghdad in November 2009, an Iraqi executive explained that his construction company preferred to do business with Turkish firms because costs were lower and the Turks "are not an occupier".

Other countries that had opposed the invasion, in particular Iran, France and Brazil, likewise became major trading partners. On condition of anonymity, a European ambassador told the *New York Times* that his country's commercial relations with Iraq improved greatly once it withdrew its troops. "Being considered an occupier handicapped us extremely," he said. "The farther we are away from that the more our companies can be accepted on their own merits." In 2009, in some of the largest government contracts since the invasion, Iraq's Transportation Ministry awarded $30 billion to rebuild Iraq's railroads to a combination of British, Italian and Czech companies. And the Russian company RusAir won an exclusive air cargo contract that forced FedEx to terminate its operations in Iraq. [349]

Despite the increasingly obvious disadvantages of military occupation, State Department officials at the occupation headquarters in Baghdad spent much of 2008 working on a process to extend and legitimize U.S. military operations in Iraq. These negotiations followed a similar path to the parallel ones over oil contracts. The Iraqis knew what the Americans wanted, and used this knowledge and the shifting power balance between them to drive a hard bargain. The United States was now occupying a country in which prime minister Maliki and the other major players were all playing a more complex game than American occupation officials could control. For the umpteenth time in its history, the United States was finding that puppet-strings can be pulled from either end, and that this makes for an improvised and unpredictable puppet show with less and less relation to its own script or the interests driving its policy.

---

349 Rod Nordland, "Rebuilding its economy, Iraq shuns U.S. businesses", *New York Times*, November 13 2009.

Even as American forces in Iraq continued to face popular armed resistance, the Iraqi government and National Assembly were establishing their authority and legitimacy with their own people by standing up to their American puppet-masters over oil contracts and the status of forces negotiations. The United States was being forced to accept conditions for its role in Iraq that served Iraqi interests, while its own commercial and strategic interests, for which it invaded and destroyed Iraq and sacrificed thousands of its soldiers' lives, were gradually and inexorably slipping away.

This must have seemed like a recurring nightmare to State Department officials. In the 1940s, successive American envoys to the Chinese Nationalist government in Chungking reported that Chiang Kai-shek was running the most corrupt regime in history, but American aid continued to fill his coffers for want of a better option. The nightmare recurred with Syngman Rhee in South Korea, the Shah of Iran, Ferdinand Marcos in the Philippines, Mobutu in the Congo, Suharto in Indonesia, successive governments in the pseudo-state of South Vietnam, a long succession of governments in Latin America, and of course Saddam Hussein in Iraq.

Once an American puppet has grasped the power that he wields over his handlers, the United States is faced with a choice between following him down this well-worn garden path or attempting to engineer a new regime change. As the United States helps to eliminate its puppet's opponents and consolidate his power, it renders the prospects for a further regime change increasingly slim and its own leverage and power are reduced.

And so it was in Iraq. But the completion of the ethnic cleansing of Baghdad and the consolidation of power in the Maliki government encouraged American policy-makers to greedily renew their commitment to the original goals of the invasion. American pressure on the National Assembly to pass the Hydrocarbon Law and the role of the "Embassy" in negotiations over the TSA contracts highlighted the obvious, that the Iraqi oil industry was a primary target of the invasion and occupation all along. As Frederick Barton at the Center for Strategic and International Studies told the *New York Times*, "We pretend it is not a centerpiece of our motivation, yet we keep confirming that it is ... And we undermine our own veracity by citing issues like sovereignty, when we have our hands right in the middle of it."

CHAPTER 18. ESCALATION AND GENOCIDE

> *Pillagers of the world, they have exhausted the land by their indiscriminate plunder, and now they ransack the sea. A rich enemy excites their avarice; a poor one their lust for power. East and West alike have failed to satisfy them ... To robbery, butchery, and rapine, they give the lying name of "government"; they create a desolation and call it peace.*
>
> *Pictish chieftain Calgacus, speaking about the Romans before the Battle of Mons Graupius in Scotland, 84 A.D.*[350]

In January 2007, the United States government announced a new strategy, a "surge" of U.S. combat troops in Baghdad and Anbar province. Most Iraqis reported that this escalation of violence made conditions where they lived even worse than before, as its effects were added to the accumulated devastation of four years of war and occupation.

The U.N. human rights report for the first quarter of 2007 found that 54% of Iraqis were now living on less than $1 per day, including 15% in even more extreme poverty, on less than 50 cents per day. 68% of the population no longer had safe water to drink. 2,000 doctors had been killed, while another 12,000 had fled the country. This had reduced the number of doctors in the country by 41% in the midst of a prolonged national emergency.[351] The violence of the American "surge" resulted in a further 22% reduction in the number of doctors, leaving only 15,500 out of an original 34,000 by September 2008, with the most severe shortages in the most desperate areas. Those who remained were disproportionately concentrated in Iraqi Kurdistan, where they were least able to serve the dire needs of the population.[352]

---

350. Tacitus, S.A. Handford ed., H. Mattingly tr., *The Agricola and the Germania*, (New York: Penguin Classics, 1971), 81.

351. http://www.uniraq.org/aboutus/HR.asp

352. Karin Laub, "Health chiefs battle to bring back Iraqi doctors," *Associated Press*, September 7th 2008.

The U.N. reported that the new U.S. offensive had already raised the prison population from 31,000 to 38,000, with most of the new prisoners in the custody of either U.S. or Iraqi interior ministry forces. The U.N. report expressed the "utmost concern" over people held by the Ministries of Interior and Defense because of "the use of torture and other inhumane treatment in detention centers." None of the promised enquiries had resulted in anyone being convicted for the crimes committed at al-Jadiriyah or other Interior Ministry prisons. And in Irbil in Kurdistan, there were demonstrations by relatives of people who had disappeared without a trace after being arrested by Kurdish authorities. And yet the number of prisoners continued to grow, soaring to 51,000 by the end of the year.

Prisoners of U.S. forces were accorded the fewest rights of all and were effectively subject to indefinite detention with no legal recourse. Subsequent human rights reports documented shifting and contradictory claims by American officials regarding their procedures for reviewing detainees' cases. The U.N. found that, even when the Americans did in fact follow their own ad hoc and ever-changing rules, their treatment of detainees did not meet minimum standards to which both Iraq and the United States were committed under the terms of international human rights treaties that both countries had signed and ratified.

The Coalition Provisional Authority had established a new Central Criminal Court in Baghdad which continued to function under successive governing institutions. UNAMI remained "concerned about procedures followed by the CCCI and other criminal courts in Iraq, which consistently failed to meet minimum fair trial standards." Under new emergency regulations, even property crimes such as theft and destruction of private and public property were now punishable by death. The CCCI had handed down 256 death sentences since 2004, of which 85 had already been carried out.

The U.N. noted a host of irregularities that effectively denied defendants access to lawyers and the ability to appeal verdicts and sentences. But perhaps the most shocking feature of these trials was that, even in capital cases, trials only lasted between fifteen and thirty minutes. And, according to UNAMI, the judges' deliberations typically did "not last more than several minutes for each trial, including in complex cases involving serious felonies resulting in sentences of life imprisonment or the death penalty." The report described the inevitable result of all these irregularities: "Such trials are increasingly leading to the imposition of the death penalty."

On February 8th, the U.N. High Commissioner for Human Rights, Louise Arbour, intervened in the case of Taha Yassin Ramadan, Iraq's former Vice President. He was sentenced to life imprisonment, but the appeals court sent the case back to the lower court effectively demanding a death sentence. The High Commissioner wrote a brief to the court, arguing that this would violate Iraq's obligations under the International Covenant on Civil and Political Rights which "provides that a death sentence may only be imposed following proceedings conducted in strict adherence to due process requirements." Ms. Arbour could have intervened with the same argument in most capital cases in Iraq, but she was ignored in any case. Yassin was hung on the fourth anniversary of the U.S. invasion of his country, March 20th, 2007. His son told *ITV News* in the U.K., "It was not an execution. It was a political assassination."

The occupation authorities in Iraq created an environment of kangaroo courts, torture, death squads, and thinly disguised lynchings, protected by absolute impunity for all involved in the perversion of justice. The complete chaos reigning in much of the country deterred most Western journalists from doing much more than hunkering down in the Green Zone and parroting the briefings they received from the Centcom press office. The Iraqi Society for the Defense of Journalists recorded the deaths of 170 journalists and media workers in Iraq by

January 2007—as with every aspect of this crisis, the vast majority of the victims were Iraqis.

Until the end of 2006, the U.N.'s human rights office received monthly figures on the numbers of civilians killed, both from a hospital survey conducted by the Ministry of Health's operations center and from the Medico-Legal Institute in Baghdad, which managed six morgues in the major cities. By adding these numbers together, UNAMI was able to provide consistent monthly mortality figures that gave some idea of the nature and scale of the deadly violence that the population was experiencing. However, following the publication of the U.N. human rights report for the last quarter of 2006, Prime Minister Maliki's office claimed that these numbers were exaggerated, even though they were official figures compiled and provided by agencies of his government.

As the new U.S. escalation of the war began, the government abruptly stopped providing these figures. On March 1st, the Interior Ministry announced that 1,646 civilians had been killed in February, but, as the U.N. report noted, "It was unclear on what basis these figures were compiled." Comparison to prior months was impossible, and any assessment of the overall scale of the conflict and its impact on civilians became dependent on conflicting reports, isolated figures, and anecdotal evidence. This in turn left journalists and their audiences more than ever at the mercy of the Centcom press office and the Pentagon's other public relations operations.

When UNAMI was able to obtain reports from the central morgue in Baghdad, there appeared to have been no overall reduction in violence since 2006 related to the new Baghdad Security Plan, which was officially launched in mid-February. The U.N. human rights office reported that,

> At the beginning of January, up to 50 or more unidentified bodies were being found on a daily basis in Baghdad

alone, with scores more in areas such as Mosul and Suwayra ... By late February, government officials announced that the number of such killings had decreased, which they attributed to the success of the Baghdad Security Plan. Despite this announced decrease, the number of victims was nevertheless high, with up to 25 bodies still being found on some days during this period in Baghdad. March again witnessed a rise in the number of casualties, with reports of large numbers of bodies found in Baghdad, al-Ramadi, al-Hilla, Kirkuk, Mosul, Khalis, Tikrit, and Himreen.

Of course, since Interior Ministry forces under U.S. command were probably responsible for about 90% of the extra-judicial killings, the occupation authorities had the power to reduce or increase the scale of these atrocities more or less on command. So a reduction in the bloodletting with the launch of the "security plan" should not have been difficult to achieve. In fact, a small reduction in violence seems to have served an important propaganda role for a couple of weeks, but then the death squads got back to work, supported by the new American offensive.

The U.N. High Commissioner for Refugees and the International Organization for Migration reported that about 740,000 Iraqis had been newly displaced within Iraq in the past year, bringing the total number of internally displaced people to almost 2 million. Another staggering 2 million had by now fled to other countries, mostly to Jordan and Syria.

This was the context in which the United States launched its escalation of the war in 2007. Millions of Iraqis had already been killed or had fled from areas which had by now been under relentless attack by U.S. forces and Iraqi and American death squads for four years. For example, the population of Adhamiya in Baghdad had already been reduced by half. The sectors of the Iraqi population being murdered, detained, tortured, and ethnically cleansed were primarily the secular middle class of the country, with Sunni Arabs always a prime target. The violence of the occupation was a full frontal assault on Iraqi civil society that transcended sect and ethnicity. The scale of the crime was therefore far greater than can be quantified in strictly ethnic terms. However, the U.S. invasion and occupation probably killed at least 10% of the Sunni Arab population and drove about half the Sunni Arabs in the country from their homes, either into exile or internal displacement. By the standards applied elsewhere in the world in recent decades, and by its definition in international treaties, the term "genocide" is an entirely accurate and appropriate description of American actions and policy in Iraq.

The escalation of American firepower in 2007, which included a five-fold increase in air strikes over 2006 and the use of Spectre gun-ships and artillery in urban areas in addition to the "surge" of additional ground combat forces, was intended as a devastating climax to the past four years of war and collective punishment inflicted on the Iraqi people. All resistance-held areas would be targeted with overwhelming fire-power, mainly from the air, until the additional U.S. ground forces could build walls around what remained of each neighborhood, control entry and exit points, and isolate each district.

In Ramadi, the capital of Anbar province, the United States was waging a kind of war that both Marines on the ground and General Petraeus in Baghdad explicitly compared to the Battle of Stalingrad, with snipers from both sides hunting each other through the rubble of the bombed-out city. The Americans seemed to have no qualms about adopting the role of the German invaders in this analogy. They completely leveled what remained of several blocks surrounding their forward operating base to deny cover to the Iraqis, give themselves a clear field of fire, and take advantage of their heavier weapons and air support. Over a period of three years, Ramadi was gradually destroyed as surely and as completely as was Fallujah in November 2004. Ramadi was Fallujah in slow-motion.[353]

By the time the U.N. issued its human rights report for the second quarter of 2007, American air-strikes and other illegal American attacks against civilians and civilian areas had become a prime concern of the human rights office. American and Iraqi authorities succeeded in delaying the publication of this report until October, following a major escalation of air strikes during the climax of the offensive between June and September. CENTAF acknowledged conducting 981 air strikes in Iraq during those four months, as many as during the previous two years.[354] The usual caveats applied regarding additional attacks that appeared to be beyond CENTAF's reporting criteria, such as the air strikes by U.S. Marine Air Wings that reduced much of Fallujah and Ramadi, the two largest cities in Anbar province, to rubble, and the nightly missions by U.S. Special Forces Spectre gun-ships.

In spite of obvious pressure from the occupation authorities, UN-AMI continued to insist that American air strikes in densely populated civilian areas were violations of international law. The section of the report headed "MNF military operations and the killing of civilians" includes the following footnote: "Customary international humanitarian law demands that, as much as possible, military objectives must not be located within areas densely populated by civilians. The presence of individual combatants among a great number of civilians does not alter the civilian character of an area." UNAMI followed up with a demand "that all credible allegations of unlawful killings by MNF forces be thoroughly, promptly and impartially investigated, and appropriate action taken against military personnel found to have used excessive or

---

353. Dennis Shanahan, "Surge working says U.S. general," *The Australian*, August 31st, 2007; also http://transcripts.cnn.com/TRANSCRIPTS/0604/17/acd.02.html
354. www.afa.org/edop/2009/2004-08CFACCstats123108.pdf
www.centaf.af.mil/shared/media/document/AFD-091103-001.pdf

indiscriminate force ... The initiation of investigation into such incidents, as well as their findings, should be made public."

CENTAF reported a decrease in air strikes in October 2007 to only 42, possibly in response to UNAMI's concerns. But this figure was later revised upward to 173, indicating that there was no real let-up in the air campaign and suggesting that the lower figure may have been pure propaganda. In fact the aerial bombardment of Iraq reached a new climax in January 2008 with 400 air strikes, making it the heaviest month of bombardment since 2003. Throughout the "surge", American claims of reduced violence concealed a strategic shift to a greater reliance on inherently indiscriminate air-launched weapons. Air strikes continued on an almost daily basis until August 2008 even as inter-Iraqi violence and American casualties declined.[355]

The U.N. human rights report published in October 2007 included the results of UNAMI's efforts to investigate 15 incidents in which 103 Iraqi civilians were killed in American air strikes and house raids. These were incidents that were brought to UNAMI's attention by news reports, grieving relatives, or local officials and were obviously only the tip of the iceberg. Without doubt, the U.S. Department of Defense was aware of many more similar incidents, hence UNAMI's urgent call for full public disclosure and investigation of all such killings.

Among other incidents, the report documented the killing of nine civilians in five villages in air strikes near Baquba on March 11th; six civilians killed in house raids on civilian homes near Mosul on April 2nd; twenty-seven civilians killed by air strikes in Khaldiya, near Ramadi, on April 3rd; four civilians killed by air strikes in Sadr City and four more killed in Taji, all on April 26th; and the killing of seven children in an

---

355. Anthony H. Cordesman, "U.S. airpower in Iraq and Afghanistan: 2004-2007," *Center for Strategic and International Studies*, December 13 2007.
http://www.csis.org/media/csis/pubs/071213_oif-oef_airpower.pdf
Revised figures at: www.centaf.af.mil/shared/media/document/AFD-091103-001.pdf

American helicopter attack on an elementary school in Diyala province on May 8th. The incidents spanned the country, from Mosul to Basra.

Even as the report was published, new incidents were being reported in the press. On the day it was released, six women, nine children, and nineteen men were killed in air strikes around Lake Tharthar, north of Baghdad. The Centcom press office immediately declared that the nineteen men killed were all "terrorists," but such claims were invariably contradicted by local residents and officials. These declarations begged the question as to how U.S. forces could tell the difference between civilians and combatants when they disregarded military and human rights laws designed to protect civilians and used such excessive and indiscriminate force. The fact that they also killed nine children and six women in these attacks made the assertion that the men they killed were all combatants especially dubious. This would imply that the air strikes selectively killed women, children, and "terrorists," without harming adult male civilians. On the other hand, with their homes under attack, all the adult males may have been trying to defend their homes and families, qualifying them as "terrorists" in the eyes of U.S. public relations officers.[356]

Given the attitudes and lack of training described in Chapter 8, the Centcom press office was probably reflecting American rules of engagement that frequently treated all military-age Iraqi males as terrorists and ignored the serious legal responsibility of American officers to train their troops to discriminate between combatants and civilians. This brings up the same point of international humanitarian law raised by the U.N. human rights report. When military forces are illegally ordered to attack civilian areas, many people will try to defend themselves, especially if they know that the failure to do so may result in arbitrary detention, abuse, torture, or summary execution for themselves

---

356. "U.S. strike kills women and children," *Associated Press*, October 12th 2007.

or their relatives. But their efforts to defend themselves do not create a legitimate justification for the attack that placed them in such an intolerable position in the first place.

Any legitimate counterinsurgency strategy would have to be based on better intelligence and target only clearly identified insurgents who were carrying out attacks. But it would first of all have to be carried out, as Michael Howard suggested in October 2001, by forces that had scrupulously safeguarded their own authority and legitimacy. Beginning with the invasion itself, the fundamental illegitimacy of U.S. policy in Iraq deprived American forces of precisely that authority from the outset.

Three more air strikes the previous week had killed five women and four children in Mussayyib, south of Baghdad on September 25th; seven men, two women and four children in an air strike in Dora on September 28th; and another seven or eight men were killed in Abu Dshir when American helicopters fired rockets and machine guns into a gathering celebrating the beginning of Ramadan, also on September 28th.[357]

All this should be understood in the context I explained in Chapter 7, that 15-25% of American "precision" air-launched weapons used in Iraq missed their targets by at least thirty feet and that exploding bombs and missiles are designed to injure and kill people over a wide radius. So the impression conveyed by the Centcom press office and CNN that these weapons could be used to safely and surgically "zap" one house in an urban area was an artful blend of propaganda and science fiction.

---

357. "Iraqi civilian deaths part of war on terror: U.S. military," *Agence France Presse*, September 29th, 2007; Alissa J. Rubin, "Two different accounts of deadly air strike in Baghdad," *New York Times*, September 29, 2007.

The U.S. "embassy" in Baghdad did reply to the U.N.'s call for an end to illegal, excessive, and indiscriminate use of deadly force by U.S. forces, and this gave UNAMI the opportunity to further clarify the legal context in its next human rights report. A U.S. official wrote that "While MNF-I agrees that, when possible, military objectives should not be located in areas densely populated by civilians, we request that UNAMI recognize that this problem flows directly from what the insurgency is doing, not from actions taken by MNF-I. MNF-I would welcome a statement from UNAMI condemning the insurgents for effectively creating involuntary human shields."

The "human shields" claim has been a standard response by U.S. officials whenever American forces kill civilians anywhere in the world, confusing the serious crime of human shielding with the existence of resistance forces among civilian populations. Such claims are rarely made in a context where they can be clearly and accurately responded to, but, in this case, UNAMI was able to clarify the difference between the crime of human shielding and the "effective" cover provided to guerillas by civilian populations:

> International humanitarian law requires all parties to the conflict to take all feasible precautions to minimize harm to civilians. UNAMI notes that the failure to do so is separate from the more serious violation of human shielding, which involves the intentional rather than "effective" use of civilians in order to deter attacks from enemy combatants and is a war crime.

This same exchange between U.S. and U.N. officials also served to clarify the American position on another important question, the actual legal status of the war in Iraq. The International Committee of the Red Cross had recognized the nominal restoration of Iraqi sovereignty in 2004 as the end of the war between the United States and Iraq, so that the civil and political rights of Iraqis should now be governed by the International Covenant on Civil and Political Rights and other human rights laws rather than by the Third and Fourth Geneva Conventions that apply during wartime. Among other things, this would have strengthened the rights of Iraqis detained by U.S. or Iraqi forces to speedy and fair trials.

However, according to the U.N. human rights report, "In December [2007], upon a request for clarification by UNAMI, the MNF confirmed that the U.S. government continues to regard the conflict in Iraq as an international armed conflict, with procedures currently in force consistent with provisions of the Fourth Geneva Convention." The ICCPR affords many of the same protections to civilians and prisoners as the Geneva Conventions, and Common Article 3 of the conventions applies to non-international conflicts in any case. But there is a stronger basis in U.S. law for holding people criminally responsible for their actions under the Geneva Conventions than under the ICCPR, because the federal War Crimes Act passed in 1996 explicitly criminalized violations of the Geneva Conventions, even providing for the death penalty in cases of death by torture (see chapter 10). The American admission that the United States was still legally engaged in an "international armed conflict" against Iraq at the end of 2007 also raised serious questions regarding the legitimacy of constitutional and political changes made in Iraq by the occupation forces and their agents during the war.

The U.N. report provided an update on court martial proceedings in the Haditha case, in which U.S. Marines killed twenty-four civilians, and it noted that four other war crimes cases against American troops were also going to trial. In the Haditha case, the report explained that none of the Marines involved were being charged with murder but instead faced charges of voluntary and involuntary manslaughter. These cases followed the same pattern as the cases involving Iraqis tortured to death by American interrogators in Iraq. Courts were unwilling to hold the junior ranks who were charged with the crimes fully responsible, because, in every case, their actions arguably fell within rules of engagement and conduct established by more senior officials. And yet in no case were more senior officials charged with the crimes for which the courts by implication held them primarily responsible. In the Haditha case, a lieutenant colonel was charged with dereliction of duty for failing to investigate the incident, but the charges against him were dismissed in June 2008, as were the charges against all but one of the Marines who actually carried out the massacre.

Another aspect of the 2007 "surge" or escalation appears to have been an increase in the use of the American special forces assassination teams discussed in Chapter 8. As reported in December 2003, Israeli *Mist'aravim* assassins trained American special forces to operate in disguise among the Iraqi population to carry out assassinations of suspected Resistance leaders and supporters. In April 2008, the American *Mist'aravim* were finally acknowledged publicly by President Bush and credited with part of the claimed success of the "surge." "As we speak," he said, "U.S. Special Forces are launching multiple operations every night to capture or kill al-Qaeda leaders in Iraq." The secrecy surrounding these operations prevented more widespread reporting, but, as with earlier covert U.S. operations in Vietnam and Latin America, we will learn more about the actual effects of these operations over time. Like the Phoenix program in Vietnam and Cambodia, this entire campaign appeared to be a murderous campaign against a civilian population in flagrant violation of the laws of war.[358]

The American escalation of the war in 2007 threatened Iraq with even more total and prolonged destruction, but a number of factors emerged in late 2007 to eventually reduce the level of violence. In August, Muqtada al-Sadr announced that he had ordered his Mahdi Army forces to cease fire and to use force only if they were directly attacked by occupation forces. This ceasefire was renewed six months later and then extended indefinitely. Maliki and the Americans launched a major new assault against the Mahdi Army in Basra and Sadr City in February

---

358. http://www.whitehouse.gov/news/releases/2008/04/20080410-2.html

2008, but al-Sadr continued to order his forces not to fight other Iraqis except in self defense, while maintaining their status as an armed militia committed to resisting foreign occupation. In spite of threats against his party's participation in provincial elections originally scheduled in 2008, al-Sadr insisted on maintaining the capacity for armed resistance. In August 2008, thousands of his followers swore new blood oaths to renew their commitment to resist the occupation, and hundreds of thousands of them took to the streets in October 2008 to protest a draft Status of Forces Agreement between the U.S. and the Maliki government.

Another little-reported factor in the reduction in violence in Iraq in late 2007, in addition to the increasing reliance on air strikes and special forces death squads, was that, as in Vietnam, American officers were finding it harder to launch "search and destroy" missions because of the plummeting morale of their troops. Troops on their third or fourth deployments were increasingly recycling a tactic from the Vietnam war: "search and avoid." This usually meant parking their Humvees in a safe place and calling in reports of fictional searches for resistance fighters and weapons.[359]

Phil Aliff, who fought with the 10th Mountain Division in Anbar province, told *Inter Press Service*, "We decided the only way we wouldn't be blown up was to avoid driving around all the time. So we would go find an open field and park, and call our base every hour to tell them we were searching for weapons caches in the fields and doing weapons patrols and everything was going fine."

Geoff Millard, who was on the staff of an American general at a Tactical Operations Center in Iraq in 2004 and 2005, told *Inter Press Service* in October 2007, "One of my buddies is in Baghdad right now and

---

359. Dahr Jamail, "U.S. soldiers shy from battle in Iraq," *Inter Press Service*, October 26th 2007.

we e-mail all the time. He just told me that nearly each day they pull into a parking lot, drink soda and shoot at the cans. They pay Iraqi kids to bring them things and spread the word that they are not doing anything and to please just leave them alone."

Tech-savvy troops even learned how to report fictitious movements on their on-board computers. Sergeant Seth Manzel commanded a Stryker vehicle in Iraq in 2004 and 2005. He explained, "On the map we would manually place our icon to the target location and then move it back and forth to make it appear as though we were actually on the ground and patrolling. This was not an isolated case. Everyone did it."[360]

This effective truce worked out by foot-soldiers on the ground was also being replicated at a higher level. In central Iraq, American officers succeeded in persuading a series of tribal leaders and former Baathists to suspend armed resistance in exchange for a new status as "Awakening Councils" or "Sons of Iraq." These local armed groups were led by local leaders who received American funds and weapons and ruled their territories in similar fashion to the American-backed warlords who replaced the Taliban in most of Afghanistan in 2001. The American government paid about $300 per month for each fighter, but the money was distributed by the warlords, creating the potential for them to keep a lot of the money themselves. Having failed to defeat the Resistance militarily or politically, the Americans were now bribing the Iraqis not to fight, and with greater success.

One of the first of these warlords was Abdul Sattar Abu Risha, who formed the first "Sahwa" or "Awakening" council in Ramadi in the summer of 2006. He was the son of the chieftain of the 160,000 strong Abu Risha tribe, a sub-tribe of the Dulaimi tribe that comprised much

---

360. Dahr Jamail, "Refusing to comply: the tactics of resistance in an all-volunteer military," *Tomdispatch*, June 30th 2009.
http://www.tomdispatch.com/post/175090/dahr_jamail_a_secret_history_of_dissent_in_the_all_volunteer_military

of the resistance to the occupation in Anbar province. Like other tribal leaders, Abu Risha's authority and wealth were undermined by his inability to protect his people and property from the Americans, their Shiite and Kurdish allies, extreme Islamist resistance groups, or criminals. The younger Abu Risha made a deal with the Americans and gathered a force of his tribesmen to police Ramadi. He was killed by a road-side bomb on September 13th 2007. The bomb may have been planted by rival resistance forces or, as many of his tribespeople believed, by agents of the Maliki government.

Even as warlords like Abu Risha proliferated across central Iraq and gathered about 100,000 men to their ranks, they were always viewed with distrust by the Green Zone government, who rightly saw them as competitors for power and a long-term threat to any central authority. Government officials were especially worried when the Americans started recruiting "awakening" groups in and around Baghdad. By December 2007, there were about 43,000 fighters affiliated with the groups in the Baghdad area. Many of these were led, not by tribal leaders as in Anbar, but by former officials of the pre-invasion government. For example, Adel Mashadani, the leader of the Sons of Iraq in the Fadhil district of Baghdad, was a former Special Republican Guard officer. Saleh Kashgul Saleh, a warlord in Dora, had been a colonel in the Mukhabarat intelligence service.[361]

The suspicion between the government and the councils was mutual. Mashadani considered the Shiite-led government as the pawns of Iranian and Shiite death squads. "These guys are a bunch of conspirators who belong to Iran," he told the *New York Times*. And, on American plans to integrate council members into the government's security forces, a Special Police Captain in Dora said, "I don't think the Awakening men should join the Iraqi police. It would be no better than putting

---

361. Alissa J. Rubin and Damien Cave, "In a force for Iraqi calm, seeds of conflict," *New York Times*, December 23rd 2007.

Al Qaeda informants into the police." Safa Hussein, the Deputy National Security Adviser who monitored the Awakening movement for Prime Minister Maliki, estimated that almost half its members were former resistance fighters and that many of them were still in contact with resistance leaders. "Will they go back to being insurgents?" he asked. "Will they be dangerous? We don't know yet."

By December 2007, out of the 43,000 Awakening fighters in and around Baghdad, only 1,700 men from a council in Abu Ghraib had in fact been given jobs in the police. By August 2008, another 3,489 out of about 100,000 fighters had been transferred to the government's security services, according to official U.S. figures. Most of the remainder were gradually becoming targets rather than allies of the U.S-backed government.[362]

Recruiting the warlords and their men to form these groups was another step in the overall American "divide and conquer" policy. The Americans were only too glad to use the warlords to keep the peace, but they had no long-term commitment to these groups or their leaders. In the spring of 2008, the Maliki government suspended the work of a committee charged with integrating the fighters into the police and army. As Maliki's armed forces became strong enough to move against them, their American allies provided no defense at all against renewed assaults by Iraqi Army and National Police (formerly Special Police) Commandos. Lieutenant Colonel Jeffrey Kulmayer told the *Los Angeles Times*, "We don't have a 'get out of jail free' card for the Sons of Iraq. There is law and order in this country, and we respect the Iraqi government."

In July 2008, the Americans agreed to a plan that would reduce the warlords' forces to 60,000 by the end of 2008 and completely abolish

---

362. Ned Parker, "Iraq seeks breakup of U.S.-funded Sunni fighters," *Los Angeles Times*, August 23rd 2008.

them by the following summer. The plan called for 20% of them to be integrated into the police and for others to be trained for civilian jobs. But Haider Abadi, a member of parliament for Maliki's Dawa party, explained to the *Los Angeles Times* that any job training offered to former fighters would be limited and temporary because, "We have the same problems around the country. We can't just create a program to pay some people and not others." By May 2009, only twenty of the 2,000 militia recruited in Dora had government jobs, according to their leader, while Lt. Col Kulmayer claimed that 17,000 out of 94,000 throughout the country had been given jobs and promised that more would be hired soon.[363]

In any case, by then many of the groups were under attack by Shiite or Kurdish Iraqi government forces, and many members were already either on the run, in hiding, or had fled the country. Abu Azzam, the U.S.-backed warlord in Abu Ghraib, fled in May 2008 when an Iraqi Army brigade moved into his district. Abu Abed, a warlord in Adhamiya, warned, "In the event that the U.S. military and government don't live up to their promises, it could turn back to a violent form of resistance. Every action breeds a reaction."

In the end, the recruitment of the warlords and their followers bought some time for the Maliki government, but the American betrayal of their nominal allies created yet another group of 100,000 Iraqis and their families who had been tricked, betrayed, and humiliated by the Americans, and would be unlikely to forgive their duplicity. The fact that these groups had played a significant role in stabilizing large areas of Iraq suggests that these were not people whose loyalties could be manipulated with impunity, and the full consequences of their manipulation and betrayal will become clearer over time.

---

363. Jack Dolan and Sahar Issa, "Iraqi militiamen frustrated that promised jobs haven't materialized," *McClatchy Newspapers*, May 20th 2009.

American leaders hailed their "surge" in 2007 and 2008 as a successful operation that reduced the level of violence in Iraq. These claims were based on the false premise that Iraqi resistance forces were the source of the violence sweeping the country, and that the escalation of U.S. military operations in 2007 finally defeated these forces or persuaded them to stop fighting. In fact, throughout the war, the U.S. occupation forces and their allies were the perpetrators of most of the violence in Iraq, and their invasion and occupation of the country was the cause of all of it. It was therefore entirely possible at any point for the occupation forces to achieve a reduction in violence simply by scaling back their own operations, as they finally did after the climax of the "surge" in 2008.

The fact that so many American casualties were the result of "IEDs" or improvised mines planted on the roads underlines this point. Mines are an essentially defensive weapon. The Iraqi Resistance used them to defend their territory from offensive U.S. operations: patrols, house-raids, and attacks. And of course the U.S. troops on the ground eventually figured this out. As Phil Alliff said, if they could "avoid driving around all the time," they "wouldn't be blown up."

This raises the important question as to what extent the "surge" was a politically motivated operation. The United States would stage one last major operation, claim that it had succeeded, and then take steps to reduce the violence of the occupation by curtailing its own offensive operations and gradually withdrawing to long-term bases. To launch such an escalation of a war for essentially domestic political reasons would have been cynical in the extreme, and this deserves to be examined in the context of investigations of American war crimes. Like the larger crime of the war itself, it would demonstrate a wanton disregard for the lives of U.S. military personnel as well as for those of their Iraqi victims.

Another significant development in 2008 was the gradual process by which the Maliki government, universally despised until then by all but a narrow segment of the Shiite population, succeeded in gaining some legitimacy in the eyes of a larger cross-section of the population. Maliki's shows of strength against al-Sadr's Mahdi Army and other resistance forces may have contributed to this. More importantly though, Maliki's new authority derived from his assertion of Iraq's sovereignty and independence from American interests.

Whatever Maliki's personal feelings about his compromised position as an American puppet installed by an occupying army, the only way his government could build the legitimacy it lacked was to call America's bluff and to treat Iraq's nominal sovereignty as the real thing. Indeed the steadfast opposition of the Iraqi people to American occupation left Maliki and his co-collaborators with no other choice. In turn, this left his American handlers, up to and including Presidents Bush and Obama, no choice but to try and salvage what they could from what was in fact a nearly total defeat.

As the negotiations dragged on over a Status of Forces Agreement, the Hydrocarbon Law and all the other "benchmarks" for American success in Iraq, it became clear that the United States had very little leverage on any of these issues. Its primary commercial goal of privatizing the oil industry would probably never be achieved, and its primary strategic goal of establishing long-term military bases could only be achieved at the huge cost of continued regional instability and guerilla war, with a virtually unlimited price-tag and without the expected commercial pay-off that justified it to most of its backers in the first place.

For such meager spoils, the United States assaulted the civilian infrastructure of Iraq for at least seven years with battlefield weapons it had built to repel a Soviet invasion of Western Europe. A million Iraqis were dead, millions more were refugees, and their country was in ruins.

As Sheldon Wolin concluded, "In Iraq, Superpower succeeded only in providing the answer to the plaintive question of 9/11, "Why do they hate us?"[364] Like the Romans in Scotland, American occupation forces and officials would eventually be expelled from Iraq, by whatever political or military means necessary, or just by the sheer futility of "staying the course." They created a desolation, but they would never be able to claim that they brought peace to Iraq.

---

364 Sheldon Wolin, *Democracy Incorporated*, (Princeton: Princeton University Press, 2008), 93.

CONCLUSION. LAW NOT WAR.

>*They are talking about peace as a distant goal, as an end we seek, but one day we must come to see that peace is not merely a distant goal we seek, but that it is a means by which we arrive at that goal. We must pursue peaceful ends through peaceful means. All of this is saying that, in the final analysis, means and ends must cohere because the end is preexistent in the means, and ultimately destructive means cannot bring about constructive ends.*

>—Rev. Dr. Martin Luther King, in a sermon on Christmas Eve, 1967

>*Foreign policy is not and cannot be amoral because it is made by men who make instant choices on the basis of one set of values or another. The important issue is what kind of moral values are encouraged or discouraged within our national security structures. However, important as it is, in my view, to have foreign policy managed by men with a very different set of values than those that have prevailed in the last generation, ... it is crucial to maintain a healthy skepticism toward everybody's morality. As I would not choose bankers and ambitious college professors to decide when duty and honor require invading other countries and killing their people, so I would not grant such discretion to saints. That is why the "rule of law," so celebrated in rhetoric and so consistently violated in practice, is such a clear, practical necessity. It is exactly because moral standards are so difficult to apply wisely to foreign policy issues that it becomes necessary for survival to submit to objective, even arbitrary standards. There are some things that should not be done, whatever the circumstances or however plausible the provocation. The rules of war and the limitations on national sovereignty in the United Nations Charter were developed out of the shared experience of nations that a world where everything is permitted is not worth living in.*

>—Richard J. Barnet, Roots of War, 1972, p. 66.

Political rhetoric and commentary in the United States treated the lack of authority or legitimacy for the American invasion of Iraq as a separate issue from its catastrophic results. In reality, the lawlessness that pervaded U.S. policy from top to bottom lay at the root of almost every aspect of the crisis in Iraq. Terrible violations of the Hague, Geneva, Genocide and Torture Conventions and other human rights laws accumulated day after day under the American regime of military occupation, compounding the overarching crime of aggression. The first step toward the resolution of the crisis remained throughout, as it had been since the very beginning, the end of American occupation and the full restoration of Iraqi independence and sovereignty, with all the support that the international community could provide.

The horror, futility, and sheer barbarism of the destruction visited on the people of Iraq by the United States is literally impossible for most Americans to grasp. But it is precisely the separation of those collectively responsible from the fate of their victims that makes technological bureaucratic killing like this possible. As we saw in Chapter 8, American attitudes toward war differ quite sharply from those of people in other countries. The fact that Americans have not experienced war on their own soil since the 19th century or foreign occupation since 1815 has combined with the nature of technological warfare and a consistent lack of relevant education to insulate the American population from the reality of the wars that its government inflicts on other countries.

The destruction of Iraq constituted a climax in the larger crisis of American militarism. The U.S. military industrial complex is a debilitating drain on the U.S. economy, an obstacle to progress on a host of critical issues and a threat to the rest of the world. As Paul Kennedy documented in *The Rise and Fall of the Great Powers* and as Britain found in the 1950s, attempts to leverage military power to reverse a great power's declining relative economic position have proven counter-productive and highly destructive.[365]

The American effort to expand its military empire and regain control of the global oil industry under the guise of combating terrorism was a classic case of the phenomenon that Kennedy described. America's confused leaders saw only an opportunity to exploit the United States' military superiority to extend its dominant position in the world economy. The catastrophe on the "central front in the war on terror" in Iraq should be a clear lesson in the terrible consequences of succumbing to this sort of temptation. America's squandering of its scarce resources, the opportunities it lost to deal with other serious problems, including terrorism, and its undermining of international law and order left it in a far worse position. To continue the dogged pursuit of the habitual goals of U.S. foreign policy can only make the inevitable transition to a productive peacetime economy more painful and its eventual success more doubtful. American leaders must be prevented from wreaking further destruction on other countries, most immediately Afghanistan, Pakistan, Yemen, Somalia and Iran. And they must be persuaded to start building the framework of a productive new peacetime economy for a post-hegemonic future.

Richard Barnet wrote *Roots of War* a generation ago, towards the end of the Vietnam War. He examined the problem of American militarism and concluded that profound changes would be necessary in American government and society to prevent a recurrence of the horrors inflicted on the people of Vietnam, Cambodia, and Laos by the United States' armed forces.[366] And yet whatever positive changes occurred in American society and policy-making in the interim were insufficient to save the people of Iraq from a very similar fate.

---

365. Paul Kennedy, *The Rise and Fall of the Great Powers* (New York: Random House, 1987).
366. Richard J. Barnet, *Roots of War*, (New York: Atheneum, 1972).

Barnet was correct that a reliance on the morality of policy-makers will always be inadequate to prevent war. George W. Bush did not prove to be a moral person by any stretch of the imagination, but even he justified his decisions according to his own twisted sense of personal morality. It was precisely such conflicting moral justifications for wars throughout history that led American diplomats a century ago to the legalist approach to international affairs, to establish clearly defined objective rules of international behavior, culminating in the United Nations Charter, the Nuremberg Principles, and other important international treaties relating to war and peace.

American policy-makers who deride and belittle international law and the United Nations Charter have a high bar to meet in offering an alternative means of preventing war. The American destruction of Iraq revealed the self-serving nature of their critique and the deadly threat it concealed. In reality, these arguments are often pretexts, not to find a more effective means of achieving peace, but to exchange peace itself for a state of limited war, based on the belief that the United States can advance its interests by becoming the principal perpetrator of international violence. They would therefore appropriate to the United States the monopoly on legitimate violence that the U.N. Charter has granted exclusively to the Security Council since 1945. They are right to see the U.N. Charter as an obstacle to their ambitions. That is its purpose.

During the Vietnam War, American policy-makers were eventually forced to view the limitations of American military power more realistically, leading to détente with the Soviets, the opening of relations with China and restraint in the direct use of military force. Today we face the danger that American leaders have not grasped the meaning of their failure in Iraq, and are determined to cling to their original strategic and commercial goals there; to escalate the war in Afghanistan and Pakistan; to threaten or even attack Iran; to continue to threaten and use military force to destabilize other countries all over the world; and to spend $700 billion or more year after year on an absurd one-

374

sided arms race, bankrupting the debt-ridden economy of the United States as surely as the last arms race bankrupted the Soviet Union.

And yet, in contrast to their leaders in Washington and despite Americans' unique lack of education regarding their country's obligations under international law, a 2006 survey of American public opinion by the Chicago Council on Global Affairs found that exactly three-quarters of Americans would prefer a legitimate, multilateralist foreign policy, in accordance with international law. The Chicago Council expressed a sense of relief that this result was consistent with surveys it had conducted regularly since 1945 and that the American war in Iraq had not resulted in any erosion of this position.[367]

Seventy-five percent of Americans told the Chicago Council that they did not approve of the United States playing the role of a "world policeman," defined (hypocritically) as working "to fight violations of international law and aggression wherever they occur." 76% agreed that the U.S. was currently playing that role "more than it should be." And 75% of Americans said that the United States should do its share to solve international problems together with other countries, *"rejecting the idea that the United States, as the sole remaining superpower, should continue to be the preeminent world leader in solving international problems (just 10% favor this view) or that the United States should withdraw from most efforts to solve international problems (only 12% favor this)."*

These results make it clear that the prevailing view of American leaders that the United States should act as "the preeminent world leader in solving international problems" is in fact an extreme fringe position held by only 10% of the American public at large. This hege-

---

367. *Global Views 2006: The United States and the rise of China and India,* (Chicago: Chicago Council on Global Affairs, 2006), 14.
http://www.thechicagocouncil.org/UserFiles/File/POS_Topline%20Reports/POS%2020 06/2006%20Full%20POS%20Report.pdf

monic view has even less popular support than the isolationist view held by 12% of the public that the United States should just give up on solving international problems altogether. Instead the vast majority of Americans hold the legitimate view that their country should base its foreign policy primarily on cooperation with other countries rather than on either a preeminent U.S. leadership role or an isolationist position.

Most Americans may not know as much about international law as they should, but their instincts are fundamentally sound and their humanity and common sense hold up pretty well under the flood of propaganda that is directed at them. The same survey found that, on nuclear weapons policy, only 20% of Americans support their government's first-strike policy, while another 20% oppose the use of America's nuclear weapons even in the event of a nuclear attack on the United States. And a PIPA poll in November 2007 found that 73% of Americans support complete, verifiable nuclear disarmament.[368] The results of indepth surveys like these illustrate why such a web of lies had to be concocted to take the United States to war in Iraq, to lead a fundamentally peace-loving people who reject the aggressive, unilateral use of force to commit this terrible crime.

The dynamic by which the American people were tricked into war was the same one explained to Captain Gustave Gilbert, an American military psychologist, by Reichsmarschall Hermann Goering during a conversation in his prison cell in Nuremberg on April 18th, 1946. Gilbert recorded the conversation in his book, *Nuremberg Diary*.[369] Senator Robert Byrd of West Virginia quoted this passage during the Congres-

---

368. "American and Russian publics strongly support steps to reduce and eliminate nuclear weapons," *World Public Opinion*, November 9th, 2007.
http://www.worldpublicopinion.org/pipa/articles/international_security_bt/432.php?nid=&id=&pnt=432
369. G. M. Gilbert, *Nuremberg Diary*, (New York: Farrar, Straus and Giroux, 1947), 278-9.

sional debate on the Iraq war resolution in 2002,[370] but his colleagues ignored him and behaved exactly as Goering described:

> "Why of course the people don't want war," Goering shrugged, "why would some poor slob on a farm want to risk his life in a war when the best that he can get out of it is to come back to his farm in one piece. Naturally, the common people don't want war; neither in Russia nor in England nor in America, nor for that matter in Germany. That is understood. But, after all, it is the leaders of the country who determine the policy and it is always a simple matter to drag the people along, whether it is a democracy or a fascist dictatorship or a Parliament or a Communist dictatorship."
>
> "There is one difference," I pointed out. "In a democracy, the people have some say in the matter through their elected representatives, and in the United States only Congress can declare wars."
>
> "Oh, that is all well and good," (Goering replied), "but, voice or no voice, the people can always be brought to the bidding of the leaders. That is easy. All you have to do is tell them they are being attacked and denounce the pacifists for lack of patriotism and exposing the country to danger. It works the same way in any country."

As Gilbert pointed out, that is not the way it is supposed to work in the United States. The division of powers under the United States Constitution gives Congress, the branch of government "closest to the people," the authority over matters of war and peace, including the power "to declare War," "to raise and support Armies," "to provide and maintain a Navy," to "provide for the common defense," and to appropriate funds for those purposes, with the proviso that "no Appropriation of Money to that use shall be for a longer Term than two Years," so that the power of the purse can be used as a check on the military and the President.

---

370. Senator Robert Byrd, *Congressional Record*, October 10th 2002, S10275.

As former subjects of the King of England, the founders of the United States understood only too well the danger of an executive with war-making powers. In 1798, James Madison wrote in a letter to Thomas Jefferson, "The Constitution supposes what the history of all government demonstrates, that the executive is the branch of power most interested in war and most prone to it. It has accordingly with studied care vested the question of war in the legislative."[371]

Alexander Hamilton was an advocate of strong presidential power, but, in *Federalist Paper Number 69, The Real Character of the Executive*, he contrasted the limits of presidential power in the draft U.S. Constitution with the far greater power of the King of England. First of all, the President would be subject to impeachment, and "would afterwards be liable to prosecution and punishment in the ordinary course of law." Second, Congress would have the last word on all legislation, with the power to override a presidential veto. Third, the President would not have the power to raise armies or to declare war.[372]

Because America's founding fathers were so acutely aware of the danger of granting war-making power to a President and his advisers, they went to great pains to craft a constitutional system in which the President would not possess this critical and dangerous power. However, since 1945, the United States Congress has abdicated the power over military affairs assigned to it by the United States Constitution, gradually fading to a cipher or a rubber stamp instead of an actual representative body, effectively protecting the executive branch of the government from accountability to anyone but the most powerful corporate institutions. Congress now acts as a buffer for the presidency, absorbing phone calls, e-mails, and protests from the public so that the execu-

371. James Madison, *Letter to Thomas Jefferson*, April 2nd 1798. http://www.constitution.org/jm/17980402_tj.txt
372. Alexander Hamilton, *The Federalist no. 69: The Real Character of the Executive*, March 14th 1788. http://www.constitution.org/fed/federa69.htm

tive branch is not disturbed in the serious business of defense policy, and war-making in particular. The role of Congress has been reversed from representing the public to insulating and shielding the government from the public. After decades of ceding its constitutional power, the Democratic-led 110th Congress earned even lower public approval ratings than Mr. Bush, the most unpopular President in American history.

Sheldon Wolin, who taught political science at Berkeley and Princeton for thirty-three years (after piloting bombers in World War II), describes the current American political system as "managed democracy" or "inverted totalitarianism." Wolin sees the present U.S. model as a more sophisticated and therefore more effective way of concentrating and merging state and corporate power than the "classical totalitarianism" of the Fascist and Communist states of the twentieth century. Standing the classical model on its head, "inverted totalitarianism" retains the outlines of the existing political structure instead of sweeping them away. Instead it uses the resources and marketing techniques of the increasingly monopolistic corporations that dominate the U.S. economy to package and sell policies and candidates that consolidate and advance the concentration of wealth and power.

Officials elected via this system are more indebted to their party leadership and to the corporate and plutocratic interests that fund both major parties than to the public, whose votes the system efficiently delivers to them on election day. Corporate interests set the government's agenda and obtain whatever they want by bipartisan consensus, behind a theatrical smoke-screen of rancorous party politics. The concerns of the general public up to and including the most critical issues of economic, social, constitutional, environmental and international crisis are marginalized by apparent "gridlock" or are just "off the table". Wolin writes, " ... the egalitarian momentum generated during the thirties and revived during the sixties of the last century has been reversed. As a result democracy has been reduced to a rearguard action, struggling not to advance and improve the lives of the Many but merely to defend the shredded remains of earlier achievements."[373]

The 2002 Congressional authorization for war with Iraq was a classic example of Congress's abdication of its constitutional powers and of its role as a facilitator for executive power under the "inverted totalitarian" system. In the House Foreign Relations Committee, Republican Congressman Ron Paul called his colleagues' bluff by introducing a resolution for an actual Declaration of War against Iraq. There was a brief debate, the roll was called, and the committee voted *not* to declare war on Iraq by a vote of forty-one to zero. Then, with millions of lives on the line, Congress abdicated the most critical power granted to it by the Constitution to give President Bush the one power that Hamilton, Madison, Jefferson, and their colleagues were most determined to keep in the hands of Congress and out of the hands of the President.[374]

"Congress would rather give up its most important authorized power to the President and the U.N. than risk losing an election if the war goes badly," Congressman Paul observed. "So members take half steps, supporting confusingly worded 'authorizations' that they can back away from easily if necessary ... By transferring its authority to declare war to the President..., Congress not only violates the Constitution, but also disenfranchises the American electorate."[375]

The deficit of democracy in the United States presents a huge obstacle to any public effort to right the wrongs of the American war in Iraq or to prevent the U.S. government from inflicting similar devastation on other countries in the future. But this makes it more important

---

373. Sheldon S. Wolin, *Democracy Incorporated*, (Princeton: Princeton University Press, 2008), 147.

374. House Committee on International Relations, *Authorization for Use of Military Force Against Iraq*, October 2nd & 3rd 2002, 122-132.

http://www.foreignaffairs.house.gov/archives/107/82194.pdf

375. Ron Paul, "Congress must say yes or no to war," *Anti-War Web Site*, October 8th 2002. http://www.antiwar.com/paul/paul50.html

than ever that public campaigns to address this crisis should have the most coherent and concrete goals possible. In addition to demanding the withdrawal of all U.S. military forces and civilian personnel from Iraq, not just "combat troops", two extremely important and effective demands that the public can and should make are for the prosecution of major American war criminals and for the payment of financial reparations to the people and government of Iraq.

These are legitimate international obligations that the United States has incurred by its actions. The first would hold individuals accountable for crimes they have committed under international, federal, and military law. The second would constitute an acceptance of collective responsibility by the American people for the crimes committed in their name, while funding the desperate needs of the people of Iraq. If civil society is able to enforce both personal and collective accountability for these crimes, this will have truly far-reaching effects on the way that future U.S. governments will behave and thus on the lives of our children and grandchildren. And part of the elegance of these remedies is that even partial success on either count will have real consequences.

The Nuremberg trials of major German war criminals established the precedent that political leaders can and should be held criminally accountable for international crimes, in particular the crime of waging aggressive war, which the judges called the "supreme international crime differing only from other war crimes in that it contains within itself the accumulated evil of the whole." In Chapter 6, I quoted U.S. Supreme Court Justice Jackson's statement to the London conference that established the Nuremberg Principles in 1945. He made it clear that they were intended to be universal principles that applied equally to every country: "If certain acts in violation of treaties are crimes, they are crimes whether the United States does them or whether Germany does them, and we are not prepared to lay down a rule of criminal conduct against others which we would not be willing to have invoked against us."[376]

And yet, while the Nuremberg Principles have formed the basis for war crimes trials for Yugoslavia, Rwanda, and other countries in conflict, they have not been applied to instances of aggression by major powers, least of all the United States. An article of impeachment was drawn up against Richard Nixon for waging a secret, illegal war against Cambodia. But the House Judiciary Committee voted against including this charge of aggression among the articles of impeachment to be introduced in Congress, choosing instead to focus more narrowly on Watergate, wire-tapping, and contempt of Congress. Nixon was pardoned by his former Vice President in any case, and was not ultimately prosecuted for any of his crimes.[377]

Because no senior American officer or civilian official has ever faced war crimes charges, there has been effective impunity for terrible crimes committed against dozens of countries, including Vietnam, Cambodia, Laos, the Dominican Republic, Grenada, Nicaragua, Panama, Yugoslavia, Haiti, and now Iraq. While junior officers and enlisted personnel occasionally face courts martial, the more senior American officials who are ultimately responsible for all of these crimes still live in a pre-Nuremberg world, with an implicit guarantee of impunity. An American President or Defense Secretary or general can order the bombing or the invasion or the complete destruction of another country secure in the knowledge that he or she will never have to justify or defend his or her actions in a court of law, no matter how blatant the crime. If the military plans offer the prospect of success, if the commercial and strategic rewards are sufficient, and if policy-makers are confi-

376. "International Conference on Military Trials," *Dept. State Pub. No. 3880*, July 23 1945, 330.

377. Elizabeth Holtzman with Cynthia L. Cooper, *The Impeachment of George W. Bush*, (New York: Nation Books, 2006), 18-19 & Appendix F.

dent that the public can be "brought to their bidding," as Goering put it, then they can count on others to fight and to die, while they go about their business with the untarnished respect, or even the acclaim, of their peers.

Prosecutions of senior American officials for aggression, torture, murder, genocide, issuing illegal rules of engagement, and other war crimes in Iraq would send shock-waves through U.S. foreign and defense policy for generations to come. The end of impunity would put every American official on notice that international treaties, Federal Law and the United States Constitution really are the "supreme Law of the Land,", as the Constitution says, and must therefore be the basis that determines what policy options may be legitimately considered and what courses of action should be unconscionable.

With a recommitment to legitimate, constitutional government in Washington, the United States could become a real partner to the rest of the world in confronting the serious environmental, economic, and societal challenges that the world is facing. Serious gaps in the development and enforcement of international criminal law could finally be addressed. The United States could sign and ratify the Treaty of Rome and join the International Criminal Court, which 71% of Americans have told pollsters they support, but which the U.S. government has consistently and actively opposed.[378] For the officials of other governments, the unwritten proviso that one of the parties to every agreement, the United States, will simply ignore it whenever it becomes inconvenient makes a mockery of the good faith that other diplomats bring to international negotiations and undermines the entire international system of collective security and cooperation. The universal ju-

---

378. *Global Views 2006; U.S. Public Topline Report,* (Chicago: Chicago Council on Global Affairs, 2006), 17.
http://www.thechicagocouncil.org/UserFiles/File/POS_Topline%20Reports/POS%2020 06/2006%20US%20Topline.pdf

risdiction of international law provides the essential legal framework for a peaceful world, as the generation of leaders who signed and ratified the U.N. Charter intended as they stared into the abyss at the end of two world wars.

The prospects for the successful prosecution of major American war criminals would be far from certain. But the critical questions of law are well established, and the U.S. federal court system has demonstrated that it can perform at least some of its legitimate functions in cases involving illegal kidnapping, detention, and show-trials of terrorism suspects, even in the face of enormous pressure from the executive branch of government. When the U.S. Supreme Court ruled that prisoners at Guantanamo Bay were entitled to the protection of *habeas corpus*, it established a precedent that will be binding on future U.S. administrations. Any success in bringing major American war criminals to justice will establish even farther-reaching precedents. The U.S. Justice Department has the responsibility to investigate all serious allegations of criminal behavior by government officials. Once investigations and prosecutions have begun, diligent investigators, prosecutors, judges, and juries must be permitted to follow the law and the trail of evidence wherever it leads. Ultimately, even if some of the most serious offenders are able to escape conviction on the most serious charges, the fact that American society took steps to hold them accountable would be a powerful shot across the bows to any of their successors contemplating similar crimes in the future.

As I explained in the Introduction, the specific crimes committed against Iraq and its people grew out of overarching U.S. policy positions that were enunciated in official documents over many years. The regression from compliance with the U.N. Charter to a policy of unilateral military action to "ensure uninhibited access to key markets, energy supplies and strategic resources" anywhere in the world was made gradually by American regimes from Truman to Clinton. Bush pulled the trigger, but his predecessors built the gun and handed it to him.

These policies have no basis in international law or the U.S. Constitution. No other country has ever accepted the oxymoronic proposition that the United States has some kind of supra-national status that places it above the rule of international law. The attempt to formulate and implement these policies has been a catastrophic exercise in collective wishful thinking by leaders drunk on fantasies of superpower and militarism. Forcing them to actually account for their actions in courts of law is the most powerful step Americans can take to restore legitimacy to their country's foreign and defense policy.

In 1951, Hannah Arendt wrote in The *Origins of Totalitarianism*, "We can no longer simply afford to take that which was good in the past and simply call it our heritage, to discard the bad and simply think of it as a dead load which by itself time will bury in oblivion. The subterranean stream of Western history has finally come to the surface and usurped the dignity of our tradition. This is the reality in which we live."[379]

As we confront the consequences of "inverted totalitarianism", Americans must face a similar reality. Like Europeans, we have much to be proud of in our country, our culture and our history. But selectively ignoring collective responsibility for aggression and atrocities has only fed the worst trends in American society. It has allowed powerful interests to exploit sincerely held values to whitewash atrocities. Patriotism has been held hostage by militarism. Freedom and democracy have been twisted into hollow political slogans to dignify terrible crimes. Like Arendt, we must find the honesty and objectivity to confront the reality of our heritage, good and bad, so that we can reclaim our roles as responsible actors in the events of our time.

Even in contemplating an entirely successful and thorough prosecution of major American war criminals, it is immediately apparent that

---

379. Hannah Arendt, *The Origins of Totalitarianism*, (New York: Meridian Books, 1958).

that would only fulfill one part of our collective responsibility for these crimes. People of all countries face challenges to their humanity, and there are particular challenges that apply to modern technological societies. Because responsibility for killing and destruction is distributed throughout many sectors of society, from civilian officials to the military to Congress to weapons manufacturers to the media to the public, nobody bears sole responsibility, but neither is anybody entirely free of responsibility. As so many Americans discovered in Iraq, the person who finally pulls the trigger or releases the bomb is only the final cog in a carefully constructed machine, with a deliberately circumscribed capacity to exercise moral judgment when the critical moment arrives.

The United States has left another country in ruins and shattered millions of people's lives. However clearly many Americans may have opposed these policies from the outset, it was America's elected government and armed forces that carried out this crime, using American tax dollars to pay for every bomb, missile, and bullet. By the same token, American tax dollars must be used to repair the damage. It is an established principle of international relations that a nation that inflicts the devastation of war on another country incurs the responsibility to provide compensation to repair the damage it has caused, to whatever extent that is possible.

Arguments that have been made against reparations in other cases do not apply to the U.S. war in Iraq. The United States will not emerge from this war as an impoverished country that cannot afford to pay for the damage it has done. Neither would this be a case of arbitrary justice. There is no question that the United States attacked Iraq and not the reverse. Nor would this be a case of an innocent people being forced to pay for the actions of a dictatorial government. The U.S. political system may be corrupted, but its genius from the point of view of the powerful interests it serves is precisely that it functions through a superficially democratic political structure.

The United States government did not want to publicly and formally accept its responsibility to pay reparations to Vietnam. Article 21 of the Paris Peace Accord committed the U.S. government only "to contribute to healing the wounds of war and to postwar reconstruction of the Democratic Republic of Vietnam ..." President Nixon sent a letter to the government of Vietnam explaining that the U.S. would fulfill this clause of the peace agreement by paying $3.3 billion for reconstruction in Vietnam in lieu of war reparations. Subsequent U.S. administrations reneged on his promise, and the International Monetary Fund held the Vietnamese government responsible for the war debts of the U.S.-backed regime in Saigon, exacerbating the economic problems of a liberated but devastated country. In light of this history, a formal and explicit acceptance of U.S. obligations to Iraq that subsequent administrations could not worm their way out of would be very helpful.[380]

Ironically, the most appropriate model for reparations to compensate Iraq would be the reparations regime imposed on Iraq itself following its invasion of Kuwait in 1990. UNSC resolution 687 established Iraq's legal responsibility for the losses of Kuwait and its people, and the Iraqi government accepted its responsibility in a letter to the Security Council three days later. The resolution created a compensation fund and directed the Secretary General of the U.N. "to recommend mechanisms for determining the appropriate level of Iraq's contribution to the fund, taking into account the requirements of the people of Iraq, Iraq's payment capacity and the needs of the Iraqi economy."[381]

The details were then spelled out in UNSC Resolution 705, which established a U.N. Compensation Commission (UNCC) in Geneva, with representatives of each country that had a seat on the Security Council but without a veto for permanent members. The UNCC received claims

---

380. Ronald J. Cima, ed. "The United States," *Vietnam: A Country Study*, (Washington: GPO for the Library of Congress, 1987).

381. http://www2.unog.ch/uncc/

against Iraq totaling $352.5 billion and eventually awarded a total of $52.5 billion to settle 1.55 million claims. A thirty percent levy against Iraqi oil export revenues funded the payment of the claims. This was later reduced to 25 percent and more recently to 5 percent. The fund disbursed $21 billion in the first 16 years, and it was decided from the outset that awards to individual victims would receive priority and be paid before those to the Kuwaiti government.

By contrast, the severe damage to Iraq's infrastructure in the present war would require that the post-occupation Iraqi government receive payment from the compensation fund from the outset, along with individual war victims. Fortunately, the United States is still wealthy enough to make substantial payments both to rebuild Iraq's infrastructure and to help its people to bind their wounds at the same time.

One may wonder what total Iraqi claims against the United States would add up to. They could quite possibly exceed the trillions of dollars already committed to the war and its consequences, but this would be up to the compensation commission. The UNCC reduced the amount claimed by Kuwait and its people by 85 percent, and it appears to have conducted its deliberations fairly and impartially. The American people and the U.S. government would hopefully have the good grace to accept the authority of a similar compensation commission and to comply with its rulings.

It may seem counter-intuitive that the American people can further their real interests by voluntarily accepting constraints and liabilities that their government has worked so hard and long to shake off and evade. But this is precisely the nature of collective security. The rule of law protects nobody if the strong or the wealthy simply refuse to submit to it. Roosevelt's vision of the United Nations, of "a universal organization in which all peace-loving nations will finally have a chance to join," rests on the good faith of the United States and other powerful countries to accept the limitations that the United Nations Charter places on their national sovereignty, just as the laws of war depend on those with the most powerful weapons to accept legal limitations on how they may use them.

Peace is the first prerequisite of survival and security in an interconnected world. As General Eisenhower explained in 1949, the false security of offensive weapons and policies of aggression has been a seductive but deadly siren for great powers throughout history. Few of us alive today have had the first-hand experience of world war that brought the nations of the world to the negotiating table in San Francisco in 1945 with a unanimous commitment to peace as a matter of survival, but renewing that commitment now is the essential precondition to solving all the other problems facing the world.

As a whole, the world has made great strides toward peace. The Stockholm International Peace Research Institute (SIPRI) monitors international conflict around the world and has charted a steady decline in war since the end of the Cold War. While SIPRI finds no two countries at war with each other in the world today, the United States is involved in nearly all of the world's 15 major internal conflicts, either directly, as in Iraq, Afghanistan and Pakistan, or indirectly as a principal supporter and arms supplier to one side, as in the Philippines, Colombia and Palestine. All these conflicts stem from or are exacerbated by U.S. policy, from the Ethiopian (and U.S. Special Forces) invasion to destroy the Islamic Courts government and newly destabilize Somalia in 2006 to the U.S.-Peru Trade Promotion Agreement that launched the Peruvian armed forces on a civil war against indigenous people over oil drilling in 2009.[382]

The aggressive ambitions of the U.S. government present the world with an existential threat. It may prove quite impossible to adequately

---

382. Lotta Harbon and Peter Wallensteen, *SIPRI Yearbook 2009*, (Stockholm: Stockholm International Peace Research Institute, 2009), Appendix 2A. http://www.sipri.org/yearbook/2009/02/02A

address global problems like climate change, resource depletion, and nuclear proliferation as long as American militarism spreads chaos and undermines the framework of international law and cooperation. Other governments have wisely continued to cooperate in building necessary institutions like the International Criminal Court, but Ben Ferencz's brainchild is itself in danger of being undermined by its inability to gain jurisdiction over the world's most dangerous criminals. A court that can indict the President of Sudan but not the President of the United States can provide only a transitional step toward universal justice. In the meantime, lawyers and civil society groups in the United States, Iraq and other countries must cooperate with existing legal institutions to investigate and prosecute war crimes by American officials.

When confronting powerful aggressors, there is a fine line between preserving peace and appeasement. Some combination of external and internal pressure can often bring about peaceful change, but aggressors tend to interpret a lack of military opposition as acquiescence or even support. The election of Mr. Obama raised hopes that the United States was capable of internal democratic change, but his first steps in foreign and defense policy soon dispelled the hopes he had raised, notably the slow and uncertain withdrawal from Iraq, the escalation of the war in Afghanistan, illegal drone strikes in Pakistan, the indefinite detention without trial of terrorism suspects and the record $700 billion budget for America's bloated military industrial complex. Regrettably, the talent for compromise that made Mr. Obama so successful as a politician was entirely inadequate to the task of reining in a government engaged in aggression and other war crimes, where a much firmer hand was needed.

The failure of the American people to take charge of their own political destiny will effectively place their fate in the hands of others as they face the inevitable transition from military superpower to whatever may come next. The United States' mountain of debt provides the most obvious point at which international pressure can be brought to bear to alter its international behavior, but the balance must be finely calibrated to avoid violent confrontation on the one hand and acquiescence in further U.S. aggression on the other. A fine balance will likewise be needed to build a healthy global economic system that is no longer distorted by American debt and over-consumption. If the United States feels too much strategic or economic pressure from China, or from any other single "threat," powerful forces in the United States will be tempted to provoke a new and even more dangerous military confrontation.

Strong multilateral peaceful pressure, both diplomatic and economic, is therefore the most effective course. American global military dominance is ultimately unsustainable, for both economic and political reasons. But it is necessary for survival that the United States give way peacefully to an effective system of collective security based on the United Nations Charter and international law, without another world war or a long debilitating struggle for military power. Laying American militarism to rest is the imperative of our time, but, as Dr. King suggested, peaceful means are the key to a peaceful end.

BIBLIOGRAPHY

Hannah Arendt, *The Origins of Totalitarianism*, (New York: Meridian Books, 1958)

Andrew J. Bacevich, *The Limits of Power: the End of American Exceptionalism*, (New York, Metropolitan Books, 2008)

Richard Barnet, *Roots of War: the Men and Institutions Behind U.S. Foreign Policy*, (New York, Atheneum, 1972)

Hanna Batatu, *The Old Social Classes and the Revolutionary Movements of Iraq*, (Princeton: Princeton University Press, 1978)

Richard K. Betts, *Soldiers, Statesmen and Cold War Crises*, (New York: Columbia University Press, 1991)

William Blum, *Killing Hope: U.S. Military and CIA Interventions Since World War II*, (Monroe: Common Courage, 2004)

Francis Anthony Boyle, *Foundations of World Order: The Legalist Approach to International Relations, 1898-1922*, (Raleigh: Duke University Press, 1999)

Kevin Buckley, *Panama*, (New York: Touchstone, 1992)

Zbigniew Brzezinski, *Out of Control: Global Turmoil on the Eve of the 21st Century* (New York: Scribner, 1993)

Michael Byers, *War Law: Understanding International Law and Armed Conflict*, (New York: Grove Press, 2005)

Albert Camus, *Camus at Combat*, (Princeton: Princeton University Press, 2006)

Antonio Cassese, *International Criminal Law*, (Oxford: Oxford University Press, 2003)

Ha-Joon Chang, *Bad Samaritans: The Myth of Free Trade and the Secret History of Capitalism*, (New York: Bloomsbury, 2008)

Abram Chayes, *The Cuban Missile Crisis: International Crises and the Role of Law*, (Oxford: Oxford University Press, 1974)

Noam Chomsky, *Hegemony or Survival: America's Quest for Global Dominance*, (New York: Metropolitan, 2003)

Noam Chomsky, *Failed States: the Abuse of Power and the Assault on Democracy*, (New York: Metropolitan, 2006)

Ronald J. Cima, *Vietnam: a country study*, (Washington: GPO for the Library of Congress, 1987)

James DeFronzo, *The Iraq War: Origins and Consequences*, (Boulder: Westview, 2010)

Aidan Delgado, *The Sutras of Abu Ghraib*, (Boston: Beacon Press, 2007)

Shadia Drury, *Leo Strauss and the American Right*, (New York: Palgrave Macmillan, 1999)

George Fielding Eliot, *If Russia Strikes*, (Indianapolis: Bobbs-Merrill, 1949)

Wilbur Crane Eveland, *Ropes of Sand: America's Failure in the Middle East*, (New York: Norton, 1980)

Richard Falk, Robert Jay Lifton and Gabriel Kolko, *Crimes of War*, (New York, Random House, 1971)

Richard Falk, Irene Gendzier & Robert Jay Lifton, *Crimes of War: Iraq*, (New York: Nation Books, 2006)

William F. Felice, *How do I save my honor?: War, Moral Integrity and Principled Resignation*, (Lanham: Rowman & Littlefield, 2009)

Robert Fisk, *The Great War for Civilization: the Conquest of the Middle East*, (New York: Knopf, 2005)

D. F. Fleming, *The Cold War and its Origins*, (Garden City: Doubleday, 1961)

General Tommy Franks, *American Soldier*, (New York: Regan Books, 2004)

Paul Fussell, *Wartime: Understanding and Behavior in the Second World War*, (New York: Oxford University Press, 1989)

Edmund A. Ghareeb, *Historical Dictionary of Iraq*, (Lanham: Scarecrow Press, 2004)

G. M. Gilbert, *Nuremberg Diary*, (New York: Farrar, Straus and Giroux, 1947)

Bob Graham and Jeff Nussbaum, *Intelligence Matters*, (New York: Random House, 2004)

Karen J. Greenberg, Joshua L. Dratel & Anthony Lewis, *The Torture Papers: the Road to Abu Ghraib*, (Cambridge: Cambridge University Press, 2005)

Greenberg Research, *The People on War Report: ICRC Worldwide Consultation on the Laws of War*, (Geneva: ICRC, 2000)

Stephen Grey, *Ghost Plane: the True Story of the CIA Torture Program*, (New York: St. Martin's Press, 2006)

Alexander Hamilton, *The Federalist no. 69: the Real Character of the Executive*, March 14th 1788

Eric Hobsbawm, *The Age of Extremes: a History of the World 1914-1991*, (Gloucester: Peter Smith, 2001)

Eric Hobsbawm, *On Empire: America, War, and Global Supremacy*, (New York: Pantheon Books, 2008)

Elizabeth Holtzman with Cynthia L. Cooper, *The Impeachment of George W. Bush*, (New York: Nation Books, 2006)

Alistair Horne, *A Savage War of Peace: Algeria 1954-1962*, (New York: New York Review of Books, 2006)

"International Conference on Military Trials", *Dept. State Pub. No. 3880*, July 23 1945

Charles Issawi and Muhammed Yeganeh, *The Economics of Middle Eastern Oil*, (New York: Praeger, 1962)

Dahr Jamail, *Beyond the Green Zone: Dispatches from an Unembedded Journalist in Occupied Iraq*, (Chicago: Haymarket Books, 2007)

Mark Weston Janis, *International Law, 5th Edition*, (New York: Aspen, 2008)

Chalmers Johnson, *The Blowback Trilogy*, (New York: Metropolitan Books, 2000-2006)

Paul Kennedy, *The Rise and Fall of the Great Powers* (New York: Random House, 1987)

Naomi Klein, *The Shock Doctrine: the Rise of Disaster Capitalism*, (New York: Metropolitan Books, 2007)

Gabriel Kolko, *Century of War: Politics, Conflicts and Society Since 1914,* (New York: The New Press, 1994)

Gabriel Kolko, *Confronting the Third World: United States Foreign Policy 1945-1980,* (New York: Pantheon, 1988)

Gabriel Kolko, *World in Crisis: the End of the American Century,* (New York: Pluto, 2009)

Barry S. Levy and Victor W. Sidel, *War and Public Health,* (Oxford: Oxford University Press, 1997)

J.G. Lorimer, *Gazetteer of the Persian Gulf, Oman and Central Arabia* (Calcutta, 1908-1915)

James Mann, *The Rise of the Vulcans: the History of Bush's War Cabinet,* (New York: Viking Press, 2004)

Michael Mann, *Incoherent Empire,* (London: Verso, 2003)

Phebe Marr, *The Modern History of Iraq,* (Boulder: Westview Press, 1985)

Robert W. McChesney, *Rich Media, Poor Democracy: Communication Politics in Dubious Times,* (New York: The New Press, 1999)

Camilo Mejia, *The Road from Ar Ramadi: the Private Rebellion of Staff Sergeant Camilo Mejia,* (New York: The New Press, 2007)

Helen Chapin Metz, *Iraq: a Country Study,* (Washington: Federal Research Division, Library of Congress, 1990)

Hans L. Morgenthau, *Politics Among Nations, 7th Edition,* (New York: McGraw Hill, 2005)

Edward L. Morse and Amy Myers Jaffe, *Strategic Energy Policy Challenges for the 21st Century*, (New York: Council on Foreign Relations, 2001)

Greg Muttitt, *Crude Designs: the Rip-off of Iraq's Oil Wealth*, (London: Platform, 2005)

Yitzhak Nakash, *The Shi'is of Iraq*, (Princeton: Princeton University Press, 1994),

National Commission on Terrorist Attacks, *The 9/11 Commission Report*, (New York: Norton, 2004)

John Pilger, *The New Rulers of the World*, (London: Verso, 2002)

Ronald Radosch, *American Labor and United States Foreign Policy*, (New York: Random House, 1969)

Ellen Ray and William H. Schaap, *Covert Action: the Roots of Terrorism*, (Melbourne: Ocean Press, 2003)

Scott Ritter, *Iraq Confidential: the Untold Story of the Intelligence Conspiracy to Undermine the U.N. and Overthrow Saddam Hussein*, (New York: Nation Books, 2005)

Michael Rose, *Washington's War: the American War of Independence and the Iraq Insurgency*, (New York: Pegasus, 2008)

Philippe Sands, *Lawless World: America and the Making and Breaking of Global Rules from FDR's Atlantic Charter to George W. Bush's Illegal War*, (New York: Viking, 2005)

Michael Schwartz, *War Without End: the Iraq War in Context*, (Chicago: Haymarket Books, 2008)

Peter Sluglett, *Britain in Iraq: 1914-1932*, (London: Ithaca Press, 1976)

Norman Solomon, *War Made Easy: How Presidents and Pundits Keep Spinning Us to Death*, (Hoboken: John Wiley, 2005)

Staff Report of the House Select Committee on Intelligence, *CIA - The Pike Report*, (Nottingham: Spokesman Books, 1977)

Joseph E. Stiglitz and Linda J. Bilmes, *The Three Trillion Dollar War: the True Cost of the Iraq Conflict*, (New York: Norton, 2008)

Leo Strauss, *Persecution and the Art of Writing*, (New York: Free Press, 1952)

Michael J. Sullivan III, *American Adventurism Abroad*, (Malden: Blackwell, 2008)

Ron Suskind, *The Price of Loyalty: George W. Bush, the White House and the Education of Paul O'Neill*, (New York: Simon & Schuster, 2004)

David Swanson, *Daybreak: Undoing the Imperial Presidency and Forming a More Perfect Union*, (New York: Seven Stories, 2009)

Tacitus, S.A. Handford ed., H. Mattingly tr., *The Agricola and the Germania*, (New York: Penguin Classics, 1971)

Charles Tripp, *A History of Iraq, 3rd Edition*, (Cambridge: Cambridge University Press, 2007)

United States Strategic Bombing Survey, *Summary Report (Pacific War)*, (Washington: Government Printing Office, 1946)

Douglas Valentine, *The Phoenix Program*, (New York: William Morrow, 1990)

Lawrence E. Walsh, "Final Report of the Independent Counsel for Iran/Contra Matters", *United States Court of Appeals for the District of Columbia Circuit*, August 4 1993

William Appleman Williams, *The Tragedy of American Diplomacy*, (New York: Dell, 1962)

Sheldon S. Wolin, *Democracy Incorporated: Managed Democracy and the Specter of Inverted Totalitarianism*, (Princeton: Princeton University Press, 2008)

Ellen Meiksins Wood, *Empire of Capital*, (London: Verso, 2003)

Haifa Zangana, *City of Widows: an Iraqi Woman's Account of War and Resistance,* (New York: Seven Stories Press, 2007)

INDEX

CPSIA information can be obtained
at www.ICGtesting.com
Printed in the USA
LVHW012043230821
695924LV00001B/86

9 781934 840986